Related Books

Implementing the IBM® Rational Unified Process® and Solutions

By Joshua Barnes

ISBN-10: 0-321-36945-9

This book delivers all the knowledge and insight you need to succeed with the IBM Rational Unified Process and Solutions. Joshua Barnes presents a start-to-finish, best-practice roadmap to the complete implementation cycle of IBM RUP–from projecting ROI and making the business case through piloting, implementation, mentoring, and beyond. Drawing on his extensive experience leading large-scale IBM RUP implementations and working with some of the industry's most recognized thought leaders in the Software Engineering Process world, Barnes brings together comprehensive "lessons learned" from both successful and failed projects. You'll learn from real-world case studies, including actual project artifacts.

Implementing IBM® Rational® ClearQuest®
An End-to-End Deployment Guide

By Christian D. Buckley, Darren W. Pulsipher, and Kendall Scott

ISBN-10: 0-321-33486-8

Implementing IBM Rational ClearQuest brings together all you need to integrate ClearQuest into an over-arching change-management system that works. Drawing on decades of experience, the authors present a detailed, easy-to-use roadmap for each step of ClearQuest deployment, from evaluating business cases to planning, design, and implementation. You will find the industry's clearest, most useful explanations of ClearQuest technology here, along with real-world examples, best practices, diagrams, and actionable steps.

Related Books of Interest

A Practical Guide to Distributed Scrum

By Elizabeth Woodward, Steffan Surdek, and Matthew Ganis

ISBN-10: 0-13-704113-6

This is the first comprehensive, practical guide for Scrum practitioners working in large-scale distributed environments. Written by three of IBM's leading Scrum practitioners—in close collaboration with the IBM QSE Scrum Community of more than 1,000 members worldwide—this book offers specific, actionable guidance for everyone who wants to succeed with Scrum in the enterprise.

Readers will follow a journey through the lifecycle of a distributed Scrum project, from envisioning products and setting up teams to preparing for Sprint planning and running retrospectives. Using real-world examples, the book demonstrates how to apply key Scrum practices, such as look-ahead planning in geographically distributed environments. Readers will also gain valuable new insights into the agile management of complex problem and technical domains.

The Art of Enterprise Information Architecture
A Systems-Based Approach for Unlocking Business Insight

By Mario Godinez, Eberhard Hechler, Klaus Koenig, Steve Lockwood, Martin Oberhofer, and Michael Schroeck

ISBN-10: 0-13-703571-3

Tomorrow's winning "Intelligent Enterprises" will bring together far more diverse sources of data, analyze it in more powerful ways, and deliver immediate insight to decision-makers throughout the organization. Today, however, most companies fail to apply the information they already have, while struggling with the complexity and costs of their existing information environments.

In this book, a team of IBM's leading information management experts guide you on a journey that will take you from where you are today toward becoming an "Intelligent Enterprise." Drawing on their extensive experience working with enterprise clients, the authors present a new, information-centric approach to architecture and powerful new models that will benefit any organization.

Related Books of Interest

Software Test Engineering with IBM Rational Functional Tester
The Definitive Resource

By Chip Davis, Daniel Chirillo, Daniel Gouveia, Fariz Saracevic, Jeffrey B. Bocarsley, Larry Quesada, Lee B. Thomas, and Marc van Lint
ISBN-10: 0-13-700066-9

If you're among the thousands of developers using IBM Rational Functional Tester (RFT), this book brings together all the insight, examples, and real-world solutions you need to succeed. Eight leading IBM testing experts thoroughly introduce this state-of-the-art product, covering issues ranging from building test environments through executing the most complex and powerful tests. Drawing on decades of experience with IBM Rational testing products, they address both technical and nontechnical challenges and present everything from best practices to reusable code.

Enterprise Master Data Management
An SOA Approach to Managing Core Information

Dreibelbis, Hechler, Milman, Oberhofer, van Run, Wolfson
ISBN-10: 0-13-236625-8

The Business of IT
How to Improve Service and Lower Costs

Robert Ryan, Tim Raducha-Grace
ISBN-10: 0-13-700061-8

Agile Career Development
Lessons and Approaches from IBM

Mary Ann Bopp, Diana A. Bing, Sheila Forte-Trammell
ISBN-10: 0-13-715364-3

Dynamic SOA and BPM
Best Practices for Business Process Management and SOA Agility

Marc Fiammante
ISBN-10: 0-13-701891-6

Multisite Commerce
Proven Principles for Overcoming the Business, Organizational, and Technical Challenges

Lev Mirlas
ISBN-10: 0-13-714887-9

Sign up for the monthly IBM Press newsletter at
ibmpressbooks.com/newsletters

Praise for *Work Item Management with IBM Rational ClearQuest and Jazz*

"Dave and Shmuel have mastered both CQ ALM and Jazz and produced a primer introducing these to the IBM Rational Tools audience. This is a great starting point for implementing the integration."

—*Robert W. Myers*
  CQ ALM Architect
  IBM Rational

"This book is an excellent introduction to how to think about workflows, a topic that has been severely lacking in discussions of implementing tools that govern workflows. Without this understanding of workflows, good tools are often poorly implemented and therefore don't yield the ROI expected. Although this book uses Rational tools to describe implementation fine points, the information presented will be very useful for doing the groundwork for implementing any workflow-supporting tools."

—*Chuck Walrad*
  Managing Director
  Davenport Consulting

"Dave Bellagio and Shmuel Bashan provide thorough and practical coverage of how to implement a work item change management process using IBM ClearQuest or the Jazz Platform. A must-read for professionals involved in implementing a change management process with IBM ClearQuest or with one of the Jazz-based products."

—*Celso Gonzalez*
  Coauthor of Patterns-Based Engineering: Successfully Delivering Solutions via Patterns

"Application Lifecycle Management (ALM) is the key to success for today's increasingly complex enterprise software delivery challenges. At the heart of ALM is work item management. This book provides an excellent review of practical approaches to work item management based on real world experience that will help you to deliver enterprise solutions more effectively. It is a great resource for the whole software delivery team."

—*Alan W. Brown*
  IBM Distinguished Engineer

Work Item Management with IBM Rational ClearQuest and Jazz

Work Item Management with IBM Rational ClearQuest and Jazz

A Customization Guide

Shmuel Bashan

David E. Bellagio

IBM Press
Pearson plc

Upper Saddle River, NJ • Boston• Indianapolis • San Francisco
New York • Toronto • Montreal • London • Munich • Paris • Madrid
Capetown • Sydney • Tokyo • Singapore • Mexico City

ibmpressbooks.com

IBM Press Program Managers: Steve Stansel, Ellice Uffer
Cover design: IBM Corporation
Associate Publisher: David Dusthimer
Marketing Manager: Stephane Nakib
Publicist: Heather Fox
Acquisitions Editor: Chris Guzikowski
Development Editors: Sheri Cain and Chris Zahn
Managing Editor: John Fuller
Designer: Alan Clements
Project Editor: Anna Popick
Copy Editor: Barbara Wood
Indexer: Jack Lewis
Compositor: The CIP Group
Proofreader: Kelli M. Brooks
Manufacturing Buyer: Dan Uhrig

Published by Pearson plc

Publishing as IBM Press

IBM Press offers excellent discounts on this book when ordered in quantity for bulk purchases or special sales, which may include electronic versions and/or custom covers and content particular to your business, training goals, marketing focus, and branding interests. For more information, please contact:

U.S. Corporate and Government Sales
1-800-382-3419
corpsales@pearsontechgroup.com

For sales outside the U.S., please contact:

International Sales
international@pearson.com

The following terms are trademarks or registered trademarks of International Business Machines Corporation in the United States, other countries, or both: IBM, Rational, ClearQuest, Rational Team Concert, Jazz, ClearCase, RequisitePro, BuildForge, PurifyPlus, WebSphere, DB2, DB2 Universal Database, developerWorks, Tivoli, PureCoverage, Quantify, DOORS, Lotus, and Sametime. Microsoft, Visual SourceSafe, ActiveX, Windows, VisualStudio, Access, Excel, and SharePoint are trademarks of Microsoft Corporation in the United States, other countries, or both. UNIX is a registered trademark of The Open Group in the United States and other countries. Linux is a registered trademark of Linus Torvalds in the United States, other countries, or both. Oracle and Java are registered trademarks of Oracle and/or its affiliates. Other company, product, or service names may be trademarks or service marks of others.

The following terms appear throughout the book: Introduction: IBM®, Rational®, ClearQuest®, Rational Team Concert™, Jazz™, ClearCase®, RequisitePro®, Visual SourceSafe®, BuildForge®, PurifyPlus™; Chapter 1: ActiveX®, Windows®; Chapter 2: UNIX®, VisualStudio®, WebSphere®, DB2®, DB2 Universal Database™, Access®, Oracle®; Chapter 4: developerWorks®; Chapter 6: Tivoli®, Linux®, PureCoverage®, Quantify®, Excel®, Java™, DOORS®, Lotus®, Sametime®, Quickr®, SharePoint®.

Library of Congress Cataloging-in-Publication Data

Bashan, Shmuel, 1952-
  Work item management with IBM Rational Clearquest and jazz : a customization guide / Shmuel Bashan, David E. Bellagio.
      p.   cm.
  Includes index.
  ISBN 978-0-13-700179-8 (pbk. : alk. paper)
  1. Business—Computer programs. 2. Teams in the workplace--Data processing. 3. Computer software—Development—Management. 4. Jazz (Computer file) 5. Rational Clearquest. I. Bellagio, David E. II. Title

  HF5548.4.M5265B37 2011
  658.4'04028553—dc22

                                                        2011011419

ISBN-13: 978-0-13-700179-8
ISBN-10:   0-13-700179-7

Text printed in the United States on recycled paper at RR Donnelley in Crawfordsville, Indiana.
First printing, June 2011

Contents

Preface   **xix**

Acknowledgments   **xxvii**

About the Authors   **xxix**

Chapter 1   Work Items   **1**

1.1 Work Item Definition   1

    1.1.1 Terms Related to Work Items in ClearQuest and Jazz   1

1.2 Work Item Classification   4

    1.2.1 Change Requests   4

    1.2.2 Activities   5

    1.2.3 Test Elements   6

    1.2.4 Project-Related Work Items   6

1.3 Work Item Elements   7

    1.3.1 Data   7

    1.3.2 Presentation Forms   7

    1.3.3 Workflow   9

    1.3.4 Other Work Item Elements   11

1.4 Customization   13

    1.4.1 Which Work Item Elements Can Be Customized?   14

    1.4.2 Customizing Jazz Work Items   17

    1.4.3 Customizing ClearQuest Record Types   18

1.5 Resources   19

1.6 Summary   20

Chapter 2   Disciplines: Requirements, Analysis & Design   **21**

2.1 Requirements   23

    2.1.1 Gathering Requirements   23

    2.1.2 Defining and Documenting Requirements   25

    2.1.3 Getting Agreement   28

    2.1.4 Using Agile Practice   28

    2.1.5 Maintaining Requirements   28

2.2 Analysis & Design 29
   2.2.1 Defining the Types of Clients 29
   2.2.2 Defining the Infrastructure Architecture 30
   2.2.3 Choosing a Database 32
   2.2.4 ClearQuest Schema High-Level Design 33
   2.2.5 Defining the Data Fields 35
   2.2.6 Defining the Workflow 35
   2.2.7 Designing the User Interface (Forms) 36
2.3 Design Patterns 36
   2.3.1 Closing Pattern 37
   2.3.2 Triage Pattern 37
   2.3.3 Parent Control Pattern 38
   2.3.4 Child Control Pattern 38
   2.3.5 Dead End Pattern 39
   2.3.6 Data Hierarchy Pattern 39
   2.3.7 Superuser Modification Pattern 39
   2.3.8 Resolution Pattern 40
2.4 Review and Sign Off Design Models 40
2.5 Resources 40
2.6 Summary 40

Chapter 3   The Workflow   43
3.1 Software Development Processes 44
   3.1.1 The Rational Unified Process (RUP) Method 44
   3.1.2 OpenUP Method 45
3.2 Process Representation 45
   3.2.1 Creating the State Transition Matrix 49
3.3 The States 50
   3.3.1 Basic Stages in Workflow 50
   3.3.2 State Types 53
3.4 Dynamic Workflow 56
   3.4.1 Background 56
   3.4.2 The Technique 56
   3.4.3 Automatically Move to Another State 57
   3.4.4 One Record Type Having Several State Machines for Each Issue Type 59
   3.4.5 A State Machine for Each Issue 61
3.5 ClearQuest ALM Schema Workflow 65
3.6 Jazz Workflow 66
3.7 Subflow 68
   3.7.1 More Information 69
   3.7.2 Build Approval 76
3.8 Summary 78

Chapter 4   The Data   **81**

4.1 Work Item Content   83

    4.1.1 Work Item Description   83

    4.1.2 Location   86

    4.1.3 Environment   87

    4.1.4 Internal Impacts   88

    4.1.5 External Impacts   89

    4.1.6 Corrective Actions   91

    4.1.7 Times   92

    4.1.8 Tests   95

    4.1.9 History   96

    4.1.10 Additional Data   98

    4.1.11 Quality Assurance   103

4.2 State-Based Objects   104

4.3 Stateless Objects   104

4.4 Object Relations   106

    4.4.1 ClearQuest Single Relationship   106

    4.4.2 ClearQuest Multiple Relationship   108

    4.4.3 Back Reference   110

    4.4.4 More on ClearQuest Unique Key   113

    4.4.5 Jazz Links   115

4.5 Data Representation   117

    4.5.1 ClearQuest Data Representation   117

    4.5.2 Jazz Work Items Data Representation   118

4.6 ClearQuest Scripts   120

    4.6.1 HasAttachment   120

    4.6.2 Limit Attachment Size (Perl)   121

    4.6.3 Convert Full_Name to Login_Name   122

    4.6.4 Create Parent from Child   123

4.7 Summary   126

Chapter 5   Roles   **127**

5.1 Understanding Typical Problems   128

    5.1.1 Enforcing Security Control   128

    5.1.2 Unassigned Change   128

    5.1.3 Assigning the Wrong Person   128

    5.1.4 Blocking Assignment   129

5.2 Understanding Terms and Concepts   129

    5.2.1 Basic Definitions   130

    5.2.2 Role Type (Cardinality)   130

    5.2.3 Roles, Areas, and Groups   131

    5.2.4 Key Roles in the Change Request Process   131

5.3 Possible Solutions   132

    5.3.1 Implementing Roles with ClearQuest Groups   132

5.3.2 Implementing Roles Implicitly   133
5.3.3 Using Roles Stateless Record Type (with Static Roles)   136
5.3.4 User-Defined Roles   137
5.4 Security and Roles   139
5.5 Roles in the ClearQuest ALM Schema   140
5.6 Roles in Jazz   142
5.7 Code Examples   144
5.7.1 SQL Command for Group Method   144
5.7.2 Hook to Automatically Set Responsible Based on Role of Type Single   145
5.7.3 Hook to Automatically Set Choices Based on Role of Type Multiple   146
5.7.4 Hook to Automatically Set Responsible Based on Role Object   147
5.7.5 Hooks for User-Defined Roles   150
5.8 Summary   151

Chapter 6   Integrations   153
6.1 Introduction   153
6.2 ClearQuest Integrations   155
6.2.1 ClearQuest Packaged (Built-in) Integrations   156
6.2.2 Creating New Integrations with ClearQuest   162
6.2.3 Third-Party Integrations to ClearQuest   176
6.3 Jazz Products Integrations   177
6.3.1 Rational Quality Manager Integrations   177
6.3.2 Rational Team Concert Integrations   187
6.3.3 Building a New Jazz Integration   192
6.4 Resources   195
6.4.1 ALM   195
6.4.2 Jazz   195
6.4.3 ClearQuest   195
6.4.4 General Information   196
6.5 Summary   196

Chapter 7   Disciplines, Part 2   197
7.1 Implementation Discipline   197
7.1.1 ClearQuest Implementation Tasks   198
7.1.2 Jazz Implementation Tasks   199
7.2 Testing Discipline   199
7.3 Deployment Discipline   201
7.3.1 Preparation   201
7.3.2 Installations   202
7.3.3 Setting Up the Environment   202
7.3.4 Deploying Customizations   203
7.3.5 Importing Initial Data   204
7.3.6 Training   206
7.3.7 Following Up on System Adoption   207

7.4 Maintenance   207
    7.4.1 Defining the Change Process   207
    7.4.2 Ongoing Support   208
    7.4.3 Improving Maintainability   208
7.5 ClearQuest Tool Mentor   208
    7.5.1 Importing Records with References   208
    7.5.2 Importing Updates   210
    7.5.3 Creating a Test Environment   212
7.6 Jazz Tool Mentor   217
    7.6.1 Creating a Jazz Project with the Common Process Template   217
7.7 Resources   220
7.8 Summary   220

Chapter 8   Development   221
8.1 ClearQuest Schema Development   222
    8.1.1 Common Schema (ALM)   222
    8.1.2 Implementing Patterns   222
    8.1.3 Employing Reusable Assets   234
    8.1.4 Using ClearQuest Packages   238
    8.1.5 Understanding Session Variables   239
8.2 Parallel Development   240
    8.2.1 Coding Hooks   241
    8.2.2 Record Types   241
    8.2.3 Designing Forms and Tabs   243
8.3 Comparing and Merging Schema Versions   245
8.4 Storing Hooks Externally   249
8.5 Releasing a Version to Production   250
    8.5.1 Developer Testing   250
    8.5.2 System Testing   252
    8.5.3 Promotion to Production   252
8.6 Globally Distributed Development (GDD) Considerations and ClearQuest
    MultiSite (CQMS)   253
    8.6.1 Upgrading the Schema   253
    8.6.2 Addressing Mastership Changes   253
    8.6.3 Testing the Mastership   254
8.7 ClearQuest Script Debugging   255
    8.7.1 Employing the `MsgBox()` Function   255
    8.7.2 Employing the `OutputDebugString()` Method   256
    8.7.3 Debugging with Tracing Information   258
8.8 Other Development Considerations   260
    8.8.1 Choosing a Scripting Language   261
    8.8.2 When Is a Stateless Record Type Required?   261
    8.8.3 Dealing with Records That Have More Than One Field as Unique Key   261
    8.8.4 Organizing Global Scripts   262

         8.8.5 Devising a Naming Convention   262
         8.8.6 Storing the old_id Field for Future Import   264
         8.8.7 Dealing with Long Selection Lists   265
         8.8.8 Updating a Dynamic List   271
         8.8.9 Using Hard-Coded Data   272
    8.9 Web Considerations   274
         8.9.1 Enable Button Hooks   274
         8.9.2 Field Dependency   275
         8.9.3 Other Limitations   276
    8.10 Preparing for the Future   277
    8.11 Resources   277
         8.11.1 ClearQuest   277
         8.11.2 Jazz   277
    8.12 Summary   278

Chapter 9   Metrics and Governance   279
    9.1 Metrics   279
         9.1.1 Types of Metrics   280
         9.1.2 Metrics Strategy   280
         9.1.3 Supporting Data for Metrics   284
         9.1.4 Tools   284
    9.2 Governance   287
         9.2.1 Process Control and Automation   288
         9.2.2 Permissions (Access Control and Security)   288
         9.2.3 Monitoring   289
         9.2.4 Governance with ClearQuest   290
         9.2.5 Governance with the ClearQuest ALM Schema   297
         9.2.6 Governance with Rational Team Concert   299
    9.3 Resources   301
         9.3.1 Metrics and Governance   301
         9.3.2 Jazz Reports   302
         9.3.3 Data Warehouse   303
         9.3.4 BIRT Reports   304
         9.3.5 C/ALM Reports   304
    9.4 Summary   305

Chapter 10   Test Management and Work Items   307
    10.1 What Is Rational Quality Manager?   307
    10.2 Understanding Test Entities and Work Items   307
    10.3 Work Items in the Test Process   310
    10.4 Customization   316
         10.4.1 Customizing Jazz Work Items   317
         10.4.2 Testing Specific Work Items   318
    10.5 Summary   324

Chapter 11   Managing Agile Projects   325
11.1 Defining Agile Development   325
11.2 Agile and Scrum in a Nutshell   326
11.3 Realization with Rational Team Concert   330
11.4 Realization with ClearQuest   337
    11.4.1 Required Data   339
    11.4.2 Understanding the Workflows of Each Record Type   343
    11.4.3 Understanding Metrics in Agile Development   345
11.5 Agile with the ALM Schema   346
11.6 Resources   350
    11.6.1 Materials by Scott Ambler   350
    11.6.2 DeveloperWorks Articles   350
    11.6.3 Other Information   350
11.7 Summary   351

Chapter 12   Sample Applications and Solutions   353
12.1 Collaborative ALM with Jazz-Based Tools   353
    12.1.1 Jazz C/ALM   354
12.2 User-Defined Fields in ClearQuest   356
    12.2.1 Defining Choice Lists   358
    12.2.2 Defining Requiredness   360
12.3 Service Level Agreements (SLAs) in ClearQuest   363
    12.3.1 Background   363
    12.3.2 The Topic   364
    12.3.3 SLA Definition   364
    12.3.4 Activate the SLA Rules   365
    12.3.5 Notifications   365
    12.3.6 Providing Governance Reports   366
    12.3.7 The External Program   366
12.4 ClearCase, ClearQuest ALM, Build Forge Integrated Solution Architecture   367
    12.4.1 Understanding the Work Projects   368
    12.4.2 Developers Work on Activities within a Project   368
    12.4.3 Continuously Validating through a Build and Validation Process   369
    12.4.4 Creating the Task to Integrate the Baseline That Includes a Defect Fix   370
    12.4.5 Releasing Periodically through Stable Composite Baselines   371
    12.4.6 Working on Test Artifacts   372
12.5 Manage Release Promotion   374
    12.5.1 Current Status Assessment   374
    12.5.2 Solution   375
    12.5.3 Process Components   376
    12.5.4 The Promotion Process Model   379
12.6 Resources   382
    12.6.1 Solutions Developed by Customers and Rational Staff   382

12.6.2 SLA 383

12.6.3 ALM and C/ALM 383

12.6.4 Application Lifecycle Management with Rational ClearQuest 383

12.7 Summary 384

Index **387**

Preface

Almost everyone has had the need at one point or another to keep a list of things that need to be done. Many people pick up a piece of paper every day and write down the things they want to attempt to accomplish that day. Such lists drive many people's lives. Some people keep them in their heads, but as we get older, we need to write things down more often so as not to forget what has to be done. When you are keeping track of a list of items for yourself to do, it is pretty easy to know what has been done and what has not. You only have to depend on yourself. Updating the list is easy. Having a list of the important things to be done and reviewing it many times a day might make many people more productive.

There are a few problems with creating a list of items to keep track of. One is that it gets much more complicated when many different people are working on the items. Now you have to coordinate updates to the list from all of those people. This problem becomes harder still when some of the people live in other time zones. Now it is much harder to understand who is doing what, what has been done, and, more important, what has not been done and why. So we typically create some sort of database to keep track of these things. In the simplest form, this database may be a spreadsheet. Some people start creating their own management system from scratch to deal with these lists. These systems tend to grow over time in both complexity and cost of maintenance. Pretty soon, as your needs grow, you may find that the process you created to keep track of the items does not scale, nor does it meet your needs anymore. The management system you created will also have its own list of items that need to be done, and you may find that the cost of maintaining your custom system outweighs the benefits you are receiving from it.

In the world of software and hardware development, lists of items tell us who is doing what, what has been done, what problems are being worked on, and which products are affected by these problems. These lists become the lifeblood for many individuals. Being able to accurately understand your product's status and exposure can help you make better decisions about what items should be worked on, what items you need to wait to be done, and what items are not as important as others.

The focus of this book is to help you implement solutions for dealing with many types of common patterns that crop up when managing items of work for large teams of people. In this introduction we briefly explain what a work item is and the business and technical environment with which work item management is involved. We will also define and explain many basic terms that are important for you to understand as you apply the techniques provided in this book.

The book's content is organized to allow selective reading by people who are interested in only specific subjects. We explain for whom the book is intended and how different roles should read the book. Many chapters include practical sections with code examples; guidance is given for you to make the most of the provided assets so that you can reuse them in your applications. The reality is, you need some sort of management system in place to help you use the knowledge that exists in the work items. Therefore, all of the example solutions provided within the book are implemented in IBM Rational ClearQuest (CQ) and/or IBM Rational Team Concert (RTC). There are many reasons for choosing these tools to highlight the solutions we explore. Some of the reasons for using ClearQuest as the tool of choice are that it is a mature product, there are many existing examples of solutions using the tool, and its customization potential is a powerful feature. It is easier to implement the patterns we explore in ClearQuest. Theory can take you only so far; we focus on reality and the details needed to implement solutions within these two tools.

What Is a Work Item?

A work item is an object that controls the process of performing a task. The work item contains the following elements: data, presentation forms, workflow, and possibly other elements and other objects. We call it the *work item triangle* (see Figure P.1).

Figure P.1   Elements of the work item (the work item triangle): workflow, data, and presentation

The bottom vertices of the triangle are the data that constitutes the work item and the presentation that allows the user to view and modify the data and interact with the system. The top of the triangle is the workflow. The workflow is a series of activities performed by people having the specific roles to produce a desired outcome. In different domains the outcome is different; to achieve the outcome the three elements of the triangle must be customized so that the organization will achieve the outcome in an efficient way, with minimal risk and with the highest quality.

Work items are the fundamental mechanisms for tracking and coordinating tasks within your development organization. They are governed by the workflows within your organization's process. This book will show you practical strategies for solving typical problems that will arise when you try to implement and deploy a work item management solution based on ClearQuest or Rational Team Concert.

Chapter 1, "Work Items," discusses work items in more detail and refers to additional materials that will help you deal with managing work items.

The Environment

The main environment to which this book pertains is the software development environment. However, many techniques can be applied to other environments, such as hardware development.

In the software development lifecycle (SDLC) there are several phases and several disciplines, as explained in the Rational Unified Process (RUP) and demonstrated in Figure 2.1 in Chapter 2, "Disciplines: Requirements, Analysis & Design."

It is possible that different organizational units will have ownership of the process in different phases or in different disciplines. For example, defects defined during testing may have one type of work item and defects found in development or in production may have different work item types. Another example is that the work items for project activities are different from the work items for software defect resolution. So within the software development environment there are subenvironments.

Another environment to which work item management is relevant is the systems development environment. In this environment chip, electronic device, and appliance designers and developers adopt a different development lifecycle and also use different types of work items. In some cases work items to manage software are combined with work items to manage hardware. We discuss this important subject in the book as well.

This book contains a lot of content that deals with work item customization, including detailed examples of how to customize. To meet the specific requirements of each environment it is necessary to customize the three elements of the work item, and we shall explain how to customize the data, the workflow, and the presentation using ClearQuest and Rational Team Concert.

This Book's Content

The following sections present brief summaries of the chapters of the book.

Chapter 1: Work Items

A work item is an object that contains the following elements: data, presentation forms, workflow, and possibly other elements and other objects.

Work items can be classified as changes (defects, enhancement requests, and features), tasks, activities, test plans, test cases, risks, builds, promotion, and others.

The chapter explains each of the elements, how they differ in types of changes, and the best practices for design and implementation (for example, when to combine defect and enhancement requests into a single element such as an issue; how to deal with both hardware and software defects).

Chapter 2: Disciplines: Requirements, Analysis & Design

This chapter is about the best practices used to develop ClearQuest and Rational Team Concert applications. We use the parts of the RUP methodology that are suitable to these types of applications. The following disciplines are discussed:

- **Requirements:** Gather requirements from customers and stakeholders, organize, prioritize, solve conflicts, and get agreement.

- **Analysis & Design:** Define types of ClearQuest clients, define the system architecture (server configuration, network topology, and firewall), databases, schema high-level design, and user interface. We have also included a section on design patterns.

This topic is continued in Chapter 7, "Disciplines, Part 2," where we discuss four additional disciplines.

Chapter 3: The Workflow

In this chapter we discuss various methods of describing the workflow and propose some patterns for designing it. In addition, ClearQuest is known to have a static state machine. In this chapter you will learn an advanced technique for creating a dynamic workflow in ClearQuest. Some implementation benefits and examples are provided.

Chapter 4: The Data

The data of work items is stored in fields of various types. For each type of work item a set of fields is required to meet the business requirements. We shall discuss what data is required for each work item and when it is required (which state in the lifecycle). We discuss classification methods, include recommendations, and give many examples. We also discuss data grouping: necessity and techniques.

The second part of the chapter explains how to make the most of the different types of fields, such as Reference, Reference_List, Date_Time, and others.

Performance considerations with certain types of ClearQuest hooks are explained.

Chapter 5: Roles

A role is a key concept in RUP; we explain how to incorporate roles into your ClearQuest schema. Three techniques are explained, each one with different complexity levels and schema structures, to meet various organizational needs.

In addition, we explain how to take advantage of roles, such as how to auto-assign owners based on roles, how to populate choice lists based on roles, and how to notify people of events based on their roles.

The last section of the chapter explains roles in Jazz and in the ClearQuest Application Lifecycle Management (CQ-ALM) schema.

Chapter 6: Integrations

The chapter starts with a brief introduction to integration types and the value of integrating applications. It is divided between ClearQuest integrations and Jazz integrations. In the ClearQuest integrations section we describe the built-in packaged integrations, that is, ClearCase, RequisitePro, Visual SourceSafe, Microsoft Project, Build Forge, Portfolio Manager, and PurifyPlus. We continue with building new integrations, explain the methods of integrating applications with ClearQuest (e-mail, import/export, API), and give some examples: expert systems, help desk, and others.

The second part of the chapter is about Jazz integrations. We describe the Jazz platform integration technology and continue with Rational Quality Manager and Rational Team Concert integrations with ClearQuest and other products.

Chapter 7: Disciplines, Part 2

This chapter is about the best practices used to develop ClearQuest and Jazz applications. We use part of the RUP methodology to meet the needs of these types of applications. In this chapter we discuss the following disciplines:

- **Implementing:** schema development, parallel implementation
- **Testing:** building the test environment, testing methods
- **Deployment:** managing multiple environments, enabling end users in the solution
- **Maintenance:** managing change to the solution by using the solution

Chapter 8: Development

Although developing a ClearQuest schema is in many aspects similar to code development, there are significant differences due to the special environment. In this chapter we explain the special development considerations. Some of the subjects discussed are

- Schema development tips
- Common schema
- Pattern implementation in CQ and Jazz
- Packages
- Parallel development (and multiple schemas, multiple databases)
- Versioning content
- Releasing a version to production
- Globally Distributed Development (GDD) considerations and ClearQuest MultiSite
- Preparing for future product releases

Chapter 9: Metrics and Governance

The first part of the chapter is about metrics. We explain some quality metrics (such as defect density); performance metrics (how fast and efficient our process is); and how to collect, measure, and present the data. We explain the tools available to create these metrics.

The second part of the chapter is about governance. There are various aspects of governance. In this chapter we discuss the following: controls such as electronic signature, setting service level agreements (SLAs), and managing audit logs.

Another important issue that we explain is the security setting with the Security Context record and additional security measures.

Chapter 10: Test Management and Work items

In this chapter we discuss work items used in the testing process. Test management requires different considerations from change management. We review the Rational Quality Manager work items and how the different types are used. Other subjects included in this chapter are the customization of work items and the customization of other test elements.

Chapter 11: Managing Agile Projects

With the emerging popularity of Agile programming methods, organizations need to adapt their workflows and automation techniques. In this chapter we briefly describe some Agile methods and how ClearQuest can be used to create a workflow for those techniques. We dive into the Scrum processes and explain how to mange backlogs and sprints with ClearQuest. A ClearQuest schema is provided for the Scrum Agile method.

We discuss in detail how Scrum is realized using Rational Team Concert. We also discuss how to implement the Agile process with the CQ-ALM schema.

Chapter 12: Sample Applications and Solutions

In this chapter we explain some special applications and solutions that extend existing applications.

We start with a description of a Collaborative Application Lifecycle Management integrated solution with Jazz-based products: Rational Team Concert (RTC), Rational Quality Manager (RQM), and Rational Requirements Composer (RRC).

We describe a solution to extend a ClearQuest schema with project-defined fields and an example of an SLA with ClearQuest.

The Application Lifecycle Management (ALM) solution is a good basis for many applications, and we provide some examples and techniques for how to map your solution needs to the ALM packages that come with ClearQuest. We describe an integrated solution with ClearCase, ClearQuest, and Build Forge.

Finally, we describe a solution to managing release promotion in a heterogeneous environment using ClearQuest.

Audience for the Book

The book will appeal to many roles and to users with a wide range of interests. This book is for everyone who is interested in software change management.

The large community of ClearQuest users will find this book valuable. This includes all users involved in ClearQuest administration, all who are interested in developing new applications with ClearQuest, and those who want to integrate ClearQuest with other applications.

The growing community of Jazz customers will also find this book interesting. In addition to the theoretical parts, we provide examples of work item management within Rational Team Concert and Rational Quality Manager, and we have dedicated Chapter 10 to test management and a focus on Rational Quality Manager.

These roles within your organization will find value in this book:

- **Project managers:** This role will learn how to use work items to help manage their project's health: what metrics are important, how to triage effectively, and obtaining visibility into potentially desired workflows that meet the organization's needs. Project managers can also learn how to use ClearQuest to manage Agile projects.

- **Technical leaders:** This role will be exposed to solutions to various problems that may shed some light on a particular issue that affects the organization's current challenges, for example, how to model and track activities related to a project's development patterns using the ClearQuest ALM workflow framework.

- **SCM administrators:** This role will be exposed to strategies for implementing solutions to problems that should benefit from a complete change management solution, for example, how the ClearQuest ALM workflows integrate with ClearCase UCM stream strategies.

- **Tools engineers:** This role will be exposed to best practices and techniques for implementing solutions to common patterns that may be important to the organization's needs.

- **Test managers:** This role will find Chapter 10 of interest, especially if adopting the Jazz platform is being considered. Test managers will also be interested in various defect-tracking techniques as well as in Chapter 9.

- **QA managers:** This role can find value in Chapter 9 as well as Chapter 10, especially if adopting the Jazz platform is under consideration.

- **Process analysts:** Process control is discussed in several chapters, in the discipline chapters and in Chapters 3 and 9. Also, the examples of using ClearQuest ALM to model the development process should be of importance.

- **Experienced ClearQuest users:** These users can deepen their knowledge of change management, learn new techniques, get new ideas for improving the system they work with, and learn how to implement ideas they have.

- **Experienced RTC and RQM users:** These users can learn how to customize the Jazz work items and how to create new work item types.

How to Read This Book

This book attempts to close the gap in the existing materials on work item management. There aren't many books or articles that discuss this subject. The book is organized in a way that will allow many users to take advantage of its contents. In each chapter we discuss the theory of the subject with examples from the industry. After discussing the theory, we dive into the practical elements of the discipline and provide implementation examples using ClearQuest, Rational Quality Manager, or Rational Team Concert. In many cases there are several solutions to the specific requirements, and we have provided proposed solutions from a lighter-weight approach to an increasingly more complex implementation.

So, how to read this book? It depends on your role and your interests.

One way is to read the book from start to finish. It is organized in a way that will make such an approach easy. For example, we have split the disciplines between two chapters in order to make sequential reading more coherent.

Another way is to first read the two chapters about disciplines: Chapter 2 and Chapter 7. They complement each other, and we have split them so that the disciplines described in each chapter are followed with the right content. If you are interested only in the theoretical part of work item management, it makes sense to read those two chapters in sequence. They include references to practical materials in other chapters so that you can learn how the discussed disciplines are implemented with the tools.

The other chapters discuss specific areas of work item management. For example, Chapter 5 discusses roles and includes implementation examples and ClearQuest scripts. If you want to improve your process governance and lifecycle efficiency, go directly to this chapter.

Another example is Chapter 11 on Agile projects. This chapter includes a theoretical part and implementation examples in ClearQuest and Rational Team Concert. If your organization is using ClearQuest and is thinking about adopting Agile practices, you must read this chapter.

You can also use it as a cookbook. If you need to resolve an issue, search in the table of contents or the index for the relevant content. You may find implementation descriptions with code examples and references to additional materials.

A Note on the Code Examples   Because of page width limitations we sometimes break command lines into two or more lines and use the backslash character (\) as the break character. Also in code examples you may see some unnatural indentations for the same reason.

Acknowledgments

This book's content is not just the effort of the authors. The material was gathered over the past ten years of using and deploying customer solutions composed of the products mentioned within this book. The authors would like to thank the host of coworkers and customers who over the years have contributed to our greater understanding of the principles of change management, the functioning of the products, and our understanding of which change management strategies work and which ones don't.

Our ever-patient editors at Pearson, Christopher Guzikowski and Raina Chrobak, deserve many thanks as well. Many thanks to our copy editor, Barbara Wood, and to our production editor, Anna Popick, for their diligence during the production process.

We would also like to thank our families for their long-suffering during the many weekends we were busy writing the book. Shmuel would like to thank his wife, Catherine, for her support and encouragement. Dave would like to thank his wife, Laura, and kids, Anthony, Jacob, and Mark, for allowing him the time to be involved in this effort.

Much of the material is directly related to the experience of the IBM Rational field teams in engagements with customers using ClearQuest. Some of the folks whom we would like to thank for their efforts in fleshing out strategies that work with many of our larger customer needs are Ariel Whol, Shai Shapira, Etan Shomrai, Alan Murphy, Allan Wagner, Daniel Diebolt, Majid Irani, Stuart Poulin, Michael Saylor, Paul Weiss, Grant Covell, Katur Patel, Marlin Deckert, David Maroshi, Bob Myers, and Raanon Reutlinger. We have probably missed someone; if so, our apologies and thanks.

Colleagues who agreed to share content deserve many thanks: Caroline Pampino for content on C/ALM; Bob Myers for content on CQ-ALM; Scott Ambler for content on Agile; David Lubanco on metrics; Sharon Weed, Bala Rajaraman, and John Wiegand for content on integrations; Patrick Streule and Nicolas Dangeville for their help with OSLC; Yuhong Yin and Steven Pitschke for assistance in building charts and content on CQ architecture; and Alan Murphy for content on CQ development and debugging.

Special thanks to those people who put in the time to review this book and provide comments to help make the information more accurate and the reading more pleasant: Scott Ambler, Bob Myers, Michael Warfield, Chuck Walrad, and Celso Gonzalez.

We have learned from every client engagement, many of them inspired with ideas and innovative solutions. Many thanks to clients who agreed to share content: Dr. Alexander Karnovsky, Gerrit Van Doorn, Joseph W. Derr Jr., and Jacob (Kobi) Welber.

Finally, our thanks go to everyone at IBM Rational Software who keeps ClearQuest and the Jazz-based product efforts moving forward. Keep up the good work.

About the Authors

Shmuel Bashan

Shmuel Bashan is a Senior Deployment Specialist and Mentor on IBM Rational Software's global services account team, covering European countries. Prior to this assignment, he worked as the Rational technical leader, solution architect, and Rational country leader in Israel.

Prior to joining Rational in 1997, Shmuel was a manager of a consulting firm, and prior to that a software developer of CAD/CAM applications. Shmuel holds a B.Sc. in mechanical engineering from Ben-Gurion University and an Information Systems Analyst Certificate from the Manufacturers Association of Israel.

Shmuel is an active member of the change management community and has contributed several articles and reusable assets: scripts for various solutions, advanced training materials, and workshops. He has also contributed to the RUP 8.0 Change Management practice.

Shmuel presented at several Rational user conferences in Europe and the United States:

"What's New in Automated Software Testing and ClearQuest" (Israel, 2004)

"From Requirements to Delivery" (Israel, 2005)

"Advanced Techniques in ClearQuest Customization" (Orlando, FL, 2006)

"ClearQuest Tips and Tricks" (Strasbourg, France, 2007)

"Automating Code Integration Activities with ClearQuest ALM, UCM, and Build Forge" (with David E. Bellagio, Orlando, FL, 2009)

Shmuel published the following articles in *developerWorks*:

"Adaptive Workflow in ClearQuest"

"Manage Scrum Projects with ClearQuest"

"Using Roles for Automatic Assignment in IBM Rational ClearQuest"

Shmuel resides in Israel with his beloved wife, three children, and two grandchildren. Shmuel enjoys jazz music, art cinema and theater, playing chess and bridge, jogging along the seashore, and hiking, but unfortunately time does not allow all these activities. He can be reached via e-mail at bashansh@il.ibm.com

David E. Bellagio

David E. Bellagio has been involved in the software development community for the past 30 years, ever since he caught the programming bug growing up in Healdsburg, California. David holds a B.S. and an M.S. in computer science, with honors, from California State University at Chico. David has worked at various companies, including Computer Sciences Corporation, Tandem Computers, Automatic Data Processing, and Hewlett Packard. He started with Rational Software as a technical field representative in the Pacific Northwest in early 1998.

David currently is a Worldwide Integration Engineering Architect at IBM Rational Software in charge of developing and deploying integrated solutions to customers around the world. He has worked on-site with numerous customers to define and manage successful deployments of Rational Software solutions. David has presented the following topics at Rational user conferences:

> "Building Software with Clearmake on Non-ClearCase Hosts" (Lexington, MA, 1995)
>
> "ClearAdmin: A Set of Scripts, Processes, and Techniques for Administrating Large ClearCase Sites" (Lexington, MA, 1996)
>
> "UCM Stream Strategies and Best Practices" (Dallas, TX, 2004)
>
> "Automating Code Integration Activities with ClearQuest ALM, UCM, and Build Forge" (with Shmuel Bashan, Orlando, FL, 2009)

David coauthored *Software Configuration Management Strategies and IBM Rational ClearCase: A Practical Introduction, Second Edition* (IBM Press, 2005).

David currently resides in the state of Washington with his lovely wife and three children. When time allows, David enjoys playing rock music, shooting pool, and brewing fine ales and mead. He can be reached via e-mail at dbellagio@us.ibm.com.

## CHAPTER 1

Work Items

This chapter is an overview of work items; it is meant to set the right context for work items within the project development process. We shall go into the details of the work item elements in Chapter 3, "The Workflow," Chapter 4, "The Data," and Chapter 5, "Roles." This book is not only about work items theory but also a practical introduction to ClearQuest and the Jazz-based products' work item management. The terms used in ClearQuest and the Jazz work items are sometimes different, so we shall provide a comparison, along with some examples.

Currently (version 3.0) the Jazz-based products that include work items are Rational Team Concert and Rational Quality Manager.

1.1 Work Item Definition

A work item is created so that people having specific roles can perform actions within the process of creating or changing (software) artifacts. This definition is taken from Jazz.net, but we can adopt a more general definition that is related to any work done in any project.

A work item is an object that controls the process of performing work during software or systems development. The work item contains the following composite elements: data, presentation forms, workflow, and possibly other elements and other objects. Each of these elements will be described in detail in the following chapters.

1.1.1 Terms Related to Work Items in ClearQuest and Jazz

Table 1.1 summarizes the basic terms that are used in ClearQuest and the Jazz products. In the book we shall use terms from both, depending on the context.

Table 1.1   Comparing ClearQuest and Jazz Work Item Terms

ClearQuest	Jazz	Comments
Schema	Process Template	The metadata definition. All the elements described in this table are defined in a ClearQuest schema or in a Jazz Process Template.
Record type (state-based)	Work item type	
Record type (stateless)	N/A	
Field	Work item attribute	In Jazz, user-defined attributes are called custom attributes.
Record type family	Work item type category	The implementation is totally different, because of the differences in architecture. In Jazz, all types of a type category share the same custom attributes and follow the same workflow. In ClearQuest, the family members do not share anything; they only have a common list of fields having the same names, so that you can retrieve data from the members in a single query.
State transition matrix	Workflow	
State	State	
State type	State group	In Jazz, Resolution is a private case similar to the Resolved state type.
Action	Action	
Forms	Editor presentations	
Tab	Tab	
Group box (in tab)	Section (in tab)	Group box and section are not exactly the same but have similar visual presentation and the same purpose.
N/A	Quick Information section	Although the Quick Information section does not exist in ClearQuest, the functionality can be customized with ReadOnly fields to provide a similar display.
GUI control	Presentation	A graphical control to present data or to interact with the user, also called a graphical user interface (GUI) widget. The Jazz work item does not include button, radio, and ActiveX controls.

Table 1.1 Comparing ClearQuest and Jazz Work Item Terms (*Continued*)

Choice list	Enumeration	ClearQuest has static, dynamic, and scripted (hook) lists. Jazz enumerations are used mainly in choice lists and are similar to the ClearQuest dynamic list. A Jazz enumeration is an independent entity that can be bound to any attribute.
		Jazz does not support hooks in choice lists.[1]
Access control (for actions)	Permission	Notice that the term *permission* means different things in ClearQuest and Jazz. In ClearQuest, permission is a field hook that at runtime sets the field behavior to Optional, Mandatory, or ReadOnly. Static values are set in the field's behaviors table.
		In Jazz, permission configures which action is permitted for each role and is part of the project configuration or team configuration (not only work item configuration).
User's privileges	Access control (for read access to a project area)	
N/A	Approval tracking	In Jazz, approval tracking defines how an approval state change can trigger a workflow action.
		In ClearQuest, approval tracking can be customized with hooks.
Action hooks	Operation behavior or extensions	In ClearQuest, an action hook is code in BASIC or Perl.
		In Jazz, operation behavior sets the required preconditions and follow-up actions for the corresponding operation and role.
		Code hooks are not supported in Jazz, but one can write a Jazz extension (in Java or another language) using the Jazz API and SDK to update work items and their attributes.
N/A	Plans	RTC 3.0 introduced plans, which present an advanced way to organize work items.[2]
Field behaviors	Preconditions in operation behavior	In ClearQuest, for each field in each state we can set the behavior to Mandatory, Optional, or ReadOnly. Behavior can be either a static value or dynamically set with code in a field permission hook.
		In Jazz, field behavior is set to either Required or Optional.

1. Jazz work item attribute value providers: RTC 2.0 introduced a preliminary capability that currently supports custom default values for attributes and calculated attribute values. For more details see Patrick Streule, "Work Item Attribute Value Providers," https://jazz.net/wiki/bin/view/Main/AttributeValueProviders, February 8, 2011 (accessed February 24, 2011).

2. RTC plans: For more information on plans see "Getting Started with Planning in Rational Team Concert 3.0," jazz.net/library/article/593, November 10, 2010 (accessed March 24, 2011).

1.2 Work Item Classification

During software project development each role performs various activities to build or modify different artifacts. Each work effort may require different flow or data during the process, thus requiring several work item types.

There are many types of work items, and you can create additional work items both with ClearQuest and with the Jazz-based products to fulfill the business requirements of your organization.

We can classify those work items as

- Change requests

- Activities

- Test elements

- Project-related work items

In the following sections we describe each work item class. We recognize that there may be other classes, depending upon the environment and the domain in which the business operates.

1.2.1 Change Requests

Change requests are work items used to track, document, and govern the process of changing a product. Examples of changes are

- **Defect:** an error in the product that should be fixed, also called a bug by optimistic people

- **Enhancement request:** a request to improve or add functionality to an existing feature of a product

- **Feature:** a request to add a new feature to a product

Different change request types usually have different data fields and different workflows; in many cases the different types are realized in a single work item type. When realized in a single work item, include a field that identifies the type, as shown in Figure 1.1.

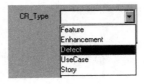

Figure 1.1   ClearQuest work item type selection

1.2.2 Activities

Activities are work items assigned to team members to perform various types of work or tasks. Activities are broken down into subclasses:

- Activities used for general project tasks, such as installation, setup, data imports, training, and so on

  These work items are usually called tasks or activities. Their workflows are simple and have very few states and actions.

- Activities used to break down change requests into smaller work elements

  The best way to explain this is with examples. An enhancement request is usually split into several activities when there is a need to deal with several artifacts such as a design model, code, and documentation; because different artifacts are owned by different roles, each activity is assigned to a different role. Another example is when an enhancement request is related to a few domains, such as components owned by two teams, both hardware and software; each child activity is assigned by role to the relevant solution provider.

- Administrative work such as defining new users and groups or organizing non-project activities (education, department social events, and so on)

In the ClearQuest ALM schema, activities are children of tasks, and tasks are children of requests. Figure 1.2 shows the ClearQuest Web client form of the ALMTask work item (id=0111).

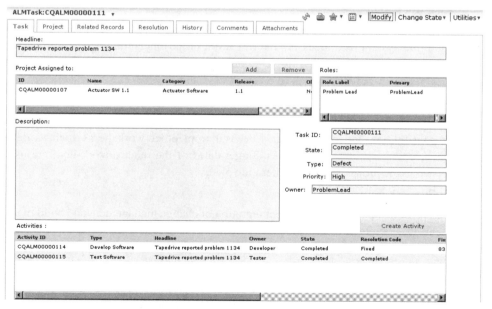

Figure 1.2   ClearQuest work item of type ALMTask with children of type ALMActivity

This record has two children of type ALMActivity. The ALMActivity (id=0114) was created for software development, and the ALMActivity (id=0115) was created for software testing.

1.2.3 Test Elements

Although often not considered as work items, test objects have their own lifecycle, data, and forms and thus conform to our definition of work item. We can identify several test work items; the obvious ones are test plans and test cases. In ClearQuest Test Management (CQTM), these objects are state-based record types just like defects and enhancement requests. A test case is created, assigned to a role, reviewed, implemented, and approved (for execution in a specific release) and thus has a workflow.

In Rational Quality Manager the test plan and test case objects also have a lifecycle, but they are of a different type from the other Jazz work items such as defects, enhancements, and requirements. In the Jazz foundation, test plan and test case are not considered work items and do not appear in the work item list, although they have all the elements that conform to the work item definition.

Test elements are described in detail in Chapter 10, "Test Management and Work Items."

1.2.4 Project-Related Work Items

If you are interested in Application Lifecycle Management (ALM), you should consider additional work items that govern projects, such as risk, release, build, promotion, and other elements of the lifecycle.

- **Risk work item**

  The risk work item is part of risk management; its function is to control the process of capturing system risk, assessing the risk level, proposing solutions, and mitigating the risk. This work item is often linked to other work items such as features and enhancement requests that may introduce risks to the system.

- **Release work item**

  The release work item controls the release process, the release content, dates, and responsibilities. Release content is derived from other work items such as defects, enhancement requests, or features. Target dates of the release work item are usually related to the project timeline or iteration plan.

- **Build work item**

  The build work item manages the integration of change management and build management. It is common to integrate this work item with build generation tools or process automation tools such as Rational Build Forge.

- **Promotion work item**

  The promotion work item governs the process of promoting artifacts from one environment to a higher environment. Some examples are promotion from the development environment to the test environment or promotion from the preproduction environment to the production environment. This work item is usually integrated with the software configuration management (SCM) system and the build system.

Rational Team Concert is an ALM tool, and therefore some of these elements are an integral part of the tool—the release and the build, for example.

The ClearQuest ALM schema also includes record types such as Project, Build, Phase, and Iteration. ClearQuest also provide packages for deployment tracking and for build tracking.

1.3 Work Item Elements

As explained in section 1.1, "Work Item Definition," *work item* includes the following composite elements: data, presentation forms, workflow, and possibly other elements and other objects. In the following sections we provide a brief explanation of each work item element, and we shall give much more detailed information in the next chapters.

1.3.1 Data

A work item contains data that is stored in fields (or work item attributes). Although all work items have a common set of fields, such as ID, State, Subject, and Owner (built-in attributes), each work item type contains fields that are exclusive and serve the specific purpose of the work item type in the organization (custom attributes).

The following are some examples of custom fields:

- Defect contains fields such as Component, Software_Version, Phase_Detected, Severity, etc.
- Feature contains fields such as Customer_Priority, Impact, Risk, etc.
- Test Case contains fields such as Pre-Conditions, Post-Conditions, Acceptance_Criteria, etc.
- Hardware Defects contains fields such as Device, Part_Number, Machine_Type, etc.

Work items for specific domains such as finance, pharmaceutical, and telecommunications will have fields specific to their domains.

See the detailed information on work item data in Chapter 4, "The Data."

1.3.2 Presentation Forms

The data of a work item is presented to the user in forms. A form usually has several tabs, and each tab contains graphic controls. Some graphic controls display the data fields, for example, check box, drop-down combo box, and various types of text boxes. Other controls like the push-button generate an action or launch an application. There are also special controls for lists, controls to deal with attachments, complex controls for parent-child relationship interactions, and many others.

Work item data is also presented outside the form, for example, in queries, charts, reports, and dashboards, but user interaction is performed in the form only.

For more detailed information on work item data presentation see Chapter 4, "The Data."

See Figure 1.2 for the Web presentation of a work item. The same record is shown in Figure 1.3 in the ClearQuest Eclipse client and in Figure 1.4 in the ClearQuest Windows native client.

As you can see, there is not much visual difference among the three ClearQuest client environments. User interaction is slightly different because of different controls and their location.

The Jazz presentation is somewhat different. You can work with work items via the Web interface or the Eclipse interface. The Web interface is based on Web 2.0, which provides the user with a richer interface and more dynamic behavior.

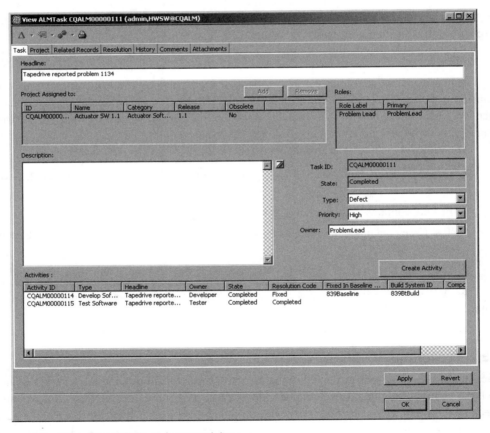

Figure 1.3   ClearQuest Eclipse form work item

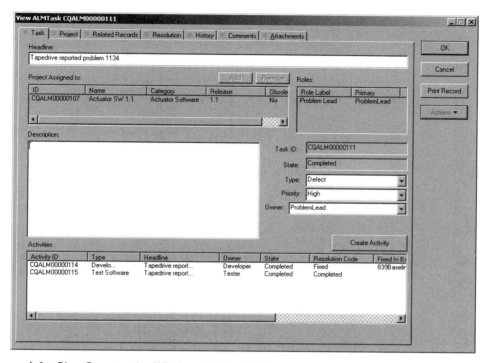

Figure 1.4 ClearQuest native Windows form work item

See section 4.5, "Data Representation," in Chapter 4, "The Data," for detailed information on this subject.

1.3.3 Workflow

The work item has a lifecycle; it is transitioned from state to state until it is closed (the end state). People with the right access control (permission) perform actions on the work item that change its state. In addition to changing the state, they are usually adding data or changing the data of the work item by typing text, selecting values from a pick list, or adding attachments. In some cases the actions are performed by automation scripts and not by people.

The workflow is designed with graphical aids like a Unified Modeling Language (UML) activity diagram and is defined in ClearQuest and Jazz with a state transition table.

An example of workflow definition in a Jazz work item is demonstrated in Figure 1.5.

The ClearQuest state transition matrix defines the workflow in a very similar way. See the more detailed information on work item workflow in Chapter 3, "The Workflow."

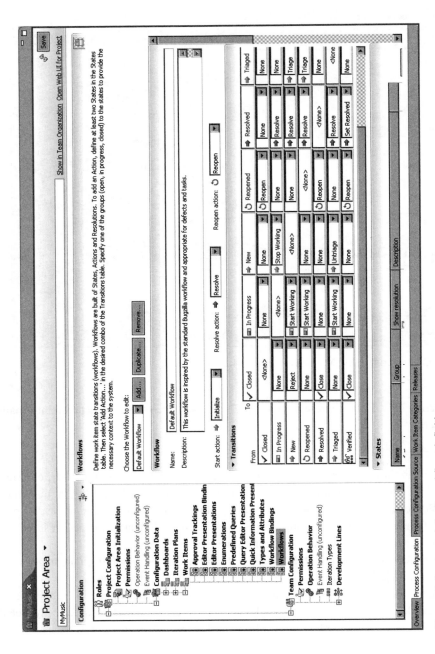

Figure 1.5 Jazz default workflow definition

1.3.4 Other Work Item Elements

Work items can have additional elements such as rules, attachments, links of various types, pictures, and more. These elements are described in the following sections.

1.3.4.1 Rules

To govern the process of change, you must set rules to control the process of the work item. Some examples of rules are as follows:

- Setting the requiredness of the fields

  Requires the users to provide a value after a specific event, or prevents them from changing the value of a field in specific states

- Access control

  Defines whether a user is allowed to perform an action, or whether an electronic signature is required prior to performing an action

- Notifications

  Notifies users by e-mail of events, for example, that the user was assigned to resolve a work item

- Perform an action

  Performs an action if conditions are met or after another event

- Integration

  Integrates with other applications when the work item reaches a specific state

Rules are implemented in various ways depending on the type of rule and on the tool. Customized rules can be installed in the metadata with packages like the ClearQuest Notification package or the ClearQuest Audit Trail package. Many times rules are defined by customized code, like the code examples we provide in section 8.1.2, "Implementing Patterns," in Chapter 8, "Development," for implementation of parent control and child control rules.

1.3.4.2 Attachments

To provide supporting information to the work item data, the user can attach a file or files to the work item. Typical attachments are screen shots, log files, or specification documents. Attachments can be divided into flow phases, such as analysis attachments, development attachments, or testing attachments.

1.3.4.3 Links to Other Work Items

The link (or reference) to other work items is important and a key feature of process management. It allows the user to see relationships such as parent-child relationships, to browse from one work item to a related work item, to derive more precise and meaningful metrics, and to automate actions based on information in related work items.

In the CQ-ALM schema the process is based on links between work items. We shall discuss this in detail in Chapter 12, "Sample Applications and Solutions."

1.3.4.4 Pictures or Graphics

We do not refer to images that are included as attachments, which are additional data, but to presentation insertions such as a company logo, icons, or other graphics to improve the user experience. Figure 1.6 shows the picture control within the palette control of ClearQuest Windows Designer. The Rational logo was inserted in the defect submit form.

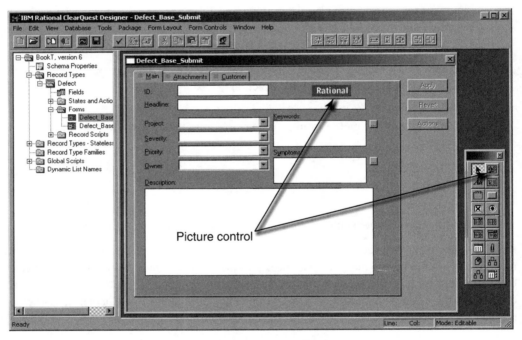

Figure 1.6   The picture control in ClearQuest Windows Designer

ClearQuest Eclipse Designer Warning   The picture control can be added only with the original ClearQuest Designer (Windows version).

1.3.4.5 Applets

Applets are pieces of code that are used to perform background operations, such as integration with other products. In ClearQuest they are actually ActiveX controls. For example, the ActiveX control is used for the ClearQuest and ClearCase (base) integration.

1.3.4.6 Roles

A role is a set of activities users are allowed to perform on artifacts. Role is a key concept in any governed workflow system.

In Jazz, roles identify the functions of team members. Permissions for specific operations can be assigned to roles at the project level or within a team area.

ClearQuest does not have inherent support for roles, and because of the importance of the subject we have dedicated Chapter 5, "Roles," to discussing how to implement roles in ClearQuest.

1.4 Customization

Work item customization means creating new work item types or changing the elements (data, workflow, presentation, and rules) of existing work item types to meet the organization's process and policy.

The customization process, which follows the requirements analysis and design phases, includes some basic stages:

1. Create new work item types.
2. Create fields of various types in each work item type to represent the required data.
3. Create the work item workflow, which includes the definition of the states, the actions, and the allowed state transitions.
4. Create the forms, tabs, and graphical controls to present data and to interact with the user.
5. Develop the rules by setting the fields' behavior, permission to perform actions, access to data, security, notification, integration, and other attributes.

The ClearQuest administrator or the Jazz administrator can create any type of work item that is required. But there is a need to balance business requirements, usability, and maintainability (in that order). What we are trying to say is that it is not advisable to create a work item type for each required business flow. In many cases you can unify two or more work items and achieve the functionality of two business requirements, without affecting the usability and possibly improving the maintainability.

Let's consider some examples. A company is managing their defect tracking with ClearQuest. They would now like to start managing enhancement requests and new features as well. They can create two new work items, one for enhancement requests and one for features. They can take a completely different approach and convert the defect work item to an issue work item that will handle the three issue types (defect, enhancement request, and feature). So what is the best approach? The company must analyze the requirements of each of the three work items, for data and workflow. Considering how much each process differs from the others, does the data required in each state differ a lot from one work item to another? If the answer is that there is much similarity, the work items should be unified. In this case a field called Issue_Type should be added that will have a closed list of the three types we have mentioned (see an example in Figure 1.1).

Work item data is discussed further in Chapter 4, "The Data," and workflow in Chapter 3, "The Workflow."

1.4.1 Which Work Item Elements Can Be Customized?

Within each work item type you can customize the following elements:

- Data (fields, permission to view and edit)
- Presentation of data (forms, tabs, graphic controls)
- Process (workflow, actions, roles, rules)

The details of how to perform the customization are described in the tools manuals and the online help and we shall not repeat them here. In the following chapters we shall discuss customization strategies and techniques that are not included in the tools manuals.

Table 1.2 shows the work item elements and indicates whether they can be customized in ClearQuest Designer and in Rational Team Concert.

Table 1.2   Comparing ClearQuest and Jazz Work Item Customization Elements and Terms

Customization Element	ClearQuest	Jazz	Comments
Data	Define fields of various types: Short String, Integer, Multiline String, Attachment_List, Reference, Reference_List, and Date_Time.	Define attributes of types Boolean, Contributor, Contributor List, Integer, Large HTML, Medium HTML, Large String, Medium String, Small String, Long, Priority, riskLevel, Severity, Tag, TimeStamp, Version, Work Item, Work Item List. Additional Jazz-specific data types are Deliverable, Process Area, Process Area List, Project Area, Project Area List, Team Area, Team Area List.	In Jazz you can develop new attribute types.

Table 1.2 Comparing ClearQuest and Jazz Work Item Customization Elements and Terms (*Continued*)

Customization Element	ClearQuest	Jazz	Comments
Field edit permission	ReadOnly, Optional, or Mandatory for each field in each state, called requiredness. Complex logic and rules to set permission are possible via the field permission hook code.	For each role and work item type a precondition of Mandatory or ReadOnly can be set for each field.	In ClearQuest it is called requiredness and in Jazz, precondition.
Hide data	Security context rules hide complete records based on group membership. Tabs can be hidden from specific groups. Hiding tabs is for usability purposes and not for security purposes.	With project area access control you can configure which users have read access to the project area (source control and work items). In RTC 3.0 you can hide attribute presentation in some conditions, such as workflow state. This is for usability and not for security.	
Presentation of data	Define tabs, position fields on the tab. Can easily set a field's size, alignment, and caption. Colors and multifonts are not supported.	Define tabs, define sections within a tab, and order fields within a section. Customized fields are placed by default on the Custom tab.	In RTC 2.0 it is possible to position custom fields in any tab via scripting. RTC 3.0 supports position custom fields in any tab with the editor presentation.
Workflow	Defined with a state machine diagram. Dynamic rules can be added in action hooks.	Define a static workflow with a state machine diagram.	Dynamic workflow customization in ClearQuest is described in section 3.4, "Dynamic Workflow," in Chapter 3, "The Workflow."
Actions	Actions can be added. Predefined action types are Submit, Change_State, Modify, Delete, Duplicate, Base, Script_Alias.	Actions can be added. Predefined action types are Start, Resolve, Reopen.	In Jazz, Duplicate is a built-in action in addition to various cloning options.

continues

Table 1.2   Comparing ClearQuest and Jazz Work Item Customization Elements and Terms (*Continued*)

Customization Element	ClearQuest	Jazz	Comments
Roles	Can be customized as described in Chapter 4, "The Data." Built-in in the ALM schema.	Built-in and can be modified.	
Notifications	Supported via the Email_ Rule record and can be customized.	Notification pop-up feeds and notification e-mails are supported.	Jazz supports Instant Messaging collaboration.
Rules	Code in BASIC or Perl can be hooked to fields for initialization and when a value is changed. Code can be hooked to an action during initialization, pre-commit, and post-commit. High level of flexibility for setting up rules via hooks.	Approval tracking and operation behavior provide limited flexibility for defining and setting up rules. XML coding provides some more flexibility.	For complex rules Jazz supports writing extensions (in Java or another language) using the Jazz API and SDK to interact with work items and update their attributes.

Note   In Jazz it is possible to edit the XML code in the Process Configuration source using the RTC client.

Some customization areas are not directly related to the work item elements but to the presentation of a data collection. These areas are

- Queries
- Charts
- Reports
- Dashboard

Table 1.3 shows these customization areas in ClearQuest and the Jazz-based products.

Table 1.3 Comparing ClearQuest and Jazz Queries, Charts, Reports, and Dashboard

Customization Area	ClearQuest	Jazz	Comments
Dashboard	Does not exist.	Built-in and can be modified and extended by adding tabs and viewlets.	Rational ProjectConsole can display dashboards with ClearQuest data. Rational InSight can display dashboards with ClearQuest data and Jazz data.
Queries	Queries can be created and modified with wizards or SQL.	Queries can be created and modified with wizards.	
Charts	Charts can be created and modified with wizards. Supported charts are 1. Distribution charts 2. Aging charts 3. Trend charts	Various chart types can be added to a dashboard, such as team velocity, release burndown, and work item status.	
Reports	Reports can be customized with 1. Built-in query editor and Crystal Reports 2. Rational SoDA 3. Exporting the query result set 4. BIRT	Reports can be created with internal (BIRT) report templates. Reports can be exported to PDF, Word, PostScript, and more.	ClearQuest Report Format is similar to RTC Report Template.

1.4.2 Customizing Jazz Work Items

Jazz work item types for both Rational Team Concert and Rational Quality Manager are customized with the Rational Team Concert Eclipse client (RTC 3.0 also supports customization with the Web client). We shall discuss customization in detail in the following chapters. To learn how to perform the work item customization, see RTC Help > Managing change and releases > Tracking work items > Customizing work items.

For the test-specific work items created with Rational Quality Manager (test plan and test case), the customization is performed with the RQM Web client. See section 10.3, "Work Items in the Test Process," in Chapter 10, "Test Management and Work Items," for more information on test plan and test case customization.

1.4.3 Customizing ClearQuest Record Types

ClearQuest record types are customized with the ClearQuest Designer. Until version 7.0 only a Windows version of the ClearQuest Designer existed. Since version 7.0.1 an Eclipse version is also available. Although both designers are similar in functionality, the operations are done in different ways. ClearQuest schema designers who are used to working with the Windows version will have to get used to the new Eclipse version, which includes several advantages over the Windows version; the basic differences are described in Table 1.4.

Table 1.4   Comparing the Eclipse and Windows Versions of ClearQuest Designer

Feature	Windows Designer	Eclipse Designer
Load schema	Only one schema can be opened in a session.	Several schemas can be loaded and opened at the same time.
Object properties	Need to select the object and open the properties.	Object properties are auto-displayed in the Properties view when an object is selected.
Graphic /image control	Available.	Not available.
Tab order	Special menu mode: Form Layout > Set Tab Order. Set as a series of field selections.	Set in the field properties extended tab.
Script editor	System provided.	The user can select the editor. The Eclipse editor is richer in functionality.
Test client type	Only the Windows client is launched.	The user can select the type of client (Windows, Eclipse, or Web) to be launched.
Schemas compare	Not available.	Available, between any two revisions.
Hooks compare	Not available.	Available.
Copy and paste elements of the schema	Not available.	Available.
Syntax error checking	Hook > Compile checks the syntax of an edited hook. Validate: Syntax check is performed during schema validation.	Validate: Syntax check is performed during schema validation. Syntax is checked also when saving the script.
Form outline view	Not available. It is an issue when one control covers another.	Available. Selecting a field in the outline will open its properties.

There are many additional differences that we have not mentioned. Most operations are done in a different way, to take advantage of the Eclipse platform.

Although you can use either version, we propose that you get habituated to the Eclipse version. Personally, we think that the Windows version is more user-friendly, but the Eclipse version has more features, and this version will probably get richer in features in the future. Most of the examples in this book are related to the Eclipse version of ClearQuest Designer.

1.5 Resources

What's new in 2.0 work items? These are the main enhancements to work items in Jazz version 2.0:

- New custom attribute types
- Custom work item presentations
- RESTful Change Management API
- Import work items from CSV files
- Message @Me
- Inline work item editor in Web UI

For details of the work item enhancement, see

> IBM Rational, "WorkItems—New Custom Attribute Types," https://jazz.net/downloads/rational-team-concert/releases/2.0?p=news#workitems, June 25, 2009 (accessed February 24, 2011).

For more on work item tracking, see

> IBM Rational, "Work Item Tracking," http://jazz.net/projects/rational-team-concert/features/wi, November 2010 (accessed February 24, 2011).

For an overview of Jazz work items, consult the following:

> IBM Rational, "Jazz Work Item Overview," http://jazz.net/library/LearnItem.jsp?href=content/docs/platform-overview/work-item-overview.html, May 28, 2008 (accessed February 24, 2011).

For more on work items in version 3.0:

> Benjamin Pasero, "What's New in Rational Team Concert 3.0: Part V—Work Item Enhancements," December 3, 2010, http://jazz.net/blog/index.php/2010/12/03/whats-new-in-rational-team-concert-3-0-part-v-work-item-enhancements/.

> "What's New in Rational Team Concert (last version)," http://jazz.net/projects/rational-team-concert/whatsnew/.

1.6 Summary

In this chapter we introduced work items. We defined a work item as an object that controls the process of performing a work or task during software or systems development. We discussed the elements of a work item: data, presentation forms, workflow, and other objects. We explained additional work item elements such as rules, attachments, links, graphics, and applets.

In the second part of the chapter we briefly discussed work item customization: create new work item types; create fields in each work item type to represent the required data; create the work item workflow, which includes the definition of the state, actions, and transitions; create the form and tabs to present data and interact with the user; develop the rule by setting the field's behavior, access to actions and data, security, integration, and so on.

We compared the customization areas in the ClearQuest record types and the Jazz work item types and explained what can and cannot be customized in each product in the current release.

Because a new ClearQuest Designer based on Eclipse technology has been introduced, we compared the main features of this version with the legacy ClearQuest Designer.

Disciplines:
Requirements,
Analysis & Design

The disciplines for developing change management applications are in many aspects different from those of a regular software project, mainly because of the development environment provided by IBM Rational ClearQuest and IBM Rational Team Concert. To define the disciplines for change management systems we have used elements from the Rational Unified Process (RUP) for small project frameworks, as shown in Figure 2.1.

We have taken elements of the RUP framework and adapted them to meet the environment for change management, specifically with orientation to ClearQuest and Jazz work items. We have removed the Environment discipline because the development environment is provided with the tools. We have removed the Project Management discipline because change management projects are usually small, and the project management element can be embedded in other disciplines. We have added the Deployment discipline because we think deployment is important to the success of a project. We have also added a Maintenance discipline.

The disciplines are discussed in two chapters. In this chapter we shall cover two disciplines:

- Requirements discipline
- Analysis & Design discipline

In Chapter 7, "Disciplines, Part 2," we shall discuss additional disciplines:

- Implementation discipline
- Testing discipline
- Deployment discipline
- Maintenance discipline

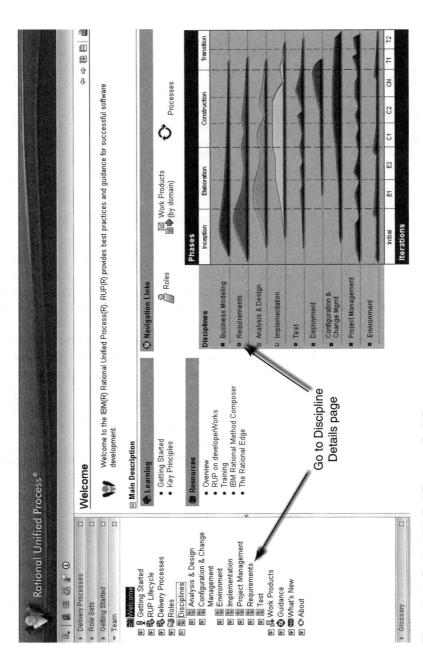

Figure 2.1 Rational Unified Process disciplines

2.1 Requirements

The Requirements discipline explains how you gather requirements from various sources, and how you manage and package them. The way requirements are managed and presented to stakeholders directly influences how the change management system will be built and will affect its success.

2.1.1 Gathering Requirements

In order to build the requirements document, you need to gather information and requirements from various sources using several techniques.

2.1.1.1 Gather Initial Documentation

The organization probably has various documents that explain its requirements for change management. These documents will give you a good picture of how the organization has managed its changes until now. You should not consider these documents as requirements until they are approved by stakeholders or managers. The documents that you can collect are

- Forms for changes, process instructions, defect reports, and similar materials
- Measurements and metrics such as key performance indicators (KPIs)
- Management guidelines, business requirements
- Regulations (internal and external)
- Observations of the current way (system) the company manages changes

2.1.1.2 Interviews

The main tool for gathering requirements is the interview. You will need to plan the interviews. The people you are interviewing are busy and will appreciate your respecting their time and be well prepared. Consider sending the interviewees a list of questions ahead of time so they can be prepared. We think that a one-on-one interview gives the best results. Your first step is to decide whom you would like to interview. Good candidates are the system stakeholders, power users, subject matter experts, and managers of development, testing, quality assurance, and IT departments. Be sure to interview a representative of every role in the organization, as their interactions with the change management system are often different.

The purpose of the interview is to identify the stakeholders' needs and to get their wish lists—things they always wanted but never dared to ask for. You also want to get their priorities for each requirement they mention. Try to find out what the limitations and problems in the previous system were; knowing that will help you to prevent mistakes during the design phase.

When interviewing technical people, you need to ask them about constraints and limitations. For example, you may find that only one physical server will be provided for the system, or that the system will be hosted on an existing server. Another example might be an IT organization policy of preferring Web client applications over native clients. Constraints and limitations may affect the system architecture in a later phase.

During the interview try to sense the interactions between teams: relationship, level of cooperation, and so on. Although this is not relevant to requirements gathering, it is important to understand while constructing the system and can only be learned while talking to people. The change management process crosses several organizational departments and will have to bridge them.

Also try to identify objections and the reasons for them.

2.1.1.3 Questionnaires

The questionnaire is an efficient technique for eliciting information from stakeholders who are not available for interview. It saves time as it allows you to reach a wider range of people than if you do direct interviews. Be careful and validate the questionnaire results during one or more of the interviews; it may be that one or more of the questions was not understood correctly. In many cases after you have finished the interviews, you will find that you need more information, and sending questionnaires to all the interviewees and possibly other people is an easy way to get the information without arranging more interviews.

Make sure the questionnaires are adapted to roles. If you have one questionnaire, group the questions by roles, so that people will not have to read questions that are not relevant to their role or are out of the scope of their knowledge.

The following are sample questions that you can use to build your customized questionnaire:

- What types of change requests do you currently manage (defects, enhancements, or new features)?
- How to you manage them?
- Do you have a document that describes the process for each type of change request?
- Who is allowed to submit a change request?
- Who decides whether to accept/reject a change request?
- Who sets the change request priority?
- What do you do with rejected change requests?
- Who is responsible for triaging a change request?
- Who is responsible for closing a change request?
- Describe the lifecycle of each change request type.
- What measurements do you perform, who gets the information, and how do they get it today?
- Can a developer make a change without an approved change request?
- How do you decide on the content of a release?
- Who decides what changes will be included in the next release?
- Do you plan or need to integrate the change management system with the version control system, or with other systems (help desk, requirements management, test management)?

- Who are the users of the system (internals, customers, contractors) and what are their roles?

- Where are the users of the system physically located?

- Are there security issues with the data?

- Does the organization have to conform to regulations?

- How do you manage the promotion process?

- Do you trace elements from requirements to change requests and to change set assets?

Open questions are important:

- What are the main problems in the current way change requests are managed?

- List the main features you think should be included in the change management system.

Regarding the last item, have the respondents tell you at least three main features they would like to have in the new system.

Questions can be classified according to subjects like flow, data, integration, security, measurements, reporting, and maintenance. Another way to organize the questionnaire is by roles. For each role list the questions you want to ask; this will create repetition as the same question may appear for many roles, but it is more efficient during the interview and can also serve you when you cannot meet the interviewee and have to mail the questionnaire.

See the "Collaborative Application Lifecycle Management with IBM Rational Products" redbook section 4.1.4, "Requirements Definition and Management Blueprint," in Part B, Chapter 4, for additional examples of questions for various roles to support the requirements planning.

Redbooks   IBM redbooks and redpapers can be found on www.redbooks.ibm.com/.

2.1.2 Defining and Documenting Requirements

The requirements can be gathered and documented in a text document, or in a tool like IBM Rational Requirements Composer or IBM Rational RequisitePro. The requirements document, however, should be presented in a format common to all involved people. A Microsoft Word document is a common format used by many, but the requirements document can be easily generated from most tools.

Use a vocabulary that is common in your organization and will be understood by both technical and nontechnical participants. Consider adding a glossary to prevent misunderstanding and future errors. This is mandatory if during the information gathering you discover that different teams are using different terms, or some interviewees are not familiar with technical terms you have used.

Use graphics and diagrams as much as possible: state transition diagrams, user interface layouts, reports, and chart examples. You can use other techniques to document the requirements as you see fit, such as storyboarding. When you use a variety of techniques and notations to elicit, capture, elaborate, discuss, and review requirements, you improve the quality of the requirements and consequently of the system itself.

Figure 2.2 is an example of a definition of use case in Rational Requirements Composer.

The requirements document should contain the information described in the following sections.

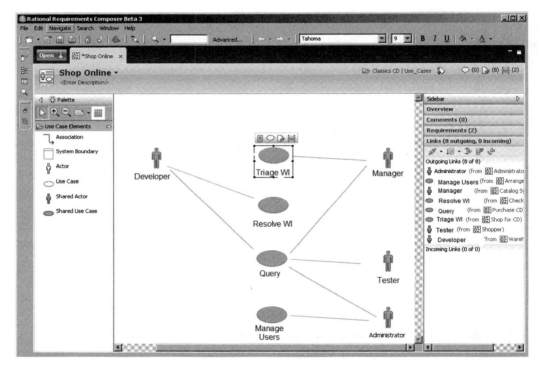

Figure 2.2   Rational Requirements Composer use case definition example

2.1.2.1 The Scope of the System

It is crucial that one of the outcomes of the requirements gathering and the interviews be the definition of the scope and the boundaries of the system:

- Who are the users: internal users only; external users such as business partners, subcontractors, and customers?

   Who the users are directly affects the definition of the requirements for security, user administration, as well as other requirements and may affect the system architecture.

- What types of change requests are we managing? Do we manage defects only or also other change requests?

  The types of change requests influence the design stage. In many cases stakeholders will want to extend the scope and include management of issues, incidents, and other activities.

- Will existing change requests have to be migrated to the new system?

  If so, do not underestimate this effort.

- Do we integrate with other systems? What level of integration is required; what data has to be shared; what are the use cases?

You can draw a high-level use case diagram to illustrate the actors and boundaries of the system.

2.1.2.2 Functional Requirements

A list of all the functional requirements should be documented with use cases, stories, or any other method and organized in a clear and concise way. The requirements can be organized as a hierarchy or as a list that can easily be classified.

Storyboards are extremely useful when the requirement involves more then one tool, or more than one work item type. For example, in one project ClearQuest ALM is integrated with RevTrack for SAP change management. The process involves three ClearQuest record types and one RevTrack work item. A storyboard was very useful in communicating and clarifying the stakeholders' needs.

2.1.2.3 Supplementary Specifications

A list of all the nonfunctional requirements should be documented as a textual description or by any one of the methods described in the preceding section. This category includes specifications for performance, environment, and compliance, among others. Another important factor that directly affects system sizing is the number of concurrent users. You can estimate the number of concurrent users from the number of total users and their roles.

2.1.2.4 Priority

Each requirement should have a priority value. It is probable that the application will be developed in several releases. Priorities will help determine what requirements will be included in which release. Stakeholders might not agree to that priority, as each one sees the priority from his or her point of view. You have the full picture, you have discussed the issue with all of them, and you are unbiased and impartial, so you should weigh in with your opinion.

2.1.2.5 Estimated Effort

When stakeholders decide which requirements will be developed in which phase, it is important that they know the amount of effort needed to implement each requirement. Therefore, it is advisable to include the estimated effort in man-hours and in calendar duration, especially if the requirement is dependent on the implementation of another requirement. This effort will be inserted into the activities in the project plan.

2.1.3 Getting Agreement

When the requirements document is ready, you should get it approved. The best way to obtain agreement on the scope and requirements priorities is in a meeting. The last version of the requirements document should be sent prior to the meeting to allow the participants enough time to read, learn, and comment before the meeting.

The following participants should be invited to the requirements review meeting:

- Key users (from the development team and the testing team)
- The change management team (who are in many cases also the authors of the requirements document)
- An authority in the organization who can make a decision in case of conflict or disagreement
- Other stakeholders such as quality assurance manager, process manager, and others, depending on the nature of the application

Sometimes people will not agree on a specific requirement, which makes sense because each one sees the system from his or her point of view. It is your role to find a solution to these conflicts, either by compromising or by taking a stand that is best for the organization.

2.1.4 Using Agile Practice

If you and the organization are used to Agile practices, it is only logical that you will use those practices in this phase. You may leave some incomplete requirements and get agreement only on the requirements that will constitute the first iteration. You will continue to gather requirements as the project goes along. After each iteration, demonstrate the change management system developed and refine the requirements based on the reviewers' comments, gather more requirements, and agree on the requirements that will be developed in the next iteration.

More on Agile, from the application lifecycle management perspective, is described in Chapter 11, "Managing Agile Projects."

2.1.5 Maintaining Requirements

Requirements will change—that is a fact of life—and you have to make sure those changes are managed properly just like the software artifacts. One simple way to manage changes in requirements is by creating a project in the change management system you develop that will allow users to submit enhancement requests and new features, as well as defects. In this way all of your change requests are documented in the change management database.

The change management system allows the organization to control the requirements approval process and to distribute any change to the stakeholders. If you are using ClearQuest, you can create a project and call it ClearQuest Maintenance, for example. All record types used in the change management system will be available for that project.

A Jazz administrator can create a new project for tool maintenance in the same way that we have described for ClearQuest. Another way is to define a category for the change management system. It is important, however, that metrics you derive do not include work items of this maintenance category.

2.2 Analysis & Design

In Rational Unified Process the purposes of Analysis & Design are

- To transform the requirements into a design of the system-to-be

- To evolve a robust architecture for the system

- To adapt the design to match the implementation environment, designing it for performance

So in this phase the requirements and constraints are analyzed, and the system will be designed based on the analysis. The design of the change management system should include at least the following elements:

- Definition of client types: Web client, Windows (native) client, and/or Eclipse client on Windows or UNIX platforms

- Definition of the infrastructure architecture: servers to use, physical or virtual configuration, systems and applications on each server

- Physical location: data center, network topology, firewall

- Database(s): database vendor, space required, other system requirements

- Schema high-level design: entities and their relations, integrations with other applications

- Data (field types) in each work item type/entity/object

- Workflow of each stateful entity

- Design of the graphical user interface (forms, tabs, and field controls)

In the following sections we shall elaborate on the analysis and design elements of the change management system.

2.2.1 Defining the Types of Clients

The human actors of most use cases (or functional requirements) are the users of the system. We have to understand whether the users are all internal users or if there are also external users. If you have external users, the system has to be designed with different security measures (see section 9.2, "Governance," in Chapter 9, "Metrics and Governance"). In most cases external users and remote clients will use a Web client. The system must be architected with Web server(s) to provide for that client type.

In some cases a terminal server client such as Citrix may be used. It is mainly required when distributed teams must use the native clients, for example, because of ClearCase-ClearQuest integration or special features that the Web client or the remote connection does not provide or not with the desired performance.

For internal users you have the choice of using each of the supported clients. Remember that there is a trade-off: A Web client is the easiest from an administrative point of view as no installation is required on the users' machines. Native clients are usually faster if used in a local area network (LAN) but may be extremely slow when used over a wide area network (WAN). Native clients are currently richer in features, but the Web client is closing the gap.

Developers working with Eclipse would prefer to have all their applications in the same Eclipse environment. The same applies to developers working with Microsoft VisualStudio. Another issue to consider is the integration with other applications. Some integrations are not supported on all platforms, which creates a restriction on the client selection and the system design. For example, the ClearQuest to RequisitePro integration works only with native clients and with the Web client. Product technical limitations should be considered when designing the system.

In general, we can say that Web client functionality is improving every year, and the latest Web 2.0 features give significant advantages to users and allow more flexibility in the design phase.

Design Advice   Although it is easier from a design and administrative point of view to limit client types, you should first consider ease of use and productivity.

2.2.2 Defining the Infrastructure Architecture

The physical infrastructure of the system should be designed to meet the nonfunctional requirements of the system. The architecture should answer questions like these:

- What database server should we use? What is the configuration? Do we need redundancy or a high-availability server?

- What Web server should we use? What is the configuration? Do we need more than one Web server to meet performance requirements?

- Where in the demilitarized zone (DMZ) topology should the servers be located?

  The DMZ is a network located between the organization's internal LAN and the Internet. It is protected by firewall and allows an additional layer of security.

- Where should we locate the license server?

We usually recommend that a license server be located on the same machine as the database server. But there are other considerations, such as

— Does the organization have a central license server?
— Is a redundant license server required?

These questions should be answered with the cooperation of the IT department specialists: system administrator, database administrator, security and network specialists.

If the system is opened to external users (customers, for example), extra care should be taken in designing the security of the system. A common configuration is described in Figure 2.3. Note that it is an example of infrastructure design and not a "fit-for-all" solution.

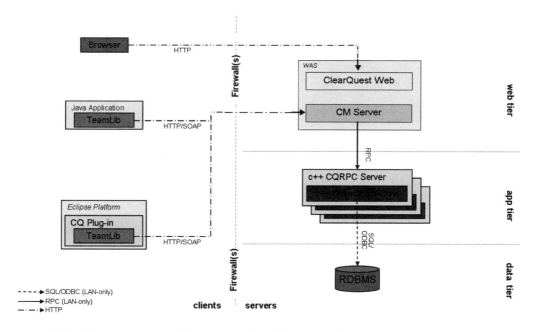

Figure 2.3   CQ components and firewall configuration example

For more information on ClearQuest firewall configurations see ClearQuest Help > Administering IBM Rational ClearQuest > Administering ClearQuest Web > Ports Used by Rational ClearQuest Web > Configuring a firewall between the Rational ClearQuest Web application and a Rational ClearQuest server.

To learn more about the ClearQuest Web Server configuration, sizing, and performance, read this article:

Ferreira, Carlos, "CQWeb: Performance and Tuning," *IBM developerWorks*, www.ibm.com/developerworks/rational/library/5503.html, 2004 (accessed February 24, 2011).

We do not recommend locating the database server and the Web server on the same machine for performance reasons. The bandwidth of the network segments of the data server and the Web server should be high; it has a significant impact on the client's response time (see Figure 2.4).

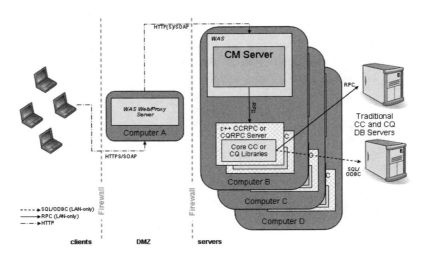

Figure 2.4   ClearQuest physical deployment example

In the figure, Computer A is the IHS server (IBM HTTP server based on WebSphere Application Server). Computers B, C, and D are CM servers.

2.2.3 Choosing a Database

As you know, ClearQuest and the Jazz-based products store data and metadata in common commercial databases. Your first step is to select the database vendor.

2.2.3.1 ClearQuest Database

ClearQuest supports the following databases: IBM DB2, IBM DB2 Express, IBM DB2 Enterprise Edition, IBM DB2 Universal Database for Rational, Microsoft Access, Microsoft SQL Server, and Oracle Database. Microsoft Access can be used as a local database for the ClearQuest administrator tests but cannot be used for production purposes. The selection among the other vendors should be mainly done according to the organization's ability to maintain the database. If your organization already has Oracle or DB2, it makes sense that you would want to use the same database. There is also a matter of cost; when you purchase ClearQuest, some free DB2 licenses are provided. Other than that, we can say that all databases mentioned are successfully used in many organizations.

After selecting the vendor, you should decide on the number of physical databases to be created. Usually you would need at least three:

- Schema repository database
- User (production) database(s)
- Test database(s)

In many cases more than one schema repository is used. This is a design decision based on the analysis made and depends on the number of ClearQuest applications developed, the organizational units that are using the applications, the number of administrators responsible for the maintenance of those applications, and whether ClearQuest MultiSite is planned.

The databases will probably be defined on the same vendor data store, but this is not required by ClearQuest and your analysis may point to some other solution. For example, you can use Microsoft Access as a test database located on the developer's machine.

The space required for the ClearQuest databases should be calculated by multiplying the number of records by 15kB; in addition, you should add the size of the attachments. The attachment size may be quite high, sometimes up to 200MB per attachment file. Given the nature of the system, you should be able to calculate the database initial size and the growth size per month. Note that you can limit the size of the attachments by including a validation hook that checks the attachment's size. For more information see the hook "Limit Attachment Size (Perl)" in section 4.6.2 in Chapter 4, "The Data."

ClearQuest allows an easy and safe utility to migrate from one database vendor to another. See section 7.5, "ClearQuest Tool Mentor," in Chapter 7, "Disciplines, Part 2," for more information.

2.2.3.2 Jazz Database

Rational Team Concert (RTC) and Rational Quality Manager (RQM) support the following databases: Derby (included in the products), DB2 (Workgroup Edition included), Oracle, and Microsoft SQL Server. The considerations for selecting the database and vendor are similar to those we described for ClearQuest in the previous section.

If your organization is small, using Derby will be an advantage from the maintenance point of view.

Note Supported databases and database entitlement are not the same for each product edition and version. Verify the product release notes for full information about supported databases and entitlement.

2.2.4 ClearQuest Schema High-Level Design

The schema high-level design includes the definitions of the entities (record types) and their interrelations, and integrations with external systems.

First decide what entities will be used and the type of each entity (state-based or stateless). In Chapter 4, "The Data," there is a detailed discussion of this subject. We prefer to represent the entities and their relations in an entity relationship diagram (ERD) or a UML class diagram.

Figure 2.5 is an example of entities and their relations in the ClearQuest ALM schema. Notice the usage of different symbols for stateless entities (record types Role, Project, Phase, and Iterations) and the other state-based entities.

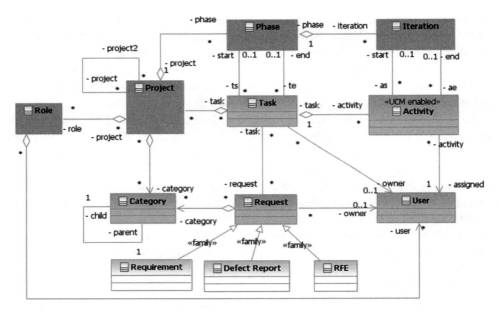

Figure 2.5   Entity relationship diagram of the ALM schema

Other elements of the high-level design that can be used are

- Interaction diagram or table

   In this diagram define all the human actors that interact with the change management system (customer, developer, tester, etc.) and the nonhuman actors (ClearCase, Requi-sitePro, help desk system, etc.).

- The main use case diagram of the system

   This is useful mainly to define the boundaries of the system by highlighting the high-level interactions of the actors with the system.

2.2.5 Defining the Data Fields

After you have decided what entities to use, define the fields within each entity. Decide what the type of each field is and complete the entity relationship diagram. Add the fields to the attributes section of the entity box, as shown in Figure 2.6.

Figure 2.6 Entity fields

Chapter 4, "The Data," provides a detailed description of the work item data.

2.2.6 Defining the Workflow

The entities defined in the high-level design are divided into two record types: stateful and stateless. For each stateful entity define the workflow in a state diagram or activity diagram. If you have defined the entities in a class diagram, add the actions from the workflow diagram to the method section of the class box, as shown in Figure 2.7.

Figure 2.7 Entity fields and actions

Chapter 3, "The Workflow," provides a detailed description of the work item workflow and a sample state diagram.

2.2.7 Designing the User Interface (Forms)

The user interface is very important, although unfortunately it is often seen as a negligible issue. Here are some basic rules for designing the user interface:

- The user interface should be clear and concise both visually and functionally.

- Tabs should be created and ordered in a way that conforms to the process and eases the user's work.

- Fields in each tab should be arranged in the order of work.

These general instructions are aimed to generate a positive user experience and an efficient work session. Users should be able to find the required fields easily. Field names (and labels) must be meaningful to the users and taken from the organization's vocabulary.

Fields that are aligned and are the same size create a pleasant experience. The need to navigate several times from one tab to another during the same operation creates an unpleasant experience and wastes time.

We strongly support the best practice of prototyping the user interface. The stakeholders will be able to provide feedback based on something close to reality. Prototyping can be easily done with a development tool like ClearQuest Designer or any other tool, but if done with Clear-Quest you can use the prototype for your implementation.

2.3 Design Patterns

A design pattern is a general reusable solution to a common design problem. Design patterns exist in many areas, such as object-oriented software development, graphical user interfaces (GUIs), and many others. ClearQuest is quite different; the ClearQuest Designer has some built-in patterns, but some patterns cannot be developed because of the special environment. This is also true for Jazz. Many of the ClearQuest packages are solutions to common design patterns.

The following are some examples that describe the ClearQuest built-in patterns:

- **State pattern:** Allows an object to alter its behavior when its internal state changes. A record can change its behavior in different states; for example, a field's requiredness can change from state to state (in both ClearQuest and Jazz).

- **Balking pattern:** Allows executing an action on an object when the object is in a particular state. The allowed actions for a given state are an inherent feature in ClearQuest (and also in Jazz).

- **Initialization pattern:** A record must have an initialization action. Every record type in ClearQuest is created with the two actions of type Submit and Import that allow its initialization.

- **Notification pattern:** Notifies users about an action they should perform. This pattern has many variants. The ClearQuest Email Notification package allows implementation of various notification patterns. Jazz also has a notification mechanism.

The ClearQuest community has invested more in building solutions to problems than in building design patterns. We shall try to establish some basic patterns, and we call on the Clear-Quest designer community to enrich the selection for the benefit of all users.

The following sections describe patterns that may (and probably should) be used in many change management applications.

Note In Chapter 8, "Development," we shall explain how to implement some of these patterns.

2.3.1 Closing Pattern

Pattern Name: Closing

Purpose: Capture the closing type and closing reason.

Reason: Help the organization to improve its processes and achieve a higher maturity level. In many cases when work items are closed, it is difficult for the submitter or for other people involved to understand why the work item was closed, if the problem was solved, and how the problem was solved. If the problem was not solved, what is the reason for not solving it? This often leads to loss of time and numerous exchanges between the submitters and the team to clarify the closure reason.

Applicability: The pattern is applicable to any state-based record type.

Content: The pattern enhances an existing record type by adding two fields, one field of type Short String for the closing type, and one field of type Multiline for the closing reason. Those fields should be mandatory for all actions that lead to an end state (examples: Close, Reject, and Postpone). Closing types can be Completed, Work as Designed, Can Not Reproduce, and other types depending on the organization's process.

Automation: For an action that implies a closing type such as Reject, a default value should automatically be filled in.

2.3.2 Triage Pattern

Pattern Name: Triage

Purpose: Assign a work item to the right solution provider.

Reason: Ensure that every change is followed up, there is no duplication of work, there are no delays, and there is no falling between the cracks. In many cases it is not clear who is responsible for the work item.

Applicability: The pattern is applicable to any state-based record type.

Content: The pattern enhances an existing record type by adding the Assignee (or Owner) field and requires the selection of a value by an authorized role prior to any work.

Automation: Automatic assignment is possible in several situations. See section 5.7.2, "Hook to Automatically Set Responsible Based on Role of Type Single," in Chapter 5, "Roles."

2.3.3 Parent Control Pattern

Pattern Name: Parent Control

Purpose: Ensure that all children of a record are in the same state before the parent state is changed.

Reason: Make sure that a complex process is controlled and managed. Ensure that all subactivities are completed before the parent activity can be declared as completed.

Applicability: The pattern is applicable to parent-child state-based record types. Parents and children are not necessarily of the same type.

Content: The pattern enhances existing record type(s) by adding a commit hook to specific actions to enforce and control the rule.

Automation: Should be used.

2.3.4 Child Control Pattern

Pattern Name: Child Control

Purpose: Ensure that the parent changes its state when all its children have reached the same state.

Reason: Make sure that a complex process is controlled and managed. Ensure that the parent state is in sync with the child states.

Applicability: The pattern is applicable to parent-child state-based record types. Parents and children are not necessarily of the same type.

Content: The pattern enhances existing record type(s) by adding a commit hook to specific actions to enforce and control the rule.

Automation: Should be used.

Variations: The pattern can have many variants depending on the organization's policy. Here are some examples:

- Once all children have reached the resolved state, the parent will automatically be moved to the Resolved state.
- Only if all children have reached the resolved state except one child that is of type Documentation, allow the parent to be moved to the Resolved state.
- Other exceptions might be low priority or nondependency.

2.3.5 Dead End Pattern

Pattern Name: Dead End

Purpose: Ensures a record cannot be reopened after closure.

Reason: Help the organization to improve its processes and achieve a higher maturity level.

Applicability: The pattern is applicable to any state-based record type.

Content: The pattern limits an existing record type by preventing actions of type Change-State and Modify in state of type Closed. The only action that is allowed is cloning, so if additional work is required, it will be performed and documented in the cloned record.

Automation: Not relevant.

2.3.6 Data Hierarchy Pattern

Pattern Name: Data Hierarchy

Purpose: Allows a hierarchy relation between records.

Reason: Organize product component relations and be able to generate a bill of materials (BOM) for the system to be tracked. The pattern prevents user errors in selecting components and their versions and in selecting related elements.

Applicability: The pattern is applicable to any user-defined stateless record type. Notice that we do not mean hierarchy between work items, but hierarchy between data (stateless) record types. The hierarchy is usually between different record types but can be done between the same record types; for example, one product can contain several other products.

Content: The pattern maintains parent-child relationships between records, to construct a hierarchy structure.

Automation: Eases automation of autoselection values in dependent fields.

2.3.7 Superuser Modification Pattern

Pattern Name: Superuser Modification

Purpose: Allows the superuser to modify a record at all states.

Reason: In many cases a record needs to be modified even when the process rules do not allow it. It may be caused by user error, schema modification, or other administrative reasons. The superuser action will be tracked and logged. From a maintenance point of view this pattern is critical in many situations to fix import errors or to "clean up" after schema changes.

Applicability: The pattern is applicable to any user-defined record type.

Content: An action of type Modify will be added to the record type; the Access_Control hook verifies that the user has superuser permission. The requiredness of all fields will be set to

Optional during that action regardless of the record state and the predefined behaviors. In an ALM-based schema, the role of ALMAdmin has this ability.

Automation: Not applicable.

2.3.8 Resolution Pattern

Pattern Name: Resolution

Purpose: Captures the resolution type, resolution reason, and resolution description.

Reason: Help the organization to improve its processes and achieve a higher maturity level. The pattern improves the organization's ability to learn from past mistakes and to resolve issues faster.

Applicability: The pattern is applicable to any state-based record type.

Content: The pattern enhances existing record types by adding two fields, one field of type Short String for the resolution type, and one field of type Multiline for the resolution reason and description. Those fields should be mandatory for all actions that lead to a resolved state. The ClearQuest Resolution Package assists the implementation of this pattern.

Automation: In some situations automation is possible.

2.4 Review and Sign Off Design Models

The purpose of the design review is to verify that the design model fulfills the requirements of the system, and that it serves as a good basis for its implementation.

The review process can identify risks, architectural problems, performance issues, design flaws, requirements not captured correctly, and other issues.

During the review you may discuss other design options that may improve the system. All the required changes should be documented and resolved for the next review. Several iterations may be required until reviewers agree to the solution and are ready to approve it.

After reviewers approve the design model, the decision is documented, the model is signed off, and you are ready for the next phase, which is constructing the system.

2.5 Resources

IBM Rational, "Rational Unified Process 7.2, RUP for Small Projects," www-01.ibm.com/software/awdtools/rup/index.html (accessed February 22, 2011).

Leffingwell, Dean, and Don Widrig, *Managing Software Requirements: A Use Case Approach, 2nd edition* (Boston: Addison-Wesley, 2003).

2.6 Summary

In this chapter we covered the Requirements discipline and the Analysis & Design discipline. We described techniques for gathering requirements, from eliciting existing documents to interviews and questionnaires. We explained the requirements document content and the importance of getting stakeholders to agree on the requirements. A sample list of questions for your questionnaire was provided.

In the second part of the chapter we explained the elements of the design document: client types, infrastructure architecture, database, and schema model. Some elements of the design, such as the work item, the data, the user interface, and workflow, were described only briefly as we dedicate special chapters to each subject.

We suggested the use of design patterns and proposed some patterns such as the Closing pattern, Parent Control pattern, Dead End pattern, and others.

The Workflow

Workflow, at its simplest, is the movement of documents, artifacts, and/or tasks through a work process. More specifically, workflow is the operational aspect of a work procedure:

- How tasks are structured
- Who performs them
- What their relative order is
- How they are synchronized
- How information flows to support the tasks
- How tasks are being tracked

Because the dimension of time is considered in workflow, workflow considers "throughput" as a distinct measure. Workflow problems can be modeled and analyzed using graph-based formalisms such as Petri nets and UML activity diagrams.

In Wikipedia a workflow management system is defined as "a computer system that manages and defines a series of tasks within an organization to produce a final outcome or outcomes. Workflow Management Systems allow you to define different workflows for different types of jobs or processes."

The ClearQuest and Jazz artifact is the work item; you can imagine the work item as a document that is physically moved from one person to another. In the change management practice the purpose of the work item is to change other artifacts such as source code, manuals, models, and even requirements. The workflow is defined by a state machine (the state transition matrix) which contains all the states through which the work item may transition. In ClearQuest the state transition is performed by an action of type Change_State.

3.1 Software Development Processes

Workflow is a key concept in several software development processes such as the Rational Unified Process (RUP), the Telelogic Harmony, the Open Unified Process (OpenUP), and others.

We shall only briefly discuss workflow in RUP and OpenUP, and then focus on a method that we think is best for change management practices.

3.1.1 The Rational Unified Process (RUP) Method

Workflow is a key concept in RUP; it is explained as follows.

A mere enumeration of all roles, activities, and artifacts does not constitute a process; we need a way to describe meaningful sequences of activities that produce some valuable result, and to show interactions between roles. A *workflow* is a sequence of activities that produces a result of observable value.

In UML terms, a workflow can be expressed as a sequence diagram, a communication diagram, or an activity diagram. Figure 3.1 presents an activity diagram from the change management discipline of the RUP practice.

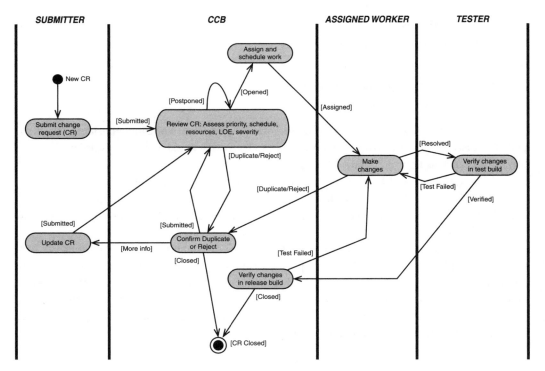

Figure 3.1   Change request activity diagram in Rational Unified Process

The area between the bars represents the responsibilities of a specific role, in other words, the actions that should be performed by the person having that role. In this diagram the actions are represented by ovals and the states by arrows.

3.1.2 OpenUP Method

OpenUP is a Lean Unified Process that applies iterative and incremental approaches within a structured lifecycle. OpenUP embraces a pragmatic Agile philosophy that focuses on the collaborative nature of software development. It is a tools-agnostic, low-ceremony process that can be extended to address a broad variety of project types.

For more information on OpenUP change management practices and workflows visit the Eclipse site and the Wiki site:

"OpenUP," http://epf.eclipse.org/wikis/openup/, November 30, 2010 (accessed February 24, 2011).

"OpenUP—Home," http://process.osellus.com/sites/wiki/OpenUP/Wiki%20Pages/ Home.aspx, January 7, 2008 (accessed February 24, 2011).

Now that we understand what a workflow is, and what the basic elements are, let's see how we can represent the process we need and how to realize it in ClearQuest and Rational Team Concert.

3.2 Process Representation

There are many techniques for representing a process; each one has advantages that manifest in emphasizing one or more aspects of the flow. For example, the state diagram emphasizes the states; the activity diagram emphasizes the activities and the flow logic. We shall later discuss a few of these methods.

Figure 3.2 represents a simple flow.

Figure 3.2   State transition diagram

In Figure 3.2 the ovals represent the *states*; the arrows represent *actions* that transition the work item from one state to another. Some of the workflow rules are defined in this diagram; other rules are defined textually, and we shall discuss them later. In the diagram note the following:

- Entering state Submitted can be done by the action Submit only (only one arrow enters that state).
- The state Closed is a dead end; you cannot transition to any other state from that state (no arrow exits from that state).
- There are only two alternative paths in this diagram.

In ClearQuest we define the flow in a state transition diagram in a very simple way in a textual matrix and not in a graphical tool, and therefore it is less informative.

We suggest that during the design phase you draw a diagram that will enable all involved stakeholders to quickly understand the workflow, in order to discuss and agree upon it. The diagram is part of the design model and the system documentation and will later be useful during user training.

A graphical representation such as the one in Figure 3.2 usually does not include all the rules; they are elaborated in an accompanying document.

Here are some basic recommended rules for the workflow definition:

- Every *state* should be given a unique name. The name is in passive tense, such as Submitted, Resolved, or Closed. The name of the state is written inside the oval, as shown in the diagram.
- Every *action* should be given a unique name. The names are in active tense, such as Submit, Resolve, or Close. The name of the action is written above the arrow, as shown in the diagram. If the arrow is not horizontal, write the action name on the side of the arrow that would be the top if the arrow were horizontal.
- Permission to perform an action is usually not granted to everyone but is limited to one or more roles. In some cases role definition is not enough, as the organization may define complex logic to allow access to actions.
- The role(s) that are allowed to perform an action are written below the arrow (or on the side of the arrow that would be the bottom if the arrow were horizontal).

  We shall discuss roles in the next chapter; for now, to complete the picture assume that a role can be represented by the user's group or by a name.

- We suggest enclosing the role name in square brackets, such as [Tester], [Developer], or [Leader]. There are two reasons for the brackets: to make the graphical syntax clear, and because with a complex flow the actions will be drawn vertically, and people may confuse the action name and the role.
- If nothing is written under the arrow, *all users* are allowed to perform the action.
- As previously mentioned, there are situations where the *access control* (permission to perform an action) logic is complex and just adding the roles is not enough. In these cases enter under the arrow [Dynamic_1], [Dynamic_2], etc.

- [Dynamic_1] is defined textually; for example, Action Integrate is always allowed to role [Tester] and is allowed to role [Developer] if the value of the field TestType is Unit-Test. It is clear that such logic requires translation to an appropriate algorithm. In Clear-Quest it is done by scripting the Access_Control hook (of the action or base action).

Figure 3.3 demonstrates a workflow diagram that uses these recommendations.

[Dynamic_1] = [Developers] if field Issue_Type = "external"; otherwise [Leaders] only

Figure 3.3   Modified state transition diagram

Another method of drawing a flow that emphasizes the roles is shown in Figure 3.4. Two vertical dotted lines mark the role name, the states are located on the lines, but the actions are between the lines and cannot cross them. In this diagram it is very clear which actions are performed by each role. The disadvantage is that the sequence of actions from Submitted to Closed (the happy path) does not always flow from left to right as in the previous diagram; this can be seen in the activity diagram of Figure 3.1. Also, in some cases the roles are not predefined; we marked such a role [Dynamic] in Figure 3.3. See an example in the next chapter.

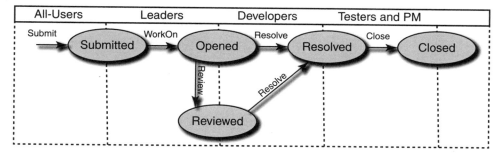

Figure 3.4   State diagram—roles presentation

In many cases the change process involves several organizational units and several tools. This makes the process presentation more complex and harder to understand. Figure 3.5 is an example of such a process diagram. The process was designed with IBM WebSphere Business Modeler (WBM).

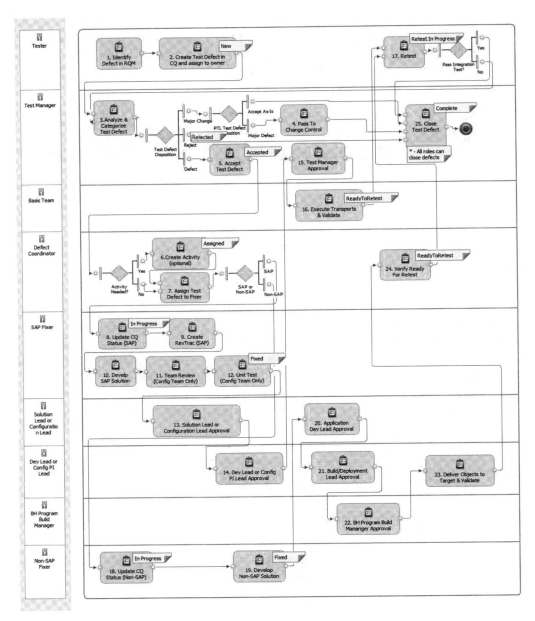

Figure 3.5 Complex change management process diagram

Notice how easy it is to see the activities of each role, to identify the decision points and which role makes the decision. The states in ClearQuest are flagged on the relevant activities. The process involves two additional tools that are integrated into ClearQuest: Rational Quality Manager and RevTrac.

3.2.1 Creating the State Transition Matrix

After you have agreed with the stakeholders on the workflow of each work item, you have to convert the graphical diagram to a state transition matrix. This is done in a similar way in ClearQuest and in Rational Team Concert:

1. Create a state in the States section for each state (oval) in the diagram.
2. Create an action in the Actions section for each action (arrow) in the diagram.
3. For each action define the source(s) state(s) and the target state.

Figure 3.6 is a realization in ClearQuest of a state transition diagram of the workflow described in Figures 3.2 and 3.3.

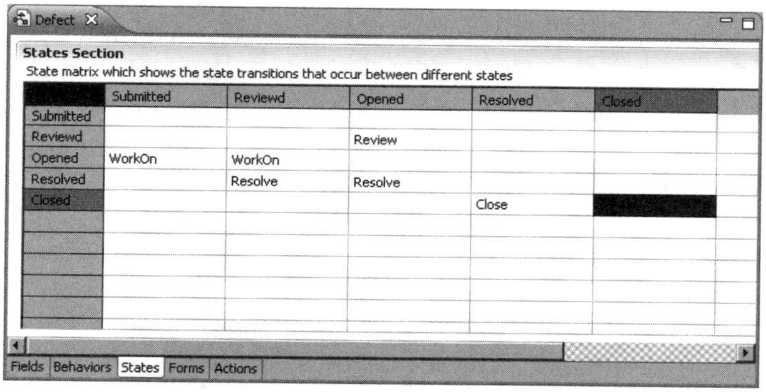

Figure 3.6 Definition of the state transition diagram in ClearQuest Designer

To verify that the state transition matrix is identical to the graphical chart, do the following:

1. For each state count the number of arrows pointing to that state in the graphic model. Now count the number of actions in the raw (to state) of that state in the state transition matrix. The numbers should be identical.
2. For each state count the number of arrows pointing away from that state in the graphic model. Now count the number of actions in the column (from state) of that state in the state transition matrix. The numbers should be identical.

We have described some techniques for how to graphically model a workflow. We now proceed with a detailed description of the states that are basic elements of the workflow.

3.3 The States

The states in a workflow can be classified by type and divided into lifecycle stages. We shall discuss here the stages in the workflow and the state types.

3.3.1 Basic Stages in Workflow

When designing the workflow model, you should consider defining states of the following stages of the work item lifecycle:

- **Submission**

  The submitter, or the person who requires the change, fills out the submission form. The submitter is obliged to fill in, at a minimum, all the mandatory fields, and to provide the required information for the roles performing the next actions, especially to the solution provider. It is important to identify and store the submitter contact information, by the login name for an internal user and by full name and company name for an external user. Submitter details are required for two reasons: to be able to contact the person for clarification of the request and for notification of the resolution status. The submit date is also an important piece of information to store. In cases where the submitter is not the reporter (for example, a customer requested the change indirectly by phone or e-mail), we need in addition to store the reporter name, his or her company name, and the report date. We shall discuss in detail in Chapter 4, "The Data," the recommended fields to include at this stage. Also note that ClearQuest allows the definition of a special form for this stage called the Submit Form. Submission is performed by an action of type Submit. Every record type must have an action of this type and therefore it is created by default.

- **Analysis**

  The information is analyzed by a subject matter expert. The analyst checks that the defect is actually a defect and can be reproduced. What is the cost of the fix/change in time and labor? Which component should be changed, and what other components are affected? Are there any external effects? What is the cost of not making the change? The analyzer should try to quantify as much as possible all of these questions as well as others that may be more relevant to the environment in which the organization operates. Organizations that use classification methods, such as the Beizer defect classification, will classify the defect in this stage.

- **Decision**

  The data provided by the analyst will be considered by the decision maker, usually the Software Change Control Board (SCCB, also called CCB). The board will have to decide whether to make a change and when, that is, in what product version the change will be included (a target date may also be supplied). The board should also decide who the solution provider is, or at least select the person who will select the solution provider. The board can decide to postpone the decision without selecting the target version (in this case the change will be discussed again in a later stage, usually when deciding on the content of the next release). The board may also decide to reject the change, usually because of high risk or high cost versus small value to the project. Another common reject reason is "Work as designed"—the submitter assumed the application would work in one way but it was designed to work in a different way. Other reject reasons are "Out of scope," "Test error," and "Not reproducible."

- **Resolution**

  After the decision is made to make the change and the solution provider has been assigned, the resolution stage starts. Software engineers will make the necessary changes in the code; technical writers will change the documentation; and so on. The solution providers will work with version control tools like ClearCase, and therefore the integration between the change management tool and the version control tool is manifested mainly at this stage. We shall discuss this matter in Chapter 6, "Integrations." In many cases the work item is split into several tasks, either because the change requires expertise in several domains, or to accelerate the project by parallel development.

- **Testing**

  After the resolution is completed and a new version is built (this version usually includes several changes from several solution providers), the test team will verify that the changes and fixes operate as required. It is well known that the preferred way is to perform full regression tests. If the testers find out that the change is not satisfactory, they will transition the work item back to the Analysis state.

- **Closure**

  After test results are analyzed, and if tests pass with no errors, the tester or the test manager will approve that the change was done, has been tested, and is ready to be released. In some workflows the submitter is the one who closes the change and approves that the result meets the requirements.

These are the very basic stages; each stage will be represented by one or more states. In some special cases two stages may be joined into a single state.

The stages may vary depending upon the nature of the work item. Some examples: A defect with low cost and no affected components may go directly to the resolution state with no need for the CCB to take action. A new feature with high cost may require more analysis and more approval stages. In some organizations every defect goes through code review and every feature through both design review and code review. Some organizations require that unit testing be an additional stage, and others include it in the resolution state.

Here are some additional stages that the organization can include in the workflow:

- **Reopening**

  After the closure, a decision may be made to reopen the change for one of the following reasons: a mistake was made in the closure decision; changes were made in the environment or in the requirements. Reopening does not necessarily require a state of its own; the change can be returned to one of the initial states as required (Submitted, Opened, or another). As this operation is not common, we suggest enforcing an explanation for the reopening. In our opinion it is not correct to reopen a closed change. If such a need arises, you can just open a new change and reference the closed change. This is correct from the process point of view and from the organizational metrics point of view.

- **Deferring or postponing**

  The CCB sometimes decides that a change is important but has a lower priority and therefore will not be implemented in the current release. There are various reasons to postpone a change, but they are usually high cost, high risk, or long implementation time versus lower priority due to no significant commercial gain. It is recommended when putting a change in the Deferred state to specify the delay time or the release in which the change is to be implemented. In this way it will be easier to identify the changes to be reconsidered when the CCB meets to discuss the content of a new release.

- **Deleting or rejecting**

  The CCB decides that the requested change has no importance to the organization and it will not be implemented now or in the future. Other examples are incorrect reports, such as defects that have been found to function correctly. The rejection reason should be documented by rejection type ("Not a bug," "Work as designed," "High risk," etc.) and by free description.

Note   *Deleted* is a state; it does not mean that the work item is physically deleted from the database.

- **Duplicating**

  This is a special state type that indicates that the change (or similar change request) was already recorded in the system. When a change request is in state Duplicated, it means that there is another record that describes the same issue, and that record is referenced from the duplicated record. It also means that a record in this state should not be worked on, as the work is done on the original (and referenced) record. A record having the state Duplicated is actually of type Completed. The reference between the changes allows us to perform operations such as notification to the submitter that a fix for the change exists when the parent record (the referenced one) was fixed.

  Duplicates can be used by the organization to understand the impact of an issue based on the number of submissions. If you get a lot, then this issue affects a lot of people. Typically, the issue is duplicated and the submitter is added to a subscription or notification list.

In Figure 3.7 you can see two records. Record 013 is a duplicate of record 011; they are links and can be accessed by just double-clicking. The state of record 013 is Duplicated and the state of record 011 is Opened.

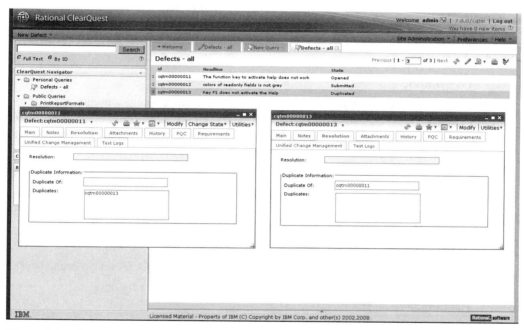

Figure 3.7 Records duplication example in ClearQuest

Note A record can have more than one duplicate.

3.3.2 State Types

The state names are proprietary and in many cases not in English. Some ClearQuest packages require you to define the type of each state. The definition is done using ClearQuest Designer by selecting the properties of each state.

Currently the following ClearQuest packages make use of state types:

- Unified Change Management (UCM) by the supporting package AMStateTypes

   This package is used for the integration of ClearQuest with ClearCase/UCM.

- Resolution

   This package adds support for tracking how a work item was resolved.

Knowing the state type enables you to automate several operations, for example, change field requiredness when entering a state of a specific type.

3.3.2.1 UCM State Types

When working with ClearCase Unified Change Management (UCM) methodology integrated into ClearQuest, there are some rules that the methodology enforces on your workflow. UCM defines four types of states: Waiting, Ready, Active, and Complete.

We shall briefly explain the types as they are well explained in both ClearCase and ClearQuest administration manuals. The state types are defined from the developer, or the solution provider, point of view.

- **[W] Waiting**

    The change was submitted and registered in the database, but no solution provider was selected. This is the early stage in the process. Either no decision was made by the CCB, or a decision was made but the team leader has not assigned the solution provider to resolve the change. Examples of states of type Waiting are Submitted, Analyzed, and Postponed.

- **[R] Ready**

    The change was assigned to a solution provider but the work has not started. Assignment means that the field Owner contains the login name of the developer.

- **[A] Active**

    The solution provider is working on the change. It means that files have been checked out, modified, and associated with this change.

- **[C] Complete**

    The developer finished the work. It means that the change was committed to the integration stream.

Each and every state in the flow must be mapped to one of these types.

Figure 3.8 shows the state transition matrix and the state Properties view. You can see in the State Types view that the state Opened is of type Active for the package AMStateTypes, 1.0; as mentioned before, this package is the supporting package for the Unified Change Management package.

3.3.2.2 Resolution State Types

The Resolution package requires you to define the type of each state. Two types are allowed:

- Resolved means that the solution provider has finished working on the work item. It does not necessarily mean that the work item is closed.

- Not_Resolved means that the solution provider has not finished working on the work item, or has not started the work.

Figure 3.9 shows the state transition matrix and the state Properties view. You can see in the State Types view that the state Opened is of type Not_Resolved for the package Resolution, 1.1.

Figure 3.8 State type definition for the UCM package

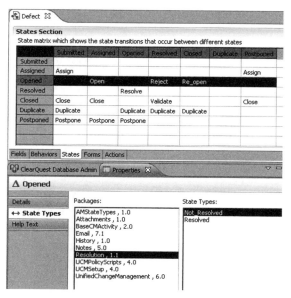

Figure 3.9 State type definition for the package Resolution

Note that the state Opened has two types, Not_Resolved for the package Resolution and Active for the package AMStateTypes. This is perfectly correct and does not create any conflict as the types are related to different packages.

3.4 Dynamic Workflow

In ClearQuest the state transition matrix defines the core workflow of a work item, or in Clear-Quest terms a *stateful record type*. Transition is done by actions performed by user selection. It means that the workflow is static. In many cases it is necessary to have a dynamic state machine, so the flow will vary depending on different conditions.

We shall demonstrate a technique that will enable a user (having the appropriate role) to change the default workflow for each and every record.

3.4.1 Background

In ClearQuest you can create work items of several types which are called record types. Usually they are Issue, Defect, Enhancement, Feature, Activity, Test Case, Build, and many others. A company may want to have only one record type to deal with change requests (there are many good reasons), but the static state transition matrix limits the implementation. Let's look at some simple examples:

- For new features and enhancements you would probably want the CCB to decide whether to implement them or not; for a bug you do not need the board to make this decision, and the flow can be shorter and faster.

- In small projects testers are familiar with the development teams; they know the developer who owns the defective component that they have just tested. So there is no need to go through some states to assign the bug to the developer; the tester can select the assignee during the Submit action.

- For features that pose a high risk to the project the project manager may want to have extra actions such as DesignReview and CodeReview. For simple features these actions may be omitted.

Each extra action is, in the best case, a waste of time for the user performing the action.

A more severe consequence is when the change delivery is delayed for a long time, or even forgotten. In the worst case someone makes a mistake and moves the issue to the wrong state, causing unnecessary delays to several users and inefficient work of the team.

In the following paragraphs we shall explain the programming technique to implement dynamic workflow, to be followed by three examples, each one with a higher complexity level.

3.4.2 The Technique

In ClearQuest performing an action of type Change_State always moves the record to a specific single state. In Figure 3.10 you can see the action Assign in the Properties view; there are two source states (multiple choice) but there is a single destination state (choice list).

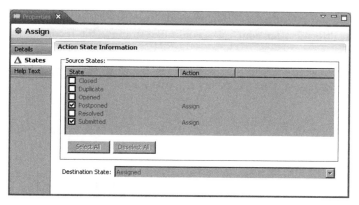

Figure 3.10 State transition in Action Properties dialog

We will use a hook to move the record to another state defined in the state transition matrix. To change the record state with the ClearQuest API one must use the session method `EditEntity()`; a correct BASIC example is

```
session.EditEntity EntityObj , "Assign"
```

Beginners sometimes try to change the state using

```
SetFieldValue("State", "NewState")
```

This call is forbidden and will not work. Another common mistake is trying to call another action in a validation or commit hook; this will result in a failure. Calling `EditEntity()` from a notification hook will not change its state. When the notification hook is fired, the record is already committed to the database and no changes to the record are possible in this context. So it seems as if there is no way to move the record to another state other than the current action destination state.

However, the fact that the notification hook is executed after the commit and the fact that it is possible to reload the record (as if it were open in a new session) enable us to perform the required action on that record.

The method of dynamic (or adaptive) workflow is based on this idea.

Note Reloading the entity is performed with the session method `LoadEntity()`.

Warning Using `LoadEntity()` is better than using a new session as it does not require a new login and does not expose the user password in the code.

3.4.3 Automatically Move to Another State

You are probably familiar with all the predefined schemas in ClearQuest. In all of them the initial state is Submitted and no owner is assigned. The default action in this state is Assign, which moves the record to the Assigned state and requires you to fill in the fields Owner and Priority.

As explained in section 3.4.1, "Background," in many cases the submitter can fill in the fields Owner and Priority, after which we would like to move the record to the state Assigned automatically.

The way to do it is by performing the action Assign in the notification hook after the record is committed to the database. This can be done in two ways:

- **New session**

  In the notification hook, create a new session, log in by providing a username and password, edit the entity, and perform the required action.

- **Reloading the record**

  This method is preferred over the new session method, as it is faster, shorter, and does not reveal the password in the code.

Listing 3.1 is an example of a notification hook code, placed in the action Submit, that automates the state change.

Listing 3.1   Auto-change State

```
Sub Defect_Notification(actionname, actiontype)

' Purpose: Change defect state to "Assign" if owner & priority were
'          set on submit
' Created by SB on 11 Dec 2003
' Date modified: 23 Sep 2007


Dim session, EntityObj
' check if both owner and priority have values
if ( "" <> GetFieldValue("Owner").GetValue AND    _
       "" <> GetFieldValue("Priority").GetValue ) then
            ThisID = GetDisplayName

  ' Get, Edit and Validate the record
     Set session = GetSession()
     Set EntityObj = session.LoadEntity ("defect", ThisID)
     session.EditEntity EntityObj , "Assign"
     status = EntityObj.Validate
     if (status <> "") then
         session.outputdebugstring "SB>>>: Fail validating " & _
"in action assign: " & status & vbCrLf
         EntityObj.Revert
  else
         session.outputdebugstring "SB>>>: Success validating " & _
```

```
"in action assign: " & status & vbCrLf
        EntityObj.Commit
  end if  ' pass validation
end  if  ' auto assign


End Sub
```

3.4.4 One Record Type Having Several State Machines for Each Issue Type

Now let's take a step forward and see a more complicated scenario. The ClearQuest schema has one record type called Issue, which deals with defects, enhancements, and features. We want to include more states when the type of the issue is Enhancement or Feature. For the sake of the example, let's assume that it must go through the additional states DesignReviewed and CodeReviewed. The states and actions are represented in the workflow diagram in Figure 3.11.

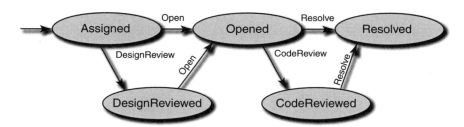

Figure 3.11   Partial state diagram

How do we change the workflow to force the transitions to the above-mentioned states?

Let's consider the portion of the state machine described in Figure 3.11. From the state Opened it is possible to move to the Resolved state using the action Resolve, or to the Code-Reviewed state with the action CodeReview. Some organizations may leave the decision to the developers, trusting their judgment or their familiarity with the company methodology. But in several situations the transition decision can be automated; the automation gives the organization better control of the process.

As mentioned earlier, if the issue is a defect, code review is not necessary, but for a new feature code review is obligatory. Other rules can be used, such as complexity value, number of lines of code changed, or function points.

When the developer has finished coding and testing, the issue needs to move to the next state. To do this, a special action we called Next is used.

The Next action has been added to the Issue record type; its type is Modify.

The notification hook of this action will determine the required final state using the required action of type Change-State which will be activated on the reloaded entity.

Listing 3.2 is a code example to perform the required state change. Notice the `Case "Opened"` section for the selection of the next action as previously explained.

Listing 3.2   Dynamic Change State

```
Sub Issue_Notification(actionname, actiontype)


' - Purpose: Change issue state to the required state
' - Created by SB on 01 Dec 2003
' - Date modified:

Dim session, EntityObj
' - check the current state
Cur_state = GetFieldValue("State").GetValue
Issue_Type = GetFieldValue("Issue_Type").GetValue
ThisID = GetDisplayName
' - Get session and reload the entity
    Set session = GetSession()
    Set EntityObj = session.LoadEntity ("defect", ThisID)
 ' - find the required action
  Select Case Cur_state
  Case "Submitted"
          NextAction = "Analyze"
  Case "Analyzed"
          NextAction = "Assign"
  Case "Assigned"
      If  ( Issue_Type = "Defect" ) then
          NextAction = "Open"
      Else
          NextAction = "DesignReview"
      End if
  Case "DesignReviewed"
          NextAction = "Open"
  Case "Opened"
      If  ( Issue_Type = "Defect" ) then
          NextAction = "Resolve"
      Else
          NextAction = "CodeReview"
      End if
```

```
  Case "CodeReviewed"
          NextAction = "Resolve"
  Case "Resolved"
          NextAction = "Verify"
  Case "Tested"
          NextAction = "Close"
  Case "Closed"
End Select



' - Edit the record using the selected action
    session.EditEntity EntityObj , NextAction
    status = EntityObj.Validate
    if (status <> "") then
       session.outputdebugstring "SB>>>: Fail validating action " & _
 NextAction  & ", the error is: " & status & vbCrLf
       EntityObj.Revert
    else
       session.outputdebugstring "SB>>>: Success validating action" & _
 NextAction  & ", the error is: " & status & vbCrLf
       EntityObj.Commit
  end if

End Sub
```

3.4.5 A State Machine for Each Issue

Now let's look at a more complicated scenario. The flow rules will be set manually by the CCB (or other authority). Consider a new feature arriving to the CCB. The CCB may reject, postpone, or accept the feature. If it is accepted, the CCB may require that the feature pass through some additional states, based on the risk it poses to the project (there may be other reasons to set different workflows, for example, the stage of the project).

The solution we propose is as follows:

In the schema we include fields to define whether a state is mandatory. For example, if the field Req_CodeReview has the value Yes, the state CodeReviewed is mandatory.

A person with a hub role (or other authority) will fill in these additional fields. The screen shot in Figure 3.12 is an example of how to select the required states in a tab form called Navigation Flow.

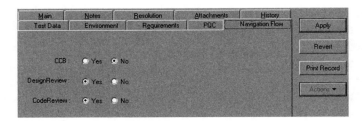

Figure 3.12   Setting the workflow navigation path

As in the previous example, we define an action of type Modify (let's call it Next_Action or just Next). The notification hook of this action will reload the entity and will perform the required action that will change the state according to the rules previously set on the form.

The code for this hook is provided in Listing 3.3.

Listing 3.3   Dynamic Workflow

```
Sub Issue_Notification(actionname, actiontype)

' - Purpose: Change issue state to the required state
' - Created by: SB on 12 Dec 2003
' - Date modified:   22 Sep 2007

Dim session, EntityObj
' - check the current state and the type of the issue
Cur_state = GetFieldValue("State").GetValue
Issue_Type = GetFieldValue("Issue_Type").GetValue

ThisID = GetDisplayName
' - Get session and reload the entity
    Set session = GetSession()
    Set EntityObj = session.LoadEntity ("defect", ThisID)

' - find the required action
  Select Case Cur_state
  Case "Submitted"
      If  (GetFieldValue("Req_CCB").GetValue = "Yes" ) then
          NextAction = "toCCB"
      Else
          NextAction = "Analyze"
      End if
```

```
  Case "Analyzed"
          NextAction = "Assign"
  Case "Assigned"
      If   (GetFieldValue("Req_DesignReview").GetValue = "Yes" ) then
            NextAction = "DesignReview"
      Else
            NextAction = "Open"
      End if
  Case "DesignReviewed"
          NextAction = "Open"
  Case "Opened"
      If   (GetFieldValue("Req_CodeReview").GetValue = "Yes" ) then
            NextAction = "CodeReview"
      Else
            NextAction = "Resolve"
      End if
  Case "CodeReviewed"
          NextAction = "Resolve"
  Case "Resolved"
          NextAction = "Verify"
  Case "Tested"
          NextAction = "Close"
  Case "Closed"
End Select


' - Edit the record using the action previously selected
    session.EditEntity EntityObj , NextAction
    status = EntityObj.Validate
    if (status <> "") then
       session.outputdebugstring ">>>: Fail in validating action " & _
    NextAction  & ", the error is: " & status & vbCrLf
       EntityObj.Revert
   Else
      session.outputdebugstring ">>>: Success in validating action " _
& NextAction   & vbCrLf
       EntityObj.Commit
  end if

End Sub
```

But something is missing in this method; the fields' requiredness defined in the behaviors table will not have any visual effect. The action the user selected is of type Modify, and it is not clear during the record editing what the final state is. Field behavior is defined by the final state of the action the user selected. Therefore it is necessary to set the requiredness of the fields before the record is edited, meaning in the initialization hook of the action Next.

Listing 3.4 is an example of how to do this.

Listing 3.4   Dynamic Workflow with Requiredness

```
Sub Issue_Initialization(actionname, actiontype)

' - Purpose: Change fields Requiredness based on final state
' - Created by: SB on 18 Dec 2003
' - Date modified:  23 Sep 2007


Dim newses , EntityObj
' check the current state
Cur_state = GetFieldValue("State").GetValue
IType = GetFieldValue("Issue_Type").GetValue
ThisID = GetDisplayName
ReqCCB = GetFieldValue("Req_CCB").GetValue

'  find the required action
  Select Case Cur_state
  Case "Submitted"
      If  (ReqCCB = "Yes" OR IType = "Feature" ) then
      Else
         SetFieldRequirednessForCurrentAction "Owner", AD_MANDATORY
         SetFieldRequirednessForCurrentAction "Priority", AD_MANDATORY
      End if
  Case "CCB"
         SetFieldRequirednessForCurrentAction "Owner", AD_MANDATORY
         SetFieldRequirednessForCurrentAction "Priority", AD_MANDATORY
  Case "Opened"
         SetFieldRequirednessForCurrentAction "Resolution", AD_MANDATORY
  Case "CodeReviewed"
         SetFieldRequirednessForCurrentAction "Resolution", AD_MANDATORY
 End Select

End Sub
```

In this example the field requiredness values are hard-coded in the hook; this is easier to code but not the best from a maintenance point of view. We shall discuss this issue in section 8.8.9, "Using Hard-Coded Data," in Chapter 8, "Development."

3.5 ClearQuest ALM Schema Workflow

The ClearQuest ALM schema takes a different approach to workflow. The workflow is built from several work item types, and the flow advances by creating new work items. The work item types that build the flow are

- ALMRequest
- ALMTask
- ALMActivity

The diagram in Figure 3.13 shows these work item types within the basic steps of the ALM workflow.

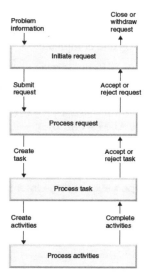

Figure 3.13   The ClearQuest ALM workflow and work items in the ALM process

An example will clarify the process.

An ALM work process begins with a request:

1. A user submits an ALMRequest. The change request could describe an enhancement request, a release requirement, or a defect. The submitter must select the ALMType, the ALMProject, the ALMCategory, as well as additional fields that define the request.

2. A triage team or change control manager reviews the ALMRequest and accepts or rejects it. If they accept it, they create an ALMTask, which is a high-level description of the work to be done to implement the ALMRequest. The request record includes a link to the ALMTask record, and the ALMTask is autolinked to the ALMProject. More than one ALMTask can be linked to the ALMRequest according to the defined ALM configuration.

3. A lead developer or other team lead reviews each ALMTask and then activates it. Activating the ALMTask creates ALMActivities to complete the ALMTask. The team lead assigns these ALMActivities to team members. Examples of ALMActivities are development activities, test activities, and documentation (doc) activities. The ALMTask record includes links to the ALMActivities records, and the ALMActivities records have links to the ALMTask.

4. Developer, test, and doc leads assign their activities to team members who update the activity records to reflect the status of their work. When they finish their work, they deliver their changes and mark their activities as Complete.

5. A release engineer integrates and builds the delivered changes and creates baselines.

6. A tester tests changes in the baselines. The test lead marks a test task as Complete after the test activities are worked on and completed.

7. The user who submitted the ALMRequest reviews the ALMTask and its ALMActivities and, if satisfied, marks the ALMRequest as Complete.

Each of the stateful ALM record types (Request, Task, and Activity) has a standard state transition workflow that completes the ALM workflow.

Note on CQ ALM Version 1.1   This new package version includes some enhancements with regard to process automation, for example, complete successors when specific resolution code values are selected, open successors when all predecessors have reached a specific state, and many others for request, task, and activity. See the release notes for full details.

3.6 Jazz Workflow

In the Jazz-based products the definition of the workflow is performed in a very similar way to ClearQuest as described in this chapter, but there is a difference. The Jazz workflow is not an integral part of the work item process as in ClearQuest. Figure 3.14 shows the workflow definition in Jazz. The workflow name is Authoring Workflow. The Jazz workflow includes the following sections:

- **States**

    A state is defined by a name. Additional optional properties of state are Description, Group, and Show Resolution. The Group value classifies the state in three groups:

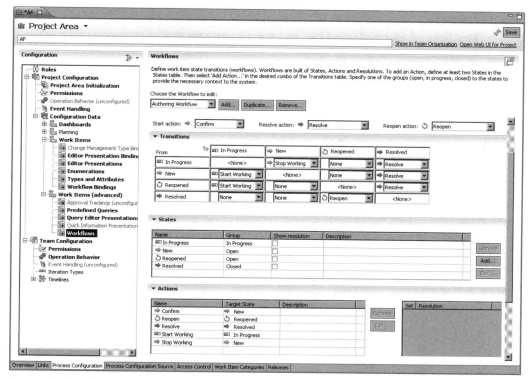

Figure 3.14 Workflow definition in a Jazz work item

Open, Closed, and In_Process. (This is similar to state types in ClearQuest.) The Show Resolution check box defines whether the resolution options will be shown in this state.

- **Actions**

  The actions are defined in the state transition matrix, and the Actions section is a read-only section. An action is defined by name and target state. Optional properties are description and icon. Note that actions are of type Change State only and there are no other types.

- **Transitions**

  This is the state transition matrix that defines which transitions are allowed and what actions will perform the transition.

- **Resolutions**

  A resolution is defined by name and brief description for the manner in which a work item can be resolved. The list of optional resolutions will be displayed when the state "Show resolution" check box is marked.

- **Icons**

  Icons can be assigned to actions and states to ease the operation and improve the user experience.

In addition, special action types can be defined; these are Start action, Resolve action, and Reopen action.

The defined workflow should be bound to one or more work item types. This is done in the Workflow Binding section of the work item. Figure 3.15 shows an example of workflow binding: the Authoring Workflow is bound to the Task-Quality work item type category.

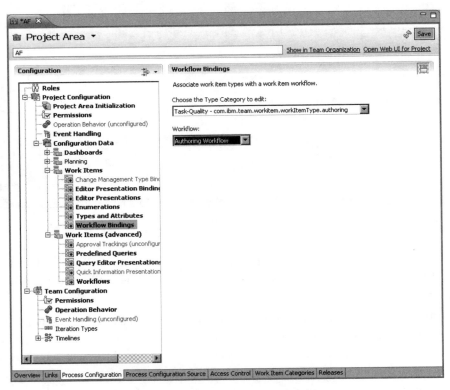

Figure 3.15   Binding workflow to type category in a Jazz work item

3.7 Subflow

Subflow is a deviation in the main workflow of a work item. The subflow may occur because of unplanned activity or a predicted yet rare situation that is not included in the main flow. This simplifies the main flow and eases the users' training and the deployment phase.

Subflow can be dealt with in many cases with child work items. For example, if during the process of change the owner identifies a need to deal with another element or an additional unpredictable task is required, he or she can create a child work item for that.

If the users can create child work items that are of a different type from the parent, it increases the flexibility of dealing with subflows. The ClearQuest ALM schema is built to deal with subflow as the workflow is based on a hierarchy of work items.

There are additional techniques to deal with subflow depending on the nature of the subflow. In the next paragraphs we explain in detail some options to deal with a subflow called More Information or Question and Answer and with build approval flow.

3.7.1 More Information

There are cases when the work item owner needs more information to continue the work. For example, the solution provider may need advice from a coworker who has more experience, or more information is required from the work item submitter, or the owner wants to ask a question and document both the question and the answer. This is a deviation from the main flow and needs to be tracked. There are several solutions to the "more info" tracking requirement.

3.7.1.1 New State

You can create a new state called More_Info. An action of type Change_State will transition from all states to this state. To return the information you need a special action to transition from the More_Info state to the original state transitioned from. Because a unique action is required to transition to a state, the designer needs to create a new action or use another action that is used in the flow. Look at the portion of the workflow in Figure 3.16. The action RequestInfo is used by the information requestor in all states. The information provider will have to use a different action to transition back to the previous state. This is a potential situation for errors, as we cannot expect the person to investigate the previous state. We need a better solution.

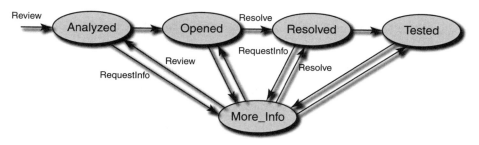

Figure 3.16   Sample sub-workflow for the More Information flow

A better solution is to have a single action of type Modify that will transition to the correct state in the background. In this solution, when the information requestor selects the action

RequestInfo, an action initialization hook stores the name of the current state and the name of the requestor. When the information provider selects the action ProvideInfo, a notification hook reads the requestor name and the required state and performs the transition. The hook examples in sections 3.4.4, "One Record Type Having Several State Machines for Each Issue Type," and 3.4.5, "A State Machine for Each Issue," are good examples of how to change the state after a Modify action.

You can use the Log_Entry field to document the information request and the information provided, or you can create additional fields for them.

3.7.1.2 Reassign

Another solution that does not involve a new state is to reassign the work item to the person whose information is required. The requestor will perform an action called RequestInfo of type Modify and will have to fill in at least two fields: Owner and Question. When providing the information, the new owner will have to perform the action ProvideInfo, also of type Modify, and fill in the field Owner (with the name of the previous owner who requested the information) and the field Answer.

You can use the Log_Entry field to document the information request and the information provided, or you can create additional fields for them.

This solution does not involve complex workflow changes, and in that regard it is better than the new state solution, but it has some disadvantages. Reassigning is not correct from a governance point of view. The new assignee is not really the owner of the work item, which may mislead managers who make status queries. The information provider is required to reassign the work item to the previous owner, and this is a potential source of errors. We recommend that this operation be automated.

This solution can be improved by adding a substate field or a check box that indicates that the work item is delayed because of the More Information subprocess.

3.7.1.3 Dedicated Actions

In this solution the designer creates two new actions of type Modify: Question and Answer. New fields are also required:

- One field is needed to identify the person to whom the question is addressed.
- The second field is a flag that indicates that a question was asked but was not answered yet. We often call this flag the substatus of the subflow.

Figure 3.17 shows an enhancement request record after the action Question. Note the mandatory fields the information requestor needs to fill in. Also note that the "Active unanswered question" check box is marked.

The Question action initialization hook is simple and is demonstrated in Listing 3.5. The Question_To (field of type Reference to users) is cleared and made mandatory, the field flag ActiveQuestion is turned on, and the Note_Entry is made mandatory.

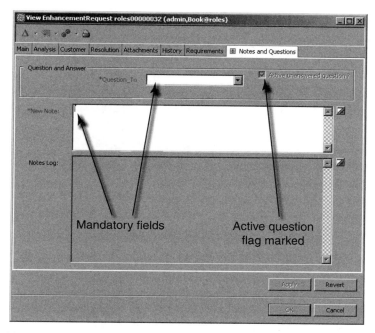

Figure 3.17 More Information subflow: the user interface after the user has selected the action Question

Listing 3.5 Question Initialization Hook

```
sub EnhancementRequest_Initialization {
    my($actionname, $actiontype) = @_;
    # $actionname as string scalar
    # $actiontype as long scalar
    # action is Question
    # record type name is EnhancementRequest
    # Start User Code
    $entity->SetFieldValue("ActiveQuestion" , "Y" );
    $entity->SetFieldValue( "Question_To" , "" );
    $entity->SetFieldRequirednessForCurrentAction("Note_Entry",
                                   $CQPerlExt::CQ_MANDATORY);
    $entity->SetFieldRequirednessForCurrentAction( "Question_To",
                                   $CQPerlExt::CQ_MANDATORY);
    # End User Code
}
```

Note that this solution uses the standard fields Note_Entry and Notes_Log to ask the questions and provide the answers. The ClearQuest screen shot in Figure 3.18 demonstrates the user interface after the action Answer.

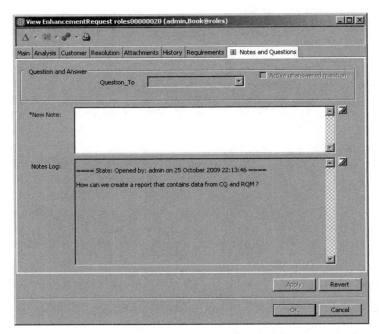

Figure 3.18   More Information subflow: the user interface after the user has selected the action Answer

The Answer action initialization hook is simple and is demonstrated in Listing 3.6. The `Question_To` is cleared and turned to be read-only, the field flag `ActiveQuestion` is turned off, and the `Note_Entry` is made mandatory so the answer will be provided.

Listing 3.6   Answer Initialization Hook

```
sub EnhancementRequest_Initialization {
    my($actionname, $actiontype) = @_;
    # $actionname as string scalar
    # $actiontype as long scalar
    # action is Answer
    # record type name is EnhancementRequest
    # Start User Code
    $entity->SetFieldValue("ActiveQuestion" , "N" );
```

```
$entity->SetFieldValue( "Question_To" , "" );
$entity->SetFieldRequirednessForCurrentAction("Note_Entry",
                              $CQPerlExt::CQ_MANDATORY);


# End User Code
}
```

As we have mentioned, this solution uses the standard Notes package; notes and comments appear in the Notes_Log fields with questions and answers. This is not wrong, but it requires more effort from users to find information. One simple solution is to use different fields for notes and for questions and answers. Another solution is to improve the log formatting so it will be easier to differentiate questions from notes. The package format for each entry header is

```
==== State: Opened by: admin on 26 October 2009 09:08:29 ====
```

The hook to the format of this header is a global subroutine that is called from the Note_Entry Value_Changed hook as follows:

```
SetLog($fieldname, "Notes_Log");
```

The SetLog subroutine can be modified as shown in Listing 3.7.

Listing 3.7   SetLog Subroutine

```
sub SetLog {
    # noteEntryField As String
    # notesLogField As String
    my ($noteEntryField, $notesLogField) = @_;
    my $session, $myName, $banner, $thisNote, $thisNoteInfo;
    my $oldNotes, $newNotes, $crLf, $month, $now;
      my $QA_head = "";


    $oldNotes = $entity->GetFieldOriginalValue($notesLogField)->
GetValue();
    $thisNoteInfo = $entity->GetFieldValue($noteEntryField);

      # hash of months and their corresponding strings in English
      %month_string = (
            "1" => "January",
            "2" => "February",
            "3" => "March",
            "4" => "April",
```

continues

Listing 3.7   `SetLog` Subroutine (*Continued*)

```perl
            "5"  =>  "May",
            "6"  =>  "June",
            "7"  =>  "July",
            "8"  =>  "August",
            "9"  =>  "September",
            "10" =>  "October",
            "11" =>  "November",
            "12" =>  "December",
    );

    if ($thisNoteInfo->GetValueStatus() eq $CQPerlExt::CQ_HAS_VALUE) {
        $thisNote = $thisNoteInfo->GetValue();
        $session = $entity->GetSession();
        $crLf = "\x0d\x0a";

        my ($sec, $min, $hour, $mday, $mon, $year, $wday, $yday, $time)
          = localtime();
        $now = sprintf("%2.2d %s %4d %2.2d:%2.2d:%2.2d", $mday,
               $month_string{$mon + 1} ,$year + 1900, $hour, $min, $sec);

        $myName = $session->GetUserLoginName();

        # Get action and alter banner for Question and Answer
        my $CurrentAction = $entity->GetActionName();
        $session->OutputDebugString(">>>Action is: $CurrentAction \n");
        if ($CurrentAction eq "Question" ) {
            $QA_head = "?? " . $CurrentAction . " to " .
                   $entity->GetFieldStringValue("Question_To") . " ?? ";
        }
        if ($CurrentAction eq "Answer") {
            $QA_head = "!! " . $CurrentAction . " !! ";
        }

        $banner = $crLf . $QA_head . "==== State: " .
                  $entity->GetFieldValue("State")->GetValue() .
                  " by: " . $myName . " on " . $now . " ====" . $crLf;

         $newNotes = $banner . $crLf . $thisNote . $crLf . $oldNotes;
    }
```

```
    else {
        $newNotes = $oldNotes;
    }

    $entity->SetFieldValue($notesLogField, $newNotes);
}
```

The SetLog() global subroutine is read-only by default, as it is owned by the Notes package. To modify the subroutine you will have to use the following command line (note that the code appears here on two lines but is actually a single line of code):

```
Packageutil enableediting -dbset mydbset admin adminPWD
 -enable CQdesignerLogin
```

Modifying package hooks is not recommended; instead of modifying the subroutine Set-Log(), you can create a new global subroutine, SetQALog(), that is called from the Note_Entry Value_Changed hook, as shown in Listing 3.8.

Listing 3.8 Note_Entry Value_Changed

```
sub note_entry_ValueChanged {
    my($fieldname) = @_;
    # $fieldname as string scalar
    # record type name is EnhancementRequest
    # field name is Note_Entry
    # Start User Code

 my $CurrentAction = $entity->GetActionName();
 if ($CurrentAction eq "Question" || $CurrentAction eq "Answer" ) {
    SetQALog($fieldname, "Notes_Log");
 }
 else {
    SetLog($fieldname, "Notes_Log");
 }
    # End User Code
}
```

Figure 3.19 shows the Notes_Log field after this change is applied to the schema. Notice the different banner for Question, Answer, and other notes. You can take this approach further and customize the note banner for various actions or subflows in your workflow.

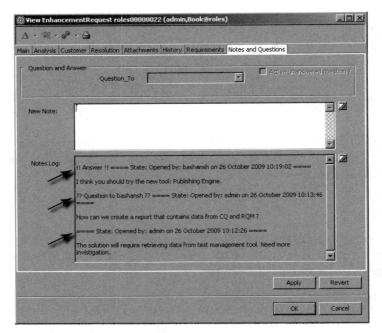

Figure 3.19   More Information subflow: the Notes Log with a distinct banner for each action

3.7.2 Build Approval

Another subflow example is when a project requires build approval from several roles: Development Manager. Deployment Leader, and Build Manager. Instead of adding three states to the flow that are not required by all projects and are not required in all work item types, we can do the following:

1. Add an action of type Modify: Build Approve.

2. Add a field of type String: Build Approval Status.

3. Add a hook to auto-assign the next role that needs to approve.

Figure 3.20 shows the new field in the Resolution tab. The field is a read-only field which is updated only by the action hook demonstrated later.

The next code examples are Perl global hooks that will be called from the Complete action validation hook to assign the first approver, and from the Build Approve validation hook to assign the next approver.

In section 8.1.3, "Employing Reusable Assets," of Chapter 8, "Development," you can find a discussion of when it is advisable to use global hooks.

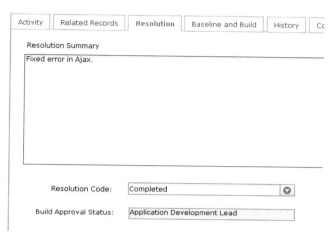

Figure 3.20 Sample subflow for build approval process

The action hook code in Listing 3.9 calls the global script `AssignApprover()` to assign the approver.

Listing 3.9 Calling Global Script

```
sub ALMActivity_Validation {
    my($actionname, $actiontype) = @_;
    my $result;
    # $actionname as string scalar
    # $actiontype as long scalar
    # $result as string scalar
    # action is BuildApprove
    # record type name is ALMActivity
    # Start User Code

    & AssignApprover();

    # End User Code
    return $result;
}
```

The global hook in Listing 3.10 is a code example to auto-assign an approver. Note that the approver is read from the ALMRole record.

Listing 3.10   Global Script to Assign Approver

```
sub AssignApprover()
{
# Purpose: Assign next approver
#          The approver is the primary in the ALMRole record
# I/O      : None

my $sapStatus = $entity->GetFieldValue("APP_Approval")->GetValue();
my $project = $entity->GetFieldValue("Project")->GetValue();
my $rolekey;
  if( $sapStatus eq "Developer fixed") {
      $rolekey = $project . " " . "Development Lead";
      $entity->SetFieldValue("APP_Approval", "Development Lead" );
  }
  if($sapStatus eq "Development Lead") {
      $rolekey = $project . " " . "Deployment Lead";
      $entity->SetFieldValue("APP_Approval", "Deployment Lead" );
  }
  if($sapStatus eq "Deployment Lead") {
      $rolekey = $project . " " . "Build Manager";
      $entity->SetFieldValue("APP_Approval", "Build Manager" );
  }

  $session->OutputDebugString(">>>>>APPassign:: key: $rolekey \n ");
my $EntityObj = $session->GetEntity("ALMRole", $rolekey );
my $primary = $EntityObj->GetFieldValue("Primary")->GetValue();
$entity->SetFieldValue("Owner", $primary );
}
# End of Global Script Process
```

3.8 Summary

In this chapter we explained different methods for designing a workflow. We recommended using a simplified state chart to design a workflow for ClearQuest and for Jazz work items.

In section 3.3, "The States," we explained the workflow stages and the states in each stage and suggested the various usage scenarios.

In section 3.4, "Dynamic Workflow," we disproved the myth that says that the ClearQuest state machine is static. We explained how to make the state machine dynamic using some script-ing. The flexibility of ClearQuest enables us to go beyond the basic functionality and allows organizations to create a (dynamic) workflow the way they need. We demonstrated how the flow can be automated in some cases; in other cases a general user action that we have called Next (the implicit meaning is that the user has finished the activity) will cause the work item to move to the required state, thus enforcing the workflow rules.

As a more complex example, we showed how to adapt a different workflow for each and every record, using user selection rules for states and flow path, set in the record itself.

The ideas presented can be developed and enhanced to meet other needs of various organizations or projects. This is the beauty of ClearQuest; most of the customization can be done using the GUI, and the complex requirements can be developed using scripting.

We explained the different approach that the ClearQuest ALM schema uses to define and manage workflow. The ALM schema defines three types of work items: ALMRequest, ALMTask, and ALMActivity. The work flows from a higher level to a lower level and is approved at the higher level.

In section 3.6, "Jazz Workflow," we explained the Jazz workflow elements, how to define a workflow, and how to bind a workflow to a work item type.

In the last section of the chapter we explained what a subflow is, provided several examples of subflows, and demonstrated some solutions to common subflows.

## CHAPTER 4

The Data

The data accumulated in the work item serves several purposes:

- **Information for analysis**

  Enables an understanding of the reason for and cause of the issue, the requirements for the change, the cost and resources needed, the possible risks, and the release in which the issue will be resolved.

- **Information for the solution provider**

  Enables an understanding of the issue location and the required changes to provide the solution, be it a defect, enhancement, or feature.

- **Information for managers**

  Enables tracking of changes and monitoring the status of issues, for example, meeting target dates, what and who is causing a delay, how to improve the process; data for statistical study regarding solution performance such as time spent at each state (also known as aging analysis), estimated times versus actual times; quality metrics such as defects per component, phase caused versus phase detected; and other information. Read more on metrics in Chapter 9, "Metrics and Governance."

- **Historical information for testers and developers**

  Enables detection of repeating defects and learning the root cause and best solution or best method to test. Historical data is also used as proof in audits.

To meet these objectives we need the following information:

- **Issue description**

  This is a very detailed description of the issue or the request. In the case of a defect the description should also include steps to reproduce it.

- **Location**

  This is information that enables you to identify the element that needs to be changed. For a software defect, the location would be the product (name and version) and the module (name and version). The product tree varies from company to company, but the information that enables you to locate the item/component to be changed must be supplied or detected.

- **Environment**

  In many cases the system configuration is important for reproducing the defect or may even influence the results. The information required for the environment varies depending on the system architecture. Examples are database vendor and version, operating system on client and server, client type, and service packs. There could be many variants to environment data.

- **Internal impact**

  Does the issue affect other components? Is the change required in other releases? A common example is a defect that was found in a recent release but exists in older releases and needs to be fixed. We may need to develop new test cases or modify existing test cases.

- **External impacts**

  External impacts are mainly customers that are affected by the change. We may need to create a patch and distribute it to affected customers; work-arounds should be investigated and if found viable should be communicated to customers. It is important to consider the cost of making the change versus the impact of not making it. Integrations with other systems should also be considered as external impacts.

- **Corrective actions**

  Who will perform the change (team, engineer, etc.)? What is the change to be performed? In many cases the actual change differs from the required change, because constraints can reduce or extend the focus of the change. An explanation and justification for performing the change (why) and a description of the actual change that was performed should be included.

- **Times**

  Included here are the amount of effort such as estimated effort and actual effort to perform the change, and estimated effort and actual effort to test the change. Also various timestamps are captured, such as due dates and actual dates for decision, resolution, and closure.

- **Tests**

  How will the test (an existing test case or a new one to be developed) be performed—with manual testing or automatic scripts? Who will perform the test (team, tester)? If internal impacts and other modules are affected, full regression testing may be required. A description of the test procedure or a link to the test case and the expected test results or a link to the test log results should be included. Important information is the required configuration of the test environment. This can be a link to the test management system that has all this information.

- **History**

  A list of all actions and changes in the work item, including username and date of action, should be included.

- **Additional data**

  It is important to include data that is required in a specific environment, such as an audit trail when regulatory compliance is needed, or hardware or firmware specifications in embedded systems.

- **Quality assurance**

  Organizations that adopt processes like CMMI (Capability Maturity Model Integration) would require additional data for improvement of process and quality. Examples are phase caused, phase detected, repeating defects, estimated effort, actual effort, and where first found.

4.1 Work Item Content

Let's examine in detail each of the previously mentioned information domains. ClearQuest and Jazz work items store data in fields, so we shall describe what fields are required to meet the information objectives.

4.1.1 Work Item Description

Work item description data consists of fields that contain the description of the change request or issue in different levels of detail. Usually the work item includes a short description used in queries and summary reports and a detailed description used by practitioners.

4.1.1.1 Headline

Headline is a one-line text field that should be carefully considered. It is sometimes called Title or Subject, but the name is not important; the content is. Users of the system should understand by reading this single line what the essence of the required change is. If the change is a defect, the line should describe the problem and possibly the domain or location. It is recommended that the organization define written procedures for the structure of the headline.

Examples of good headlines are

Module administrating does not print list of users.

SQL injection is allowed via search field.

These types of structures enable every reader to focus on the essence of the problem. The organization should not allow "freedom of speech" in this field. Some companies even define a list of known problems for the user to select from. While this may sound excessive, it definitely makes the headline clear.

UCM Note   When working with UCM, there must be a field called Headline with a length of 125 characters.

4.1.1.2 Description

Description is a free-text multiline field where the submitter of the work item describes in detail the required change. Depending on the type of the work item, the field can contain the description of the task. In the case of a defect the submitter should include the steps to reproduce the problem (see also section 4.1.1.3, "Steps to Reproduce"). It is advisable to copy system messages or other output to this field that will help to clarify the problem. If there is a lot of information, it is best to store system messages and logs as attachments and include a note in the description regarding the additional information in the Attachments tab.

For example, in Figure 4.1 the check box indicates that an attachment exists in the Attachments tab. The check box is filled automatically by the Value_Changed hook of the Attachment field. This check box allows the user to see at a glance if there is an attachment without the need to navigate to that tab. Similarly, you can add a check box for other data such as Log_Note or other fields in other tabs. This is somewhat similar to the Jazz Quick Information view but less detailed.

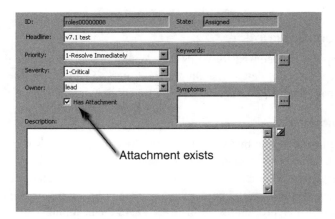

Figure 4.1   Description field with adjacent attachment check box; the checkmark indicates that an attachment exists.

ClearQuest Hook Example   A Perl script to mark the Has_Attachment check box if an attachment has been added is included in section 4.6.1, "HasAttachment."

4.1.1.3 Steps to Reproduce

The Steps to Reproduce field is related mainly to defects (but may also be relevant to some enhancement requests) and includes a detailed description of step-by-step actions that lead to the reproduction of the problem. In some companies, if the defect was detected during system tests, it is enough to specify the test procedure or the automatic test program, because the test procedure specifies the steps to reproduce the defect. Developers spend a lot of time trying to reproduce issues during the debug and resolution process, so we want to emphasize that a link to the test case or configured test case in the test management system is important information for understanding and reproducing the issue.

We do not exclude the option of capturing a sequence of snapshots or even video of the steps causing the issue and attaching the file to the defect. The trade-off between disk space and clarity should be considered.

4.1.1.4 Test Case

The Test Case field contains the name or the reference to the test case in the test management system. When using ClearQuest-TestManager integration, that information is inserted automatically by Rational TestManager; that is, if a defect is reported during the execution of a test case, the test case name (or reference) data is included in the defect form. That information is used in two ways: to verify coverage, and to obtain traceability to use cases or requirements for QA metrics. It is very important to trace defects to requirements. Chapter 9, "Metrics and Governance," goes into more detail on metrics.

This information will ease the work of the testers when validating the fix; they will know immediately which test case they should use to verify whether the problem was correctly fixed.

See also section 4.1.8, "Tests."

The Jazz environment is similar. If a tester working with Rational Quality Manager identified a defect during test case execution and reported it, the test case name will be automatically included in the Summary field and in the Description field of the defect work item. Also in the Links tab, under the Links section, a link is created to the test case. A tester can hit the link and the test case artifact will open in Rational Quality Manager. An example of such a defect is shown in Figure 4.2.

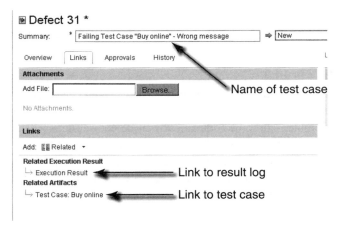

Figure 4.2   Jazz defect with a link to the test case

Table 4.1 provides a list of suggested fields and their types for the work item description. Some of the fields are included in ClearQuest built-in schemas and in the Jazz process templates.

Table 4.1   Suggested Fields for Description Data

Field Name	Field Type	Comment
Headline	Short_String	
Description	Multiline_String	
StepsToReproduce	Multiline_String	These fields names are relevant for defects. For new features or enhancement requests, similar fields are required: Story and UseCase.
TestCase	Short_String	

4.1.2 Location

Location information describes the physical artifact involved in the change. This is usually a set of fields that include information regarding the component/module where the change is required. A full hierarchy of the element should be defined (product tree). In many software cases we see the following data to define the location: Product Name > Product Version > Module Name > Module Version. In most cases there is a dependency between the elements, so building the system in a dependent manner is recommended so that the user will not be able to select a wrong element. For example, if the product name is selected, then the versions of only that product will appear in the product version list. After the user has selected the product version, only the modules that are part of that product version will appear in the list of modules, and so forth for the whole product tree. In section 4.4, "Object Relations," we further discuss this matter and provide examples.

In complex products it is likely that more information will be required to identify the location. For products that include both hardware and software, we shall have to designate fields for elements and versions of both disciplines.

Figure 4.3 shows the ALMCategory record for hardware and software practice. Here a record type was allocated for item identification. Note that the category type is Hardware, the name of the category is TapeDrive, and there are two subcategories for hardware and for software.

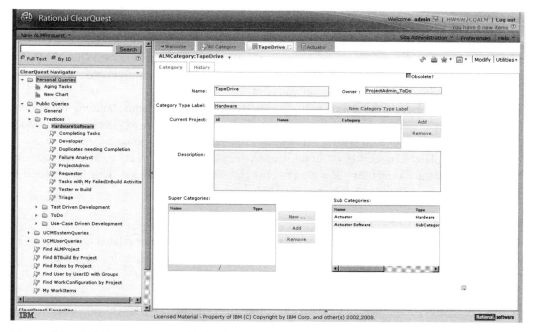

Figure 4.3 ALMCategory record in hardware and software disciplines

It is important that this data be easy to maintain, ideally by the project team. Commonly the structure changes and items are added. This information is owned by the project teams, and they should be able to update it easily.

4.1.3 Environment

This field (or set of fields) specifies the environment configuration of the system where the defect was detected. For other types of change the environment is less likely to be interesting. Required information for configuration varies tremendously from one system to another and generally includes information such as

- Operating system (OS)
- OS version

- Service pack (SP) (if relevant in both client and server)
- Other software products (such as database, networking, and licensing)
- Software libraries

In some systems the hardware configuration should also be specified.

In Command and Control Systems, specifying the exact system configuration may be critical to identifying the problem, reproducing it, and fixing it. It is also recommended that the information *not* be stored in a free-text field but as a set of fields with closed value lists; this allows precise definition and enables easier search. In many cases the development team cannot reproduce a problem that was discovered by the testing team; the problem or defect did not disappear and certainly was not resolved as some optimistic developers tend to assume. The reason for the inability to reproduce, in most cases, is differences in the system configuration between the development environment and the test environment.

As mentioned previously, if there is a dependency between elements, building the system in a dependent manner is recommended so that the user will not be able to select a wrong value; for example, after the OS field is selected, only SPs related to that OS should appear in the list.

As we explained in section 4.1.2, it is important that this data be easy to maintain, ideally by the project team. Commonly the structure changes and items are added. This information is owned by the project teams and they should be able to update it easily.

4.1.4 Internal Impacts

When analyzing the change, we should examine whether it affects other related components, or whether the changes are required only in the current release or in previous releases as well.

4.1.4.1 Impact on Components

During the analysis of the change we must check the impact of the change on other software components; in some cases a change may require fixes in more than one component. In these cases we must consider the complexity and the risk of affecting the related components. A special field of type Reference_List is required to store the list of the related (affected) component.

If there are affected components, the testing team must analyze the influence of the change on existing test cases and test procedures, that is, what tests to run to ensure that the issue was fixed and that errors will be detected, if they still exist, during regression tests.

4.1.4.2 Impact on Releases

In addition, we must examine previous releases and find in what releases the change is required. For example, a defect was detected in release 7.5; we now need to examine whether the defect was generated in release 7.5 or was generated in an earlier release and just detected in this release. So if we find that the defect also exists in releases 7.4 and 7.3, the organization has to decide whether to fix only the next release (i.e., 7.6), or to fix all previous releases having that defect. If only the new release is fixed, some administrative action has to be taken, such as including a note in the release notes document, or even reporting to customers and suggesting upgrading to the new release.

If the defect was not detected in internal tests (reported by customers), the test plan has to be modified so that the defect will be detected in the future during formal tests.

4.1.5 External Impacts

Making a change to an application can also impact actors, documentation, training, and other applications.

4.1.5.1 Users

All of the users of the system may be affected by the change: customers, internal users, partners, and others. The following questions should be considered:

- Do we need to create a patch and distribute it to affected customers?
- Are there viable work-arounds?
- What is the cost of making the change versus the impact of not making it?
- Do we need to modify the training materials and train the users?

So we must include fields to track that information, such as

- Affected_Customers (list of customers)
- Customer_Severity
- Customer_Priority
- Estimated_Cost

This customer data must be populated from the system containing the master customer data. Usually corporations have this data somewhere else, so ClearQuest must be populated periodically to keep in sync.

Not making the change can have negative commercial impact, such as a bad reputation, customer complaints, and unsatisfied users, which can cause a decline in future sales.

Synchronizing Customer Data   In section 6.2.2.3, "Creating Integration with Perl and BASIC API," in Chapter 6, "Integrations," we provide a Perl script to update Devices information from an ERP (enterprise resource planning) system. A similar method can be used to update customer data from a CRM (customer relationship management) system.

4.1.5.2 Applications

In some cases external impact is related to external applications that are integrated into the system under test. In such cases we should include the application names or their interfaces to the system.

4.1.5.3 Documentation

A change may affect relevant documentation, especially if the change is an enhancement or a new feature. This may require changes or additions to the user manual or other technical documentation. Software artifacts have documents related to them, and we may want to include fields that define whether a documentation change is required, which documents need to be changed, and what sections should be changed.

We believe that if this is the case, a new work item(s) should be opened (as a referenced child) to manage the process of these additional changes. Because documentation change is handled by the Technical Writer role, it is even more important to create a new work item for this additional change.

The ClearQuest ALM schema auto-creates child tasks and activities to deal with these different types of activities, providing an advantage that allows defining such a process without modifying the schema. Figure 4.4 shows an ALMTask with three child activities of types Dev, Test, and Doc Assess.

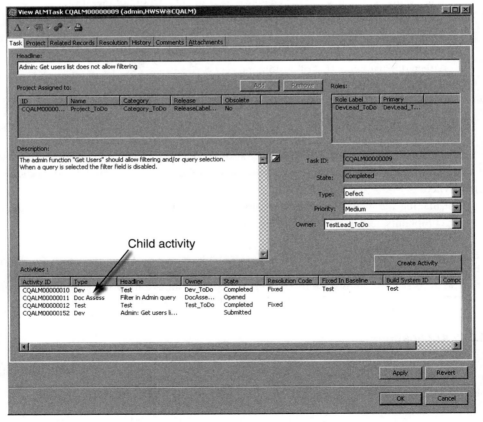

Figure 4.4   ALMActivity of type Doc Assess as child of ALMTask of type Defect

In many cases an application change requires an update in the release notes, which are considered as documentation. Work items often include a special field with notes to be included in the release notes.

4.1.5.4 Training

The considerations for training materials changes are similar to those for documentation, as described in the preceding section. Changes of type New Feature will most likely require additions or modifications to the training materials.

4.1.6 Corrective Actions

When the SCCB decides to approve a change, it has to make some more decisions: who the solution provider is, exactly what they will change, when they will provide it, and what the priority is.

4.1.6.1 Assign the Solution Provider

The first stage is to assign the work item to the solution provider (also known as the assignee or owner). In many cases the work item is assigned to the group leader of the relevant component (this is auto-assigned in the ClearQuest ALM schema based on the ALMRole > Primary setting), and the group leader assigns the work item to the developer to develop the change.

We have seen cases where a work item is assigned to a group, for example, the group developing the component. We believe that this is a mistake and that only one person should be assigned to a work item at a given time. We hear claims like "We do not know now who will do it, but it is certainly someone from the GUI group." Several assignees mean that nobody is responsible! The answer to this claim is "Let the group leader be the owner of the work item until he or she decides who will actually be the owner." Another advantage of setting a single owner is the ability to create process automation by auto-assigning a work item by roles.

See section 5.3.2, "Implementing Roles Implicitly," in Chapter 5, "Roles," for a more detailed description, and section 5.7.2, "Hook to Automatically Set Responsible Based on Role of Type Single," in the same chapter for a code example.

When working with ClearCase/UCM there must be a field called Owner; this field contains the user login of the solution provider. (This is created with the ClearQuest package Unified Change Management.)

In section 5.2.1, "Basic Definitions," in Chapter 5, "Roles," we discuss the differences between the responsible role and the solution provider role. In some situations having just a single field for the owner does not provide the required governance level.

4.1.6.2 Prioritize

Users usually have more than one task to do at a time. Therefore, when we assign a task to a user, we must set the priority (a field) and possibly set another field with the target date, or target release (which implicitly sets the target date).

4.1.6.3 Document the Solution

The solution provider should carefully document the changes performed. At a minimum the type of change (a field with a choice list such as code, configuration, data, documentation, etc.) should be defined, but it is advisable that the organization have more detailed information on the substance of the change and versions of files that were changed (this information is created automatically when working with a version control system integration such as ClearCase or Rational Team Concert). Also, when relevant, recommendations for testing, documentation that needs to be changed, or the documentation that was changed should be provided.

When working with UCM, the ClearCase Stream, View, and Change-Set (the versions of the changed files) are automatically filled in special fields provided by the integration package.

Table 4.2 provides a list of suggested fields and their types for the work item corrective actions. Some of the fields are included in ClearQuest built-in schemas and in the Jazz process templates.

Table 4.2   Suggested Fields for Corrective Actions Data

Field Name	Field Type	Comment
Owner	Reference	
Priority	Short_String	Closed list
SolutionType	Short_String	Closed list
SolutionDescription	Multiline_String	
DueDate	Date_Time	

4.1.7 Times

Each action timestamp is automatically stored in the database history table. In many cases this is not enough and we shall propose additional fields to improve system quality, ease of use, and the ability to easily create queries and charts.

4.1.7.1 Termination Dates

By termination we mean setting additional fields to store the expected and the actual termination dates of some important actions, for example, the SCCB decision date, the solution provider termination date, the release date, and the closing date. Each organization will set additional (or other) terms according to its needs.

ClearQuest, Rational Team Concert, and Rational Quality Manager enable the organization to set controls on the defined times; here are some examples:

- A query to display all changes for which the target date is almost due
- Sending an e-mail to a manager with details of each change for which the target date has passed
- Generating a periodic lag report

It is possible and recommended that several methods be combined, according to the type of the term. E-mail is recommended if the work item has related items and a delay will affect or cause a delay in the related item too. E-mail is also recommended for high-priority work items. Refer to this article for more information:

> Staff, IBM Rational, "External VB Application to Do 'Something' with Records Not Touched in 14 Days," *IBM developerWorks*, www.ibm.com/developerworks/rational/library/3895.html, 2004 (accessed February 23, 2011).

4.1.7.2 Amount of Effort

The amount of effort performed by practitioners is important information. It is stored in a field of type Integer and can have values measured in hours or days. This is not the duration or the elapsed time, which is the calendar time between two actions, but the actual work time. The duration can be calculated from the history table.

We usually store the amount of effort in two types of work tasks:

- **Resolution:** The time that the solution provider actually worked on resolving the change or the issue
- **Testing:** The time that testers worked on testing the solution; for new features the time may include the time to develop a new test case or modify an existing one

Another possible effort time we may want to capture is the analysis time.

Other actions in the process of change are less time-consuming (although they may take much calendar time) and therefore are not very interesting to capture.

This information allows us to calculate the cost of the change and enables us to estimate more accurately similar changes in the future. Moreover, we can evaluate the actual amount of effort versus the estimated amount of effort and improve either the estimation during the analysis phase or the actual development in the solution phase.

Table 4.3 provides a list of suggested fields and their types for the work item times. Some of the fields are included in ClearQuest built-in schemas and in the Jazz process templates.

Table 4.3   Suggested Fields for Times

Field Name	Field Type	Comments
ResolutionDate	DateTime	
CloseDate	DateTime	
SubmitDate	DateTime	
ResolutionEffort	Integer | DateTime	For DateTime: On the ClearQuest form control, select Properties, clear the Date, and mark only the Time check box in the Date/Time tab.
TestingEffort	Integer | DateTime	
EstimatedResolutionEffort	Integer	The effort is estimated during the analysis phase.
EstimatedTestingEffort	Integer	

A few words about field types and time units. As previously mentioned, for ClearQuest you can use either DateTime or Integer, but you still have to decide what the measurement unit will be. In most cases hours is appropriate for work item amount of effort. Days might work, but then the minimum unit of work is one day, because ClearQuest does not support the floating-point field type.

If decimals are required to define the time units, review this article from the *IBM developerWorks* library:

Muse, William, "Getting around a Decimal," *IBM developerWorks*, www.ibm.com/developerworks/rational/library/4498.html, 2003 (accessed February 24, 2011).

In a Jazz work item the user can specify the unit of work, for example, 2 w (for two weeks), 3 d, 20 h, 30 m. The user can also combine units, for example, 2 d 4 h, as seen in Figure 4.5.

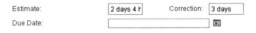

Figure 4.5   Jazz work item times: estimated and actual effort, and due date. Note the units of time in Jazz.

Note on SLA   See Chapter 12, "Sample Applications and Solutions," for an example of an SLA solution that makes extensive use of terms data.

4.1.8 Tests

After the new release is built, a tester should verify whether all required changes were resolved and the quality of each change:

- If the change is a defect that was detected in system tests, it is probable that a test case exists and just has to be executed.
- If the change is a new feature, you will probably need to develop a new test case(s).
- If the change is an enhancement request, you will probably need to modify an existing test case and possibly develop a new one.

The tester should provide the following information:

- The identification of the product tested, that is, build number or product version and other information about it
- Environment configuration of the system under test
- The test case name
- The test script name and type of test script (automatic, manual, etc.)
- Test results (pass, fail, inconclusive, etc.); if the result is not "pass," additional information is required: failure description and tester opinion, screen shots, system outputs, and other references and supporting evidence of the failure
- Results log (log file name or reference to database log)

Many of these fields are already included in the schema for ClearQuest Test Manager and Rational Quality Manager. In Figure 4.2 you can see that in the Rational Quality Manager defect there are links to the test case and the test log. The links are created automatically when the defect is reported from Rational Quality Manager during test execution.

Another field that is useful in improving the quality of the solution and the change process is the FailCount. In many cases a defect claimed to be fixed fails again and again during tests. High fail count indicates an unhealthy situation that should be mitigated. The reasons can vary from unclear requirements to poor quality of coding.

Table 4.4 provides a list of suggested fields and their types for the work item test data. Some of the fields are included in ClearQuest built-in schemas and in the Jazz process templates.

Table 4.4 Suggested Fields for Test Data

Field Name	Field Type	Comments
TestCase	Short_String	Reference	
BuildNumber	Short_String	Reference	
ProductVersion	Short_String	Reference	

continues

Table 4.4   Suggested Fields for Test Data (*Continued*)

Field Name	Field Type	Comments
TestScript	Short_String	Reference	Required if not included in the test case information
TestType	Short_String	Closed list: automatic, manual, functional, performance . . .
Result	Short_String	Closed list: pass, fail, inconclusive, halt ...
ResultLog	Short_String	Reference	Log file name or reference to database log
FailureDescription	Multiline_String	Mandatory if test failed
FailCount	Integer	Auto-augment on Fail action

4.1.9 History

We need to save the history of a work item mainly for the following reasons:

- Tracking information for audits; finding out who has performed an action, when the action was performed, and what has been changed
- Generating quality metrics
- Statistical information

ClearQuest aging charts and trend charts are generated from the history table.

For organizations that must comply with regulations, history is not only important, it is a necessity because they must provide proof that actions were performed according to regulations, and in case of exceptions, they must identify the cause and take action to prevent irregularity in the future. ClearQuest automatically stores the following information for each action:

- Time_stamp
- User_Name: login name of the user who performed the action
- Action_Name
- Old_State: the state of the record before the action
- New_State: the state of the record after the action; it may be the same as Old_State if the action was of type Modify

There are additional fields that are not presented to the user when building a query; some of them are

- Entity_Name: the name of the entity that the history record is related to, such as Defect, Project, etc.
- Entity_DBID: the database ID of the record on which the user performed the action

The History stateless record type is read-only and cannot be customized via ClearQuest Designer. Neither the user nor the administrator can change the history data (or the metadata).

You can get history data by querying the history records; you can also get data using Clear-Quest API. See the article "Getting the Last Line in the History Tab" for an API BASIC hook example at www.ibm.com/developerworks/rational/library/4319.html.

Figure 4.6 shows the History tab of a defect record in the ClearQuest Eclipse client.

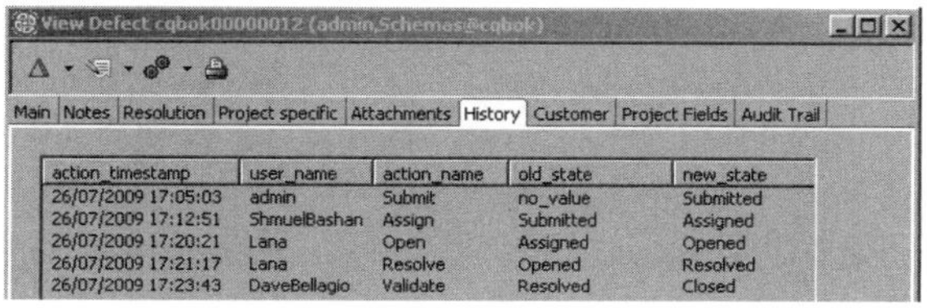

Figure 4.6　The ClearQuest History tab

In some cases more detailed history information is required by the organization; for example, what was the value of some fields before and after a change, or who is the user who changed the priority and what was the previous value?

In some medical and financial systems every field change must be tracked for audit reasons. ClearQuest provides a package called Audit Trail that allows you to keep the timestamp, the user login, the action performed, and a list of fields with previous value and current value. The Audit Trail package can be customized; for example, you may want to display changes in some fields but not all of them, as your organization sees fit.

Figure 4.7 shows the Audit Trail tab of a defect record in the ClearQuest Eclipse client.

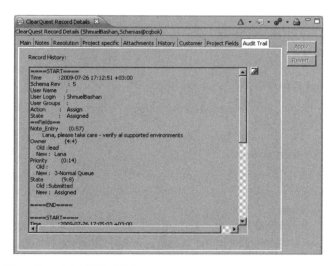

Figure 4.7　The ClearQuest Audit Trail tab

The Jazz work item automatically stores a full audit trail. Users can see in the History tab who performed an action, at what time, and what data was added or changed.

Figure 4.8 shows the History tab of a defect record in the Jazz work item. Notice how easy it is to detect when a user made a change and the exact change of each field.

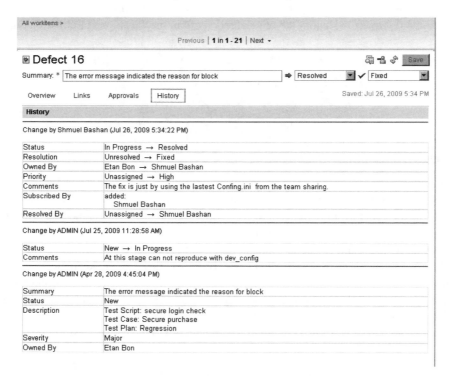

Figure 4.8   The Jazz work item History tab

4.1.10 Additional Data

In this category we include information that is required to manage the work item or to support information in other categories.

4.1.10.1 Requestor Information

Although the submitter login and the submit timestamp are stored in the history record, it is common to include these two fields in the change record: Submit_Date (of type DateTime) and Submitter (of type Reference).

Some organizations allow customers to submit changes to the ClearQuest database. Usually each customer gets a ClearQuest login, but several persons in the customer organization may use the same login. You should be able to identify when the requestor is a customer and require him or her to fill in a few more fields to identify the reporting person. There is a package called Customer that adds those fields. We suggest including a hook to change the requiredness of those fields if the requestor is a customer.

Figure 4.9 shows the Customer tab in the EnhancementRequest record.

Figure 4.9   The ClearQuest Customer tab

4.1.10.2 Ownership

As previously explained, the user login name is stored in a field called Owner. In many cases the login name is just a code or initials, which makes it hard for the assigner to identify the person. In these cases it is recommended that the user's full name be used. But we also need the field Owner (of type Reference) because it is mandatory for UCM and important in other cases, for example, to easily get the owner e-mail in a hook, to make the login name selectable in a query filter, to pop up the linked record form to see the user details. A simple solution is to have two fields: Owner_ Fullname (of type Short String) and Owner (of type Reference). A Choice_List hook attached to Owner_Fullname will display of course the User.Full_Name values, and a Value_Change hook will insert the correct value in the Owner field.

In section 4.6.3, "Convert Full_Name to Login_Name," see hooks in Perl and VBA for how to convert Full_Name to Login_Name.

Another example is "User Fullname Drop-down List," which explains how to keep the Login_ID in a field while allowing the user to select a human-readable name; the article can be found at www.ibm.com/developerworks/rational/library/4369.html.

In Chapter 5, "Roles," there is an additional discussion of ownership. We propose using two fields: Responsible and Owner. Having two fields helps differentiate the current owner and the solution provider.

4.1.10.3 Attachments

Attachments are files that contain information that cannot be displayed in a regular field, for example, images, colored or formatted text, or very large files that require a special viewer. Screen shots, system logs, and files created by the application are good candidates to be stored as attachments. Attachments may be huge, so it is recommended that large text files be compressed; images should be stored in compressed formats like .jpg or .gif rather than .BMP.

Many large attachments can rapidly increase the database size and cause degradation in performance. You can add a hook to limit the size of the attachment. The hook checks the size of the file, and if it exceeds a given size, the Commit action will fail with the appropriate error message. See the article "Restricting Attachment Size" with a VBA code example at www.ibm.com/developerworks/rational/library/3883.html.

A Perl example is provided in section 4.6.2, "Limit Attachment Size (Perl)."

Some companies limit not only the single attachment size but also the total size of all attachments per work item. For example, a single attachment size limit can be 3MB and the total size limit of attachments per record can be 5MB.

To use attachments in ClearQuest you can install the Attachment package to your schema, or do it manually in the following way. In ClearQuest Designer define a new field of type Attachment_List and add the field to a Form tab; there is a special control for attachments.

Each field of type Attachment_List may contain several attachment files. You may create several fields to store files for various purposes, for example, Test attachments, Development attachments, Customer attachments, or Internal attachments. Notice that the user can include a comment on each attachment he or she adds. We believe that it is better to include comments that explain the type and reason for the attachment because the file name may not be descriptive enough, for example, "Testing screen dump with the error message" or "Installation instructions."

Figure 4.10 shows the Attachments tab of a defect record in ClearQuest Web client.

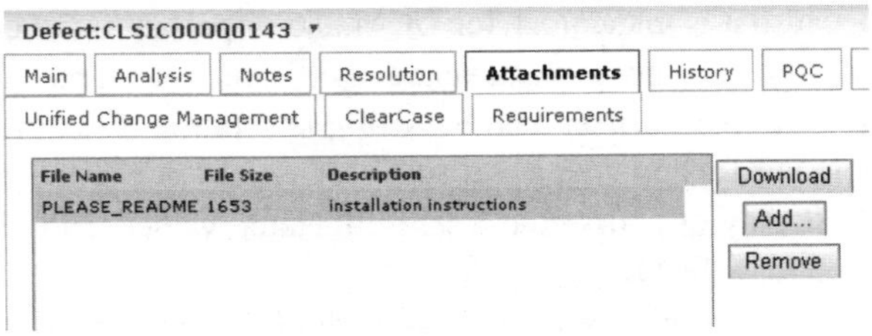

Figure 4.10 The ClearQuest Attachments tab

ClearQuest Hint In the ClearQuest Windows client the attachment list can be displayed in several ways. The comment (or the file description) is shown only in the Details mode, similarly to the way it is displayed in the Web client in Figure 4.10. To change the view mode, right-click on the attachment area (field control) and select View > Details, as shown in Figure 4.11.

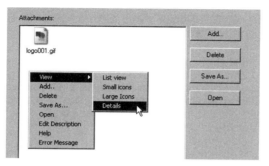

Figure 4.11   Attachments field: setting the View format to Details in CQ Windows client

Another way to deal with attachments is by creating a link to the attachment file. The file is not stored in the ClearQuest database but in the file system. To create a link to a file the user just writes in any multiline field a line in URL or UNC format, for example:

```
\\server_name\shared_directory\directory_name\File_Name

H:\DevData\Bashan\ideas\dialogue_control.doc
```

Figure 4.12 displays some links in the Description field.

Figure 4.12   Links to external files

There is an important difference between the two methods.

- In the first method (database attachments) the files are stored in the database and users can access them only via ClearQuest. Also, it is not possible to change the original attachment file, so the data is trustable as evidence.

- In the second method (external attachments) the files are stored in the file system and can be changed without leaving any information about the change in ClearQuest, but there are some advantages such as the ability to version the file, the ability to access the file without the need to enter ClearQuest, and the fact that there are no limits on the size.

Link with Spaces   If the file path contains spaces, use the Unicode character %20.

External Attachments (FTP)   Attachments 2.0 is a new ClearQuest package that upgrades the Attachments 1.0 package to provide external storage of CQ attachments in off-site locations such as FTP servers.

Attachments 2.0 uses the existing Attachments 1.0 Add button as usual when the CQ record is being edited and changed, temporarily displays the new attachment(s) in the usual Attachments 1.0 window, then, when the record is saved, moves it to the external storage site. The attachment is removed from the CQ display and a URL link to the attachment's location is stored in a field in the CQ Attachments tab.

Another useful use of attachments is the ability to take a screen shot and insert it right in the work item as an attachment. This is especially important for testers who want to include the screen showing an error, both for clarity and in case the defect is not reproduced in the development environment. A user can capture a screen or a window, save it to a file, and then add the file as an attachment to ClearQuest or to the Jazz work item.

But there is an easier way, when using an Eclipse client either for Rational Team Concert or Rational Quality Manager:

1. To take a screen capture and attach it, click Add Screenshot.

   Figure 4.13 shows the Attachments section in the Rational Team Concert Eclipse client. Note the Add file… button and the Add Screenshot… button.

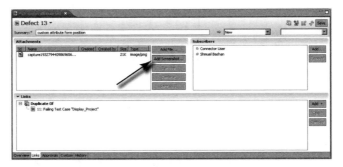

Figure 4.13   Jazz work item attachment; note the Add Screenshot… button

2. Click the Add Screenshot… button; the screen shot tool will pop up.

3. Position the frame on the area that you want to capture. Use the arrows on the sides of the frame to expand or reduce its size to fit the area.

4. Click the camera icon. You can use the pen, oval, and rectangle icons to highlight specific areas of the screen capture.

5. Specify the graphics format in which to save the image.

6. Under Attach to: click Work Item <*ID*>. This is used to enter the screen shot file as an attachment to the current work item that you edit, or to another work item.

7. In Figure 4.14 you can see that the current work item is 13. Click it to add the .PNG attachment to this work item.

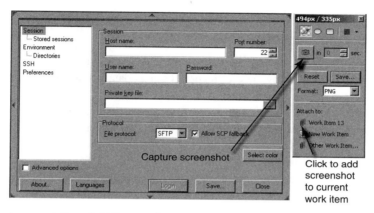

Figure 4.14 Jazz work item Add Screenshot... tool

Warning on the RTC Web Client Screen shot attachments in the RTC Web client are available only in RTC version 3.0.

When using a ClearQuest Windows client, a ClearQuest hook allows you to add the clipboard content—for example, an application window or an error message window—as a .jpg image to the Attachments section of a defect.

For the hook code and instructions see the article "Save Clipboard Content as .jpg Image Attachment" at www.ibm.com/developerworks/rational/library/3927.html.

Warning on the Web Client This solution makes use of the ActiveX control and will not work on the ClearQuest Web client.

4.1.11 Quality Assurance

Organizations that adopt processes like CMMI would require additional data for improvement of process and quality. For example, capturing "phase caused" and "phase detected" can indicate how well the organization is doing in testing in all phases. If most defects are detected in the same phase, the organization's testing is good.

Another example is capturing "estimated effort" and "actual effort," which can allow us to improve during the analysis phase (wrong estimation) or indicate flaws in the change process (excessive fix effort).

Repeating defects are defects that were discovered in previous versions, were fixed, and appear in newer versions. These can be measured by counting the number of times the same work item returns to the testing state.

Capturing "where first found" is useful for validating testing and finding areas where improvement may be needed. It is important because it indicates problems found internally even if customers found them eventually.

4.2 State-Based Objects

State-based objects are in most cases the work items that contain the data discussed in this chapter. We do not recommend using stateful record types as data containers; for that purpose use stateless record types, described in section 4.3, "Stateless Objects." There are situations where a data container seems to have a status, like open/close, active/obsolete, etc. Consider the workflow rules to decide whether the object is a data container or a work item with real workflow. If it is a data container, use a stateless record type, and add a field with a check box or radio button on the form to set the status of the record.

An example of a state-based object used as a data container is in the ClearQuest ALM schema; the ALMProject record type is a state-based record.

Stateless objects are powerful for presenting data and creating hierarchy relations, bills of materials, and more. These types of objects do not exist in Jazz. We can create Jazz work items as replacements for stateless objects (similar to the ALMProject previously mentioned). In the current Jazz version they do not have the same power as in ClearQuest because the referencing mechanism is not the same, but they can be advantageous over using fields with no container.

4.3 Stateless Objects

Stateless objects are meant to collect data that is logically related in a physical element. The object is defined in ClearQuest as a *stateless record type*.

What advantage do we gain by collecting the information in these objects?

- The data model becomes simpler.
- We can improve the users' experience by lowering the number of fields that they have to fill in.
- We can reduce errors by automating operations that are related to the same object.
- We can improve the user experience and reduce errors by generating choice lists with correct items only.
- We can improve response time and flexibility because the responsibility for generating the stateless records can be assigned to a member or members of the group dealing with the object, as opposed to being the ClearQuest administrator's responsibility. For example, instead of having the project manager request that the ClearQuest admin open a new project record, the project manager can generate the new project record and later modify it as necessary without the mediation of the ClearQuest admin.

Let's review some examples:

- A *project* object may contain the following fields: Name, Leader, Manager, QA_Manager, Team_Members, Current_Release, and Components.

- A *component* object may contain the following fields: Name, Leader, Team_Members, In_Project, and Modules.

- A *module* object may contain the following fields: Name, Leader, Team_Members, and In_Component.

- A *customer* object may contain the following fields: Name, Location, Contacts, Products_ Used, and Licenses.

It is recommended that the same field names be used in all objects; for example, instead of Project_Name use Name, instead of Project_Members use Team_Members. Doing so will make the scripts you are coding simpler, more readable, and *reusable*.

For example, it is easier to code one hook GetMembers() that will operate on all objects having the field Members. See section 8.1.3, "Employing Reusable Assets," in Chapter 8, "Development," for more information and code examples.

ClearQuest stateless record types contain the following elements:

- **Fields of various types**

  Some of the fields are auto-defined and are read-only (Version, Record_Type, etc.). You can define more fields of any predefined type as required.

- **Actions of any type except Change_State**

  The actions Submit and Import are created automatically.

- **Field behaviors**

  Field behaviors define a field's requiredness (Mandatory, Optional, and ReadOnly).

- **Unique key**

  The unique key allows you to select one or more fields that define the database primary key. For state-based record types the primary key is the record ID, which is unique and automatically created; here you will have to define it. Extra care should be taken, and a lot of thinking is required when selecting the unique key or keys. Using the previous examples, for the Project record type it is quite clear that the Name field is a good choice for the unique key. Now what about the Component record type? Is it possible that we shall have in two projects a different component with the same name? In many cases the answer is yes; that means that selecting just the field Name as the unique key of a component is not enough. In this case we shall have to select a second field as a unique key, and because the component is unique in a project it is correct to select the In_Project field as the second unique key.

In some cases it is necessary to select three fields to define the uniqueness of a record. Figure 4.15 shows how to define three fields as a combined unique key for the record type Roles.

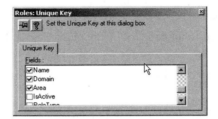

Figure 4.15   Unique key constructed of three fields

Note that ClearQuest always creates a field called DBID for every newly created record; this field is unique and may be used as the unique key, although we do not recommend it because this field has no meaning. See section 4.4.4, "More on ClearQuest Unique Key," for additional information on referencing record types with multiple unique keys and for an explanation of how to replace a field in a unique key.

- **Form**

  A form displays the fields and interacts with the user.

4.4 Object Relations

A very important feature of a change management system is the ability to create relationships between objects. In ClearQuest you can create relationships between record types, and in Jazz you can link artifacts such as work items and service providers. In section 4.4.5, "Jazz Links," we discuss the Jazz links.

In ClearQuest there are two types of relationships:

- Single or Reference
- Multiple or Reference_List

4.4.1 ClearQuest Single Relationship

In this relationship, one record is referenced from another record. The relationship is realized by a field of type Reference. Note that the reference points to the unique key of the referenced object. Some examples of such a relationship are the field Owner, which is a reference to the Users record type, and the field Project, which is a reference to the Project record type. As you can see, any object can be referenced: state-based, stateless, built-in, or user-defined.

The control used for this field is usually a drop-down combo or list box. A nice feature is that users can right-click on the field and select View Details; Figure 4.16 shows how this is done with the field Owner.

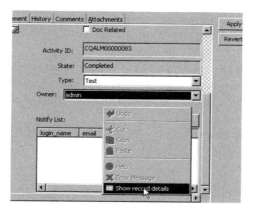

Figure 4.16   View the details of the referenced record

This will pop up the referenced object form—in this example the Users record whose unique key (field Login_Name) is "admin"—so the user can see the values of all the fields of this specific record and even perform actions.

Figure 4.17 shows the Users record that was popped up after the selection. Note that this operation is not available in the ClearQuest Web client.

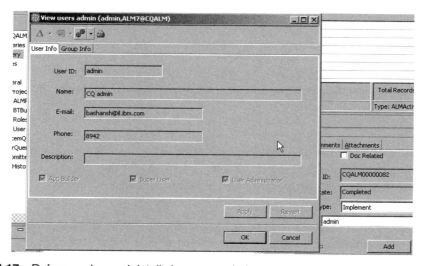

Figure 4.17   Referenced record details in pop-up window

4.4.2 ClearQuest Multiple Relationship

In this relationship, several records are referenced from one record. The relationship is realized by a field of type Reference_List. A reference list can point to any record type, either of the same type (defect to defect) or a different type (feature to activity), from state-based to stateless and vice versa. Some examples of such relationships in the Defect record type are the field Related_Defects, which lists references to the Defect record type, and the field Activities, which lists references to the Activity record type.

There is a special graphic control for a field of type Reference_List. This control has a kind of table format, and it allows the designer to select the fields (columns) to be displayed to the user. See Figure 4.22 and the explanation in section 4.4.3, "Back Reference," for how to set the columns.

In Figure 4.18, a state-based record type called Task is referencing a stateless record type called Config_Item whose fields—Name, Platform, Promotion_ID, DB2_info, CI_Action, and CC_Component—are displayed in the control.

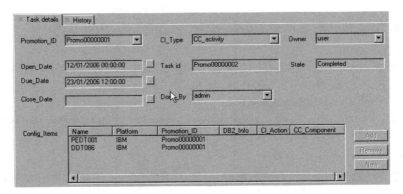

Figure 4.18   Reference list graphic control example

The control also includes three buttons, Add, Remove, and New, which are related to the same field.

- **Add**

  Add enables the user to include existing records as referenced records (children). To add objects, a wizard allows the user to run a query, and the user can select from the result set one or more records to be included in the list of referenced objects.

- **Remove**

  Remove allows the user to select an object from the list and remove it from the list, thus disconnecting the referencing. Note that Remove does not delete the object.

- **New**

  Pressing New opens the Submit form, allowing the user to fill out the form. When the user presses OK, the record is committed to the database and is referenced from the parent record.

Each button has pre-action and post-action hooks that enable the designer to perform advanced features, such as cloning a child from a parent or copying some fields from the base record to the referenced one. Another powerful usage of these hooks is to set global variables (in the pre-action hook) and clear them in the post-action hook. The global variables are used to pass information between the parent and the "future" child, that is, before the child record is committed to the database and the reference link between the parent and the child records is established.

Figure 4.19 shows how to define the PreAction Hook of the Add button of the Parent/Child control.

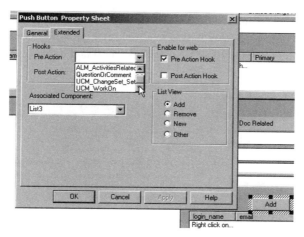

Figure 4.19 Button properties and action hooks

Associated Component The List View and the button controls should have the same Associated Component. This assures that pre-/post-action hooks are related to the correct list. If there are multiple parent/child controls on a single form, and in the case that you have added buttons, extra care should be taken in relating the buttons to the correct component.

In ClearQuest Eclipse Designer the association selection is done by field label and not by arbitrary name such as List1, List2, and so on.

4.4.3 Back Reference

The Back Reference field creates a link from the referenced record back to the parent record. This field is a read-only field (which means that hooks cannot be added to that field). The Back Reference field is always of type Reference_List, whether the pointing field is of type Reference or Reference_List.

Also for this field there is a special child-parent control called List View, which is similar to the parent-child control but does not have the buttons Add, Remove, and New. It means that the user *cannot* link a parent to a child, but only a child to a parent. Usually there is no need to link a parent from the child, but in the rare cases where this feature is required, we hereby provide an advanced scripting solution. See the script and explanation in section 4.6.4, "Create Parent from Child."

This field is not created as a usual field with Add Field. When you create the Reference or Reference_List field, type the name of the Back Reference field in the dialog.

For example, we can see in Figure 4.20 the Properties window of the field Tasks of the ALMRequest record type. This field references the record type ALMTask. When you type the name of the Back Reference field Request, a read-only field of type Reference_List will be created in the ALMTask record type. Its name will be Request and it will point to the ALMRequest record type.

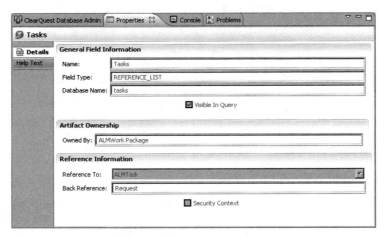

Figure 4.20   Reference List field with Back Reference and field properties window in ClearQuest Eclipse Designer

There are two special controls for multiple relations: the Parent/Child control for the Reference_List field and the List View for the Back_Reference_List field. In Figure 4.21 you can see the two controls. Note that usually the Parent/Child control has three buttons (New, Add, and Remove). The schema designer can remove a button or add a button. For example, if we want

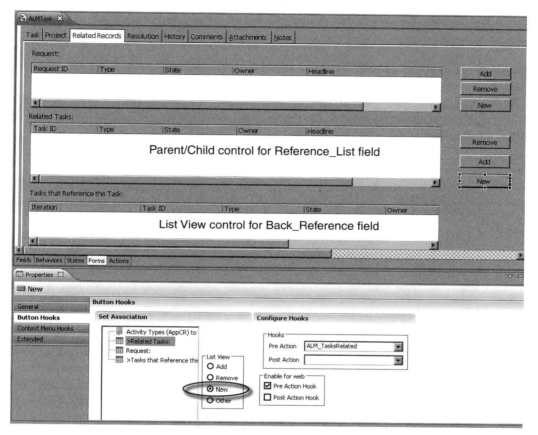

Figure 4.21   Reference and Back Reference List graphic controls

to create relationships only from existing records, we can remove the button New. This is demonstrated at the top of Figure 4.21 for the field Request. In other cases the schema designer can add a fourth button; for example, we may want to have two types of New buttons, one to submit a blank child record and the second to submit a clone child record that inherits some of the parent fields. There are many cloning techniques; we explain one technique in section 4.6.4, "Create Parent from Child," and you can read about others in *IBM developerWorks*.

Figure 4.21 shows a form with three field controls. The two Parent/Child controls have buttons associated with them. The association is set in the Properties view: right-click on the button and select > Show Properties View. Click on the Button Hooks tab. This tab is shown at the bottom of Figure 4.21; note that the button type is set to New and it is associated with the field control labeled Related Tasks. Also note the hooks that are associated with the button; this is explained in section 4.6.4, "Create Parent from Child," and a hook example is provided in Listing 4.5.

Note that the columns in each control are not the same. The designer can customize the control by selecting which columns will be displayed, what the title is (by default the title is equal to the field name), and what the initial column width is. Figure 4.22 shows the same ClearQuest Designer forms. To set the columns, select the field and select the Columns tab. Click the New button and select the field from the Selected Source Field list. Arrange the fields with the up/down buttons. In the Selected Column's Attributes section you can change the label and set the initial width. This is very important, as it will help the user to see important information without changing the width. Also note that the column label for the field was changed to Task ID; in many cases accurate labeling can prevent confusion.

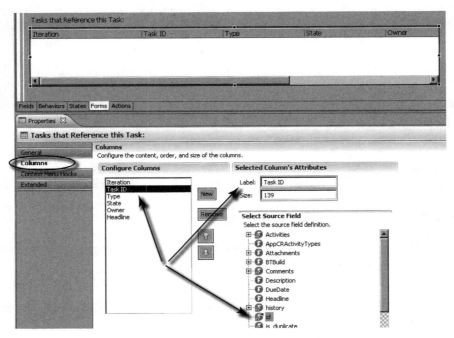

Figure 4.22   Setting the columns of the List View graphic control

When the user adds a record to the list, the column values in this field are automatically filled. The user can right-click on a record in the list and select Open Record; the referenced record form will open and the user will be able to perform any allowed action.

Back Reference is powerful in two aspects:

- It allows the user to see the relationship from both directions, and not only see the relationship but also access the related record. When a line (a record) in the Reference or Back Reference control is double-clicked, the parent record pops up, allowing you to view all the details in the tabs and even perform an action.

- It is easier to query the records when you have the Back Reference field, especially if the records are of different types. As you know, the query wizard requests a record type before building the filter and the display, so when you have a Back Reference field you can select either the parent type or the child type, whichever is more convenient and appropriate.

But back referencing also has a performance drawback. When displayed, each record retrieves from the database all the data of the records referenced (not just the fields displayed in the control). So it is recommended that reference lists be used with some caution and that the trade-offs be considered.

Another important issue is the *direction of the reference*. Let us take an example of a product that contains several components. Also, let's assume that we need only a Reference_List connection without a Back Reference List connection. We should now ask ourselves, Do we create the Reference_List field in the Product record type or in the Component record type? To answer this question we suggest you examine the user scenario. How will the users work? Will they create a component and immediately relate it to the product that contains it, or will they create a component and in a later stage edit a product and associate all the components to that product? Another use case to consider is Open New Product: if the reference list field is in the Product record type, it will be easy to associate all the components with that record. If the Reference List field is in the Component record type, it will be harder to associate all the components with that record. This is opposed to the other scenario: run a query to identify all components, mark them all in the result set view, perform the Modify operation, and select the new product. (In the Web client it is slightly different; mark the records in the result set view, right-click, and select Multi-Record Update > Modify.)

In most cases each product will contain several components, and each component may be associated with several products, so to realize this model we also need a Back Reference field. But once again we have to ask ourselves in what direction to set referencing, that is, in which record type to create the Reference_List field. The considerations are very similar to the use cases we have previously described.

Another issue to consider when selecting the direction is who is doing the reference operation, the administrator or the user? The administrator is usually doing a bulk operation; thus up-down reference is suggested. A user is usually doing a single operation, so bottom-up reference is suggested.

Think how the users will work and what will make their work easier and faster. Usability is a more important factor than the amount of scripting or maintenance.

4.4.4 More on ClearQuest Unique Key

The usage of reference fields that point to the unique key(s) of another stateless record type can be complex in some situations. How is the key displayed when multiple fields are defined as a unique key? How can we retrieve information from the database in such cases? What is the procedure to replace a key when the schema changes?

In the following sections we shall answer these questions.

4.4.4.1 Referencing

We explained before that a field of type Reference points to the unique key of the referenced object. If the field Owner is a reference to the Users record, the value of the field login_name (which is the unique key of the Users record type) will be displayed in the field Owner. See the Owner field in Figure 4.1 for an example.

If the referenced object has more than one key, all the keys will be displayed in that field. In the following example, the Product record type has two fields as a unique key: Name and InProject; see the special icon for the unique key field of the ClearQuest Eclipse Designer in Figure 4.23. The Defect record type has a field of type Reference that points to the Product record type. The form control for this field is a drop-down list box. When the user selects this control, he or she will see double values in the list: Project Name Product Name.

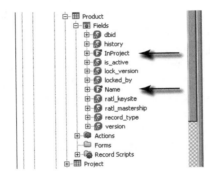

Figure 4.23   Referencing a record with two unique keys

Sometimes this feature is good, but at other times you want the user to first select the project and then select the product. To do this you must replace the field of type Reference with *two* fields of type Short_String. You also have to write a choice list hook for each field to display the correct values.

Your choice list hook should implement the following query:

```
"select productname from Products where InProject = "myProject"
```

The choice list hooks are simple and largely discussed in IBM DeveloperWorks ClearQuest Hook Index as a field dependency. Several examples of such choice list hooks are provided in the following link: www.ibm.com/developerworks/rational/library/4517.html.

4.4.4.2 Access Records

To access a record that has multiple fields in a unique key from a hook, we have to construct the unique key. A common method to get record data is by calling the session method

```
GetEntity(entity def_name, display_name)
```

If we use the same example, the entity `def_name` is Product and the `display_name` is a string that is constructed from the values of the two fields of the unique key with a space between them. In a hook, constructing the `display_name` is done like this:

In BASIC:

```
GetFieldStringValue("ProjectName") & " " & _
GetFieldStringValue("ProductName")
```

In Perl:

```
$entity->GetFieldStringValue("ProjectName") . " " .
$entity->EntityGetFieldStringValue("ProductName");
```

4.4.4.3 Replacing a Unique Key

We have witnessed some cases where the schema data model was changed and consequently one of the fields creating the unique key had to be replaced. This is a multistep operation and requires caution. Fortunately, ClearQuest protects you from making errors that cannot be recovered. Do the following:

1. Create a new field.
2. Add the field to the record form and check in the schema. (ClearQuest does not allow you to add a field and make it unique in the same operation.)
3. Upgrade all databases.
4. Check out the schema, open the Unique Key dialog, and add the new field by marking the check box. Now you have three fields as a unique key!
5. Check in and upgrade the databases.
6. Run a query to display all records with all the fields that construct the *new* unique key.
7. Carefully verify if there are records that will not be unique by replacing the unique keys, manually modifying them as required. If there are many records, a manual operation may take a long time, and you should consider creating an external script to add data.
8. Check out the schema, open the Unique Key dialog, and remove the unnecessary field by clearing the check box.
9. Test, check in, and upgrade the production database.

As you can see, the procedure to replace a unique key is quite complex; it requires changes in the schema and in the users database. We suggest that you carefully examine the requirements before defining the unique keys.

4.4.5 Jazz Links

Jazz links represent relationships between the project area and service providers such as project areas on other servers or even links to a ClearQuest service provider. Link types reflect the nature of the service that a provider makes available to the project. Establishing links for the project area enables linking between artifacts in this project area and artifacts made accessible by the service provider.

In a work item you can create links of the following types to other work items or artifacts like the SubVersion or Rational Team Concert artifacts:

- Blocks
- Children
- Depends On
- Duplicate Of
- Duplicated By
- Parent
- Related
- Related Artifact
- SVN Revisions

Figure 4.24 demonstrates how to link child work item(s) to a defect work item. In the same way you can link other work items with the available linking types.

Figure 4.24   Link types in a Jazz work item

4.5 Data Representation

Data representation is the way the data stored in the database is presented to the user, and how the user can interact with it. In the following sections we shall discuss some design considerations to improve the user experience and ease of use, and describe how to represent the data in ClearQuest forms and in Jazz work items.

4.5.1 ClearQuest Data Representation

The data is presented to the ClearQuest user in forms. There are only two types of forms: the Submit form (used during the action of type Submit) and a Record form used in all other action types. Each form includes tabs. In each tab you put graphic controls that are associated with data fields. The ClearQuest control palette includes various controls. Each field type has a default control, but you can override it when necessary.

In ClearQuest Designer the fields are dragged and dropped from the Record Field View to the tab, positioned, resized, and aligned to other fields. Alternatively, select a control from the palette, position it on the tab, and set the field source in the Field Properties view.

A lot of attention is required when designing the forms. Users do not like to navigate back and forth, wasting time to enter data or read information.

An important design factor is the physical size of the form. Constantly scrolling up and down or right and left does not improve the user experience. To decide what the physical size of the form should be, investigate the users' screen resolution and design the forms to fit that resolution. Usually it would be 1024 × 768, but it may be higher.

Another important factor is the client type. The Windows and Eclipse clients look almost identical to the ClearQuest Designer forms, but the Web client is slightly different, so check that you get what you want in all client types and in various resolutions. The ratio between the length and width of the form should be about 4:3; this ratio is optimal to view all the elements of ClearQuest (workspace, result set, record form) without the need to scroll a lot. The ALM schema forms were designed to fit a screen resolution of 1280 × 1024.

The tab organization is also very important. Try to position all the fields that a specific role needs during an action in a single tab. It is not an easy task and it is not always achievable. It may require some time to put the same field on two tabs; that is OK because it serves a good purpose—user efficiency and satisfaction. The order of the fields in a tab is also very important; try to organize the fields in a logical manner. If a user has to select the product name and then the product version, put the version field below or to the right of the name field (assuming the form language direction is left to right).

Fields that are related to one another can be grouped in a box. Position the fields on the form, in the order explained above, and if possible set their size to be equal, align them to the top and then to the left (or to the right, but be consistent). Now select the group box object from the control palette and surround the fields with the box. The last thing is to enter the label of the group box in the group box property sheet. When using the CQ Eclipse Designer, position the group control first and then position the fields on the group control.

The screen shot in Figure 4.25 shows how three fields and a button of the Project record type of the ALM schema were grouped together.

Figure 4.25   Grouping fields to improve presentation

For power users who use the tab key for navigation instead of the mouse, ClearQuest allows setting the tab order. In the ClearQuest Designer (Windows version) top menu select Form Layout > Set Tab Order and click the fields in the order you find correct. The fields are numbered so you can see and verify the order. When using the CQ Eclipse Designer the tab order is defined in the Field Properties view, Extended tab.

To learn more about creating forms and form controls see ClearQuest help > Developing > Developing schemas with the ClearQuest Designer > Working with Forms.

4.5.2 Jazz Work Items Data Representation

With Rational Team Concert the terms are a bit different. The form is called presentation and only one presentation can be linked to a work item type. You can define new tabs and define sections within each tab. This is a very easy way to physically arrange fields with logical similarity. User-defined fields (called custom attributes in Jazz) will default to a tab called Custom. This can be overriden so you can put your custom fields on any tab. Although the tab organization is somewhat limited, it has some advantages such as ease of use and nifty visualization.

Figure 4.26 shows the Jazz editor presentations. Note the hierarchy of the presentations:

- **Tabs:** These are Overview, Links, Approvals, Custom, History.
- **Sections:** Some tabs have a single section (History and Approval); others have two, three, or four sections. In the Custom tab there are two sections: Quality Metric and Project Metric.
- **Presentations** (field controls to present attributes): In the Quality Metric section, there are two presentations: PhaseCaused and PhaseDetected.

The designer uses the button on the right side to add a new tab, section, and presentation. The presentation can be moved up and down with the relevant buttons.

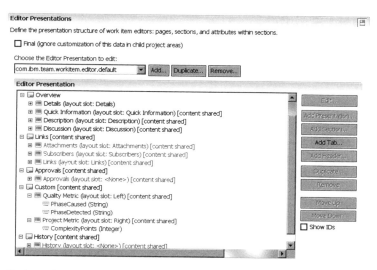

Figure 4.26 Rational Team Concert Editor presentation

The user sees the sections and attributes presentations on the Custom tab as shown in Figure 4.27.

Figure 4.27 Rational Team Concert: client view of custom attributes

In Jazz the editor presentation is not part of the work item type (as in ClearQuest). You have to bind the editor presentation ID to the work item type in the Editor Presentation Binding window. One editor presentation ID can be bound to several work items. Jazz provides some built-in editors that you can use, duplicate, and further customize.

To learn more about creating presentations in Jazz work items, see Rational Team Concert Documentation > Managing change and releases > Tracking work items > Customizing work items > Customizing the work item editor.

RTC 3.0 Customization Note Rational Team Concert version 3.0 supports customization from the Web client as well. The customization method is identical to that for the Eclipse client. The Web editor presentation even has some WYSIWYG capabilities.

4.6 ClearQuest Scripts

This section provides some examples of scripts that are related to data and data presentation. We have included references in each section to the relevant script section. The scripts described are the following:

- A script that limits attachment size and indicates on the main tab that attachments exist.
- A script to ease the selection of owner by selecting full name instead of login name and populating the login after the user's selection.
- A script that demonstrates how a click on a button creates a cloned record. The script is special because a cloned record is not of the same type as the base record. Also, the script creates a parent record from the child, a feature that is required in several cases.

4.6.1 HasAttachment

Listing 4.1 is an example of how to set the HasAttachment check box on the main tab, so that the user does not have to navigate to the Attachments tab to see if there are attachments. The `ValueChanged` hook of the Attachments field calls the `hasAttachment` global subroutine. The example is related to section 4.1.1.2, "Description."

Listing 4.1   HasAttachment Hook in Perl

```perl
sub attachments_ValueChanged {
    my($fieldname) = @_;
    # $fieldname as string scalar
    # record type name is Issue
    # field name is Attachments
    # Start User Code
      my $ExistAttach = hasAttachments();
      $entity->SetFieldValue("HasAttachments",  $ExistAttach);
    # End User Code
}


sub hasAttachments {
      # Purpose: Check if the record has attachments
      # Input  : None, checks $entity
      # Output : 0= no attachment, 1= at least one attachment

    my $attachmentfieldslist = $entity->GetAttachmentFields();
    for (my $index = 0; $index < $attachmentfieldslist->Count();
        $index++)
    {
        my $attachmentfield = $attachmentfieldslist->Item($index);
```

```
        my $attachments = $attachmentfield->GetAttachments();
        return 1 if ($attachments->Count());
    }
    return 0;
}
```

4.6.2 Limit Attachment Size (Perl)

The script in Listing 4.2 verifies the total number of all attachments and checks whether they exceed a value that is hard-coded in the hook. A better solution is to store this value externally. One location can be a stateless record with a "limitattachmentssize" field (a stateless record to store various maintenance fields). A second solution is to use a dynamic list with a single value.

Listing 4.2 Limit Attachment Size Hook in Perl

```
sub Limit_Attachment {
# Purpose: Sum the size of all attachments and return error if it
#          exceeds a defined value (1024).
# Input  : None, checks $entity
# Output : empty string if OK
#          The total size if exceeds


$limitattachmentssize = 1024;
my $attachfields = $entity->GetAttachmentFields();
my $attachfieldscount = $attachfields->Count();
$result = "";

my $totalattachmentssize = 0;
for (my $attachfieldindex = 0; $attachfieldindex < $attachfieldscount;
     $attachfieldindex++)
{
   my $attachfieldlist = $attachfields->Item($attachfieldindex);
   my $attachments = $attachfieldlist->GetAttachments();
   my $numattachments = $attachments->Count();
   for (my $attachindex = 0 ; $attachindex < $numattachments ;
         $attachindex++)
   {
     my $attachmententity = $attachments->Item($attachindex);
     my $attachmentfilename = $attachmententity->GetFileName();
     my $attachmentfilesize = $attachmententity->GetFileSize();
```

continues

Listing 4.2   Limit Attachment Size Hook in Perl (*Continued*)

```perl
    if ($attachmentfilesize == 0)
    {
      my ($diskfiledev, $diskfileino, $diskfilemode,
     $diskfilenlink, $diskfileuid, $diskfilegid, $diskfilerdev,
     $diskfilesize, $diskfileatime, $diskfilemtime, $diskfilectime,
     $diskfileblksize, $diskfileblocks)= stat $attachmentfilename;

      $attachmentfilesize = $diskfilesize;
    }

    $totalattachmentssize = $totalattachmentssize + $attachmentfilesize;
  }
}
 if ($totalattachmentssize > $limitattachmentssize) {
    $result = "Total attachments size ($totalattachmentssize)" .
             " exceeds the $limitattachmentssize byte limit";
 }
   return $result;
}
```

4.6.3 Convert Full_Name to Login_Name

This section provides hook examples of how to get the user login name from a given full name.
It is related to section 4.1.10.2, "Ownership." The hook is provided in Perl in Listing 4.3 and in
BASIC in Listing 4.4.

Listing 4.3   Getting Login from Name—Hook in Perl

```perl
sub GetLoginfromFullName {
    my( $value ) = @_;
    my $result = "" ;
# Purpose: Get a string of user full name and return the login name
# Input   : $value as string

    my $session = $entity->GetSession();
    my @myname = ( $value );
    my $queryDefObj = $session->BuildQuery("users");
    $queryDefObj->BuildField("login_name");
    my $filterOp = $queryDefObj->BuildFilterOperator($CQPerlExt:
:CQ_BOOL_OP_AND);
```

```
    $filterOp->BuildFilter("fullname", $CQPerlExt::CQ_COMP_OP_EQ, \@
myname);


    my $resultSetObj = $session->BuildResultSet($queryDefObj);
    $resultSetObj->Execute();


    if ( $resultSetObj->MoveNext() == $CQPerlExt::CQ_SUCCESS) {
        $result = $resultSetObj->GetColumnValue(1);
    }
return $result
}
```

Listing 4.4   Getting Login from Name—Hook in BASIC

```
Function GetLoginfromFullName (sName)
REM Purpose: Get a string of user full name and return the login name
REM Input   : sName as string

    Set oSession = GetSession()
    Set oQuery = oSession.BuildQuery("users")
    oQuery.BuildField("login_name")
    Set oFilter = oQuery.BuildFilterOperator(AD_BOOL_OP_AND)
    oFilter.BuildFilter "fullname", AD_COMP_OP_EQ, sName
    Set oResultSet = oSession.BuildResultSet(oQuery)
    oResultSet.Execute
    If oResultSet.MoveNext = AD_SUCCESS Then
        GetLoginfromFullName = oResultSet.GetColumnValue(1)
    End If
End Function
```

4.6.4 Create Parent from Child

In this example we demonstrate how to create a parent record from a child record. Not only is the link created but also some fields are copied. To generate the parent the user clicks on a button CloneParentCR, and the record script attached to the button creates the record.

In Figure 4.28 you can see the ClearQuest Designer view. Note that the button is of type Other.

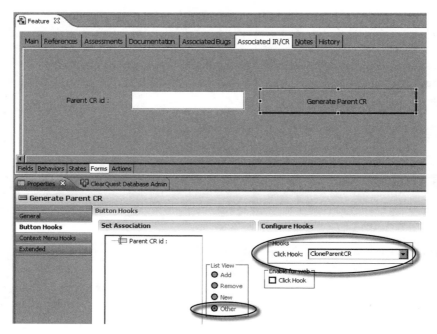

Figure 4.28   Creating a parent record from a child

The code in Listing 4.5 is the record script CloneParentCR. The code creates a new record CR, copies some fields from the Feature record, and creates the link by adding the CR ID to the Feature Reference_List field.

Listing 4.5   Cloning Hook

```
sub feature_CloneParentCR {
    my($result);
    my($param) = @_;
    # record type name is Feature
    # Start User Code

# Purpose: To clone a "Feature" record type to "CR" record type
#            and connect them as child(Feature)<--parent(CR)
# Author: Shmuel B
# Consideration: As mandatory fields altered, possible changes
#                   to the script may be needed
#
    my $session = $entity->GetSession();
    my $ircr = $session->BuildEntity("CR");  # create the CR
    my $id = $entity->GetDisplayName();
```

```perl
      my $value;
      # pairs of : GetFieldValue from Feature
        #          SetFieldValue to CR
      $value = $entity->GetFieldValue("Product")->GetValue();
          $ircr->SetFieldValue("Product", $value);
      $value = $entity->GetFieldValue("Module")->GetValue();
          $ircr->SetFieldValue("Module", $value);
      $value = $entity->GetFieldValue("Function")->GetValue();
          $ircr->SetFieldValue("Function", $value);
      $value = $entity->GetFieldValue("Priority")->GetValue();
          $ircr->SetFieldValue("Priority", $value);
      $value = $entity->GetFieldValue("Description")->GetValue();
          $ircr->SetFieldValue("Description", $value);
      $value = $entity->GetFieldValue("Initiator")->GetValue();
          $ircr->SetFieldValue("Initiator", $value);
      $value = $entity->GetFieldValue("Assign_To")->GetValue();
          $ircr->SetFieldValue("AssignTo", $value);
      $value = $entity->GetFieldValue("Risk")->GetValue();
          $ircr->SetFieldValue("Risk", $value);
      $value = $entity->GetFieldValue("Customer")->GetValue();
          $ircr->SetFieldValue("CustomerAppeal", $value);
      $value = $entity->GetFieldValue("Notes_Log")->GetValue();
          $ircr->SetFieldValue("Notes_Log", $value);
      $value = $entity->GetFieldValue("Option")->GetValue();
          $ircr->SetFieldValue("Option", $value);
      $value = $entity->GetFieldValue("Dev_NC")->GetValue();
          $ircr->SetFieldValue("DevNC_T", $value);
      $value = $entity->GetFieldValue("Dev_Infra")->GetValue();
          $ircr->SetFieldValue("DevInfra_T", $value);
      $value = $entity->GetFieldValue("Dev_Total")->GetValue();
          $ircr->SetFieldValue("DevTotal_T", $value);
      $value = $entity->GetFieldValue("CQA")->GetValue();
          $ircr->SetFieldValue("CQA_T", $value);
      $value = $entity->GetFieldValue("Feature_Type")->GetValue();
          $ircr->SetFieldValue("ReqType", $value);
#   Create the Parent-child link
          $ircr->AddFieldValue("Features", $id);
# Set CR Mandatory fields NOT copied above
          $ircr->SetFieldValue("ReqClass", "CR");
```

continues

Listing 4.5   Cloning Hook (*Continued*)

```
    $result = $ircr->Validate();
    if (!$result) {
          my $ircrid = $ircr->GetDisplayName();
          #  Mark the Parent (CR) id in the child (feature)
          $entity->SetFieldValue("ParentCR", $ircrid);
          $ircr->Commit();
    } else {
          $ircr->Revert();
    }
  # End User Code
  return $result;
}
```

Cloning Records of the Same Type   When cloning records of the same type, you can use the entity method GetFieldNames() and loop on all fields because fields in both records are identical. In the case described in Listing 4.5, the records are of different types and many of the field names are not the same, so we have to copy field by field.

4.7 Summary

In this chapter we discussed the data in the work item, the purposes the data serves, and the various roles that use the data. We classified the data as to description, location, environment, internal and external impacts, corrective actions, terms, testing, history, and quality. For each class we included a table with suggested fields.

In the second section of the chapter we explained objects and their relationships along with some common usage and implementation samples. We explained the importance of data representation to the user experience. We described how to use ClearQuest Designer to create the forms and how to use the Rational Team Concert editor presentation to customize the user interface.

In the last section we provided script examples for some common data implementations that were discussed in this chapter.

Roles

The Rational Unified Process (RUP) defines a role as "an abstract definition of a set of activities performed and artifacts owned. Roles are typically realized by an individual, or a set of individuals, working together as a team. Roles are not individuals; instead, they describe how individuals behave in the business and what responsibilities these individuals have."

In the RUP the use of roles in a process is a key concept, but there is no specific role object in ClearQuest. ClearQuest schema designers use roles in their schema implementations without a defined methodology.

Some designers have used the ClearQuest group concept as a method for implementing roles, but ClearQuest groups are designed to implement permissions. In this chapter we shall propose other implementation methods for roles.

Roles are used mainly in the following areas:

- Setting the action's access control, thus verifying if the logged-in user is allowed to perform the action selected (this subject is quite obvious and we shall cover it only briefly)
- Automating some actions within the ClearQuest application process
- Manipulating assignment choices or pick lists based on roles
- Notifying users based on their roles

In the following sections we describe typical problems that occur when roles are not implemented in the change management system. We define basic terms related to roles in the change process. We then propose several solutions that the ClearQuest schema designer can use, each one with a different degree of complexity. We describe how roles are implemented in the ClearQuest ALM schema. In section 5.6, "Roles in Jazz," we describe roles in the default Jazz process template. The last section includes code examples for the solutions proposed.

5.1 Understanding Typical Problems

As your successful software project grows, it is inevitable that there will be new releases for different customers, organizational changes, architectural changes, or new technologies adopted. These changes will likely increase the number of people involved in the project and introduce new stakeholders. These changes force the project to change the business process that was previously adopted successfully and are likely to cause changes in the roles that individuals take on and what their responsibilities may be. These changes also affect the processing of work items or change requests. As the number of people on the project grows or changes, it is not always clear who should perform a specific task. As the number of stakeholders increases, the volume of work items increases very quickly, and the amount of time involved in determining who should handle each work item may overwhelm the team.

Let us consider some examples of problems faced when creating the work item workflow in ClearQuest.

5.1.1 Enforcing Security Control

Every ClearQuest action is secured by an Access_Control hook that prevents unauthorized users from performing the action. By default, access is given to all users. Access control is set either according to the user's groups or with a hook (Perl or BASIC scripting).

If roles are not managed, it is harder to enforce security for actions. To overcome this security issue, some ClearQuest administrators hard-code in the Access_Control hook script the names of the allowed users or groups. This method is definitely not good from a maintenance point of view, because each change in a role requires changes in the ClearQuest schema (i.e., schema checkout, modify, test, check-in, backup, and upgrade).

5.1.2 Unassigned Change

In the built-in schemas (defect tracking, UCM, and enterprise), after the Submit action the defect (or the enhancement request) has no owner. Furthermore, after the Resolve action the owner is the developer. That is literally not correct, unless we mean something else by the term *owner*. A work item that is Resolved should be owned by the tester who verified the solution. When a work item is unassigned, nobody is working on it and probably nobody is responsible for delivering the work. For this reason we introduce a new term, Responsible; see section 5.2.1, "Basic Definitions."

5.1.3 Assigning the Wrong Person

Because a change request has to be owned by a user, ownership is given by a manager (project or product manager), group leader, or even the submitter. We have witnessed cases where ownership is given to the wrong person. In some organizations ownership is taken and not given, in many cases by the wrong person.

In one of the organizations in which we have implemented a defect-tracking system, assignment was dependent on the following factors: project, subproject, product, and application. There were many dozens of options, far too many for manual assignment without making mistakes.

Reasons for such mistakes are

- Lack of knowledge of the organization
- Lack of understanding of the process
- Misunderstanding the roles within the process

Also, the higher the turnover in the company/project, the more difficult it is to know the right person to assign.

So the outcome is that the next owner of the change request is set by assumptions, which often cause errors.

5.1.4 Blocking Assignment

Blocking assignment means that a change request is assigned to a person who can't perform the next step in the process.

For example, the UCM methodology defines the owner as the solution provider. In most cases the solution provider is a developer, but what about other parts of the workflow? Who is responsible for the work item when it is not owned by someone in the development group (R&D)?

As previously mentioned, there is no owner before the Assigned state. After the action Resolve the owner is no longer responsible for the work item; it should be handled by the testing group. This can create confusion among users.

The result is loss of time until the next action occurs, because someone has to assign a person to the change request in order for work to begin on it, and that takes time. Also, each time the wrong person is assigned, time is spent on reassigning.

The rest of this chapter introduces examples of implementing roles in a ClearQuest schema so that a change request is assigned to the right person automatically throughout the change request lifecycle, and so that the automation of that assignment is robust in the face of changes: new projects, changes in personnel, or changes in the role to which a person is assigned on a given project. The result will be that every change request has a valid owner, and that the team can process change requests accurately and quickly. We shall also give examples of how to use roles to efficiently set the action's access control.

5.2 Understanding Terms and Concepts

Before diving into techniques and solutions, we need to define some basic terms, the types of roles, and their relationship to user groups.

5.2.1 Basic Definitions

We are using new ideas and solution techniques, so first we have to define the terms used to set a common baseline.

- **Owner:** the user who currently has ownership of the work item

  It is important to note that the owner does *not* own the work item for the entire lifecycle. For example, in the Rational Unified Change Management method (UCM) the solution provider is the owner of the change request only in the states Assigned and Opened, or in UCM terms in the states of type Ready and Active.

- **Responsible:** the user who has general responsibility for the work item

  The responsible user should follow up on work item status, in some cases triage responsibly, and resolve ownership issues. The responsible user may or may not be the owner.

- **Role:** a set of activities to be performed by one or more users

  For our purposes we are implementing only one aspect of the RUP roles that can be automated while processing a work item in ClearQuest.

- **Area:** the organizational domain or product domain that characterizes the work item

  Every domain that users belong to (or work for) can be defined as an area. Some examples are software product, project, component, and module. In the ClearQuest ALM schema the area is defined in the Category Type field.

5.2.2 Role Type (Cardinality)

We can define two types of roles:

- **Single:** Only one user can have this role in a specific area.

  Project Manager, for example, is a role of type Single. There is typically only one project manager for any project.

- **Multiple (Many):** Multiple users can have the same role in a specific area.

  For example, Developer is a role of type Multiple. There are typically several developers for a given project.

Automation   If the role is of type Single, it is likely that some automation can be achieved, such as automatic assignment.

Roles in Jazz   In Jazz the role type is called *cardinality* and has the values Single and Many.

5.2.3 Roles, Areas, and Groups

A user may have different roles in different areas. A user may have several roles in one or more areas, and the role of a user may change over time.

The fact that different users can fulfill the same role does not mean that the role is a Multiple role. Only if there is more than one user who can fulfill a role in a specific area is the role of type Multiple.

For example, if several users have the role Component Leader, but only one user is the leader of the component Messaging, the role is of type Single.

Roles of type Single and areas can be pictured in a two-dimensional matrix: for each role and area couple there is only one user.

5.2.4 Key Roles in the Change Request Process

The following are key roles in the defect and change management process:

- *Customers* are persons who actually use the product or service.

  They report defects and have requests for changes in the product they use. The success of the product or service depends upon how these requests are managed. When customers have access to the change management system, extra attention should be given to security.

- The *Software Change Control Board (SCCB)* reviews the incoming change requests and determines how each individual request will be handled.

  The board sets the priority and assigns the work item to a solution provider or team leader.

- The *solution provider* gets the assigned change requests from the SCCB and develops the proper solutions to resolve them.

- The *tester* evaluates the resolution when a change request has been declared Fixed or Resolved.

  It is the tester's responsibility to ensure that resolved claims provide satisfactory answers to a change request.

- A *stakeholder* is affected by the outcome of the process.

  A customer is a stakeholder, but a stakeholder is not always a customer. Frequently, stakeholders prefer to participate directly in the process to influence decision-making or evaluation methods.

In complex processes more roles will be introduced, for example, Product Manager, Component Owner or Manager, Group Leader, R&D Moderator, QA Manager, Test Leader, QA Moderator, and Analyst.

5.3 Possible Solutions

This section describes some solutions for implementing roles in various ClearQuest applications. The solutions are based on different methods, and each method has its advantages, limitations, and disadvantages.

The level of complexity of each solution is different; we present the solutions from the less complex and thus the easiest to implement to the more complex, which requires more effort. The value to the organization does not necessarily match the level of complexity.

5.3.1 Implementing Roles with ClearQuest Groups

One way of implementing roles is by creating a group for each role. But because roles are relevant in the context of a specific area (such as project roles), such roles must be created for each area. Here is an example: For a project called Andromeda we can create groups such as Andromeda_developers, Andromeda_testers, and so on. We must do the same for each and every area. The advantage of such an implementation is that we do not have to script the Access_Control hooks, and we can just select the group or groups. The disadvantages are that for large organizations a huge number of groups have to be created and maintained, and for strict security scripting will be needed anyway. So the group solution is good for relatively small organizations, and for projects that are isolated from one another or for schemas that are designed for a single project.

A better solution is to create two types of groups:

- Groups for roles (Project Manager, Developer, Tester, Leader, etc.)
- Groups that include members of each area (Project_A, Project_B, Component_A, Component_B, etc.)

So how do we achieve this? If a user is a member of both the Project_A group and the Leaders group, then he or she has the Leader role in Project_A. Determining the exact role that a user fulfills in a particular area is done by a query in a script.

We can create a query that returns the users having the role Tester in the project Andromeda (users who are members of the group Tester AND in the group Andromeda). Such a query is presented and explained in section 5.7.1, "SQL Command for Group Method."

The ClearQuest Access_Control hook contains a call to a global script to verify that the logged-in user has the specified role in the specified area, for example:

```
HasRole("UserName" "AreaName", "RoleName")
```

The code in Listing 5.1 is a simple example of a `Defect_AccessControl` BASIC script.

Listing 5.1   ClearQuest Access Control BASIC Script

```
Function Defect_AccessControl(actionname, actiontype, username)
REM - Allow action if user is leader or developer in the selected
project
  project = GetFieldStringValue("Project")
```

```
If (HasRole(username, project, "Developer")
   OR HasRole(username, project, "Leader") )
Then
        Defect_AccessControl = TRUE
   Else
      Defect_AccessControl = FALSE
   End If
```

A significant disadvantage of this solution is that setting up a new role or changing roles requires administrator changes in the IBM Rational ClearQuest User Administration tool. Usually very few people have the privileges to use this tool, so the project team must have the ClearQuest administrator perform changes in roles. Also, the ClearQuest User Administration tool is not available from the Web, which poses an additional limitation.

5.3.2 Implementing Roles Implicitly

To handle multiple projects running concurrently, a more data-driven solution would be to define fields that indicate a role for a particular area (project, component, or module). This is more practical because we are using the project structure to capture the different roles, and we do not have to create as many groups as in the previous example (5.3.1), which reduces the maintenance effort.

Figure 5.1 displays the relationships between the Area objects and the users. The role fields of type Reference build the relationship by linking the objects. Think about each box as a database table and the arrows as links. Using ClearQuest terms, each table is a record type and each arrow is a reference or a reference list.

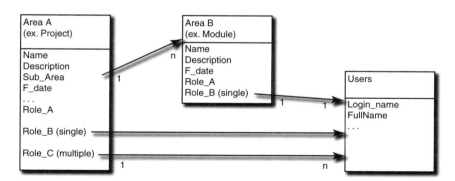

Figure 5.1   Roles implemented as fields in project and module

What we have are two stateless record types for Area A (for example, Project) and for Area B (for example, Module). They are linked with a field (here called Sub_Area) of type Reference_List, which means that each project contains several modules.

Each Area record type has fields for roles:

- A field representing a role of type Single is of type Reference to the Users stateless record type (represented as a one-to-one relationship in Figure 5.1).

- A field representing a role of type Multiple is of type Reference_List to the Users stateless record type (represented as a one-to-n relationship in Figure 5.1).

See section 5.7.2, "Hook to Automatically Set Responsible Based on Role of Type Single," for a hook that demonstrates how to automatically set the Responsible field according to the role Leader related to the module (an area) previously selected by the user. Because the Leader is a role of type Single, we can automatically assign the change request to the user having this role.

A somewhat more complicated example is when the role is of type Multiple. We cannot assign the change request automatically because there are several choices, so what we shall do is populate the choice list with all the users having the required role for the selected area.

See section 5.7.3, "Hook to Automatically Set Choices Based on Role of Type Multiple," for a hook that demonstrates how to set the Responsible choice list field according to the role Moderator related to the project (an area) previously selected by the user.

Figure 5.2 shows a project record with the Roles tab. Three roles are defined: manager, qa_manger, and developers. The ClearQuest administrator or the project manager can add or remove users from the developers role. It is a significant advantage that the area team can maintain their roles, and they do not require the ClearQuest administrator to do that work for them; as teams change, people move from one role to another or from one team to another.

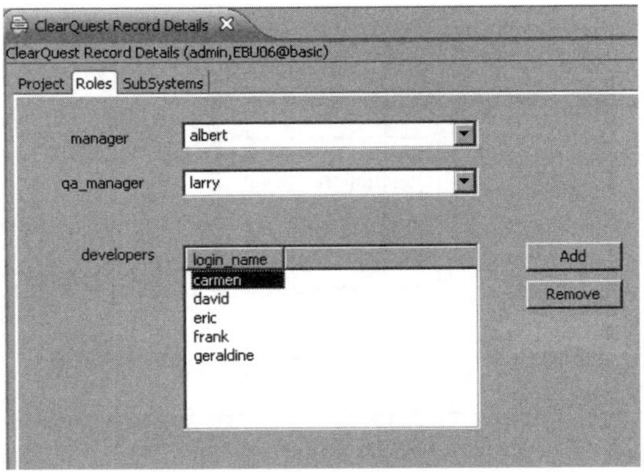

Figure 5.2   Roles defined in the Project record

In a similar way the roles of the area SubSystem are defined and maintained in the SubSystem record. Figure 5.3 shows the SubSystem record and the lead role.

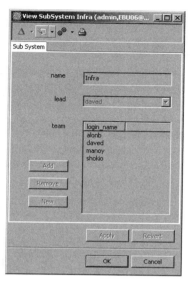

Figure 5.3   Roles defined in the SubSystem record

Figure 5.4 shows the Defect record. When the user selects the Project field, the Subsystem choice list is populated. When the user selects the Subsystem field, now two things happen: the Value_Changed hook is fired and fills the value of the Owner field with the value of Lead Role, and the choice list is populated with the subsystem team users. The user can change the default value that was set by the hook and select another user from the list that was auto-populated; Figure 5.4 shows this operation.

Figures 5.2, 5.3, and 5.4 demonstrate the relationship between the work item (of type Defect in this example) and the Areas record types (Defect > Project > SubSystem) and the relationship between the owner of the defect and the role area (SubSystem Leader). Note that the Defect form includes fields that reference the Project stateless record (an area) and the SubSystem stateless record (an area).

In the Project record there are three role fields (Project Manager, QA Manager, and Developers); each one references the Users record.

In the SubSystem record there are two role fields (Leader and Developer Team Member) that reference the Users record.

Note also that the Project record has three tabs; the SubSystems tab includes a field of type Reference_List that links the project and the related subsystems.

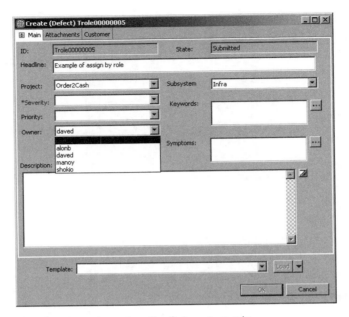

Figure 5.4   Selecting the owner based on the Subsystem role

5.3.3 Using Roles Stateless Record Type (with Static Roles)

In this section we shall demonstrate a more general but somewhat more complicated solution. The method is to define a role object, a stateless record type that defines the relationship between the different areas and the roles.

We recently used this method with a customer that captures both hardware and software change requests with a single record type. Assignment was complicated and correct assignment was important.

Table 5.1 gives definitions of fields in the Roles record type. The example is tied to a specific customer configuration. The ClearQuest designer will design this record type to meet the organization's configuration and roles.

Table 5.1   Fields in the Roles Stateless Record Type

Field Name	Field Type	Comments
Project	Reference	Unique key. Reference to Project stateless record type.
Product	Reference	Unique key. Reference to Product stateless record type.

Table 5.1   Fields in the Roles Stateless Record Type (*Continued*)

Field Name	Field Type	Comments
Component	Reference	Unique key. Reference to Component stateless record type.
IsActive	Short_String	Yes OR No
Description	Multiline	
Leader	Reference	Reference to Users stateless record type. Role of type Single.
Testers	Reference_List	Reference to Users stateless record type. Role of type Multiple.
Developers	Reference_List	Reference to Users stateless record type. Role of type Multiple.

Roles other than the ones delineated in Table 5.1 are possible.

For each combination of project, product, and component there may be one Leader user, several Testers and Developers, and possibly more fields for other roles.

See section 5.7.4, "Hook to Automatically Set Responsible Based on Role Object," for an example of an action validation hook that demonstrates how to automatically set the Responsible field based on the Roles record type for a dynamic workflow.

5.3.4 User-Defined Roles

In the previous examples the roles were predefined in the schema. In many cases this is sufficient, as the roles are defined in the organization's process and are not subject to frequent changes. The area structure (project, product, and component) was also predefined, which is relevant to many organizations but not all of them.

Adding a new component requires creating a new role record, but if the company starts managing new types of changes such as hardware they may include new areas like Board or Firmware that will require changing the schema. Our aim is to create such a schema so that many of the maintenance changes are performed on the client side rather than in the schema.

In large enterprises we find that different projects have different roles. For those organizations the previous example is not good enough.

To ease the customization process and to componentize it, we have created a role stateless record type. In this solution the area owner creates a record for each role in his or her area. This means that you can identify exactly if a user has specific role. The role record may include the allowed actions for each record type. With a list of allowed actions (or denied actions) you can dynamically and easily determine the user's Access_Control for each action performed.

Table 5.2   Suggested Fields for Stateless Record Type Roles (User-Defined Roles)

Field Name	Field Type	Comments
Name	Short_String (50)	Unique key.
Domain[1]	Short_String (30)	List of all the stateless record types (e.g., Project, Product).
Area[2]	Short_String (30)	Unique key. List of all instances of the selected domain (e.g., if domain Project was selected, list of all projects).
Description	Multiline	
IsActive	Short_String	Yes OR No
AllowedActions	Multiline	List of RecordType::ActionName. The list can be a dynamic list or generated by a hook.
RoleType	Short_String	Single OR Multiple
Member	Reference	Reference to Users. Mandatory if RoleType = Single.
Members	Reference_List	Reference to Users. Mandatory if RoleType = Multiple.

1. If the area name is *not* unique, the Domain field should also be the unique key.

2. In this case the Area field cannot be of type Reference; ClearQuest Designer requires you to specify a record type to be pointed to. Because we want the selection to be dynamic, we put the value in a Short_String field.

There are advantages to using the user-defined roles method:

- It reduces the schema customization and the level of maintenance.
- It reduces the amount of repeated work, especially when new products are introduced or after organizational changes.
- The previous methods used predefined roles such as Project Manager, QA, Developers, Testers. An organization/project may want to define its specific roles such as Technical Writer, Controller, or Integrator.
- When roles are not defined as a general object, it is hard to write a single global script to perform a general function with regard to roles, such as security, automatic assignment, or notification.
- Enterprises usually have many projects and many products. Roles may differ from one project to another. This method allows each project manager (not the ClearQuest designer!) to define the roles for the areas in his or her project.

Figure 5.5 shows an example of a role record; the authorized user defined the roles and the allowed actions for that role. This record defines the Product Manager role for the product Alfa and the actions allowed on the Defect and BaseCMActivity record types. The role is of type Single and the user having that role is bashansh.

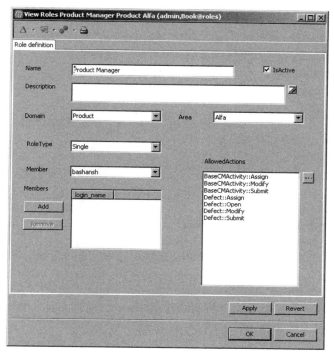

Figure 5.5 Example of roles stateless record with user-defined roles

See section 5.7.5, "Hooks for User-Defined Roles," for a hook example that shows how to populate the allowed actions.

5.4 Security and Roles

We shall discuss security in detail in Chapter 9, "Metrics and Governance," but because security is often related to roles, we will make a few remarks here. If you implement security with the ClearQuest Security Context feature, you probably know that visibility to records is set by groups, and currently there is no other option. Therefore, when you design roles, think about the groups that you already have. We have specified that one of the disadvantages of implementing roles using groups is the difficulty of managing groups with the ClearQuest User Administration. This may be an advantage if groups are already managed for the purpose of security.

In all our examples for roles of type Multiple, we have used the Reference_List field to the Users record type. If all of those users are already grouped in users' groups, it is advisable to use a field of type Reference that points to the Groups record type. This will save time and reduce errors.

5.5 Roles in the ClearQuest ALM Schema

The Application Lifecycle Management (ALM) schema includes roles as an integral part. The ALM role is similar to the user-defined roles previously described in section 5.3.4, "User-Defined Roles," but in a somewhat more general way.

Roles are realized with two stateless record types:

- ALMRoleLabel
- ALMRole

To use roles in the ALM schema an ALMRoleLabel must first be created. A role label is a stateless record type that includes the role name, description, and the actions allowed to this role (represented as a pair list of recordtypename::actionname).

The ALMRole record type includes two fields that reference the ALMProject and ALMRoleLabel records; these fields are the record's unique key fields. The members having this role can be specified as a list of users and/or groups of users.

The ALMRole does not have a type (Single or Multiple) but has a field Primary that references a user. That allows automation via auto-assignment, similar to what we explain in section 5.7.2, "Hook to Automatically Set Responsible Based on Role of Type Single."

Because a role is related to a project which is related to a category, the same role can have different attributes in each project.

When a user performs an action (in either an ALMRequest, ALMTask, or ALMActivity), the ClearQuest system uses the members list and the ApprovedActions list to verify the access control.

To understand the details see the code in the global subroutine `IsUserApproved()` in the ALMAuthorization script.

Figures 5.6, 5.7, and 5.8 are snapshots of an ALMRole record and display the various tabs and fields. The Role tab in Figure 5.6 includes the Project and the Role Label fields which are the combined record unique key.

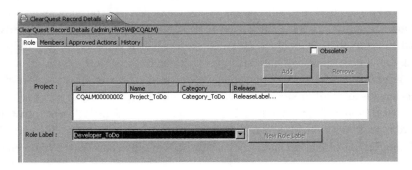

Figure 5.6   The ALMRole record

Figure 5.7 shows the Members tab. You can select individual members and/or groups. At least one of these two fields must be filled in. The primary field is also mandatory and is used to auto-assign the user depending on the record role.

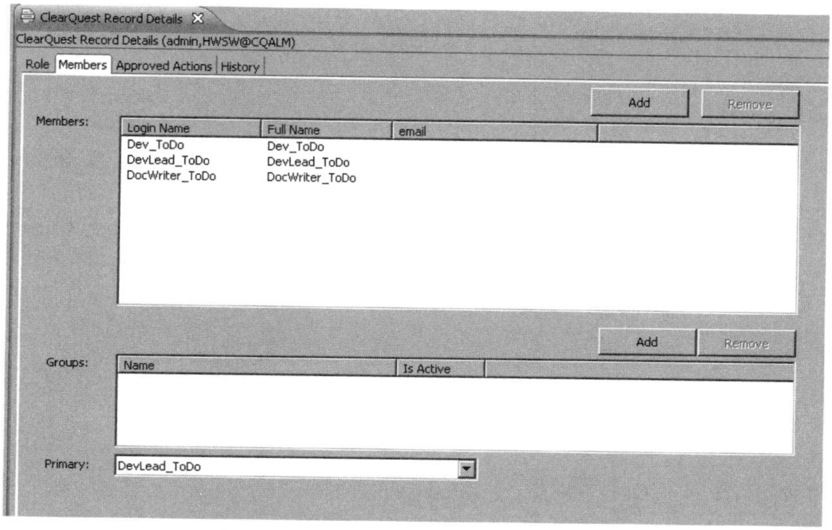

Figure 5.7 Member in the ALMRole record

Figure 5.8 shows the list of actions that the members of this role are allowed to perform in each record type.

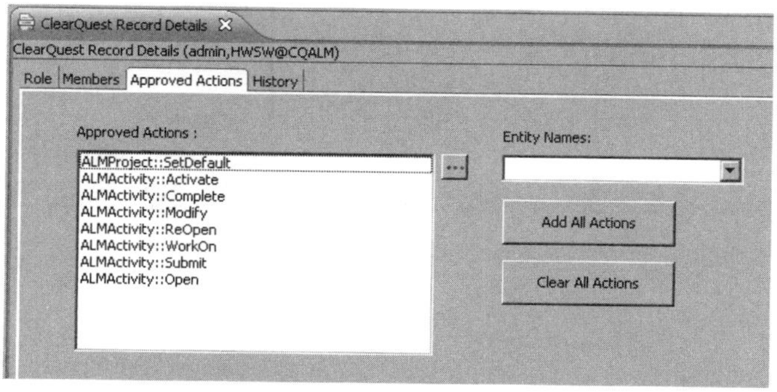

Figure 5.8 The ALMRole approved actions for each record type

5.6 Roles in Jazz

In the Jazz server roles identify the functions of team members. Permissions for specific operations can be assigned to roles at the project level or within a team area. This is realized in three elements:

- Roles for the project area
- Members of roles
- Permitted actions for roles

The following examples include screen shots from a Jazz project area. Roles are identical in Rational Team Concert and Rational Quality Manager projects.

The first stage is to define the roles for the project area. Figure 5.9 shows an example of roles definition. Note that a role has an identifier (which is the role name or label; in Figure 5.9 the role label is GroupLead), a description, and cardinality (in this case Many).

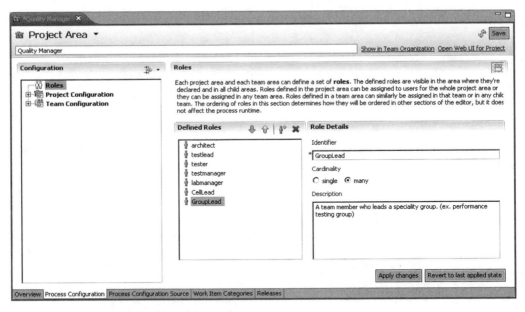

Figure 5.9   Roles definition in a Jazz project area

The second stage is to assign each project member to one or more roles. This is done in the Overview tab of the project area, in the Members section. Figure 5.10 demonstrates the members and their Process Roles.

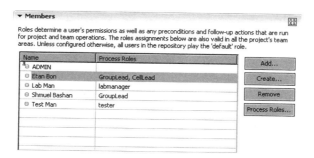

Figure 5.10 Assigning roles to team members in a Jazz project area

The third stage is to define the permitted actions for each role. This can be done in the Project Configuration or the Team Configuration section of the project area; click on Permission to open the Permission definition section. Figure 5.11 demonstrates permitted actions for the testlead role.

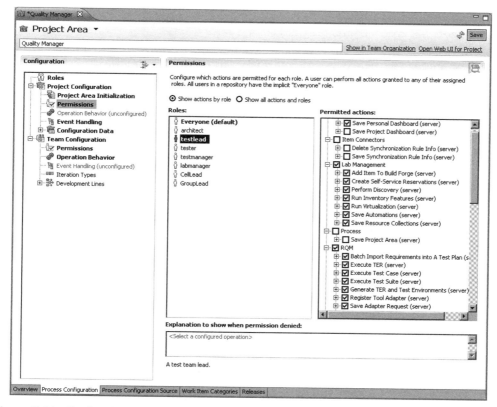

Figure 5.11 Setting the permitted actions for each role

5.7 Code Examples

The following ClearQuest code examples demonstrate how to use the techniques explained in this chapter for

- Access control hook
- Auto-assign
- Choice list population

5.7.1 SQL Command for Group Method

The query in Listing 5.2 returns the list of users who are members of the ProjectLeads group and are also members of the Andromeda group. As you see, the query is quite complex but will do the job. The query in Listing 5.2 is related to section 5.3.1, "Implementing Roles with ClearQuest Groups."

Listing 5.2   Identifying the User Role with a SQL Query

```
select distinct T1.dbid,T1.login_name
from (((  ( users T1 LEFT OUTER JOIN
    [select * from parent_child_links ]. AS T4mm
    ON T1.dbid = T4mm.parent_dbid  )
    LEFT OUTER JOIN groups T4 ON T4mm.child_dbid = T4.dbid  )
    LEFT OUTER JOIN [select * from parent_child_links ]. AS T5mm
    ON T1.dbid = T5mm.parent_dbid  )
    LEFT OUTER JOIN groups T5 ON T5mm.child_dbid = T5.dbid  )
where T1.dbid <> 0
 and (T5.name =   'ProjectLeads' )
 and  T1.dbid <> 0
 and ((T4.name = 'Andromeda'))
```

In the query example the groups are hard-coded; a more practical solution would be to insert the groups as parameters.

This query can be used in a Choice_List hook by using the session method BuildSQL-Query and passing the query string as parameter; see the following examples in Perl and BASIC:

```
$session->BuildSQLQuery(SQL_string);
session.BuildSQLQuery(SQL_string)
```

In the previous query we used hard-coded names (ProjectLeads and Andromeda). This is not a good practice; the hard-coded names should be changed to variables when coding the hooks.

For example, instead of using a hard-coded project name, get the project value:

```
ProjVal = GetFieldStringValue ("project")
```

When including a variable in a query, you must wrap it as follows:

```
BASIC:   '"&ProjVal&"'
Perl:    '$ProjVal'
```

For a full example of a script that uses BuildSQLQuery, see the code in section 5.7.4, "Hook to Automatically Set Responsible Based on Role Object."

BuildSQLQuery versus BuildQuery   We recommend using the session method Build-Query over BuildSQLQuery. Although BuildQuery is less flexible, it protects you from platform or database vendor changes.

5.7.2 Hook to Automatically Set Responsible Based on Role of Type Single

The hook in Listing 5.3 demonstrates how to automatically set the Responsible field according to the role Leader related to the module (an area) previously selected by the user.

In this case the Leader is a role of type Single, so we can automatically assign the work item to the user having this role.

If you are not using the Responsible field, replace it with the field Owner.

Listing 5.3   Automatic Assignment

```
Function Defect_Validation(actionname, actiontype(
  ' actionname As String
  ' actiontype As Long
  ' Defect_Validation As String
  ' action is Assign_owner
  ' record type name is Defect


'  --- This hook sets the responsible field based on the selected
module.
'  --- It is a Base action hook, so that responsible will be set
'      for all types of actions.
'  --- The Module field should be mandatory so the role field can be
read.

Dim moduleObj, sessionObj
'  ---Check if module value was changed (or selected)
originalValue = GetFieldOriginalValue("module").GetValue
currentValue = GetFieldValue("module").GetValue
If currentValue <> originalValue AND currentValue <> "" Then
  ' ---Look for the Group Leader of this Module
```

continues

Listing 5.3   Automatic Assignment (*Continued*)

```
set sessionObj = GetSession
set moduleObj = sessionObj.GetEntity("Module",currentValue(
lead = moduleObj.GetFieldValue("leader").GetValue
SetFieldValue "responsible", lead
End If


End Function
```

> **Note**   If the Module field is of type Reference, it is simpler to get the Leader value by using the following call:
>
> ```
>     lead = GetFieldValue("Module.leader").GetValue
> ```

5.7.3 Hook to Automatically Set Choices Based on Role of Type Multiple

Now let us see an example where the role is of type Multiple. We cannot assign Responsible automatically because there are several choices, so what we shall do is populate the choice list with all the users having the required role area.

The hook in Listing 5.4 demonstrates how to set the Responsible choice list field according to the role Moderator related to the project (an area) previously selected by the user. Again, in this case the Moderator role is of type Multiple, so we *cannot* automatically assign Responsible. Instead, we set the choice list of the field Responsible to all the users having this role, in this case through reference to a group.

If you are not using the Responsible field, replace it with the field Owner.

Listing 5.4   Populating a Choice List Based on Role

```
Sub responsible_ChoiceList(fieldname, choices)
  ' fieldname As String
  ' choices As Object
  ' record type name is Defect
  ' field name is responsible

  Dim actionname
    Dim oCQSession, oProj
    Dim oCQQuery, oCQFilter,oCQResultSet

actionname = GetActionName
originalValue = GetFieldValue("module").GetValue
```

```
originalState = GetFieldValue("State").GetValue
if (actionname = "Assign" OR originalState = "Submitted" ) _
                                AND originalValue = "" then
'  ---No module selected put all leaders in choice list      '
    Set oCQSession = GetSession()
    proj = GetFieldValue("project").GetValue
    set oProj = oCQSession.GetEntity("project" , proj (
    moderators_group = oProj.GetFieldValue("Moderators").GetValue
' ---Query the users database
    Set oCQQuery = oCQSession.BuildQuery("users")
    oCQQuery.BuildField ("login_name")
    Set oCQFilter = oCQQuery.BuildFilterOperator(AD_BOOL_OP_AND)
'  ---Return only those members of moderator (read from Project)
    oCQFilter.BuildFilter "groups", AD_COMP_OP_EQ, moderators_group
    Set oCQResultSet = oCQSession.BuildResultSet(oCQQuery)
    oCQResultSet.Execute

    Do While oCQResultSet.MoveNext = AD_SUCCESS
        choices.AddItem oCQResultSet.GetColumnValue(1(
    Loop
End If

End Sub
```

5.7.4 Hook to Automatically Set Responsible Based on Role Object

The Defect_Validation hook in Listing 5.5 is related to section 5.3.3, "Using Roles Stateless Record Type (with Static Roles)."

The hooks first read the data in the Defect record that uniquely defines the role area (i.e., project, subproject, and component). The next step is to create an SQL query (using the session method BuildSQLQuery) to retrieve the user who is the responsible user (using the ResultSet object).

In this script rules for setting the responsible/owner are also based on the defect state which is done in the last part of the script.

If you are not using the Responsible field, replace it with the field Owner.

Listing 5.5   Populating a Choice List Using Role Object

```
Function Defect_Validation(actionname, actiontype)
  ' actionname As String
  ' actiontype As Long
```

continues

Listing 5.5   Populating a Choice List Using Role Object (*Continued*)

```
' Defect_Validation As String
' action is Update
' record type name is Defect

        Dim manager, fullname
Dim sessionObj, my_proj
    Dim NonBase_action
Dim proj, subproj, compon
    Dim qry , resultset

    set sessionObj = GetSession

Rem ---  Get the areas values
    proj = GetFieldValue("Project").GetValue()
    subproj = GetFieldValue("SubProject").GetValue()
    compon = GetFieldValue("Component").GetValue()


Rem --- Build the query to retrieve user having the application
Rem     responsible role
Rem --- Note the triple wrapping ('"&) around the variables within
Rem     the SQL command

qry = "select T9.login_name
        from Roles T1,users T9,Project T5, subproject T6, components T7
        where T1.responsible = T9.dbid and T1.project = T5.dbid and
            T1.subproject = T6.dbid and T1.component = T7.dbid and
            (T5.name = '"&proj&"' and T6.name = '"&subproj&"' and
             T7.name = '"&compon&"') "

    set resultset = sessionObj.BuildSQLQuery(qry)

Rem --- Run the query and get the result
    resultset.Execute
    stat = resultset.MoveNext
  If stat = AD_SUCCESS then
        manager = resultset.GetColumnValue(1)
  Else
```

```
Rem --- If no value retrieved from the roles record-type set
Rem     the project manager
    set my_proj = sessionObj.GetEntity("Project" , proj)
    manager = my_proj.GetFieldValue("manager").GetValue()
  End if


Rem ---   Set the Owner/Owner_Display based on action and role

          NonBase_action = GetActionName
    select case NonBase_action
       case "Submit"
          fullname = GetUserDisplayName(manager)
         SetFieldValue "Owner_Display" , fullname




       Rem   -- Deal with some other action cases
. . .
. . .
. . .

    case "Resolve"
          fullname = GetFieldValue("Resolver_Display").GetValue()
          SetFieldValue "Owner_Display" , fullname

    case "Verify"
          fullname = GetFieldValue("Verifier_DIsplay").GetValue()
          SetFieldValue "Owner_Display" , fullname
       case else
    end select
'
Rem ---  The Owner_full_name is set , Now set the Owner too

    login = GetUserLoginFromFullName(fullname)
    SetFieldValue "Owner", login


End Function
```

5.7.5 Hooks for User-Defined Roles

The `allowedactions_ChoiceList` hook in Listing 5.6 is related to section 5.3.4, "User-Defined Roles."

This choice list hook builds a list of pairs RecordType::ActionName. This list can be used in Access_Control hooks to find out whether the user is allowed to perform the action.

Listing 5.6   Allowed Actions List

```
sub allowedactions_ChoiceList {
    my($fieldname) = @_;
    my @choices;
    # $fieldname as string scalar
    # @choices as string array
    # record type name is Roles
    # field name is AllowedActions
    # Start User Code
  my $entityDefObj, $value;
  my $nameList, $value;
  my $sessionObj = $entity->GetSession();
  my $entityDefNames = $sessionObj->GetEntityDefNames();

    # Iterate over all the record types
    foreach $EntityName (@$entityDefNames){

      #  Check if the entity is statebased (REQ_ENTITY)
      $entityDefObj = $sessionObj->GetEntityDef($EntityName);
      if ($entityDefObj->GetType() == $CQPerlExt::CQ_REQ_ENTITY) {
          $nameList = $entityDefObj->GetActionDefNames();
          foreach $actionName(@$nameList)  {
                  $value = $EntityName . "::" . $actionName;
                  push( @choices, $value);
            } # foreach action
      } # endif statebased
} # foreach entity
    # End User Code
    return @choices;
}
```

5.8 Summary

In this chapter we explained some of the problems that may arise during the process of change without having a proper methodology. We demonstrated several methods to solve those problems by using roles within a ClearQuest schema. The ClearQuest schema designer will have to analyze the organization's structure, the product structure, and the process requirements before selecting the preferred method to define roles as described in this chapter. The method described in section 5.3.4, "User-Defined Roles," will probably fit many large organizations but can also be applied in small organizations. In section 5.7, "Code Examples," we included several code examples that will help you implement the required method for your organization.

The ClearQuest ALM schema roles implementation includes two special record types, the ALMRoleLabel, which is general, and the ALMRole, which is specific to a project; this allows the definition of roles for each project.

We described how roles are defined in the Jazz-based products, how roles are assigned to users, and how permissions are set by roles in each project area.

Whenever possible we strongly suggest using automatic assignment. If this is not possible, limit the choice list to only those users having the required role; this will minimize errors, save time, and improve the user experience.

Integrations

The chapter is divided into two main parts: the ClearQuest integrations and the Jazz-based product integrations. The chapter starts with a brief introduction to product integrations and the advantages they provide to an organization. The ClearQuest integration section starts with a description of the ClearQuest packaged (built-in) integrations with Rational products such as ClearCase and RequisitePro, and with third-party products like Microsoft Visual Source Safe and Microsoft Project. The ClearQuest section continues with a description of building new integrations. We explain the various methods of integrating applications with ClearQuest and give some examples.

The second part of the chapter focuses on integrations of the Jazz-based products, Rational Quality Manager and Rational Team Concert. We discuss integrations between one Jazz product and another Jazz product and continue with integrations with Rational legacy products such as ClearQuest, ClearCase, and RequisitePro. An explanation is provided on the REST API that allows business partners and customers to build integrations to third-party applications.

6.1 Introduction

Most companies use various tools for creating software and to manage the process of change. Using ClearQuest, ClearCase, and RequisitePro is a common example. The fact that several tools are used in the process, and that each tool has its own repository in which to store data, may have a negative effect on process management. When a team is working on a specific change, they would like to know the source of the change, the reason for the request, who has requested it, and who will be affected by it. All of this information exists without integrations between the tools, so why bother integrating them?

Each time you work in one tool and you look for information in another tool, you are required to have access to that tool, which means having a license, sometimes a local installation, and some level of knowledge of the tool itself. This means investing in enablement and in licensing. When the tools are integrated, some of that pain is removed and you have direct access to data in your working environment. The level of integration also defines the value that you gain from establishing the integration.

For quality assurance purposes and the ability to generate quality reports that require data from several tool repositories, the integration between the tools will improve significantly the organization's ability to get value from the tools.

Tool integrations can help close the gap between separated teams such as development and testing, business analysts and development, development and operations. Integration allows one team to have direct access to the data of another team. This seamless integration helps smooth the process and increases cooperation of the practitioners.

Integrating a change management application with other lifecycle management applications can help an organization on several levels:

- **The practitioner's level**

  Integration increases the efficiency of the practitioner's work and allows easy access to data, quick transition from one tool to another, and a user-friendly experience.

- **The management level**

  Integration provides a clear view of information and process status, although data spans over several repositories. It also enables better governance of the business process.

- **The quality assurance level**

  Integration provides the ability to generate quality metrics from several repositories and on several organizational levels.

From an architectural point of view integration can be performed on one or more of the following levels: data, tools, and process. Figure 6.1 illustrates an architectural view of the three levels of integration between development (IBM Rational tools) and operations (IBM Tivoli tools).

- **Data level**

  Data-level integration allows applications to share data, exchange data, or view data. The Rational Quality Manager to ClearQuest Connector integration is a good example of two applications exchanging data in a synchronized manner.

- **Process level**

  Process-level integration allows an organization to create a single process that spans several tools and environments. The integration between Tivoli Service Request Manger (TSRM) and ClearQuest is an example of how the process in the development organization is unified with the process in the operations organization.

- **Tools level**

  Tools-level integration allows users direct access from one tool to another, or allows one application to perform actions in another application. One example is the Rational Test Lab Manager launching Rational Functional Tester to execute automated test scripts.

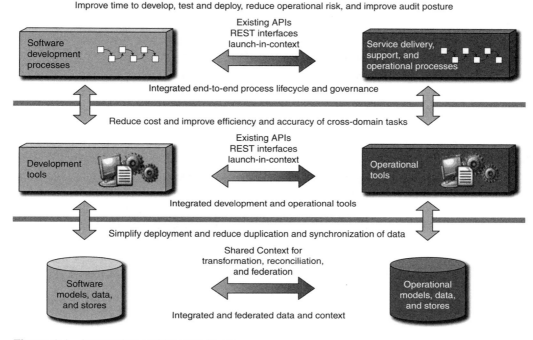

Figure 6.1   Integration architecture levels

But integrations also have disadvantages that we need to consider. The integration between two tools usually depends on the version of the tools, so we are limited to a specific version of each. When we need to upgrade a tool, we usually also have to upgrade the tools integrated with that tool and sometimes even set up the integration again. If you plan to move your repository to a newer server, the process is more complex and requires careful planning.

When you plan the backup procedure, make sure the integrated repositories are backed up at the same time; otherwise when restoring the database, the integration can be out of sync.

Some integrations require additional administrative and maintenance effort. For example, a process that synchronizes data between two repositories should be treated like an additional application that needs to be maintained.

6.2 ClearQuest Integrations

ClearQuest integrations are divided into two main categories. The first category is integrations provided by Rational that you can implement by installing a package or packages and following some configuration instructions. The second category includes integrations that you create using tools and techniques or that you develop with one of the programming tools made available by

Rational, such as the ClearQuest Application Program Interface (API) and the Representational State Transfer (REST) API.

6.2.1 ClearQuest Packaged (Built-in) Integrations

You can integrate Rational ClearQuest with other software applications by adding the required Rational ClearQuest packages to an existing schema. The package will add to the schema the required entities that build the integration, such as fields and hooks and in some cases new record types.

Some Rational ClearQuest integrations are independent integrations that require adding only the appropriate package to the ClearQuest schema. Other integrations are dependent integrations that require adding one or more packages in a specific order and may also require additional configurations of Rational ClearQuest and the integrated application.

It is important to note that not all ClearQuest integrations can be applied to the Web client; therefore, fields, forms, reports, scripts, and other functionality added to the Rational ClearQuest client for Windows, UNIX, and Linux by an integration package may not be available through the Web client. Examples of integrations that do work with the Web client include UCM and RequisitePro. Integrations that do not work over the Web include Microsoft Visual Source Safe.

Notes on Packages   Before you add new integrations to your schema, you should find out which packages are already in the schema and what the versions of the packages are. If you need to upgrade an integration or package, see the help topic in the IBM infocenter "Applying Package Upgrades."

After you add a package to a schema, you cannot remove it. You must delete all schema versions in which the package exists. You can delete schema versions only if you have not applied them to a user database. We shall discuss this in Chapter 8, "Development."

6.2.1.1 ClearQuest Independent Integrations

The following integrations are independent integrations. Note that you can use the same installation process for all independent integrations. For more information on how to add independent integration packages to your ClearQuest schema, see ClearQuest help > Managing change and releases > Integrating Rational ClearQuest with other products > Rational ClearQuest integration packages > Adding independent integrations.

The following are the independent integrations:

- **IBM Rational ClearCase and Rational ClearQuest**

  This integration allows the developer to associate one or more Rational ClearQuest change requests with one or more Rational ClearCase artifact versions (during check-in). We would like to emphasize that this is a base ClearCase (non-UCM) integration. The change set information that is created during the association of the checked-in versions and the ClearQuest records is copied into the ClearQuest field. A hyperlink is also created in the ClearCase version that points to the ClearQuest record ID. So, from either tool's point of view, you can see the associated data without having to access the other tool's data store. This means there is also no authentication required into ClearCase to access the change set data.

The required package is ClearCase.

- **IBM PureCoverage and Rational ClearQuest**

    This integration allows you to submit code coverage data to a Rational ClearQuest database and track it. Developers can submit a defect directly from the PureCoverage result log.

    The required package is PQC (an acronym for Purify, Quantify, and Coverage).

    The PurifyPlus *Installation and Getting Started Guide* includes instructions for setting up the ClearQuest integration for each ClearQuest client type.

- **IBM Purify and Rational ClearQuest**

    This integration allows you to submit data to a Rational ClearQuest database and track it. Developers can submit a defect directly from the Purify result log.

    The required package is PQC.

    The PurifyPlus *Installation and Getting Started Guide* includes instructions for setting up the ClearQuest integration for each ClearQuest client type.

    In Figure 6.2 you can see how a ClearQuest defect is submitted from an error in Rational Purify.

Figure 6.2   Submitting a ClearQuest defect from Rational Purify

- **IBM Quantify and Rational ClearQuest**

    This integration allows you to submit performance data to a Rational ClearQuest database and track it. Developers can submit a defect directly from the Quantify result log.

    The required package is PQC.

    The PurifyPlus *Installation and Getting Started Guide* includes instructions for setting up the ClearQuest integration for each ClearQuest client type.

- **Your e-mail system and Rational ClearQuest**

    This integration enables Rational ClearQuest to communicate with users through their e-mail systems.

    The required package is E-mail.

6.2.1.2 ClearQuest Dependent Integrations

The following integrations are dependent integrations. A dependent integration requires the installation of one or more additional packages and possibly additional configuration steps. The order in which the packages are installed is important.

For more information and instructions for installation and setup of the dependent integrations, see ClearQuest help > Managing change and releases > Integrating Rational ClearQuest with other products > Rational ClearQuest integration packages > Adding dependent integrations. This help page contains links to each integration help page.

The following are the dependent integrations:

- **IBM Administrator and Rational ClearQuest**

    This integration associates IBM projects with Rational ClearQuest databases. A common IBM project is required to integrate ClearQuest with RequisitePro and ClearQuest with TeamTest. The package adds the field Project which is common in the integrated tools and is required to establish the integration.

    The package required is the Repository package.

    For more information go to the "Adding dependent integrations" help page and click on the link "Adding an IBM Administration integration."

Note   In older versions of the Rational products this IBM project was called RA Project or Rational Administration project.

- **IBM Rational ClearQuest Project Tracker and Rational ClearQuest**

    This integration allows you to exchange project data between the two systems. It allows the creation of a ClearQuest record from tracker actions and synchronized data between tasks in Microsoft Project and records in ClearQuest.

For installation and detailed setup information see ClearQuest help > Managing change and releases > Integrating Rational ClearQuest with other products > Rational ClearQuest integration packages > Adding Rational ClearQuest Project Tracker integrations.

For information on the integration usage and use cases see ClearQuest help > Managing change and releases > Integrating Rational ClearQuest with other products > Using Rational ClearQuest with Project Tracker (PDF).

- **IBM RequisitePro and Rational ClearQuest**

  This integration associates RequisitePro requirements with Rational ClearQuest records. It can be used in more than one way. To set up the integration you need to install the Repository and RequisitePro packages and enable the record types you need to integrate. The next step is performed using the RequisitePro administration. You need to add properties of type ClearQuest Integrations to each requirement type that you want to integrate with ClearQuest. The last step is performed from the Rational Administrator. Select the common RA project and define the integration properties.

  One use case is when an enhancement request record is captured in ClearQuest. The workflow continues until the request is approved; once the request is approved in ClearQuest, the relevant requirement in RequisitePro is updated and linked to the ClearQuest record. In this way you establish traceability between the requirements and the requests.

  The second use case is when an approved requirement record in RequisitePro is linked to a ClearQuest change request record that will govern the implementation process of that requirement.

  Combining the two use cases, you have full traceability from the stakeholder request to the requirement to the change work item.

  For information on how to add the Rational RequisitePro and Rational ClearQuest integration, go to the "Adding dependent integrations" help page and click on the link "Rational RequisitePro and Rational ClearQuest integration."

  Also see the help in Let's Go Rational RequisitePro and in Rational Administrator.

  Required packages are Repository and RequisitePro.

- **IBM TeamTest and Rational ClearQuest**

  This integration allows you to submit defects found through TeamTest to Rational ClearQuest databases and to track them.

  For more information see ClearQuest help > Managing change and releases > Integrating Rational ClearQuest with other products > Rational ClearQuest integration packages > Adding an IBM TeamTest integration.

Note   Rational TeamTest is no longer available as end of marketing was announced.

- **IBM Unified Change Management (UCM) and Rational ClearQuest**

  This integration links Rational ClearCase UCM projects and activities to records in Rational ClearQuest. It is probably the most used integration among ClearQuest implementations. When applying this integration, the UCM activity (which physically lives in the ClearCase data store) is represented as a ClearQuest record (that is UCM-enabled), and it allows linking the ClearCase versioned artifacts to the ClearQuest activity containing the change instructions. Figure 6.3 shows a ClearQuest record that stores the ClearCase Change Set information. This allows you to know for each change request what artifact versions were changed to resolve the change.

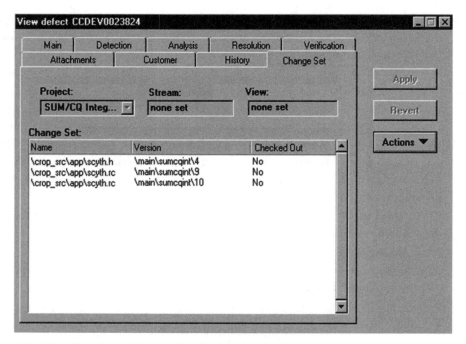

Figure 6.3   The ClearCase Change Set displayed in the ClearQuest record

For more information see ClearQuest help > Managing change and releases > Integrating Rational ClearQuest with other products > Rational ClearQuest integration packages > Adding a ClearCase UCM integration.

Required packages are AMStateTypes, UCMPolicyScripts, and UnifiedChangeManagement. The package BaseCMActivity, which adds an Activity record type, is optional.

The UCM integration from ClearQuest to ClearCase does not copy change set data as the base ClearCase integration. Instead, an ActiveX client plug-in allows ClearCase commands to be executed from the ClearQuest client on Windows. So developers have direct access to ClearCase from ClearQuest, which is a huge benefit. For platforms that don't support ActiveX, the change set is displayed at runtime. This means that the user does have to authenticate once to the ClearCase system to present the change set, or perform other exposed ClearCase actions.

- **Microsoft Visual Source Safe and Rational ClearQuest**

  The required package is Visual Source Safe.

  This integration associates Visual Source Safe versioned artifacts with Rational Clear-Quest records. It is similar to the base ClearCase and ClearQuest integration. Figure 6.4 shows the Source Safe tab in a ClearQuest record with the versioned artifacts that were changed to resolve this change request.

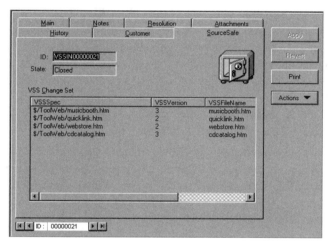

Figure 6.4 Visual Source Safe integration in the ClearQuest Windows client: the VSS change set is displayed in the ClearQuest record.

For more information and setup instructions see ClearQuest Help > Managing change and releases > Integrating Rational ClearQuest with other products > Adding a Microsoft Visual Source Safe integration.

- **Rational Build Forge and Rational ClearQuest**

  In order to integrate Rational Build Forge with ClearQuest you need two packages. The DeploymentTracking package supports the deployment approval process, and the BuildTracking package enables traceability between the build and deployment phases.

  While these two packages are not specific to the Build Forge integration, they are used by the integration to create and update the build records in ClearQuest. This integration requires you to add Build Forge environment variables that tell Build Forge how to log in to ClearQuest in order for the integration to update the ClearQuest build records.

For more information on this integration, how to set it up, and use cases, we suggest the following white paper:

> Duer, Kristofer, "Integrating Build Forge with ClearQuest," *IBM White Paper*, www-01.ibm.com/support/docview.wss?uid=swg27015041, 2009 (accessed February 24, 2011).

- **Rational Quality Manager and Rational ClearQuest**

  This integration is described in section 6.3, "Jazz Products Integrations."

- **Rational Team Concert and Rational ClearQuest**

  This integration is described in section 6.3, "Jazz Products Integrations."

- **IBM Tivoli Provisioning Manager (TPM) and Rational ClearQuest**

  If your organization is using ClearQuest and IBM Tivoli Provisioning Manager (TPM), you can integrate the two products. The integration bridges development and operations, associating your release with the location of an IBM Tivoli Provisioning Manager server, which helps better govern the release and deploy process. You can use the TPM package functionality to add a URL link to the Tivoli Provisioning Manager Web user interface to your deployment record, providing simple user interface integration between Rational ClearQuest and Tivoli Provisioning Manager.

  To create the integration apply the TPM package to your schema. The package creates three state-based record types: BTBuild, DTApproval, and DTDeployment. The package creates the following stateless record types: DTEnvironmnet, DTRelease, DTRoles, TPMServer, and TPMServer. In addition the package makes use of the eSignature, NotesLog, and UCM packages.

6.2.2 Creating New Integrations with ClearQuest

When you plan to integrate ClearQuest with another application, you should carefully examine and define the needs. Based on the requirements you will select the integration method. You have several methods of integration:

- Data exchange through importing and exporting records
- E-mail to exchange data using the E-mail Reader service
- API (ClearQuest includes several API libraries that can be used to integrate it with other applications)
- Web services

In the next sections we shall describe these integrations and provide some examples.

6.2.2.1 Import and Export

This integration is appropriate only when we need to exchange data with another application or data source, and if the required data update rate is not high. For example, if you need to import part numbers once a month or even once a day, this can be a good solution. To export and import data from the ClearQuest database you can use the ClearQuest Import Tool and ClearQuest Export Tool utilities. Because these utilities do not have a command-line interface and can be operated only via the GUI interface, we think they are useful for one-time operation, such as the initial import from an old system or adding data after schema changes. For integration we need a utility that can be operated automatically with tools such as Windows AT scheduler or UNIX Cron.

Note that before version 7.0 the ClearQuest Import Tool and ClearQuest Export Tool utilities were stand-alone utilities. Since version 7.0 these utilities are incorporated in the ClearQuest Eclipse client, and the import and export utilities can be used only from the Eclipse client. They are activated from the file menu as shown in Figure 6.5.

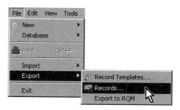

Figure 6.5   Exporting and importing records from the ClearQuest Eclipse client

The mode of import is defined in the ClearQuest Eclipse client in the following way: Select Windows > Preferences and open ImportTool. Figure 6.6 shows an example of the default preferences. Also note that the default directory, c:\temp, can be changed on the ClearQuest > Advanced preferences page.

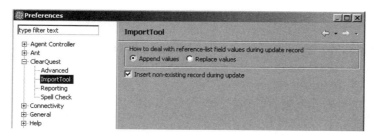

Figure 6.6   Setting the import records preferences in the ClearQuest Eclipse client

For more information on importing data, configuration of the ClearQuest Import Tool, and the format of the import file, see ClearQuest help > Developing schemas with the Rational Clear-Quest Designer > Importing and exporting data > Importing data into Rational ClearQuest. Also see section 7.3.5, "Importing Initial Data" in Chapter 7, "Disciplines, Part 2."

6.2.2.2 E-mail Reader

The E-mail Reader is a service that reads formatted e-mails from a specific e-mail box, parses the e-mails, and performs an action in the ClearQuest database. E-mails should be well formatted; otherwise the parser will reject them. You can extend an application so that it will send an e-mail to the E-mail Reader and perform the following operations:

- Submit a new record
- Modify an existing record
- Change the state of a record

The mail can include field names and their values to be updated.

Using the E-mail Reader as an integration tool has advantages and disadvantages.

The advantages are that it is easy to use and to configure, and it can be applied to many applications.

The disadvantages are that the integration is unidirectional—from an external application to ClearQuest. The sender does not get a confirmation that the e-mail was processed. The integration is not very stable; for example, if there is an error, the recovery process is manual; the administrator has to examine the log file and take corrective action or notify the submitter by e-mail.

Here is an example of using the E-mail Reader for integration: A company has teams developing in Windows using ClearCase/UCM and a ClearQuest integration, and teams developing in UNIX using CVS and ClearQuest Web. They have integrated CVS with ClearQuest so that artifact versions are included in the ClearQuest record. For that they wrote a CVS check-in trigger that sends an e-mail to the E-mail-Reader mailbox with the values to modify.

This trigger in CVS sends an e-mail upon check-in to the E-mail Reader e-mail address. They used the action Modify to add the file name and the file version to a specific field in the ClearQuest defect record.

The E-mail Reader is configured by executing the following application:

```
<Installation Directory>\RationalSDLC\Common\mailreader.exe
```

Figure 6.7 shows the E-mail Reader application with one E-mail Reader mailbox configured: Book:scrum (Book is the ClearQuest repository name and scrum is the ClearQuest user database name).

Click on Add... to add another mailbox or click on Properties to view and modify the selected mailbox properties. After clicking on Add... a wizard will guide you to provide the SMTP and POP server addresses (in many cases they are the same) as well as the e-mail address and login for the user to log in to the POP3 server. We strongly suggest creating a new dedicated user for the E-mail Reader.

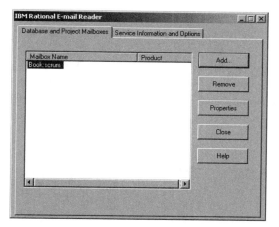

Figure 6.7   Configuring the E-mail Reader

Note on E-mail Protocol   Since version 7.x MAPI is not supported and you can configure the E-mail Reader only with the SMTP protocol.

The next step is to define the e-mail handler (the options are ClearQuest and RequisitePro). Select ClearQuest and click Configure... The wizard page is shown in Figure 6.8.

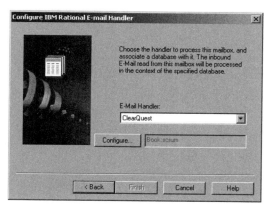

Figure 6.8   Configuring the E-mail Reader: selecting the ClearQuest handler

The wizard requires you to provide the following information: ClearQuest repository, ClearQuest user database, user and password to log on to the ClearQuest database; one or more record types that actions will be performed on; and a default action and default field for each record type. We suggest when you create the e-mail that you do not use the default action and field and always explicitly define the action and field in the e-mail. This will be discussed later in the e-mail format section.

In the second tab, Service Information and Options, fill in the log file path. It is not mandatory but highly recommended as it can help in solving problems in case they occur. Also the error notification e-mail is recommended; in this way the ClearQuest admin can address problems immediately as they occur. Figure 6.9 is an example of a trace log file and the admin error notification e-mail.

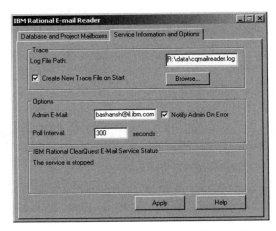

Figure 6.9   Configuring the E-mail Reader: setting service information and administrator options

After the E-mail Reader is configured, you need to start the E-mail Reader service. In the control panel > Services open the Rational ClearQuest Mail Service. Configure the logon account, set the type to Automatic, and click the Start button.

The e-mail sent to the mailbox must be well formatted as in Listing 6.1.

Listing 6.1   E-mail Format for the E-mail Reader

```
Subject: <record type> <action> <record ID>
Body:
    [<fieldname>:]< field value>
    [<fieldname>:]< field value>
    {[<multiline_fieldname>:] This is an example of a field value
        for a field whose data type is a multiline text field.
        It requires braces.
    }
```

E-mail messages must be in ASCII text only; HTML, MIME encoding, and attachments are not supported by the Rational E-mail Reader.

Figure 6.10 is an example of an e-mail sent to the E-mail Reader POP3 e-mail address cqiladmin@il.ibm.com. The record type is Defect and the record is BHALM00001982. The action to perform on that record is Assign; the e-mail body includes the values for the fields Owner and Priority.

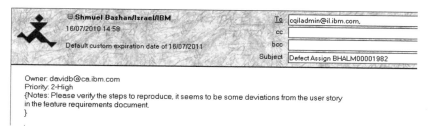

Figure 6.10   Configuring the E-mail Reader: example of e-mail format

---

Notes on E-mail Format: The right brace (}) must be on a separate line from the multiline text it encloses.

Use the <action> even if it represents the default values; it will help resolving problems and understanding the log.

<record ID> must be used for any action except actions of type Submit.

The mail body is in ASCII text only.

Detailed instructions for how to configure the E-mail Reader can be found in ClearQuest help > Administering > Administering ClearQuest > Administering the E-Mail Reader.

6.2.2.3 Creating Integration with Perl and BASIC API

The well-known BASIC and Perl API can be used either from within hooks in the schema or from an external program. Such a program can access an external application database, check for status, read the values of some table columns, and update ClearQuest records with those values. In a similar way the program can take data from the ClearQuest database and update records of an external application database, or perform actions on ClearQuest records based on field values in the external database.

When using the API in an action hook, we assume that the user has performed an action and we want to synchronize with or update another application with the changed data. In most cases this is the real use case—we are updating the integrated application whenever a change occurs. But in some situations we want to verify whether an operation was performed, for example, when the due date is approaching. In these situations we shall have to use an external program utility that is not dependent on user actions.

Another disadvantage of creating integrations from hooks is that it slows down the user. It takes some time to perform the integration, and if it is more than a second, the user will experience it as slow application performance.

The code in Listing 6.2 is an example of how to log in to ClearQuest from an external BASIC program.

Listing 6.2   Importing a Record from an Excel File

```
' Remember to add ClearQuestOLEServer as a reference to your VB project
' to access the ClearQuest OAd* object types below
' Remember to add the clearquest.bas module to your VB project
' to access the AD_* constants

Dim oSession As Session
Set oSession = CreateObject("CLEARQUEST.SESSION")
oSession.UserLogon "user", "password", "DB_Name", _
AD_PRIVATE_SESSION, "DB_set"
```

The code in Listing 6.3 is an example of how to log in to ClearQuest from an external Perl program. Note that the number of parameters passed to the session method `UserLogon()` is not the same in BASIC and Perl, and the `session_type` parameter is not required in Perl.

Listing 6.3   ClearQuest Logon—Perl

```
use CQPerlExt;
use Env;

#  Get  a CQ session
my $CQsession = CQPerlExt::CQSession_Build();
$CQsession->UserLogon("user","password","DB_Name","DB_set");
```

The following is an example of an integration that we have built for a customer:

The customer needed their ClearQuest defect-tracking system to recognize all devices stored in their ERP system so that the tester would be able to select the tested device from a closed choice list, to prevent typing errors. Because their product included many devices, each one having many configurations, and devices could be purchased from several vendors, a daily update was required. The solution was to have the ERP system export the list of devices with the properties of each device to an electronic data sheet (Microsoft Excel). The export from the ERP system is done nightly and the file is saved to a shared directory in the server. A ClearQuest Perl utility that runs nightly reads the data sheet and updates the Device stateless records.

The Windows AT scheduler executes this Perl utility nightly one hour after the ERP export utility is started.

A few explanation notes:

- The utility queries the ClearQuest database. If a record exists, it is updated; if the record does not exist, a new record is created.
- Note that the stateless record type has two fields as unique key; see how the key is constructed to get the entity.

Listing 6.4 ClearQuest Import Script—Perl

```
# Purpose:  Update the Device records with data from file
#           If record does not exist create new record.
# Input  :  Excel file - location and name are hard-coded in the script
#           All cells must have values. The program exists on empty row.
#           CQ database name and user login are hard-coded
# Output :  Operation log to stdout.
# Execution: cqperl Import_device.pl

use CQPerlExt;
use Env;
use strict;
use Win32::OLE qw(in with);
use Win32::OLE::Const 'Microsoft Excel';
my $EntityObj;
my $DevicePN, $MemoryPN, $MemConfig, $MemVersion;

$Win32::OLE::Warn = 3;                          # die on errors...

my $session= CQPerlExt::CQSession_Build();
#  Replace user/db values on next line.
$session->UserLogon("user","password","connection","database");
my $Excel = Win32::OLE->GetActiveObject('Excel.Application')
    || Win32::OLE->new('Excel.Application', 'Quit');
my $Book = $Excel->Workbooks->Open("P:\\Bench\\Data\\Devices.xls");

# We use the first worksheet, columns 1 through 4.
my $Sheet = $Book->Worksheets(1);
# First row includes headers
my $row=2;
while (1 == 1){
```

continues

Listing 6.4 ClearQuest Import Script—Perl (*Continued*)

```perl
# - - - - Get the Device for edit ( CQ record ) - -
  $DevicePN = $Sheet->Cells($row,1)->{'Value'};
  $MemoryPN = $Sheet->Cells($row,2)->{'Value'};
  $MemConfig = $Sheet->Cells($row,3)->{'Value'};
  $MemVersion = $Sheet->Cells($row,4)->{'Value'};

#  we stop reading when we encounter an empty row
 last  if ($MemoryPN eq "" || $DevicePN eq "");
 if ( dev_exist ( $session, $MemoryPN ,  $DevicePN ) == 1 ) {

# - - - - Construct the CQ Unique key from the two fields
  my $ukey =  $MemoryPN . " " . $DevicePN ;
  print "++++++ Device exists ++++++ update Entity $ukey \n";
  $EntityObj = $session->GetEntity("Device", $ukey );
  $session->EditEntity( $EntityObj, "Modify" );
#           - - - - Enter the field to CQ - - - - -
  $EntityObj->SetFieldValue("MemConfig" , $MemConfig );
  $EntityObj->SetFieldValue("MemVersion" , $MemVersion );
 }
 else {
  print "++++++ NO device in CQ  ++++++ Build new Entity\n";
  $EntityObj = $session->BuildEntity("Device");
  $EntityObj->SetFieldValue("DevicePN", $DevicePN  );
  $EntityObj->SetFieldValue("MemoryPN", $MemoryPN  );
  $EntityObj->SetFieldValue("MemConfig", $MemConfig );
  $EntityObj->SetFieldValue("MemVersion", $MemVersion );
 }
   my $result = $EntityObj->Validate();
   if ($result) {
      $EntityObj->Revert();
    print "Error: $result ,  in row: $row \n";
   }
   else {
      $EntityObj->Commit();
    print "Record  successfully Modified from line $row \n";
   }
 print "\n";
 $row++;
}
CQPerlExt::CQSession::Unbuild ($session);
$Book->Close;
```

```
sub dev_exist {
 my ( $session, $MemoryPN ,  $DevicePN ) = @_;
 my $sql_query = "select Controller from Device where
          Memory_PN = '$MemoryPN'  AND  Device_PN = '$DevicePN' ";
 my $sql_result = $session->BuildSQLQuery($sql_query);
 $sql_result->Execute();
 if ( $sql_result->MoveNext() == $CQPerlExt::CQ_SUCCESS) {
     return 1;
 }
 else {
     return 0;
 }
}
```

The previous examples showed how to connect to ClearQuest from an external application. You can connect from a ClearQuest hook to an external database to perform various operations such as running a query to verify data consistency, updating a table column with data from ClearQuest, or retrieving data to update ClearQuest records. This will allow you create bidirectional integration.

The following code is an excerpt of a hook to perform a lookup on external databases not under IBM Rational ClearQuest control:

```
set objConn = CreateObject("ADODB.Connection")
set objRs = CreateObject("ADODB.Recordset")

REM --- Supply connection string and open connection
objConn.ConnectionString = "DSN=prio;uid=xxxx;pwd=yyyy;database=
prio;"
objConn.Open
```

The full hook example can be downloaded from the following source:

> Drexler, Michael, "Hook to Perform Lookup on External Databases Not under IBM Rational ClearQuest Control," *IBM developerWorks*, www.ibm.com/developerworks/rational/library/4388.html, 2004 (accessed February 24, 2011).

Another way of using the BASIC API is via the ActiveX control. Use of ActiveX controls applies only to the Rational ClearQuest for Windows client.

The ActiveX control provides a way to incorporate any registered ActiveX control into a form. For example, you might use an ActiveX control to access and update an external database. You write the initialization record script that runs when the form that contains the control is opened and the action record script that runs when a user initiates an action (such as Submit), or the action is completed or reverted.

The ClearQuest and Base ClearCase integration uses an ActiveX control to establish the integration.

The ClearQuest API reference manual contains detailed information on the architecture and the methods that can be used for integration: ClearQuest help > Reference > API Reference.

6.2.2.4 Rational CM API

The CM API provides one unified Java API for access to both Rational ClearQuest and Rational ClearCase. This capability to use the same library to access two products provides a significant advantage for customers that use both products. In addition, this library extends the WVCM (Workspace Versioning and Configuration Management) API, which is a standard Java API for configuration management.

Having an API allows you to develop a Java program that will access ClearCase, ClearQuest, and external applications to exchange data and perform other actions. For example, the integration between IBM Tivoli Service Request Manager (SRM) and ClearQuest is implemented using the CQ CM API JNI (Desktop) provider.

Figure 6.11 demonstrates how the products are evolving to use the CM Library to connect to the repository. ClearCase Remote Client (CCRC) uses the CM library to connect to the Web server over HTTP. ClearQuest Web uses the CQ CM API WAN (Network) provider to connect to the ClearQuest core that connects via ODBC to the repository. You can also write your integration with ClearCase or ClearQuest core using the CC/CQ CM API interfaces.

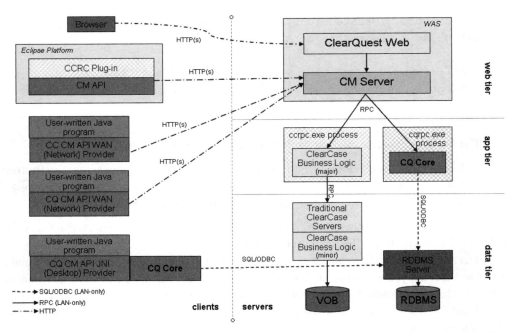

Figure 6.11   Usage of the CM Library: client's interaction with the CM Server and the repositories
Courtesy Yuhong Yin

It is important to note that in release 7.1.x for ClearQuest CM API, only the JNI desktop provider is officially supported. Our focus here is on the Customer Integration client component, so for creating a new integration using the CM Library at this release HTTP is not supported (as in CCRC) and JNI should be used.

The CM API programming model comes from the WVCM standard. A client application is started by generating a *provider*. A provider object connects a single user on the client to one or more *servers*. A server consists of a collection of *resources* of different types. Resources

- Live in *repositories*
- Have *locations* so that clients can uniquely address the repository
- Have a set of type-specific *properties*, such as version number or field content
- Optionally have *content*, such as an attachment
- Support a type-specific set of *operations* that involve interaction with the server and are identified in the interface by beginning with the word *do*

Clients access resources on the server by using strongly typed *proxies* to

- Read/write resource properties
- Read/write resource content
- Apply an operation to a resource

Figure 6.12 shows the relationship of the provider and the proxies on the client and the resources on the server.

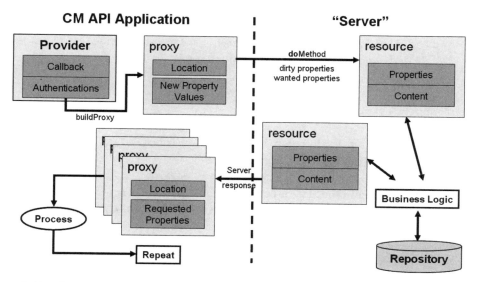

Figure 6.12 Client's interaction with resources on the server

The code in Listing 6.5 is an example of a method that uses the CM API to shows a list of all records. Note how a provider is created, then a record proxy is built, then wanted properties are defined, and finally the operation `doReadProperties` is used to read records.

Listing 6.5   CM API example

```
static void showRecord(String location) throws Exception {

    CqProvider provider = (CqProvider) ProviderFactory
            .createProvider(CQ_ONLY_PROVIDER_CLASS, g_callback);

    CqRecord record = provider.buildProxy(CqRecord.class, location);

    PropertyRequest wantedProperties = new PropertyRequest
            (CqRecord.LEGAL_ACTIONS.nest(CqAction.DISPLAY_NAME),
             CqRecord.ALL_FIELD_VALUES
            .nest(CqFieldValue.VALUE
                .nest(CqFieldValue.VALUE,
                    CqFieldValue.FIELD_DEFINITION
                        .nest(CqFieldDefinition.IS_SYSTEM_OWNED)))));

    record = (CqRecord)record.doReadProperties(wantedProperties);

    StringBuffer buf = new StringBuffer("Fields...\n");

    for (CqFieldValue field: record.getAllFieldValues())
        if (!field.getFieldDefinition().getIsSystemOwned())
            buf.append("  " + field.getName() + " = "
                            + field.getValue() + "\n");

    buf.append("\nLegal Actions...\n  ");

    for (CqAction action: record.getLegalActions())
        buf.append(action.getDisplayName() + ", ");

    showMessageDialog(null, buf.toString(), location,
                                INFORMATION_MESSAGE);

    provider.terminate();
    System.exit(0);
}
```

For more information see ClearQuest help > Extending product function > Programming with CM API and ClearQuest help > Tutorial > CM API tutorial.

6.2.2.5 RESTful Change Management API

The HTTP-based REST API that is compliant with Open Service for Lifecycle Collaboration (OSLC) allows creating, modifying, and querying work items from non-Java clients. In addition to direct modification and query functionality, the API also exposes complete HTML components that allow searching and creating work items.

Adhering to the OSLC specification lets you write clients that will work with any OSLC-compliant implementation of the Change Management API, including Rational ClearQuest.

To learn more about the ClearQuest OSLC REST API visit

> Padgett, Samuel, "ClearQuest OSLC CM REST API," https://jazz.net/wiki/bin/view/Main/RcmRestCmApi, December 7, 2010 (accessed February 23, 2011).

More information about OSLC can be found at OSLC Change Management: http://open-services.net/bin/view/Main/CmHome.

ClearQuest pre-7.1.1   In version 7.1.1, OSLC is installed with the ClearQuest Web Server. But prior to that release, to integrate ClearQuest using the OSLC REST API you needed a Jazz server to act as proxy. You have to configure the Jazz server to ClearQuest Bridge as explained in section 6.3.1.2, "ClearQuest Bridge."

From the ClearQuest Web client you can create a REST URI template. A wizard will assist you in creating URI templates that can be used to integrate ClearQuest Web with other Web applications.

To run the wizard:

1. Click the New button, and select New REST URI.
2. Fill in the required fields and click the Create button. The REST URI template is created.

You can edit the template by adding field values, username, and password.

The following URI line is an example of a template created with the wizard. Note that the double curly brackets {{Enter}} are placeholders for data that you should provide.

```
http://sak09.mega.ibm.com/cqweb/restapi/SAKDev/DMLM/RECORD/{{recor
dId}}?format=HTML&recordType=ALMActivity&action=Activate&fieldsXml
=<Field><Name>FailedInBuilds</Name><Value><![CDATA[{{Enter}}]]></V
alue></Field><Field><Name>FixedInBaselines</Name><Value><![CDATA[{
{Enter}}]]></Value></Field>&autoSave=true&loginId={{loginid}}&pass
word={{password}}&noframes=true
```

For more information see ClearQuest Help > Managing change and releases > Using your Rational ClearQuest Web client > Creating REST URIs to log on and perform common tasks.

OSLC REST API VERSUS CLEARQUEST WEB REST API

ClearQuest Web has offered a REST API since version 7.1.0.0. While this API will continue to be supported, the ClearQuest OSLC REST API documented here is strongly preferred because

- It is standards-based.
- It offers more capabilities.
- It is more robust and performs better.

New projects should use the ClearQuest OSLC API rather than the legacy REST API from ClearQuest Web for programmatic access to ClearQuest data.

6.2.2.6 Other Integration Types to ClearQuest

The following are examples of integrations to ClearQuest created by customers that take advantage of open technology to create a solution to integrate with ClearQuest:

- **Web services**

  This solution uses Web services to create a nonhuman integration with ClearQuest. The following link is a paper that shows the use of SOAP and Web services for integrating a testing tool within a ClearQuest hook:

  Jalammar, "Invoking a SOAP Web Service through Hooks," www.ibm.com/developerworks/forums/thread.jspa?threadID=189932, January 9, 2008 (accessed March 3, 2011).

- **XML**

  This is a TCP socket-based service layer on ClearQuest that enables platform-independent clients to execute ClearQuest commands via XML. The solution documentation and download are available from "cqxmlintf—ClearQuest XML Interface," http://code.google.com/p/cqxmlintf/, October 2008 (accessed February 24, 2011).

6.2.3 Third-Party Integrations to ClearQuest

Some third-party vendors and system integrators have developed integrations with ClearQuest to improve their offerings:

- HP Mercury Test Director and Quality Center integration to ClearQuest

  This integration allows users using HP's test management tools to report defects in ClearQuest.

- ClearVision Subversion integration to ClearQuest

  This integration is bidirectional, meaning users can also record ClearQuest information against the Subversion version history.

- VersionOne and ClearQuest

  This integration creates defects in VersionOne based on defects in ClearQuest. Using this integration your organization can manage and triage defects reported by customers and promote them to VersionOne once you determine a fix is necessary.

- An IBM internal project has developed an integration between SAP Solution Manager and ClearQuest to improve the change management process in SAP deliveries.

The previous examples are only a few of the many third-party integrations that exist in the market.

If you need an integration to an application and it is not available, you can either develop it using one of the techniques that we have described, or you can contact Rational Services or one of the Rational partners that provide such a service.

6.3 Jazz Products Integrations

Jazz includes built-in integrations to several applications that are provided by Rational, and you can install and use them. In addition, you can develop your own integrations to external applications.

In the next sections we shall describe the Rational Quality Manager integrations and the Rational Team Concert integrations to be followed by a section on the Jazz integration architecture and how to build a new integration.

6.3.1 Rational Quality Manager Integrations

Rational Quality Manager (RQM) and Rational Test Lab Manager (RTLM) include the following built-in integrations: ClearQuest, RequisitePro, DOORS, test automation tools, software inventory and automation tools, Rational Team Concert, and Rational Requirements Composer.

The following sections describe these integrations.

6.3.1.1 ClearQuest Connector

The Rational Quality Manager to ClearQuest Connector allows synchronizing between records in ClearQuest and work items in Rational Quality Manager. The synchronization rules define the mapping of the objects to be synchronized, such as fields, the values of pick lists, and the states. Whenever a record changes in one system, the Connector service reads the changes and updates the equivalent record in the second system. For example, if a ClearQuest user changes the defect state to Resolved and adds data to the Resolution field, the Connector will pick up the changes and according to the synchronization rules change the state of the defect work item in Rational Quality Manager to Resolve and will add the data from the ClearQuest Resolution fields to the Jazz Discussion field. Note that the state names and the field names are not the same, but the sync rule mapping is what enables the Connector service to copy the correct value to the correct field. The diagram in Figure 6.13 shows the interaction between the Connector service, the ClearQuest and Rational Quality Manager applications, and the synchronization rules data.

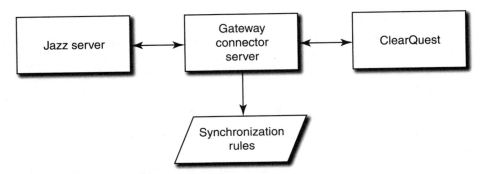

Figure 6.13 Jazz to ClearQuest Connector service: Connector service interaction with the integrated applications

The following steps describe the general creation stages of the integration:

1. Download the ClearQuest Connector from Jazz.net; note that the Connector is under Rational Team Concert downloads (and not Rational Quality Manager). Also note that the Connector is not available for Jazz Express version servers.

2. Install the Connector on the selected server.

3. Add the package JazzInterop to the ClearQuest schema. The package comes with the Rational Quality Manager installation.

4. Enable the ClearQuest record type that will be synchronized to this package.

5. Create a special ClearQuest user and give it the SQL Editor privilege.

6. Edit the properties to match your environment in the file:
   ```
   <ClearQuest Connector installation directory>\gateway\
   cqconnector.properties
   ```

7. Use the Rational Team Concert client to create a new repository connection. The dialog form is shown in Figure 6.14.

8. Enter the Rational Quality Manager server information and then click Finish.

9. Ensure that the user in the Authentication section in the dialog has the same name as the user that was created in ClearQuest.

10. Open the Jazz Project area, and in the Process Configuration include Item Connectors in Permitted actions for the role.

11. Create a new External Repository Connection in Jazz repository connection > Administrator > Synchronization Rules, and provide the InterOpGateway connection information.

12. Import the synchronization rules.

Figure 6.14 Creating a ClearQuest connection to a Jazz repository: defining the Jazz URI and the authenticated user

13. Modify the synchronization rules and create additional rules as required.

14. In the Advanced Properties of the Rational Quality Manager Jazz Server Administration set the correct values in Item Interoperation. Figure 6.15 shows an example of that section.

Item Interoperation

com.ibm.team.interop.service.internal.InteropService   Edit

Property	Current Value	Default Value
Concurrent Synchronization Tasks	2	2
Outgoing Synchronization Enabled	false	false

com.ibm.team.interop.service.internal.OutgoingSyncScheduledTask   Edit

Property	Current Value	Default Value
Outgoing Synchronization Task Fixed Delay	300	300

Figure 6.15 Configuring the Jazz to ClearQuest Connector: setting the Interoperation properties in the Jazz server administration

15. Start the integration process by running

```
<Connector Install Dir>\jazz\connectors\gateway\server.startup.bat
```

See the detailed instructions for building the integration and synchronization rules in the Rational Team Concert online help: Integrating > Rational Team Concert and Rational Clear-Quest > Configuring and using the Rational ClearQuest Connector.

Most of the operations required to set up the ClearQuest Connector can now be accomplished with a Web-based setup wizard. Once you install and start the ClearQuest Connector Gateway, the wizard can be accessed with a Web browser at the URL http://*hostname*:8081/cqconnector/setup.

Here is some additional reading and information on the Connector:

> IBM Rational, "Rational Team Concert 2.0," https://jazz.net/downloads/rational-team-concert/releases/2.0?p=news#cq-connector, June 25, 2009 (accessed February 23, 2011).

> Mehra, Maneesh, "Setup ClearCase & ClearQuest Connectors in a ClearQuest-Enabled UCM Environment," http://jazz.net/library/article/30, July 2009 (accessed February 23, 2011).

6.3.1.2 ClearQuest Bridge

The ClearQuest Bridge integration to the Jazz work item enables you to work with a Rational Team Concert or Rational Quality Manager Web client while the work items are stored in the ClearQuest database. Unlike the ClearQuest Connector integration, there is no synchronization involved, so there is no duplication of data. The disadvantage is in creating reports, as the reporting tool needs to retrieve the data from two repositories. This solution is good for customers having a ClearQuest implementation for work item (or just defect) management that would like to move to Agile development with Rational Team Concert or manage their test effort with Rational Quality Manager, yet do not want to divide their defect data into several repositories.

The following steps describe the creation stage of the integration:

1. In the Jazz Web, select Admin > Server Administration > Advanced Properties.
2. Scroll down to the ClearQuest Bridge section and click Edit.
3. Set the ClearQuest parameters as required. Make sure that the Enable ClearQuest Bridge WebUI is set to "true." See an example in Figure 6.16.
4. Save the change.

Set ClearQuest as "friend," as described in the following steps:

1. In the Jazz Web, select Admin > Server Administration > Cross-Server Communication.
2. Fill in the fields in the form as required. You can give any value to the Title and the OAuth Secret fields.
3. Mark the Trusted check box.
4. Click Request Access.

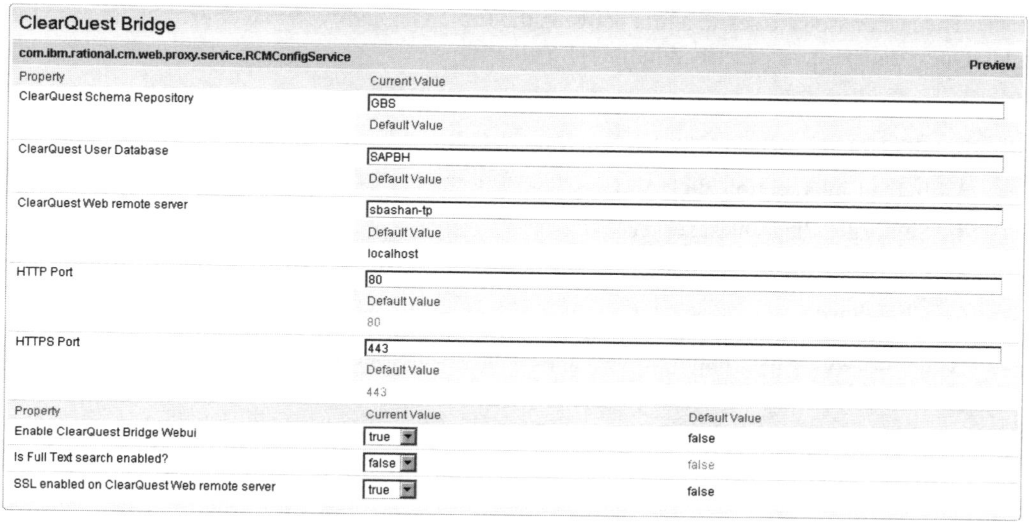

Figure 6.16 ClearQuest Bridge integration definition

The result is added to the Server Friends List. Figure 6.17 is an example of a ClearQuest server defined as a friend.

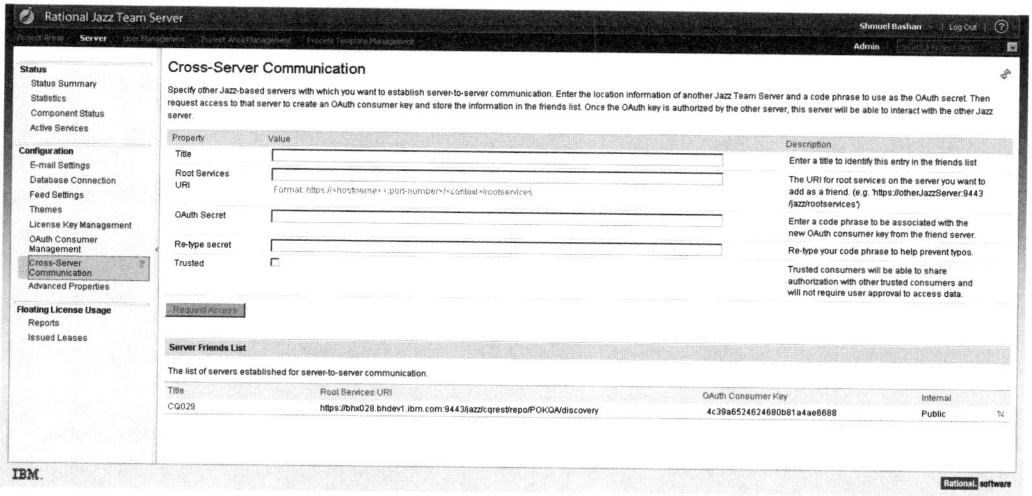

Figure 6.17 Add a ClearQuest server to Friends List

The last phase is to set up a link between the Rational Quality Manager project area and the ClearQuest database, as described in the following steps:

1. In the Jazz Web, select Admin > Project Area Management.
2. Click on the project area that you want to link.
3. In the Links section click Add.
4. Select the ClearQuest server.
5. Click Finish.
6. Click Save.

The ClearQuest user database will appear under the Service Provider column as demonstrated in Figure 6.18.

Figure 6.18   ClearQuest as service provider to a RQM project area

Now when you enter Rational Quality Manager as a user and hover over the Defect icon, you will see new options as shown in Figure 6.19.

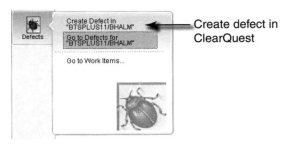

Figure 6.19   Defect section in RQM after Bridge integration with ClearQuest was established

Clicking on Create Defect in "CQ user DB" will open the ClearQuest Submit form of the default record type.

ClearQuest Record Type Created It is very important to note that in Rational Quality Manager version 2.x only one ClearQuest record type can be created from Rational Quality Manager. The type is not selectable and the default record type (as defined in ClearQuest) is the one created and linked.

When you click on Go to Defects on "CQ user DB" it will open the ClearQuest Web client. If you want to create work items in Jazz, click on Go to Work Items....

When the tester reports a defect during test execution, a ClearQuest form will be opened and the ClearQuest defect will be associated with the result log. When a user hovers over the Defect link in the result log, the record data will pop up, as shown in Figure 6.20.

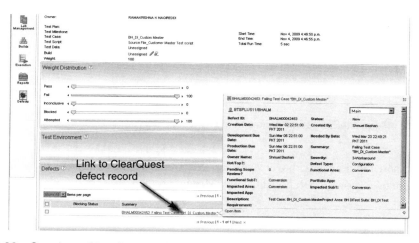

Figure 6.20   Opening a ClearQuest defect from the RQM test results log

Clicking on the link will open the ClearQuest form of that record.
The ClearQuest Bridge provides viewlets for

- Listing queries/records registered as ClearQuest Favorites
- Displaying the results for a specified ClearQuest query
- Showing Rational Team Concert work items and their links to ClearQuest records

For more information see Rational Team Concert Help > Integrating > Rational Team Concert and Rational ClearQuest > Configuring and using the Rational ClearQuest Bridge.

6.3.1.3 RequisitePro

The Rational Quality Manager and RequisitePro integration allows you to import requirements from a RequisitePro project. For each imported requirement a work item of type Requirement will be created in Rational Quality Manager. The Rational Quality Manager and RequisitePro requirements are synchronized, automatically or manually. Figure 6.21 shows the definition of the RequisitePro Web server in Rational Quality Manager system properties. The RequisitePro Web components must be installed and the Web server must be configured and running.

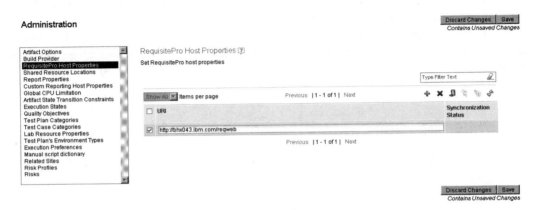

Figure 6.21 RequisitePro server definition in RQM Jazz server

To import requirements, hover over the Requirements icon and select Import Requirements. Figure 6.22 shows the Rational Quality Manager screen.

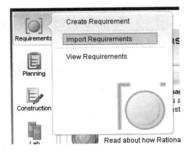

Figure 6.22 Import requirements from RequisitePro to RQM

For more information see Rational Quality Manager Help > Integrating > Rational Quality Manager and Rational RequisitePro.

The requirements can be associated with the test plan and with test cases. When testers create test cases, they associate the requirement(s) (in the Requirement section of the test case). These requirements are the reason for creating the test case and one of the basic sources of information when writing the test design and test procedure. When the Requirement link in the test case is selected, the RequisitePro Web displays the requirement. The integration to the test plan is identical. In this way the test manager can generate a report of all requirements that are not covered with test cases for a specific release. It also allows traceability from requirements to test cases to defects to get you closer to a full ALM implementation.

6.3.1.4 IBM Rational DOORS

When you integrate IBM Rational Quality Manager with IBM Rational DOORS, you can export requirements from Rational DOORS directly into the Requirements view in a test plan or test case. This integration is similar to the Rational RequisitePro integration described in the previous section.

For more information see Rational Quality Manager Help > Integrating > Rational Quality Manager and Rational DOORS.

6.3.1.5 Rational Test Automation Tools Integrations

Rational Quality Manager and Rational Test Lab Manager are integrated to the following Rational test automation tools:

- Rational Functional Tester (RFT)
- Rational Performance Tester (RPT)
- Rational AppScan

The integrations allow testers to execute automated scripts from a Rational Quality Manager test suite or test case.

You need to install and configure the integration by running the adapter that sets up the integration between Rational Quality Manager and the test automation tool. For each Rational test automation tool there is a different adapter; we shall describe in brief the Rational Functional Tester adapter.

The first step is to configure the adapter. Run the adapter program from Start > Program Files > IBM Software Delivery Platform > IBM Rational Functional Tester > Adapter to Rational Quality Manager > Configure Adapter.

The Rational Functional Tester Adapter dialog box opens. Fill in the Jazz server URL and the login and password of a user with access to Rational Quality Manager; the list of available project areas will appear. Select one and provide a name to the adapter. See an example in Figure 6.23.

To activate the adapter hit the Start Adapter button. In the tab Adapter Console you can see the connection status and additional messages.

Figure 6.23   Functional Tester adapter to Quality Manager

The next step is connecting the Rational Functional Tester script to a Rational Quality Manager script. This is done in Rational Quality Manager in the following way:

1. Go to Construction > Create Test Script.
2. In the Create Test Script dialog, enter the name of the script (this is the Rational Quality Manager script, but we recommend giving it the same or a similar name as the Rational Functional Tester name).
3. Select Functional Tester as Type.
4. Select "Use test resource from a shared location." Figure 6.24 is an example of creating a functional test script in Rational Quality Manager.

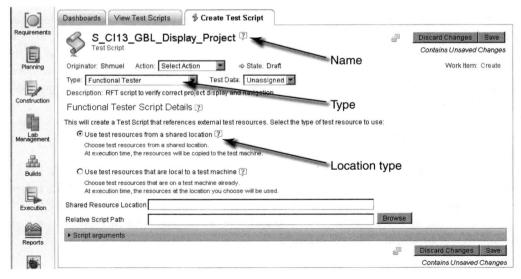

Figure 6.24   RFT integration to Rational Quality Manager: importing an automated script

5. To select the script from the test resource, click on Browse.

6. In the dialog that opens, browse and locate the test script file in the shared directory. Note the extension of the file. Select the file and click OK.

7. The last step is to add the script to a test case. Now when you execute the test case the adapter will copy the script to the Rational Functional Tester machine and execute it.

For additional information see Rational Functional Tester Help > Integrating > IBM Rational Functional Tester and Rational Quality Manager.

6.3.1.6 Build Forge

You can integrate IBM Rational Build Forge with IBM Rational Quality Manager to define and run projects that build and package software from Rational Quality Manager. This allows easy setup of the machines in the test lab for easy execution of integration and system tests.

You must have the Rational Test Lab Manager (RTLM) installed with available licenses and permission set.

For more information see Rational Quality Manager Help > Integrating > Rational Quality Manager and software inventory and automation tools > Rational Quality Manager and Rational Build Forge.

6.3.1.7 Rational Quality Manager and STAF STAX

Software Testing Automation Framework (STAF) is a framework that improves component reuse and automation in test environments. It is an open-source multiplatform framework for reusable components such as services for resource management, logging, and monitoring. Software Testing Automation Framework Execution Engine (STAX) is an XML-based execution engine implemented as an external STAF client. STAX automates the workflow of test cases and test environments.

These integrations allow the Rational Test Lab Manager to manage the test lab processes and execute automated test scripts on remote lab machines, collect results, and display logs on the Rational Quality Manager client. You need to install STAF and STAX on the Rational Quality Manager server and to install STAF on each test agent machine.

For more information and for installation and configuration instructions see Rational Quality Manager Help > Integrating > Rational Quality Manager and software inventory and automation tools > Rational Quality Manager and STAF STAX.

6.3.2 Rational Team Concert Integrations

Rational Team Concert can be integrated with other applications. We can classify those integrations as

- Integration with Jazz-based applications such as Rational Quality Manager or Rational Requirements Composer
- Integration with Rational legacy products such as ClearCase and ClearQuest

- Integration with third-party applications such as Subversion (SVN)
- New integrations creation with the API

The technology used for the integration differs, but the roadmap is to use the REST API. In the next sections we shall describe some of those integrations.

6.3.2.1 Rational Team Concert and Rational ClearCase

Rational Team Concert includes a ClearCase Connector that supports flexible interoperation between Rational Team Concert source control using the ClearCase Synchronizer and the ClearCase Importer. The ClearCase Connector also supports associations between Jazz work items and Rational ClearCase UCM activities using the ClearCase Bridge.

- **Using the ClearCase Connector for Rational Team Concert source control**

  The Connector supports two integration methods. The synchronizer is a bidirectional synchronization between ClearCase and Rational Team Concert. This allows organizations that use both ClearCase and Rational Team Concert to synchronize versioned artifacts.

  The ClearCase Importer is a unidirectional importing tool to import ClearCase/UCM and base ClearCase files and folders to Rational Team Concert source control. This allows teams to gradually move from ClearCase to Rational Team Concert using legacy assets by importing small portions of the assets each time.

- **Using the ClearCase Bridge to Rational Team Concert**

  Rational Team Concert includes a ClearCase Bridge that supports associations between Jazz work items and Rational ClearCase UCM activities. The integration allows you to integrate ClearCase source control with Rational Team Concert so that you can use work items and other change management functionality and continue using source control in ClearCase.

6.3.2.2 Rational Team Concert and Rational ClearQuest

The Rational Team Concert and ClearQuest integrations are identical to the Rational Quality Manager and ClearQuest integration that was described in section 6.3.1, "Rational Quality Manager Integrations," as they are both based on the Jazz server.

This is as good a place as any to compare the two integration types: Connector and Bridge.

The *Connector* integration duplicates data. The same defect exists in ClearQuest and in the Jazz server (Rational Team Concert or Rational Quality Manager) but the defects have different IDs and possibly other fields that are not synchronized. Duplication of data is considered risky as it is possible that at a specific time the two records will not have the same data. Another known issue is the stability of the synchronization; unsynchronized records may be in the queue and the administrator is required to manually force the synchronization from the Rational Team Concert client.

Figure 6.25 is an example of the list of unsynchronized records as displayed in the Rational Team Concert client.

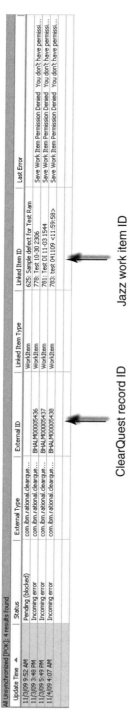

All Unsynchronized [POK]: 4 results found

Update Time ▲	Status	External Type	External ID	Linked Item Type	Linked Item ID	Last Error
11/3/09 9:52 AM	Pending (blocked)	com.ibm.rational.clearque…		WorkItem	625: Sample defect for Test Ram	
11/3/09 3:48 PM	Incoming error	com.ibm.rational.clearque…	BHALM00005436	WorkItem	778: Test 10-30 2306	Save Work Item Permission Denied You don't have permissi…
11/3/09 5:49 PM	Incoming error	com.ibm.rational.clearque…	BHALM00005437	WorkItem	781: Test 0111-03 1544	Save Work Item Permission Denied You don't have permissi…
11/4/09 4:07 AM	Incoming error	com.ibm.rational.clearque…	BHALM00005438	WorkItem	783: test 041109 <11:59:58>	Save Work Item Permission Denied You don't have permissi…

ClearQuest record ID   Jazz work item ID

Figure 6.25   Rational Team Concert to ClearQuest Connector: synchronization status

The big advantage is the reporting. You can create queries and reports by extracting data from a single repository. Various defect reports can be created from both Rational Quality Manager and ClearQuest using the internal reporting utilities, without the need to use a tool (such as IBM Rational Insight) that can access two repositories. See Chapter 9, "Metrics and Governance," for an additional discussion of reporting.

The *Bridge* integration uses the OSLC technology to create a link from one tool to another. The advantage is that there is only one record where the data exists and no synchronization is required. There is only one ID for each defect, which eliminates confusion and mistakes.

The disadvantage is that the end user response time is higher (slower), and some users are very sensitive to performance issues. Another disadvantage is the reporting. It is harder to generate reports when the data is in two repositories; tools like Rational Insight are required to derive reports that include data from both Rational Team Concert and Rational ClearQuest.

6.3.2.3 Subversion (SVN)

Rational Team Concert enables Subversion users to take advantage of Rational Team Concert source control and work items to collaborate more effectively when working with a Rational Team Concert community.

Two styles of collaboration are supported:

- You can import the contents of a Subversion repository to one or more Rational Team Concert source control components.

- If you install a Subversion client for Eclipse into the Eclipse instance that supports Rational Team Concert, you can link Subversion revisions to work items.

Teams that use Rational Team Concert source control and Subversion can use either or both of these capabilities.

6.3.2.4 Build Engines

The Jazz technology platform provides support for the automation, monitoring, and awareness of a team's builds. The following generic build-related items are stored in the Jazz repository and support the build process:

- **Build definition:** defines a build, such as a weekly project-wide integration build
- **Build engine:** represents a build system running on a build server
- **Build request:** represents a request to run a build
- **Build result:** represents the output from a build

While Jazz users can make use of the build items incorporated in Jazz Build Engine, they can also use other build engines such as IBM Rational Build Forge or CruiseControl. When you set up a build that does not use the Jazz Build Engine, you need to create build definition and build engine objects in Rational Team Concert.

For more information see RTC Help > Managing change and releases > Building with Jazz Team Build > Jazz Team Build setup variation.

Also see "Team Build Examples" on Jazz.net; select TWiki > Main Web > BuildMain > BuildExamples.

6.3.2.5 Other Integrations

The following is a list of the available integrations to Rational Team Concert organized by category:

- **Build and process automation**

  IBM Rational Build Forge

  Hudson

  CruiseControl

  Maven

- **Collaboration**

  IBM Lotus SameTime

  IBM Lotus Quickr

  IBM Lotus Connections

  GoogleTalk

  Microsoft SharePoint

  Skype

- **Defect tracking**

  IBM Rational ClearQuest

  BSD Group—RTC Adaptor for HP QualityCenter

  cm-logic—JazzConnect for JIRA

- **IDEs and development**

  Eclipse

  IBM Rational Application Developer

  IBM Rational Software Architect

  Microsoft Visual Studio IDE

- **Modeling, code generation, and asset reuse**

  IBM Rational Rhapsody

  IBM Rational Software Modeler

  IBM Rational Asset Manager

- **Project management and governance**

  IBM Rational Project Conductor

  IBM Rational Method Composer

  QSM

  WebLayers

  Black Duck

- **Quality management and security testing**

  IBM Rational Quality Manager

  IBM Rational Software Analyzer

- **Requirements management and requirements definition**

  IBM Rational DOORS

  IBM Rational Requirements Composer

  IBM Rational RequisitePro

  iRise

  Ravenflow

- **Version control**

  IBM Rational ClearCase

  Subversion

  Git

  CVS

To learn about each of these integrations visit the Rational Team Concert Integrations page:

> IBM Rational, "Rational Team Concert Integrations," jazz.net/projects/rational-team-concert/integrations/ (accessed February 24, 2011).

6.3.3 Building a New Jazz Integration

This section describes how to build integrations to Jazz work items. In version 1.0 the work item Java API was presented and it is still supported. In version 2.0 the focus is on the work item REST API.

6.3.3.1 Jazz Integration Architecture (JIA)

The goal of the Jazz Integration Architecture (JIA) is to enable diverse tools to be used together, providing an integrated experience to their users.

At the center of JIA is the Jazz Team Server (JTS). The JTS provides the Jazz Foundation Services (JFS) that enable groups of tools to work together.

The main elements powering much of JIA are

- Standard RESTful APIs
- Standard resource definitions
- Reusable building blocks
- Specifications

The API and resource definitions enable participating tools to easily share data. The reusable elements speed the development of new projects and the adoption of existing tools, and the specifications enable better integration of, and navigation between, the user interfaces of the various tools.

The tool exposes its data and services through a resource-oriented Web service called RESTful Web Services.

A REST API provides three key things:

- Stable URLs for the tool data resources
- Documented representations for those data resources
- A protocol and operations for manipulating those data resources based on standard HTTP methods

Figure 6.26 on the next page is a schematic visualization of the OSLC services that will be exposed to the Jazz repository.

A detailed description of JIA can be found in the Jazz Community Site; select Projects > Jazz-foundation > Jazz-integration-architecture.

Jazz Community Site   Visit and register at http://jazz.net.

6.3.3.2 Rest API

This section describes the Resource Oriented Work Item API 2.0. The API allows you to get, create, modify, and query work items using standard HTTP methods, allowing integrations with minimal requirements for the clients. The API adheres to the OSLC CM specification.

Here are some things that can be done with the API:

- Load work items in different formats such as JSON, XML, ATOM, HTML, and in different levels of granularity.
- Update work items by modifying the JSON or XML representation and storing it back.
- Create work items by obtaining an HTML creation dialog module.
- Create work items by posting their JSON or XML representation to a factory URL.
- Add or remove links.
- Query work items (full text and structured queries).

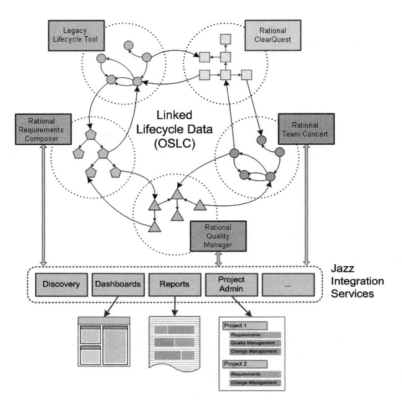

Figure 6.26   RTC REST API and OSLC services
Courtesy Edward J. Gentry

For example, if you want to get the title, state, and severity of a work item whose ID equals 27, you can use the following call:

```
https://<your-jazz-server-name>:9443/jazz/oslc/workitems/27.json?
   oslc_cm.properties=dc:title,rtc_cm:state,oslc_cm:severity
```

The return result is demonstrated in the next lines. Notice that for the severity and state the enumeration is returned.

```
{"dc:title":"Pop-Up in IE is not identical to FireFox",
"rdf:resource":"https:\/\/server-name:9443\/jazz\/resource\
/itemOid\/com.ibm.team.workitem.WorkItem\/_tSWJgC6iEd-IPrWkm3if_A",
"rtc_cm:state":{"rdf:resource":"https:\/\/localhost:9443\/
jazz\/oslc\/workflows\/_RBPUELlhEd61VPTKNlAXiw\/states\/
bugzillaWorkflow\/2"},
```

```
"oslc_cm:severity":{"rdf:resource":"https:\/\/localhost:9443\/
jazz\/oslc\/enumerations\/_RBPUELlhEd61VPTKNlAXiw\/severity\/3"}}
```

More information about OSLC can be found at http://open-services.net, and more on OSLC change management at

> Speicher, Steve, "Change Management," http://open-services.net/bin/view/Main/ CmHome, December 14, 2010 (accessed February 23, 2011).

More information on the Resource-Oriented Work Item API 2.0 can be found here:

> Streule, Patrick, "Resource Oriented Work Item API 2.0," https://jazz.net/wiki/bin/view/ Main/ResourceOrientedWorkItemAPIv2, April 13, 2010 (accessed February 23, 2011).

6.4 Resources

This section includes various resources to complete the integration picture for ClearQuest and for the Jazz-based products. If you are about to create an integration, we suggest looking at the relevant additional readings proposed.

6.4.1 ALM

Gothe, Mats, Carolyn Pampino, Philip Monson, Khurram Nizami, Katur Patel, Brianna M. Smith, and Nail Yuce, *Collaborative Application Lifecycle Management with IBM Rational Products: IBM Redbook* (Poughkeepsie: IBM, International Technical Support Organization, 2008), www.redbooks.ibm.com/abstracts/SG247622.html (accessed February 22, 2011).

Forziati, Rich, and Mats Gothe, "Collaborative ALM Interoperability," IBM White Paper, www-01.ibm.com/support/docview.wss?uid=swg27017757, 2010 (accessed February 22, 2011).

6.4.2 Jazz

Lemieux, Jean-Michel, "Integrating and Extending Rational Team Concert (the SDK)," https://jazz.net/wiki/bin/view/Main/RtcSdk20, November 19, 2010 (accessed February 22, 2011).

Lemieux, Jean-Michel, "Extending Rational Team Concert 2.0," presentation SDP023 delivered at the Rational Software Developer Conference, Orlando, FL, May 31–June 4, 2009, https://jazz.net/wiki/pub/Main/RtcSdk20/RSDC2009-extendingrtc.ppt (accessed February 22, 2011).

"Jazz Integration Architecture Overview," http://jazz.net/projects/DevelopmentItem.jsp?href=content/project/plans/jia-overview/index.html, September 22, 2008 (accessed February 22, 2011).

6.4.3 ClearQuest

Padgett, Samuel, "ClearQuest OSLC CM REST API," https://jazz.net/wiki/bin/view/Main/RcmRestCmApi, December 7, 2010 (accessed February 22, 2011).

Exum, Mike, "A Primer on ClearQuest Integrations," *IBM developerWorks*, www.ibm.com/developerworks/rational/library/1051.html, 2003 (accessed February 22, 2011).

Drexler, Michael, "Hook to Perform Lookup on External Databases Not under IBM Rational ClearQuest Control," *IBM developerWorks*, www.ibm.com/developerworks/rational/library/4388.html, 2004 (accessed February 22, 2011).

Hicks, Leesa, "ClearQuest CRM Synchronization Solution," *IBM developerWorks*, www.ibm.com/developerworks/rational/library/4678.html, 2002 (accessed February 22, 2011).

6.4.4 General Information

Speicher, Steve, and Samuel Padgett, "Get to Know Open Services for Lifecycle Collaboration Change Management," *IBM developerWorks*, www.ibm.com/developerworks/rational/library/10/openservicesforlifecyclecollaborationchangemanagement/index.html, 2010 (accessed February 22, 2011).

Allamaraju, Subbu, *RESTful Web Services Cookbook* (O'Reilly Media, 2010), http://oreilly.com/catalog/9780596801694 (accessed February 22, 2011).

6.5 Summary

In this chapter we described different types of integrations to work items. In the first part we introduced product integrations and the advantages they provide to the organization. The ClearQuest integration section started with a description of the ClearQuest packaged (built-in) integrations with other Rational products like ClearCase and RequisitePro, and with third-party products like Microsoft Visual Source Safe and Microsoft Project. We discussed several methods for building a new integration and explained the advantages of each method.

In the second part of the chapter we focused on integrations of the Jazz-based products, mainly Rational Quality Manager and Rational Team Concert. We discussed integrations between one Jazz product and another Jazz product and continued with integrations from Rational Jazz products to Rational legacy products such as ClearQuest, ClearCase, and RequisitePro. An explanation was provided of the Open Services for Lifecycle Collaboration (OSLC) REST API. Rational is building the integrations with this standard, and it allows business partners and customers to build integrations to Jazz work items as well as to ClearQuest records.

## CHAPTER 7

Disciplines, Part 2

This chapter is a continuation of Chapter 2, "Disciplines: Requirements, Analysis & Design." We have divided the disciplines to maintain a logical flow in the book's chapters. As we mentioned in Chapter 2, the disciplines for developing change management applications are in many aspects different from those of a regular software project, mainly because of the special development environment provided by IBM Rational ClearQuest and IBM Rational Team Concert. To describe the disciplines for change management systems we have used elements from the Rational Unified Process (RUP) for a small project framework and have adapted them to meet the environment for change management, specifically with an orientation toward ClearQuest and Jazz work items.

The disciplines that we discussed in Chapter 2 were

- Requirements
- Analysis & design

In this chapter we shall cover four additional disciplines:

- Implementation
- Testing
- Deployment
- Maintenance

7.1 Implementation Discipline

The purpose of implementation is to

- Define the organization of the code, in terms of implementation subsystems organized in layers
- Implement the design elements in terms of implementation elements (record types, hooks, forms, integrations, and others)

- Test the developed components as units
- Integrate the results produced by individual implementers (or teams) into an executable system

The scope of the Implementation discipline is limited to how individual schema elements (usually record types or packages in ClearQuest and work item types in Jazz) are to be unit tested. System testing and integration testing are described in the Test discipline.

Our mission is to use the design model to build the schema elements that will generate the change management system.

The tasks of implementing the design elements produce an implementation of elements such as record types and a code library. The result is typically new or modified work item types, referred to generally as implementation elements.

The work breakdown differs depending on whether implementation is performed with a single implementer or multiple implementers.

7.1.1 ClearQuest Implementation Tasks

The recommended tasks for the ClearQuest implementer are as follows:

1. From the entity relationship diagram (ERD) or the class diagram create the record types.
2. For each record type add the fields. We suggest adding fields to one record type at a time, as it is easier to test your work in this way. Also, we suggest adding the fields to the stateless record types first and then to the stateful record types.
3. Build the forms and tabs, and add the field controls.
4. For stateless record types define the unique key(s).
5. For stateful record types add the states.
6. Add the field behaviors.
7. Add the actions and their transitions; for stateless record types just add an action of type Modify.
8. Verify the state transition matrix.
9. Add hooks and scripts to complete the solution rules.
10. Import test data to populate the records.
11. Test your work with a test database; make sure to test the system in all required environments (Windows, UNIX, and Web).

    Generally large deployments will have a separate ClearQuest Schema Repository as well as user databases for the test environment. ClearQuest has schema migration utilities for moving changes from a test environment to production.
12. Develop additional utilities for importing record data, importing user definition data, backup and restore, synchronization in multisite implementations, integrations, and so on.
13. Develop queries, charts, and reports for the various roles.

7.1.2 Jazz Implementation Tasks

The recommended tasks for the Jazz implementer are as follows:

1. From the entity relationship diagram (ERD) or the class diagram create the work item types.

2. For each work item type add the attributes (fields).

3. Create one or more editor presentations and add to each one tabs, sections, and attributes. Bind each editor presentation to a work item type.

4. Create one or more workflows: add states and actions and construct the transition. Bind the workflow to each work item type.

5. Define roles.

6. Define permitted actions for each role.

7. Define the operational behaviors and the attribute preconditions.

8. Define the predefined queries and the dashboard templates.

9. Import test data to populate the records.

10. Test your work with a test project; make sure to test the system in all required environments (Windows, Linux, and Web). Generally, large deployments will have separate servers for the test environment.

11. Develop additional utilities as required.

12. Develop queries, reports, and dashboards for the various roles.

This list of implementation tasks is just an overview; the detailed activities in each task are described in the product documentation. In Chapter 8, "Development," we shall cover additional subjects and provide additional information on implementation.

7.2 Testing Discipline

Testing focuses primarily on evaluating or assessing product quality. This is realized through the following core practices:

- Find and document defects in software quality.

- Advise on the perceived software quality.

- Validate and prove the assumptions made in design and requirements specifications through concrete demonstration.

- Validate that the software product works as designed.

- Validate that the requirements are implemented appropriately.

After the change management application has been developed and all units tested by the developer have passed, the system is deployed to the system test environment. Large organizations will implement the system tests in a dedicated and isolated environment. The test environment should be as similar as possible to the production environment, that is, the same software versions of all components, database, application server, Web server, client OS, application versions, active directory, and so forth. For example, the ClearQuest schema designer may work with a Microsoft Access database for implementing and unit testing, but for the system test environment the same vendor database must be used as is deployed in the production environment. If the system has integrations to other applications, the test environment should include those applications. A bill of materials of all production artifacts can help in achieving the correct environment.

Another important factor is database size and the variety of test data. The test database for system tests can be copied from the production environment, or imported from the same source used to populate the production database. This will keep the test environment as close as possible, if not identical, to the production environment.

In section 7.5.3, "Creating a Test Environment," we provide instructions for how to create a test environment for ClearQuest.

The tester should check that all requirements are actually met. Testers will validate that there are no ways to circumvent the process and that the quality of the solution meets the organization's standards. To achieve a high-quality application it is advisable to use automated tests, with tools like Rational Functional Tester. When using automation, testers can perform large and frequent series of regression tests that will speed up the testing and improve the test quality.

If you need to validate that the solution meets certain performance requirements, tools like Rational Performance Tester can assist with this testing work. Rational Performance Tester can simulate hundreds and thousands of users to generate load on the Web server and the database, measuring response time in various use cases. IBM Rational ClearQuest Web administrators can learn a method for benchmarking the performance of their deployment and test environments in this article:

> Covell, Grant C., "IBM Rational ClearQuest Web Performance Benchmarking Kit," *IBM developerWorks*, www.ibm.com/developerworks/rational/library/07/0619_covell/, 2007 (accessed February 24, 2011).

Testers should report defects on the same system that they test. The CM administrator needs to create a special project or category for system tests. Ideally, the process of the system will be used to manage the deployment of the system. In this fashion you will only have to create another project that signifies the deployment effort of the system. This project will hold the defects, enhancements, and other metadata related to the deployment. This will help the development and test teams identify process usability issues early on.

7.3 Deployment Discipline

The Deployment discipline describes the activities associated with ensuring that the software product is available for its users. These include

- Installation of all infrastructures and applications
- Setup and configuration of the environment
- Deployment of customizations
- Population of the databases
- Training the users
- Following up with users and collecting feedback to ensure that the solution is successfully adopted

7.3.1 Preparation

Preparation includes the creation of a bill of materials and a deployment plan.

The bill of materials (BOM) is a list of all components involved in the deployment. The BOM should include required hardware, operating systems, database, application server, application software, license files, utilities, training materials, and more. Each component in the list should include the required version.

The deployment plan is a list of tasks that includes the task name, task description, the owner, start and end dates, prerequisites, and tasks dependencies. The deployment plan can be created in project management tools like Microsoft Project.

Figure 7.1 is an example of a section of a high-level deployment plan. You can see the activities for application installations.

324		0%	xSeries: App installs	17 days	Mon 1/5/09	Tue 8/25/09		
325		0%	Enterprise Lic Upgrade required on 7 windows boxes	0 days	Fri 8/21/09	Fri 8/21/09		
326		0%	FS required for app installs	0 days	Tue 8/18/09	Tue 8/18/09		
327		0%	Sudo Root access provide for all installations	0 days	Thu 8/20/09	Thu 8/20/09		TEAM
328		0%	DB2 UD (DB2 ESE V9.5) for ClearQuest, ReqPro and RQM (sub-system) on z/OS	0 days	Wed 8/19/09	Wed 8/19/09		Rich
329		0%	Rational ClearCase (windows)	4 days	Fri 8/21/09	Tue 8/25/09		Joe
330		0%	Rational ClearCase 7.1.0.2 and WBM Publisher	1 day	Fri 8/21/09	Fri 8/21/09	328,325	Ken
331		0%	Build Forge v7.1.1	1 day	Sat 8/22/09	Sat 8/22/09	330	Ken
332		0%	Rational License server v7.1.0.2	1 day	Mon 8/24/09	Mon 8/24/09	331	Ken
333		0%	TSM client configuration	1 day	Tue 8/25/09	Tue 8/25/09	332	
334		0%	Rational ClearQuest (windows)	4 days	Fri 8/21/09	Tue 8/25/09		
335		0%	Rational CQWEB v7.1.0.2	1 day	Fri 8/21/09	Fri 8/21/09	325,328	Shmuel
336		0%	Rational ClearQuest v7.1.0.2	1 day	Sat 8/22/09	Sat 8/22/09	335	Shmuel
337		0%	Rational License server v7.1.0.2	1 day	Mon 8/24/09	Mon 8/24/09	336	Shmuel
338		0%	TSM client configuration	1 day	Tue 8/25/09	Tue 8/25/09	337	
339		0%	Rational Quality Manager (windows)	17 days	Mon 1/5/09	Tue 8/25/09		
340		0%	Rational REQWEB v7.1.0.2	1 day	Fri 8/21/09	Fri 8/21/09	325,328	Shmuel
341		0%	Rational Quality Manager v2.0	1 day	Sat 8/22/09	Sat 8/22/09	340	Shmuel
342		0%	Rational Insight (bundled with RQM) NOTE: This machine is also running a Cognos engine for custom reporting	1 day	Mon 8/24/09	Mon 8/24/09	341	Shmuel
343		0%	Rational License server v7.1.0.2	1 day	Tue 8/25/09	Tue 8/25/09	342	Shmuel
344		0%	Rational REQPRO 7.1.0.2	1 day	Tue 8/25/09	Tue 8/25/09	342	Shmuel
345		0%	TSM client configuration	1 day	Mon 1/5/09	Mon 1/5/09		

Figure 7.1 Deployment plan: section of a deployment plan showing the installation phase activities

7.3.2 Installations

The installation effort usually includes several individuals and therefore it is important to prepare a deployment plan to coordinate the work.

Servers are usually installed by IT operations. Initially these machines need to have basic software installed like the required OS, service packages, and any other software required by the organization and the products. The databases reside on a database server. This software is usually installed by the database administrator (DBA). The change management administrator must coordinate the database installation with the DBA, making sure to communicate the special requirements for the CM application. For example, the page size, code page, database names, usernames, and other detailed information needed by the system should be provided to the DBA in advance.

The change management administrator should perform the installation of the specific applications. The ClearQuest server components, license server, administration components, and other components must be installed following each product's documented installation steps.

For a Jazz server, similar installation steps are required.

The client installation is time-consuming and requires careful planning. For all users who do not use the Web client a local install is required. The CM administrator and IT operations need to decide on the right approach to performing the installation of the clients. Who will do the installation and how will it be done? With the Installation Manager GUI or with the silent install? For more information on silent install see ClearQuest Help: Installing and Upgrading > Deploying Rational ClearQuest > Installing Rational ClearQuest > Installing silently.

Another important factor is the prerequisites for each installation, especially for products that are integrated with other products. Also, the version of software products that are installed on the same machine must match.

7.3.3 Setting Up the Environment

Setting up the environment includes the configuration of the database, the application and Web servers, the users' login definition, e-mail notification rules, and integration with Lightweight Directory Access Protocol (LDAP). The environment setup instructions differ for each tool and each version.

7.3.3.1 ClearQuest

The ClearQuest environment setup includes

- Creating a schema repository and user databases
- Creating a connection to the database set
- Configuring the Rational ClearQuest CM Server
- Configuring the reporting solution
- Configuring the license server

- Configuring Rational E-mail Reader
- Defining users and groups and LDAP connections

The client setup includes the definition of the connection to the database repository.

The details of the setup are listed in ClearQuest Help: Installing and Upgrading > Deploying Rational ClearQuest > Configuring your environment after installing.

7.3.3.2 Jazz

The Jazz environment setup includes

- Creating a Jazz server repository for the product in context: Rational Team Concert or Rational Quality Manager
- Importing the licenses
- Configuring the application server
- Creating project areas with the desired process configuration
- Configuring the reporting solution
- Defining users and groups and LDAP connections
- Assigning users to license types

For detailed information on the Jazz server setup see Rational Quality Manager Help > Installing and upgrading > Setting up the Jazz server.

For the Rational Team Concert setup see the help pages of the specific edition, for example, Rational Team Concert Help > Installing and upgrading > Installing Rational Team Concert Standard edition.

The client setup includes the definition of the connection to the Jazz server, which usually means accepting the e-mail invitation to join the project.

7.3.4 Deploying Customizations

After the production environment has been set up, the customized schema model must then be set up. In the next sections we shall show how to import the ClearQuest schema and how to import the Jazz process template.

7.3.4.1 ClearQuest

For ClearQuest you need to import the schema that was developed in the test environment to the production master repository. This is done with the command

```
cqload importschema -dbset proddbset . . .
```

The next step is to apply the schema to the user production database and to the test database. This is performed in two stages. First, create empty databases with the database vendor tools (see the server installation instructions for detailed information for each database vendor).

Second, initialize the empty database from ClearQuest Designer. From the ClearQuest Eclipse Designer, right-click on the schema version and select Show > User Databases; the ClearQuest Database Admin window opens (Figure 7.7 shows this window). Click the icon Create Database and provide the physical database details. That will create the database table according to the schema definition.

You may wish to create additional test environments for future enhancements. Test environments can be created with database vendor tools or with ClearQuest Maintenance Tool and ClearQuest Designer. More information on creating test environments is presented in section 7.5.3, "Creating a Test Environment."

7.3.4.2 Jazz

For Rational Team Concert or Rational Quality Manager you need to import the process template that was developed in the test environment to the Jazz production server. After the process template has been imported, you need to create a new project area with this process template. The procedure is described in section 7.6, "Jazz Tool Mentor."

7.3.5 Importing Initial Data

Most organizations have change management data in an old system; this data is valuable, and it is essential to import it to the new ClearQuest system. The import process is a mini project and requires careful planning and execution.

The first decision is what to import. Some ask only for open work items; others ask for data from the past year. We suggest importing everything and closing the connection to the old database.

The next step is to perform the export of the data from the current system to files in comma-separated-value (CSV) format. The exporting method depends on the old system. If an export utility exists, that would be the easy way; otherwise use SQL commands to retrieve the database tables. Another method is to use scripting (such as VB or Perl); this method allows you to do data cleansing while exporting. Each ClearQuest record type should have a separate CSV file to import from.

After the data has been exported to a CSV file, you need to verify its correctness; the data must be valid for the system you are importing into. Extra notice should be taken of the following situations:

- A field contains more characters than the ClearQuest Short_String size.
- A field has a value that is not included in the ClearQuest choice list and Limit to List is checked.
- State field values do not match.
- A field references another record.

Once you have the import files clean and ready, you can start the import process. The importing order is important.

First, import the dynamic lists using the command-line utility

```
importutil importlist ...
```

Second, import stateless record data; you must import records in order of dependency. The lower level in the dependency hierarchy should be imported first. For example, if record type Application references record type Module, and record type Module references record type Function, import Function first, then Module, and then Application. After each import open the ClearQuest client and test the import. The import utility reports errors, but make sure you also perform some tests with the client to be safe.

Third, import state-based records. If you have a huge number of records to import, we suggest that you split the file into chunks of about one thousand records.

Performance Hint   You can run a few import processes in parallel, if there are no dependencies between them. Because the import is a sequential process, each record is processed one after the other and the process is slow, so splitting the import files can save time.

When dealing with fields that reference other stateless records, the ClearQuest Import Tool requires you to import the referenced record first. References to stateful records require a special process. The reference field contains the value of the unique key of the referenced record, which is the ID field. Because the ID is provided by the system during record creation, the record ID from the old system is not valid. It is even more complex when you have back-referenced fields. There are methods for importing records with references, and we recommend the following:

- Import the records without the referencing fields. Make sure to import the old ID to a special field called "old_id" (this is the most common approach).

- From the new ClearQuest database export the newly imported records; the only fields required for export are "old_id" and "id" (the new ID).

- In a copy of your original import file replace the values of the referencing fields (old_id) with the new ID. This can be easily done with a script.

- Now import the records in update mode; this will add the correct values to the referencing fields.

See section 7.5.1, "Importing Records with References," and section 7.5.2, "Importing Updates," for further discussion of importing challenges with ClearQuest Import Tool version 7.1.

7.3.5.1 Fixing Import Errors

The ClearQuest Import Tool creates a discarded records log file containing all records that were not imported because of errors. The error log file format is identical to the import format so it is easy to fix the errors and import again.

It is important to use a naming convention to ensure you are not missing data. A common naming convention is the following format: RecordType_Batch_Iteration.csv.

If there are many thousands of records, they can be split into manageable batches (one to three thousand); in this way you can easily open the file with your favorite spreadsheet tool. The iteration represents the import cycle; the first cycle number is 0, the second is 1, and so on.

For example, the first iteration will have the following files: Defect_1_0.csv, Defect_2_0.csv, Defect_3_0.csv, Product_1_0.csv, Module_1_0.csv, and so forth.

If there are errors during the import of defects in batch 3, rename the error file, augmenting the iteration to be Defect_3_1.csv, examine and fix the errors, and import again. If there are still errors in this iteration (1), repeat the process in a new iteration (2).

7.3.5.2 Import Validation

After data is imported with no errors, the import must be validated. Validation is usually performed by some stakeholders who are familiar with both the legacy system and the new system. They should check that no data is missing, that the change process can be completed according to the definition, and that dependencies between data objects are correct. You should allocate enough time for the validation as it is time-consuming.

7.3.6 Training

In large organizations the administrative tasks are divided among several roles; therefore, the administrator training should be adapted to those roles. The training for administrators should include the following:

- User administration
- Schema customization, possibly with parallel development
- Creating report formats with Crystal Reports, Rational SoDA, BIRT, or other reporting tools such as Rational Insight
- Importing and exporting data
- Security administration

The users of the change management system should be trained using the customized solution as it is more effective than general user training. The training for the end users should include the following:

- The user interface description
- The workflow process and the data required in each action
- Understanding and analyzing the results of queries, charts, and reports
- Creating queries and charts (this is not required for all users but mainly for leaders, power users, and quality assurance roles)

Rational University provides various public training classes. The Rational services organization can provide on-site customized training that meets your organization's needs.

7.3.7 Following Up on System Adoption

Training is not the last task of deployment. To ensure that the system is successfully adopted, and that users are satisfied and get the most out of the system, follow-up is required. The following are some suggestions for methods to obtain feedback:

- Allow users to enter defects and enhancement requests in the system itself. To do that, create an additional project, type, or category and call it ClearQuest (or RTC). This is a great way to get suggestions from the users of the system.

- Meet with the users face to face, talk to them, and learn from their experience. When required, deal with objections by enablement, suggesting better usage techniques and proposing enhancements in the next release.

- Request feedback either by a special form, in conversation, or via a system work item.

In various sections of the book we have suggested creating a project in the system so that users will be able to report enhancement requests and defects or even just add suggestions. This improves the users' experience and the trust between the users and the system owners. Needless to say, these requests should be followed up on a daily basis and handled with a sense of importance.

It is also important to maintain direct contact with the users. It is not possible to talk to every user, especially in global companies, but getting direct feedback is important to understanding the level of system adoption. A questionnaire is one technique for getting feedback. Another way is to create a special work item of type Feedback.

7.4 Maintenance

The purposes of change management system maintenance are

- To provide ongoing support to users
- To capture and fix defects and enhancements
- To improve system functionality and performance
- To support migrations to new platforms and upgrades to new revisions
- To provide a process to add new features and new integrations

In most cases the same team that deploys the change management system is also responsible for its maintenance, so there is no delivery to another role. This actually eases the maintenance process.

7.4.1 Defining the Change Process

The change management system, like any other software system, will change over time. Users will find defects and will ask for enhancements. So you need a process in place to

- Capture change requests
- Analyze and estimate effort and risks

- Prioritize and schedule a release date with stakeholders
- Design the solution and develop the required changes
- Perform the user acceptance tests with the requestor in the test environment
- Deliver changes to production
- Communicate changes to users and enable them when required

7.4.2 Ongoing Support

The primary role of support is being able to protect the users' data. For that a backup/restore plan is required. A periodic (daily) backup of the repository is essential. A test restoration of the data is required so you know how to restore it and how much time it takes.

Another support feature is the help mechanism. Users should have a way to contact a subject matter expert (SME) to ask questions and get help with issues. This could be a phone line, e-mail support, or a help-desk-like system, but the best is to use the change management system itself. You can create a work item type called Support where users can submit help requests; requests can be simple, such as adding a user to a group, requesting a query or report, or fixing errors and requesting modifications of forms and workflow. The SME will follow up and respond as required.

7.4.3 Improving Maintainability

Maintainability can be improved by

- Tools and utilities
- Design

Tools and utilities that are developed to maintain the system include utilities to import data into records, adding users, creating a new database, exporting data to various other tools for analysis, and exporting data to a sharing portal.

When the system is designed, maintenance issues should be considered; we discuss this topic in Chapter 8, "Development." Make your code reusable; eliminate hard-coding data in hooks by keeping data in records or dynamic lists that can be extracted using hook code. Keep the hook's code out of the schema to enable the ability to change the hook's functionality without having to modify the schema and upgrade the database. This subject is also discussed in Chapter 8.

7.5 ClearQuest Tool Mentor

In this section we include explanations of tools implementation subjects that are not described in other chapters and are important to complete the information on the relevant discipline.

7.5.1 Importing Records with References

Since ClearQuest version 7.1 the import and export tool is part of the Eclipse client and not a stand-alone utility. It has some minor advantages; for example, if you mark a query and start the export, the tool will export only the record that the query returns.

A new and important feature is the ability to deal with records that have references. Although this feature does not cover all options and situations, it saves a lot of the manual work required to replace the values in the import file, and the need to import twice: once in create mode and once in update mode.

Importing References in Pre-7 Releases   The process for importing references before the 7 release includes several steps:

Import records without the referencing fields.

Update the import file to include the new record IDs.

Import the referencing fields in update mode.

The import of records with referencing fields is done by checking the box Importing Self-reference Relationship and selecting the field that contains the record ID from the old system (the real reference will point to the ID of the record having the value in the old_id field). Figure 7.2 shows a screen shot of this step in the process.

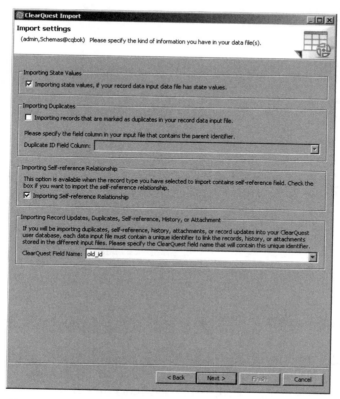

Figure 7.2   ClearQuest import settings: definition of self-referencing records import

The next step is field mapping, as most probably field names are not the same in the two systems. ClearQuest will automatically map fields with the same names. But if you import references, you have to check that all fields of type Reference_List that are imported have the Original_Identifier value as the field name you have previously selected (old_id) and the field old_id in the destination is mapped to id in the source. The example in Figure 7.3 shows that the field Children of type Reference_List is being imported.

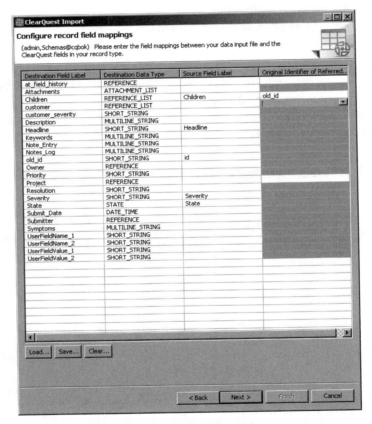

Figure 7.3   ClearQuest import: configure record field mappings

7.5.2 Importing Updates

Over time when the schema evolves and you add more fields, you may also need to update older records by inserting data into the new fields. For example, if you create a new field that is mandatory, you may wish to import value to existing records, so that users will not get errors when they modify these records. The ClearQuest Import Tool can operate in update mode, when the

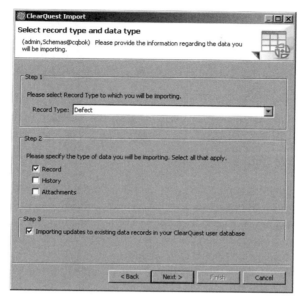

Figure 7.4   ClearQuest import of updates to existing records

"Importing updates to existing data records . . ." in step 3 of the import process is checked. This is shown in Figure 7.4.

Another issue is the ClearQuest Eclipse client preferences, as the default setting will enter a new record during update if the record to be updated is not found. Change this if it is not the desired feature, as shown in Figure 7.5.

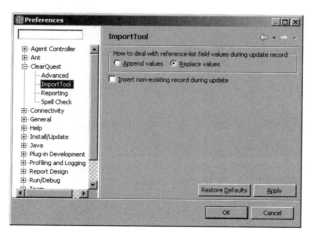

Figure 7.5   Setting ClearQuest Import Tool preferences: behavior with reference list fields

7.5.3 Creating a Test Environment

The best way to create a test environment is by copying the production environment to another environment. The test environment can be on another physical machine or on the same server if enough resources are available. You can perform the procedure with ClearQuest tools or with the help of the database vendor tools.

7.5.3.1 Creating a Test Environment with Database Vendor Tools

The fastest technique is to use the database vendor tools to copy the databases. The DBA can restore the backup to the new environment. After the master repository and the user production databases are copied, change the properties of the repository as the database contains the properties of the production environment.

Using the ClearQuest Maintenance tool, add a new connection to the new test master repository; Figure 7.6 shows a new connection called QATest. Select the new connection and you will see that the server properties are the production server properties. As shown in Figure 7.6, select Schema Repository > Update > Selected Connection.

Replace the properties with those of the new environment; in this example it is the server name.

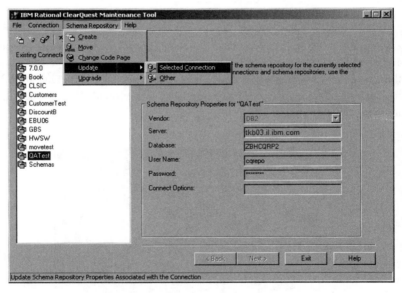

Figure 7.6   Updating the properties of the master repository for the test environment using the ClearQuest Maintenance tool

The master repository was updated to the new environment but the user database still points to the production environment. To change the user database properties, open ClearQuest

Designer. In the ClearQuest Schema Repository Explorer select the newly created repository and connect to it. Open the list of databases by right-clicking and selecting Show > User Databases.

Figure 7.7 is an example of the same QATest repository with the user database.

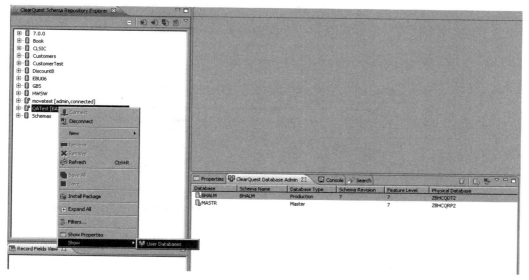

Figure 7.7 A ClearQuest Designer (Eclipse) view of database properties in a repository. Database types are Master, Production, and Test.

Select the production database, right-click, and select Properties. In the General Database Information form modify the properties for the new environment. In Figure 7.8, the DB2 server name needs to be replaced.

If additional user databases were copied to the test environment, repeat the modifications for each one of them.

WINDOWS CLEARQUEST DESIGNER

If you are still using the Windows version of ClearQuest Designer, the procedure is a bit different:

1. Open the Designer, but do not open the schema.
2. Select Database > Update User Database Properties ....
3. Select the database, and click the Update button.
4. Modify the properties to meet the new environment.
5. Click the Update button.

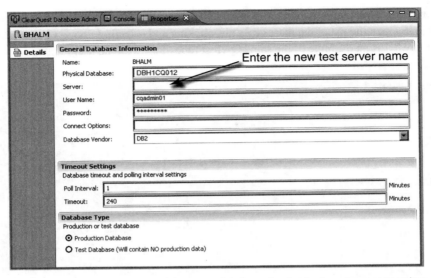

Figure 7.8   Updating the properties of the user database for the test environment using ClearQuest Designer (Eclipse)

7.5.3.2 Creating a Test Environment with ClearQuest Tools

You can create the test environment with ClearQuest tools only. The advantages are that you can copy the database to a different vendor repository and you are not dependent on others. The disadvantages are that the process takes much more time, and during the process the database is locked and users cannot log in to ClearQuest.

The process can be performed with the ClearQuest Maintenance tool to move the repository and ClearQuest Designer to move the user databases. But we propose using the `installutil` command as it is simpler. It is a two-step copy: first you copy the schema repository and then you copy the user database(s).

To copy the schema repository to another location, open the command prompt and run the `installutil` command. Before running the `installutil` command, make sure that Clear-Quest Designer is closed or the `dbset` is disconnected. The command syntax is as follows:

```
installutil copyschemarepo -dbset dbset_name
          cq_login
          cq_password
          to_db_vendor
          to_server
          to_database
          to_dbo_login
          to_dbo_password
          to_rw_login
```

```
to_rw_password
to_ro_login
to_ro_password
connect_options
```

NOTES ON INSTALLUTIL COPYSCHEMAREPO

cq_login is the superuser.

to_* are all the parameters of the target (test) environment.

The three users (dbo, rw, and ro) are for backward compatibility; in most systems a single user is used, so just repeat the same values for the three users. For Microsoft Access use " " for all users.

Connect options for each vendor are as follows:

- Oracle: HOST=host;SID=sid;SERVER_VER=[9.2,10.1];
    CLIENT_VER=[9.2];LOB_TYPE=[clob];PORT=port_number)
- SQL_SERVER: PORT=port_number
- DB2: PORT=port_number;DB2_SECURE_LOGIN;
    SERVER_VER=[8.1,8.2];HOST=host;DATABASE=database
- MS_ACCESS: " "

The following is a command example:

```
installutil copyschemarepo -dbset dbset_name admin password \
DB2 abc21z.dcenter.il.ibm.com cq_master db2admin db2password \
db2admin db2password db2admin db2password PORT=2002
```

After the master repository has been successfully copied, you need to create a new connection to the new schema repository. This is done with the ClearQuest Maintenance tool as previously explained and as demonstrated in Figure 7.8.

The next stage is to copy the user(s) database(s) using the following command:

```
installutil copyuserdb -dbset dbset_name
        cq_login
        cq_password
        user_dbname
        to_user_db_vendor
        to_user_server
        to_user_database
        to_user_dbo_login
        to_user_dbo_password
        to_user_rw_login
```

```
to_user_rw_password
connect_options
```

Note   The previous notes on `copyschemarepo` are valid also for the `copyuserdb` command.

After the user database has been copied successfully, you need to set the database properties, as the master database still stores the production information for the user database. This is done with ClearQuest Designer as follows:

1. Open ClearQuest Designer.
2. Connect to the new test environment repository.
3. Open the ClearQuest Database Admin view as shown in Figure 7.9.
4. Select the user database, right-click, and select Properties.
5. Change the properties in the dialog to those of the new database (see Figure 7.8).
6. Save the changes by selecting File > Save.

Figure 7.9   ClearQuest Designer database view

If you have copied more than one user database, repeat the steps to change the properties of each user database.

Now you have a new test environment that is identical to the production environment and is ready for development and testing.

Database Locking and Unlocking   When running the command `installutil copyuserdb ...` the source database is locked; when the database is copied successfully (i.e., exit code = 0), the database is unlocked. But if an error occurs during the process, because of network failure, for example, the source database remains locked. To unlock the user database use the command

```
installutil unlockuserdb db_vendor server database dbo_login
dbo_password connect_options
```

To unlock the schema repository after copy failure there is an equivalent command:

```
installutil unlockschemarepo db_vendor server database dbo_login
dbo_password connect_options
```

7.6 Jazz Tool Mentor

In this section we include explanations of tools implementation subjects that are not described in other chapters and are important to complete the information on the relevant discipline.

7.6.1 Creating a Jazz Project with the Common Process Template

The next sections describe the process of creating a Jazz process template file and using this file to create a new Jazz project area.

7.6.1.1 Generating the Process Template

To create a process template from a customized Jazz process configuration, use the Rational Team Concert Eclipse client IDE.

1. In the Rational Team Concert Team Artifacts view, select the project area and use Generate Process Template from the context menu.

2. In the dialog provide a meaningful name, such as SAPBH_process_template.

3. The new template appears in the Process Template view (see Figure 7.10).

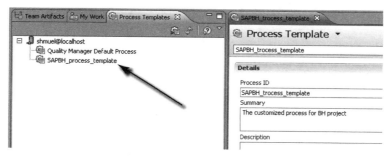

Figure 7.10 Creating a process template with Rational Team Concert Eclipse

7.6.1.2 Exporting the Process Template

To export a process template from the (development) repository, you can use either Rational Team Concert Eclipse or the Web client.

To export with Rational Team Concert Eclipse, follow these steps:

1. In the Rational Team Concert client click File > Export. The wizard will guide you.

2. In the Export window, expand the Team Process folder, select Process Template, and click Next.

3. Select the development repository that contains the process template that you want to export and click Next.

4. Select a customized process template and click Next.

5. Click the Archive file radio button, choose the destination archive folder, and click Finish.

To export with the Web client, follow these steps:

1. Log in as Jazz Admin to the Web interface to the development repository.

2. Select the Process Template Management tab.

3. Under the Actions column click the Export Template icon of the template you want to export. See Figure 7.11.

4. Select the export .zip folder location and click OK.

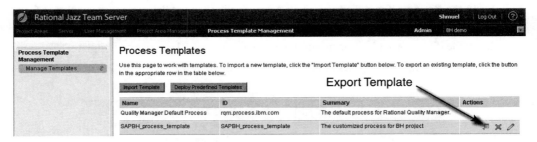

Figure 7.11   Export process template with the Web client

7.6.1.3 Importing the Process Template to Another Repository

Now we want to import the process template that we have exported from the development environment to the production repository. We can use either Rational Team Concert Eclipse or the Web client.

To import with Rational Team Concert Eclipse, perform the following steps:

1. Click File > Import.

2. In the Import window, expand the Team Process folder, select Process Template, and click Next.

3. Select the production repository where you want to add the process template and click Next.

4. Enter the path and directory where the process template .zip file was previously saved and click Finish.

To import with the Web client, perform the following steps:

1. Log in as Jazz Admin to the Web interface to the production repository.

2. Select the Process Template Management tab.

3. Click the Import Template button.

4. Click Browse and navigate to the .zip file that contains the process template saved in the previous steps and click OK.

7.6.1.4 Creating a New Project Area with the Imported Process Template

To create a new project using the imported process template you can use either Rational Team Concert Eclipse or the Web client.

To create a project with Rational Team Concert Eclipse, follow these steps:

1. Click File > New > Project Area.

2. Enter the project name.

3. Select the process template.

4. Click on the radio button to select "automatically initialize…" and click Finish.

To create a project with the Web client, follow these steps:

1. Log in as Jazz Admin to the Web interface to the production repository.

2. Select the Project Area Management tab.

3. Click the Create Project Area button.

4. In the Process section select the new process template (as shown in Figure 7.12) and click Save.

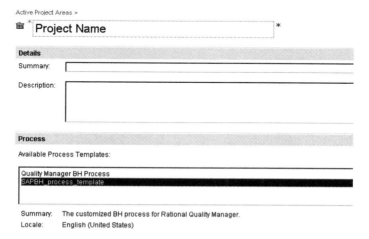

Figure 7.12   Creating a project area with a common process template

7.7 Resources

Grubb, Penny, and Armstrong A. Takang, *Software Maintenance: Concepts and Practice, 2nd ed.* (River Edge: World Scientific, 2003).

IBM Rational, "Rational Unified Process, RUP for Small Projects," www-01.ibm.com/software/awdtools/rup/index.html (accessed February 22, 2011).

Staff, IBM Rational. "Deployment Solutions for Rational ClearQuest," *IBM developerWorks*, www.ibm.com/developerworks/rational/library/5211.html?S_TACT=105AGX15, 2004 (accessed February 22, 2011).

7.8 Summary

In this chapter we discussed the Implementation, Testing, Deployment, and Maintenance disciplines. We explained the purpose of each discipline and the recommended stages of each discipline process. For each discipline we described the recommended tasks, split into ClearQuest tasks and Jazz tasks. For some of the tasks we referenced other chapters in the book or the tool mentor section in this chapter.

For each discipline we discussed the roles involved, such as schema developer, administrators, testers, trainers, and support engineer. Roles may differ from one organization to another.

The tool mentor section of the chapter provided examples of tools usage related to the discussed discipline, such as the ClearQuest Import tool and creating the environment for system testing.

In the Jazz tool mentor section we explained how to create a common process template, exporting and importing the process template, and how to create new project area with this template.

Development

Developing change management applications is in many aspects different from a regular software project, mainly because of the special development environment provided by IBM Rational ClearQuest and by IBM Rational Team Concert.

In this chapter we shall explain the special development considerations for preparing the development process and discuss techniques that can help large organizations overcome the limitations in ClearQuest.

We start by demonstrating how to implement the design patterns explained in Chapter 2, "Disciplines: Requirements, Analysis & Design," using ClearQuest and Rational Team Concert (RTC). We continue with reusable assets: schemas, packages, and code. In section 8.2, "Parallel Development," we explain methods that allow a team to work in parallel and accelerate the ClearQuest application delivery. In section 8.3, "Comparing and Merging Schema Versions," we explain development techniques using the new Eclipse Designer; we focus on comparing versions and merging, features that are not available in ClearQuest Windows Designer. Section 8.4, "Storing Hooks Externally," deals with techniques to improve maintainability by storing hooks outside the schema. The following sections are more relevant for large organizations; we provide a procedure for releasing a new version to production. We briefly discuss some of the additional considerations for customers who have ClearQuest MultiSite when developing their ClearQuest applications. In section 8.7, "ClearQuest Script Debugging," we discuss unit testing and debugging techniques. Section 8.8, "Other Development Considerations," is a collection of various subjects that ClearQuest administrators struggle with. Among others we discuss listing techniques, good administration practice, utilities assisting in maintenance, and more. In section 8.9, "Web Considerations," we discuss the needs of applications that will be used with Web browsers. The last section includes some tips regarding expected future changes.

8.1 ClearQuest Schema Development

After your organization has defined the requirements and you have made the ClearQuest application design, it is time to start developing the application. Where should you start? ClearQuest provides some schemas; should you start with one of those, or should you start with a blank schema? Most of the built-in schemas are related to integrations with other Rational products: AnalystStudio with RequisitePro, TestStudio with TestManager, UCM with ClearCase, and Enterprise with all of the above. The DefectTracking schema is often used as a starting point for software defect tracking.

Another option is to look for a good schema at developerworks.com or in one of the forums. We definitely suggest looking at some schemas that may be candidates to be your starting baseline. You can also take elements from other schemas that work for you and add them to your base schema. In the next paragraphs we shall discuss some development considerations.

8.1.1 Common Schema (ALM)

A common schema is an idea raised by ClearQuest community members who asked themselves the same the questions we have just raised: how to start developing a schema. The idea is to gather requirements and best practices that will cover the needs of many organizations. The 80-20 rule is very relevant here—a common or base schema that will cover 80 percent of the requirements of the organization with minimal development effort to get started. The other 20 percent will be developed to cover the specific and unique requirements of each organization, and they can be developed over time. This idea led Rational to develop the Application Lifecycle Management (ALM) schema that is now provided with ClearQuest. This is a good starting point for many organizations.

Organizations coming from the same domain such as finance or electronics could probably use a common schema that will cover many of their basic needs.

8.1.2 Implementing Patterns

In section 2.3, "Design Patterns," in Chapter 2, "Disciplines: Requirements, Analysis & Design," we discussed design patterns. In this chapter we shall provide some examples of implementations of those patterns (also called idioms). You can use patterns that meet the requirements of the system you develop. We provide some of the implementations in Perl and others in BASIC, but each one can be implemented in both languages.

8.1.2.1 Closing Pattern

The purpose of the Closing pattern is to capture the closing type and the closing reason. (See section 2.3.1, "Closing Pattern," in Chapter 2, "Disciplines: Requirements, Analysis & Design," for the definition.) The pattern is implemented by adding two or more fields to each state-based record type.

Table 8.1 Suggested Fields to Implement the Closing Pattern

Field Name	Field Type	Comments
CloseType	Short_String	Choice list proposed values: Resolved, Rejected, Deferred, Not a Defect, Work as Designed, Can't Replicate, Enhancement.
CloseReason	Multiline_String	
CloseDate	DateTime	Optional field, as the CloseDate exists also in the history table, but querying against the history table is complex and slow. We do recommend adding this field.

The CloseType choice list values can be divided into two types:

- **Type one:** The action was done to close the work item; values would be Fixed, Fixed Indirectly, Coding, Configuration, and so on.

- **Type two:** No work was done on the product; values would be Not a Defect, Work as Designed, Can't Replicate, and so on.

ALM Note   In the ALM schema the CloseType field is called ResolutionCode.

The Perl script in Listing 8.1 is an example of implementing the Closing pattern in the ClearQuest action Reject initialization hook. Notice that values are autoset for the fields Close-Date and CloseType and that the requiredness of the field CloseReason is set to Mandatory. We could, of course, set the requiredness of the field CloseReason in the behaviors table.

Listing 8.1   Implementing the Closing Pattern

```
sub Bug_Initialization {
    my($actionname, $actiontype) = @_;
    # $actionname as string scalar
    # $actiontype as long scalar
    # action is Reject
    # record type name is Bug
    # Start User Code
    # Do any setup for the action here.

    # purpose: Set close type and date, and require close reason

    my $date = GetCurrentDate() . " " . GetCurrentTime();
    $entity->SetFieldValue("CloseDate", $date);
```

continues

Listing 8.1   Implementing the Closing Pattern (*Continued*)

```
$entity->SetFieldValue("CloseType", "Rejected");
$entity->SetFieldRequirednessForCurrentAction("CloseReason",
        $CQPerlExt::CQ_MANDATORY);


# End User Code
}
```

A similar hook should be used for all actions that lead to an end state, for example, Close and Reject. It is also possible to set the fields' CloseReason and CloseType behavior values to Mandatory in the Closed state column in the behaviors table.

Implementing the Closing Pattern in Jazz

To implement this pattern in Rational Team Concert you have to set the preconditions of the relevant properties (fields) for the closing states. This is done in several steps; in the initial steps you define the operational behaviors and in the following steps you define the preconditions.

1. In Rational Team Concert open the project and select the Process Configuration tab.

2. Under Configuration expand Team Configuration and select Operation Behavior.

3. In Operation Behavior expand Work Items and mark the role for the Save Work Item (server). In Figure 8.1 you can see that the role Everyone (default) was selected, but you can select other roles depending on your process.

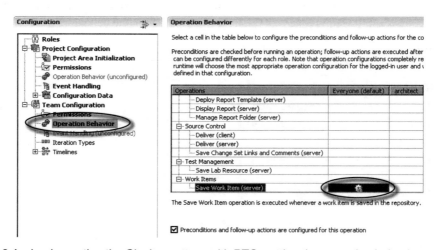

Figure 8.1   Implementing the Closing pattern with RTC: setting the operation behavior

4. Check the box "Preconditions and follow-up actions are configured for this operation."

5. Under Preconditions select the Required Properties precondition (see Figure 8.2). If it is not in the list click Add... and select it.

6. Under Category or Type select the work item type that is relevant to this pattern. You can repeat this operation for more than one work item type. In Figure 8.2 you can see that com.ibm.team.workitem.workItemType is the one we expanded.

7. Mark the Closed state and click on the Edit... button to select the attribute. The attribute is actually the required property. In Figure 8.2 you can see that the property Resolution_Description was selected. Resolution_Description is a custom attribute that we have created for this pattern.

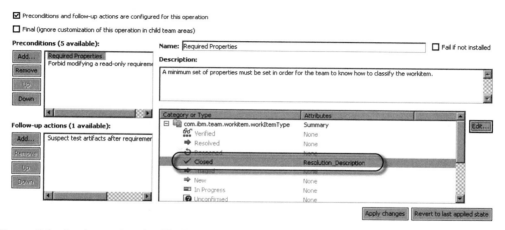

Figure 8.2 Implementing the Closing pattern with RTC: setting preconditions

When the user selects the Close action, the Resolution_Description property will be marked as required (red star); the user will not be able to save the work item without filling in the Resolution_Description property.

8.1.2.2 Triage Pattern

The purpose of the Triage pattern is to assign a work item to the right solution provider and to set the priority of the work. Implementing the Triage pattern involves setting the Owner (or equivalent) field to Mandatory prior to changing the state to Opened (or equivalent). In ClearQuest implementing the Triage pattern involves setting the fields Owner and Priority to Mandatory for state Opened and all states that follow this state in the workflow.

Figure 8.3 displays the ClearQuest behaviors table of the Defect record type. The triage action is Assign which will transition the record to the Assigned state. Note that both Owner and Priority are set to Mandatory for the states Assigned, Opened, Resolved, and Closed.

	Submitted	Assigned	Opened	Resolved	Closed	Duplicate	Postponed	Default Behavior
Attachments	OPTIONAL	OPTIONAL	OPTIONAL	OPTIONAL	OPTIONAL	OPTIONAL	OPTIONAL	OPTIONAL
customer	OPTIONAL	OPTIONAL	OPTIONAL	OPTIONAL	OPTIONAL	OPTIONAL	OPTIONAL	OPTIONAL
customer_severity	OPTIONAL	OPTIONAL	OPTIONAL	OPTIONAL	OPTIONAL	OPTIONAL	OPTIONAL	OPTIONAL
dbid	READONLY	READONLY	READONLY	READONLY	READONLY	READONLY	READONLY	READONLY
Description	OPTIONAL	OPTIONAL	OPTIONAL	OPTIONAL	OPTIONAL	OPTIONAL	OPTIONAL	OPTIONAL
Headline	MANDATORY	MANDATORY	MANDATORY	MANDATORY	MANDATORY	MANDATORY	MANDATORY	MANDATORY
history	READONLY	READONLY	READONLY	READONLY	READONLY	READONLY	READONLY	READONLY
id	READONLY	OPTIONAL	READONLY	READONLY	READONLY	READONLY	OPTIONAL	OPTIONAL
is_active	READONLY	READONLY	READONLY	READONLY	READONLY	READONLY	READONLY	READONLY
is_duplicate	READONLY	OPTIONAL	READONLY	READONLY	READONLY	READONLY	OPTIONAL	OPTIONAL
Keywords	OPTIONAL	OPTIONAL	OPTIONAL	OPTIONAL	OPTIONAL	OPTIONAL	OPTIONAL	OPTIONAL
lock_version	READONLY	READONLY	READONLY	READONLY	READONLY	READONLY	READONLY	READONLY
locked_by	READONLY	READONLY	READONLY	READONLY	READONLY	READONLY	READONLY	READONLY
Note_Entry	OPTIONAL	OPTIONAL	OPTIONAL	OPTIONAL	OPTIONAL	OPTIONAL	OPTIONAL	OPTIONAL
Notes_Log	READONLY	READONLY	READONLY	READONLY	READONLY	READONLY	READONLY	READONLY
old_id	READONLY	READONLY	READONLY	READONLY	READONLY	READONLY	READONLY	READONLY
Owner	OPTIONAL	MANDATORY	MANDATORY	MANDATORY	MANDATORY	OPTIONAL	OPTIONAL	MANDATORY
Priority	OPTIONAL	MANDATORY	MANDATORY	MANDATORY	MANDATORY	OPTIONAL	OPTIONAL	MANDATORY
Project	OPTIONAL	OPTIONAL	OPTIONAL	OPTIONAL	OPTIONAL	OPTIONAL	OPTIONAL	OPTIONAL
ratl_mastership	OPTIONAL	OPTIONAL	OPTIONAL	OPTIONAL	OPTIONAL	OPTIONAL	OPTIONAL	OPTIONAL
record_type	READONLY	READONLY	READONLY	READONLY	READONLY	READONLY	READONLY	READONLY

Figure 8.3   Implementing the Triage pattern

It is possible to perform automatic assignment in several situations. In section 5.7.2, "Hook to Automatically Set Responsible Based on Role of Type Single," in Chapter 5, "Roles," we discussed this subject in detail.

Implementing the Triage Pattern in Jazz

The Triage pattern is implemented in Rational Team Concert in a similar way to the Closing pattern described in section 8.1.2.1, "Closing Pattern." You have to set the operational behavior. In this idiom you select the Triaged state, click Edit…, and select the properties Owned By and Priority. In Figure 8.4 on the next page you can see that the property Due Date was selected in addition to Owned By and Priority that we have defined in the pattern. That is absolutely fine as many rules can be applied as well as variants of the pattern.

8.1.2.3 Parent Control Pattern

The purpose of the Parent Control pattern is to ensure that all children of a record are in the same state before the parent state is changed. (See section 2.3.3, "Parent Control Pattern," in Chapter 2, "Disciplines: Requirements, Analysis & Design," for the definition.)

The code in Listing 8.2 demonstrates how to implement the Parent Control pattern. In the parent record add a validation hook that calls the `ChildrenStatus()` subroutine; the code for `ChildrenStatus` is provided in Listing 8.3.

This validation hook should be added to any action you want to check, such as Resolve or Close. Listing 8.2 is a defect validation hook for the action Resolve.

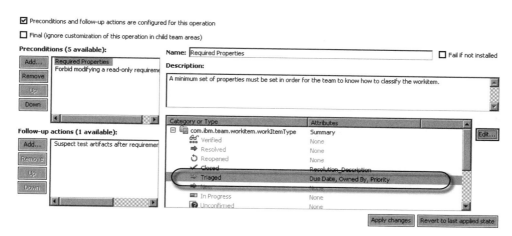

Figure 8.4 Implementing the Triage pattern in RTC

Listing 8.2 Implementing the Parent Control Pattern

```perl
sub Defect_Validation {
   my($actionname, $actiontype) = @_;
    my $result;
    # $actionname as string scalar
    # $actiontype as long scalar
    # $result as string scalar
    # action is Resolve
    # record type name is Defect
    # Start User Code

    # Purpose: Enforce the Parent-Control Pattern

    my $id = $entity->GetDisplayName();
    my $children = ChildrenStatus ($id, "Resolved");
       $session->OutputDebugString("Children status: $children \n");
    if ( $children == 2) {
         $result = "To Resolve this record all children must be
                    in status Resolved.";
      }
    # End User Code
    return $result;
}
```

The global subroutine `ChildrenStatus()` checks the states of all child records and denies the action if at least one of the children has not reached the relevant state. This pattern can be applied to the Closed state or the Resolved state or any other state where child status affects the parent status. This implementation assumes that parent and children are of same type, but it can be easily converted to a more general solution.

Listing 8.3   Checking the Status of Child Records

```
sub ChildrenStatus {
    my ($parentid, $closed_state) = @_;

# Purpose:  return the status of children records
# Input:  parentid
#         closed_state- The name of the state to verify
#
# Output:  return value:  0 = no children,
#                         1 = all children closed
#                         2 = at least one opened child

    my $session = $entity->GetSession();
    my $entitytype = $entity->GetEntityDefName();
    my $parentObj = $session->GetEntity($entitytype, $parentid);
    my $children = $parentObj->GetFieldValue("Children")-
>GetValueAsList();

    my ($total_children, $total_closed_children) = (0, 0);
    my $result = 0;

    foreach my $childid (@$children) {
        my $childObj = $session->GetEntity($entitytype, $childid);
        my $childrentate = $childObj->LookupStateName();
        $total_children++;
        if ($childrentate eq $closed_state) {
            $total_closed_children++;
        }
    }
    if ($total_children) {
        if ($total_closed_children == $total_children) {
            $result = 1;
        } else {
            $result = 2;
```

```
        }
    } else {
        $result = 0;
    }
    return $result;
}
```

Note We pass the parent record ID to get the parent entity, although this is not necessary when the hook is running from a parent action. This is done so that we can use the same hook in other situations, such as to check the status of other records. This makes the subroutine more general and easier to reuse in other parent/child control situations.

8.1.2.4 Child Control Pattern

The purpose of the Child Control pattern is to ensure that the parent changes its state when all its children have reached the same state. In this pattern the child autosets the state of the parent. (See section 2.3.4, "Child Control Pattern," in Chapter 2, "Disciplines: Requirements, Analysis & Design," for the design pattern definition.)

The code in Listing 8.4 is an example of an implementation of the Child Control pattern. In the child record add a commit hook with the BASIC code in this listing.

Listing 8.4 Implementing the Child Control Pattern

```
Sub Defect_Commit(actionname, actiontype)
' actionname As String
' actiontype As Long
' action is Resolve
' record type name is Defect
' Start User Code

' Purpose: Move the parent record to state Resolved if all siblings
'          are resolved.
' Method:  Get the parent record (we assume there is only one parent)
'          Get all children of the parent and check their states.
'          If all children are resolved edit the parent record with
'          action Resolve to change its state.

Dim ParentObj
Dim sessionObj
Dim defectChildEntityObj
```

continues

Listing 8.4   Implementing the Child Control Pattern (*Continued*)

```
set  = GetSession
ThisID = GetDisplayName
ActionJustPerformed = GetActionName
StateStatus = ""
SameState = 0

parent_id = GetFieldValue("Parent").GetValue()
if parent_id <> "" then
 set ParentObj = sessionobj.GetEntity("defect", parent_id)
 ChildRefList = ParentObj.GetFieldValue("Children").GetValue
 ChildArray = split (ChildRefList, vbLf)

 For Each ChildID In ChildArray
  set defectChildEntityObj = sessionobj.GetEntity("defect", ChildID)
  CurrentState = defectChildEntityObj.GetFieldValue("State").GetValue


  if StateStatus = "" then
   StateStatus = CurrentState
   SameState = 1
  elseif StateStatus = CurrentState then
   SameState = 1
  else
   SameState = 0
  end if

 Next

if SameState = 1 then
  ' Change the parent state
  sessionobj.EditEntity ParentObj, ActionJustPerformed
  status = ParentObj.Validate
  if (status <> "") then
  end if
  ParentObj.Commit
 end if
end if
  ' End User Code
End Sub
```

This will do the job, but if you want to apply the same pattern not only to the Resolved state but also to the Closed state, you will have to copy the same hook to the Close action commit hook. This is not very efficient from a maintenance point of view. We therefore suggest creating a global hook and calling it from the required actions, as demonstrated in the Parent Control pattern in Listing 8.3.

Jazz Note In the current version of Jazz (2.0) the Child Control pattern and the Parent Control pattern cannot be implemented.

8.1.2.5 Dead End Pattern

The purpose of the Dead End pattern is to ensure that a record cannot be reopened after closure. (See section 2.3.5, "Dead End Pattern," in Chapter 2, "Disciplines: Requirements, Analysis & Design," for the definition.) The Dead End pattern is implemented by ensuring that no action of type Change_State can be executed when the record is in Closed state. It can easily be checked in the ClearQuest states table, as demonstrated in Figure 8.5. The state Delivered (the Closed state) column has no actions; therefore the schema conforms to the Dead End pattern.

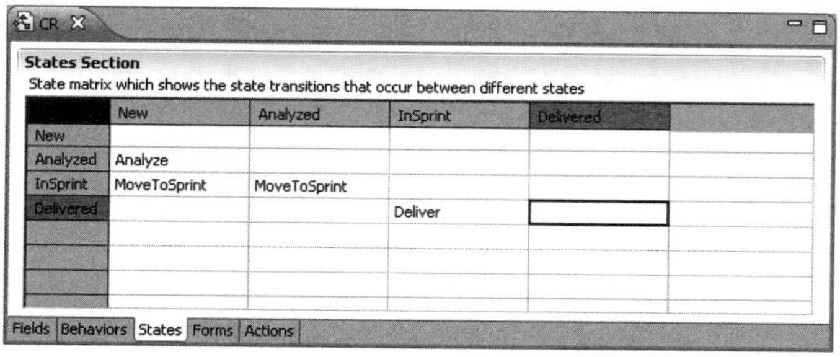

Figure 8.5 Implementing the Dead End design pattern: preventing a change state

A firmer policy of this pattern is to not allow any modifications to the record once it is in the Closed state. This is achieved by clearing the Closed states from any action of type Modify. In Figure 8.6 you can see that the Modify action is not allowed when the record is in state Delivered, which is the Closed state.

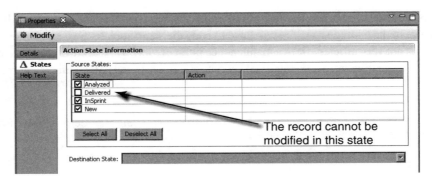

Figure 8.6   Implementing the Dead End design pattern: prevent field changes

Implementing the Dead End Pattern in Jazz

Implementing the Dead End pattern in Rational Team Concert work items is very similar to the procedure we have described for ClearQuest.

1. In Rational Team Concert open the project and select the Process Configuration tab.
2. Under Configuration expand Configuration Data and expand Work Items (advanced).
3. Click on Workflow to open it, and choose the workflow from the choice list.
4. In the Transition table, examine the row of the Closed state (the From row). Make sure all selections in this row are None.

Figure 8.7 demonstrates how the Eclipse Way workflow was altered to include the Dead End pattern by selecting None in the transition to the Reopened state.

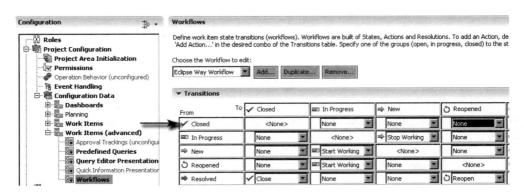

Figure 8.7   Implementing the Dead End pattern in RTC

8.1.2.6 Data Hierarchy Pattern

The purpose of the Data Hierarchy pattern is to allow a hierarchical relation between data records. This allows you to organize product component relations and to generate bills of materials (BOMs) for the system to be tracked. Using the pattern will prevent user errors when selecting components and their versions and when selecting related elements such as modules of products or functions of modules.

To implement the pattern use a field of type Reference_List to point to a lower level in the hierarchy. See Figure 8.9 for an example of a hierarchy of records and the code in Listing 8.6 as an implementation of the Data Hierarchy pattern.

The pattern is applicable to any ClearQuest stateless record type.

Jazz Note The pattern is not applicable to Jazz work items, as the stateless record type is not supported.

8.1.2.7 Superuser Modification Pattern

The purpose of the Superuser Modification pattern is to allow the superuser to modify a record in all states even when the process rules do not allow it. See section 2.3.7, "Superuser Modification Pattern," in Chapter 2, "Disciplines: Requirements, Analysis & Design," for more information.

The pattern is implemented by adding an action of type Modify to each stateful record type. To this action we add two hooks: an Access_Control hook to verify that the user has superuser permission, and an initialization hook to set the requiredness of all the fields to Optional. This allows the superuser to modify fields that are read-only for other users. Note that the action is stored in the history table, and if the Audit Trail package is applied, the fields that the superuser changed will be registered in the log.

In Figure 8.8 you can see an action called SuperModify of type Modify and the Access_Control hook that is set to the group Admin.

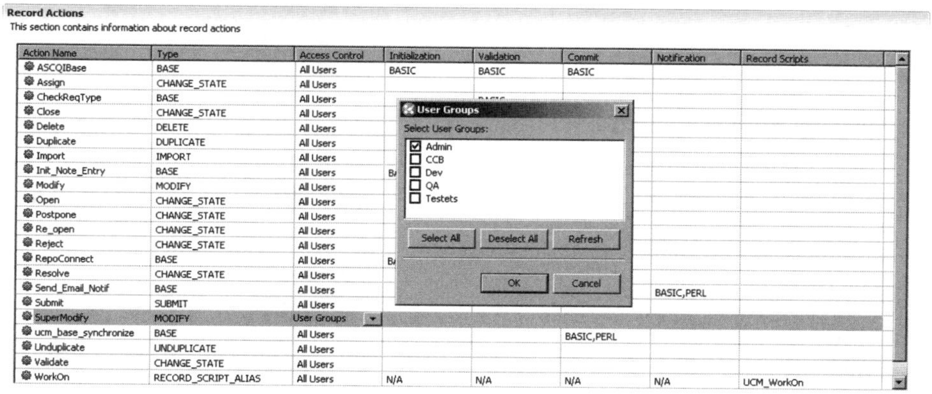

Figure 8.8 Implementing the Superuser Modification design pattern

The Perl code in Listing 8.5 is an example of the initialization hook for the action Super-Modify. Note that in this script all fields are set to Optional; if this is not desirable you can revert some of the fields to ReadOnly or Mandatory by using the session method

```
SetFieldRequirednessForCurrentAction()
```

Listing 8.5   Implementing the Superuser Modification Pattern

```
sub Defect_Initialization {
    my($actionname, $actiontype) = @_;
    # $actionname as string scalar
    # $actiontype as long scalar
    # action is SuperModify
    # record type name is Defect
    # Start User Code
 my $sessionobj = $entity->GetSession();
 my $fieldnamelist = $entity->GetFieldNames();
 foreach my $fieldname (@$fieldnamelist) {
$entity->SetFieldRequirednessForCurrentAction($fieldname,
          $CQPerlExt::CQ_OPTIONAL);
 }
    # End User Code
}
```

8.1.3 Employing Reusable Assets

Reusable assets are any part of the schema that can be saved or exported and later can be used, by you and by others, in another schema or another record type. Hook code is the obvious example, as many times we need to perform the same functionality or use the same pattern again. Many elements of the ClearQuest schema can be reused: record types, action hooks, field hooks, global hooks, and forms. In order to be effectively reused, the asset should be well documented, published, and accessible.

8.1.3.1 Writing Reusable Code

You spend a lot of time on writing code, testing, and debugging, so this is the most rewarding area in which to invest in creating reusable assets. The following are just few common examples:

- Convert user LoginName to User_FullName
- Many variants of choice list population
- Automatic assignment
- Auto-change state

- Many variants of cloning a record
- Time calculation and formatting

The developerWorks site contains a list of hooks and code examples organized by category. It is important that you be familiar with that site:

> ClearQuest Users, "IBM Rational ClearQuest Hooks Index," *IBM developerWorks*, www.ibm.com/developerworks/rational/library/4236.html (accessed February 24, 2011).

The following is an example of how to write a hook in such a way that it will be easy to reuse, but first some explanation. The schema was designed to track defects in a computer-aided design/computer-aided manufacturing (CAD/CAM) system. The CAD system has several products; in each product there are modules, and in each module there are functions. Product is a stateless record type and has a Reference_List field to Module, which is also a stateless record type. Module has a Reference_List field to Function, which is also a stateless record type. In the Defect record type there are three fields of type Reference that point to the stateless record types just mentioned (Product, Module, and Function). These three fields need to be dynamically populated as they depend on each other. When the user selects a product, the choice list of modules needs to be populated, and when Module is selected, the choice list of functions needs to be populated.

Figure 8.9 demonstrates the described ClearQuest record types and the way they reference each other.

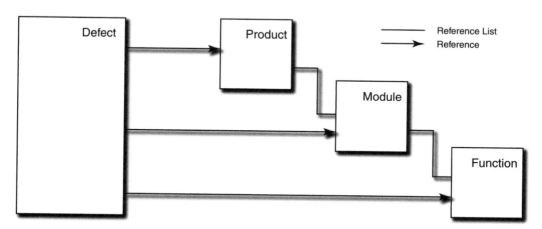

Figure 8.9 Record types and referencing relations

The choice list hooks for the dependent fields are very similar to each other, so it is easier to write a subroutine that will be called from all fields. The calling function syntax is

```
ChoiceList(RefField, RefedRecord, FilterField,
          RefFieldInRefedRecord);
```

The choice list hook of the field Module is

```
@choices = ChoiceList ("Product", "Product", "name", "Modules");
```

The choice list hook of the field Function is

```
@choices = ChoiceList ("Module", "Module", "name", "Functions");
```

The code for the global subroutine is provided in Listing 8.6.

Listing 8.6   Reusing the `ChoiceList` Library Subroutine

```
sub ChoiceList {
# Purpose: build the choice-list of a dependent list
# Input:
#     dep_field - Parent field of type reference that the list
#                 is dependent on (e.g. "Product")
#     dep_rectype - The parent referenced record type (e.g. "Product")
#                   that contains the reference field to the list
#     filter - field for the compare equal query filter (e.g "name")
#     list_field - The field in the parent record type that references
#                  the list we want to build (e.g., "Modules")
# Output:
#     Returns @list       - the dependent choice list
# Written By: Etan Shomrai

my ($dep_field, $dep_rectype, $filter, $list_field) = @_;
my $session = $entity->GetSession();
my @list ;

my @dep_field_val = ($entity->GetFieldValue($dep_field)->GetValue());
my $queryDefObj = $session->BuildQuery($dep_rectype);

my $filterOp = $queryDefObj->BuildFilterOperator(
                    $CQPerlExt::CQ_BOOL_OP_AND);
$filterOp->BuildFilter($filter, $CQPerlExt::CQ_COMP_OP_EQ,
                                    \@dep_field_val);
$queryDefObj->BuildField ($list_field) ;
my $resultSetObj = $session->BuildResultSet( $queryDefObj );
$resultSetObj->Execute();
while ($resultSetObj->MoveNext() == $CQPerlExt::CQ_SUCCESS) {
            push ( @list, $resultSetObj->GetColumnValue (1) );
}
return @list;
}
```

The `ChoiceList` subroutine may look complex because we need to pass four parameters, but consider the advantages of being able to use it for any dependent field and in any record type. If you have several state-based record types, each one having some fields that reference dependent stateless record types, your schema may have quite a lot of hooks that are very similar and that you need to maintain.

A similar code example is given in section 8.8.7.4, "Creating a Tree-like List."

8.1.3.2 Exporting and Importing Schema Portions

ClearQuest allows you to export part of the schema using the command

```
cqload exportintegration … begin_rev end_rev …
```

So if you have developed a special feature or a new record type, you can export it to a file and import it later to another schema. In this way you have a development artifact in one schema that can be reused in another schema. When maintaining this schema element, you should consider the fact that it is reused in another schema.

The full syntax of the export command is

```
cqload exportintegration
        [-dbset dbset_name]
        clearquest_login
        clearquest_password
        schema_name
        begin_rev
        end_rev
        record_type_to_rename
        schema_pathname
```

The `exportintegration` command has an optional parameter `record_type_to_rename` that allows you to rename a record type while importing. If you do not plan to rename the record type, provide an empty string: `""`.

The import command is similar:

```
cqload importintegration … to-schema …
```

The full syntax is

```
cqload importintegration
        [-dbset dbset_name]
        clearquest_login
        clearquest_password
        schema_name
        new_record_type_name
        integration_name
        integration_version
```

```
schema_pathname
form_name
```

Some of the parameters are optional; if you are not using an optional parameter, enter an empty string: `" "`.

- `record_type_to_rename` allows you to rename a record type that you are importing.

- `integration name` and `integration version` are used for documentation purposes; you can use any string values for integration name such as "Role record" or "New role record type" and any string to indicate integration version such as 2 or 2.0 to indicate that you are importing version 2 of the Role record. We strongly suggest using these optional parameters.

- `form name` is used to identify the entity form on which new tabs will be included; if not relevant use `" "`.

In section 8.2, "Parallel Development," you can see more examples of `importintegration` and `exportintegration`.

8.1.4 Using ClearQuest Packages

ClearQuest packages are reusable solutions to application problems. We can divide the packages into three types:

- **Integration packages:** packages that are related to integration between ClearQuest and other products such as RequisitePro, ClearCase, Microsoft Project, and others.

- **Functionality packages:** packages that provide functionality to change management problems such as requiring an electronic signature, tracking customer details, storing users' notes and discussions, storing resolution types, and others. Most of these packages are actually realizations of design patterns that we discussed in section 2.3, "Design Patterns," in Chapter 2, "Disciplines: Requirements, Analysis & Design."

- **Schema packages:** packages that provide an out-of-the-box schema solution. Currently the two packages that construct a full solution are ClearQuestALM and DefectTracking.

The significant advantage of using packages is that the effort is minimal. Rational has developed them and is maintaining them. However, there are some disadvantages that you should be aware of:

- After a package is installed, you cannot remove it from the schema.

- Some element (fields, actions, hooks) of the packages may be read-only and you cannot modify them directly. If the provided functionality does not entirely meet your needs, you should consider the value versus the limitations. (See section 8.1.4.1, "Enabling a Package for Editing," for an explanation of how to enable a read-only package for editing.)

- If you modify a package, your changes maybe overwritten when a newer version of the package is installed.

You should consider these disadvantages before installing a package. If you need to integrate ClearQuest with another product, we suggest that you use the package that performs integration, and we suggest using it as is. For functionality packages you are free to decide; for example, creating the Attachment package or the Notes package is very simple. If you intend to change it, maybe you are better off creating this functionality in the schema rather than installing the package.

For a full list of available packages see the ClearQuest Designer help under Developing > Developing schemas with the Rational ClearQuest Designer > Schemas and packages.

8.1.4.1 Enabling a Package for Editing

As we explained in the previous section, some of the packaged created elements are read-only. For example, the Resolution package changes all the hooks of the Resolve action to read-only. This is a severe limitation that in many cases is unacceptable. There is a solution that must be used with caution. The following command line enables a record type for editing so that you can make changes:

```
packageutil enablepackageediting -dbset dbset_name \
    cqadmin_login cqadmin_password -enable cquser_login
```

After this command is executed, the user cquser_login is granted the ability to edit package-owned components in the schema. This user can now make the changes in the schema. Extra care should be taken to prevent conflicts with the package components. When the work is done, the ClearQuest administrator should deny the ability to edit by using the command

```
packageutil enablepackageediting -dbset dbset_name \
    cqadmin_login cqadmin_password -disable cquser_login
```

8.1.4.2 Creating Your Package

It is possible to create a new package using the packageutil utility. However, Rational does not recommend and does not support the creation of packages by customers.

Partners that want to create integration packages or packages as part of their solution can contact Rational to get the required documentation.

8.1.5 Understanding Session Variables

Session variables are variables that are persistent for the entire session. For example, if one hook sets a session variable, it can be read from other hooks as long as the users have not terminated the session by logging out.

Naming Session Variables   Session variables have no naming convention, but we suggest using the underscore character as the first letter of a session variable, for example, _ParentID, _AllowedUsers.

Session variables are not set and read as regular variables; you should use special methods to do that. The following are examples in Perl, to set the session variable in one hook:

```
# Perl example- Set session variable
my $RecId = $entity->GetDisplayName();
$session->SetNameValue("_ParentID", $ RecId);
```

You read the session variable in another hook:

```
# Perl example- Get session variable
my $ParentId = $session->GetNameValue("_ParentID");
```

The following are examples in BASIC. Note that the method names for setting the session variables and getting the values are not the same in Perl and BASIC.

```
' Basic example - Set session variable
RecId = GetFieldValue("id").GetValue
curSession.NameValue "_ParentID", RecId
```

In the next example we first check if the session variable contains values before getting it:

```
' Basic example - Get session variable
If curSession.HasValue ("_ParentID") Then
  ParentId = curSession.NameValue("_ParentID")
'     Get the parent entity and copy fields
'     . . .
End if
```

You can use session variables to do the following:

- Cache data to speed up user operations, for example, a long users list in a choice list.
- Store values from one record to be read by another record, for example, in cloning operations.
- Verify session type.

  ClearQuest autostores the session type in a global variable; for example, if the variable _CQ_WEB_SESSION has value, the current session is a Web one. As using MsgBox() is not allowed in Web sessions (the message will pop up in the Web server and not in the client desktop), you can avoid this call in Web sessions.

For additional information see ClearQuest Help > Reference > API Reference > Working with sessions > Using Session variables.

8.2 Parallel Development

ClearQuest designers maintain the versions of their work in the schema. When the schema is checked out by one user, it cannot be edited by others but can be opened for view only. Only after you have checked in the schema version you have worked on will another user be able to check it out for editing. This limits significantly the development speed and the ability to provide the organization with solutions in an agile manner.

ClearQuest Eclipse Designer version 7.1 introduced new features that help the members of the development team to work in parallel, and we shall discuss them in section 8.3, "Comparing and Merging Schema Versions."

In the following paragraphs we shall explain some of the methods that allow a team to work in parallel and accelerate the ClearQuest application delivery. The methods for users still using versions below 7.1 are different; we shall discuss both methods.

8.2.1 Coding Hooks

Whether your schema scripting language is Perl or BASIC, most of the work of developing the schema is spent on coding. So the obvious place to look for parallel development is hooks coding.

The simplest method is to write the code externally with one of the many editors that fits Perl or BASIC and when you think it is ready, send it to the ClearQuest designer to copy to the main schema and test it. Another way is to have the second schema developer work on a different repository, develop the hooks within ClearQuest Designer, do minimal local tests, and send the code to the ClearQuest designer to copy to the main schema and test it.

This is basic; it takes some of the load from the main designer, but the problem is that the secondary hooks developer cannot test the code in a real environment and so cannot provide reliable hooks. It is recommended that the secondary developer have the same schema version as the main developer to make the tests resemble reality as much as possible. The final tests and debugging are left to the main developer.

If you are using ClearQuest Eclipse Designer version 7.1, the two schemas can be compared and merged. See section 8.3, "Comparing and Merging Schema Versions," for a detailed description of how this is done.

8.2.2 Record Types

Another way to split the work is to componentize the schema. Select a component that is independent of the others, so that two (or more) developers can work on their own component independently. If designed carefully, a record type can be independent and thus allow two (or more) developers to work in parallel, each one on a different record type. But they still cannot work on the same schema because it can be checked out by one user only.

If the record type is referenced, then creating the referencing fields will be left for the merging phase. Another option is to create a stub record type that will later be replaced with the one the secondary developer is working on.

The following describes the method step by step. For simplicity we describe it with two users, DevA and DevB, though the method can be used with more developers. First let's describe the environment: DevA is working on the schema called UCM that is connected to the production database and to a test database (Main DBset in Figure 8.10). DevB is working on a test environment, having another schema repository and a test database (Test DBset in Figure 8.10).

The environment is described in Figure 8.10.

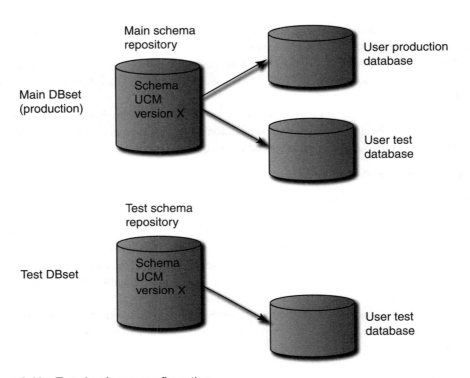

Figure 8.10   Two-developers configuration

To create a common baseline the schema version X is exported from the main DBset using the command

```
cqload exportschema -dbset Main DevA_name DevA_pw UCM \
  c:\UCM_X.txt
```

The file c:\UCM_X.txt is copied to the test environment or to a shared directory and imported into the test repository using the command

```
Cqload importrtschema -dbset Test DevB_name DevB_pw c:\UCM_X.txt
```

Now two developers have the same version of the schema and can start working in parallel. A caution: Coordination and planning are required because ClearQuest does not support real merge. If the developers work on the same objects, conflicts may arise. We recommend that each one work on a different record type; this ensures no conflicts. Also, global hooks should be considered as a single object, and only one developer should work on the global hooks.

After DevB has finished his or her work, tested it against the test database, and checked in the schema to create a new version X+1, the changes from DevB should be merged to DevA's schema. This is performed by exporting only changes from version X to version X+1. DevB will use the following command:

```
cqload exportintegration -dbset Test DevB_name DevB_pw UCM X X+1 \
    rectype_to_rename c:\UCM_X+1.txt
```

Needless to say, versions X and X+1 will be replaced with the correct schema version. Also the `cqload exportintegration` command allows you to export more than one version, but it is rarely required.

DevA has finished his or her work, tested it against the test database, and checked in the schema to create a new version X+1. Now DevA needs to import the changes from DevB. First the export file is copied to DevA's environment, and the following command is performed:

```
cqload importintegration -dbset Main DevB_name DevB_pw UCM \
    rectype_to_rename integ_name integ_version c:\UCM_X+1.txt
```

Now a new schema version is created, X+2, that includes the work of the two developers.

Some notes on the `importintegration` command: The `integ_name integ_version` parameters are for documentation purposes and help track the merges. `rectype_to_rename` is used if you want change the name of the imported record type, but this is rarely used; in our case both developers coordinated their work. There are additional parameters for import forms, which we shall discuss in the next section.

With ClearQuest Eclipse Designer the record type from the secondary schemas can be merged into the main schema. See section 8.3, "Comparing and Merging Schema Versions," for a detailed description of how this is done.

Using Test Environments A more prudent approach is that both developers work in isolated test environments and merge their work into a different test environment. After the changes are verified and validated in the test environment, they will be exported and merged into the production environment. The disadvantage is the additional effort required to manage the environment and the promotion from one environment to another.

8.2.3 Designing Forms and Tabs

The user interface should be designed and created by professionals; programming skills are not required. The best case is that a professional with the required skills will design the forms and tabs and select the required controls. Such a person can do this using ClearQuest Designer working on another schema, so the main schema developer can continue the work in parallel. When the GUI designers finish their work, the forms can be copied to the main schema. This is done in the following way:

1. From the Schema Repository Explorer of the GUI designer schema (secondary development environment), expand the schema tree.

2. Select the form you want to export, right-click, and select Export Form from the dialog that appears. This dialog is shown in Figure 8.11.

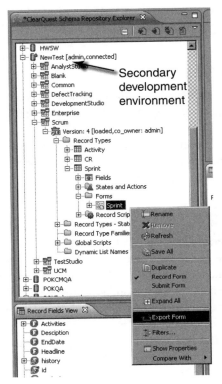

Figure 8.11 Export a form using ClearQuest Eclipse Designer

3. Enter the file name for the exported file (for example, SprintRecord.form).

4. From the Schema Repository Explorer of the main designer schema (primary development environment), expand the schema tree.

5. Select the Forms folder, right-click, and select Import Form from the dialog.

6. Pick the exported file and click the Save button.

7. Expand the form folder, select the newly imported form, and make it active by right-clicking and marking it as Record Form or Submit Form. This is shown in Figure 8.12.

The user interfaces were graphically designed in another schema and imported to the main schema; by doing this we have achieved parallel development of another element of the schema.

Note To copy forms it is also possible to use the utilities

```
cqload exportintegration . . .
cqload importintegration . . .
```

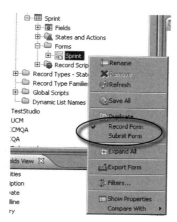

Figure 8.12 Setting the type of the imported form to Record Form using ClearQuest Eclipse Designer

See the following article:

Glockner, Christian, "Collaborative Schema Design with IBM Rational ClearQuest," *IBM developerWorks*, www.ibm.com/developerworks/rational/library/10/collaborative-schemadesignwithibmrationalclearquest/index.html, 2010 (accessed February 24, 2011).

8.3 Comparing and Merging Schema Versions

The ClearQuest schema is versioned sequentially, in a linear manner and not in a tree manner. The schema designer can open any old version for viewing, but until version 7.1 there was no mechanism to indicate what changes were introduced from one version to another. ClearQuest designers can enter a description of their changes every time they check in a schema, and they should, but this is optional and does not ensure the correctness and completeness of the information.

ClearQuest Eclipse Designer version 7.1 introduces some new and very important features that help administrators better manage their schemas. Some of the features are

- A generic History view that displays the history of all schema revisions
- The ability to make a structural comparison of schema versions
- The ability to merge changes from one schema version to another

To open the schema History view, select the schema, right-click, and select Show > History.

The version comparison is a significant step forward, and it is especially important in large organizations where more than one person is working on the schema. You can select and compare two versions of the same schema from the History view. More important is the ability to select two versions of two different schemas from the Schema Repository Explorer. This is done in the following way: Hold the CTRL key and select the two versions, right-click, and select Compare With > Each Other.

Figure 8.13 shows a History view of a schema.

Figure 8.13   Schema Revision History view: compare schema revisions

The technique for parallel development as explained in section 8.2, "Parallel Development," is becoming much simpler. Consider again the two developers we described in that section and the environment shown in Figure 8.10; instead of exporting and importing, the main designer will compare the changes made in the secondary schema and can easily import the required changes to the main schema. The process is as follows:

1. Expand the two repositories in the Schema Repository Explorer.

2. Check out the main schema.

3. Press CTRL and select the checked-out schema version and the secondary schema version.

4. Right-click and select Compare With > Each Other.

   The Schema Compare window opens; it has three sections (views). The upper section is the Schema Structure Compare with all the schema elements that are different. The lower two sections display the elements of each schema. Special icons for Added, Removed, and Conflict indicate the type of change for each element in the structure. Figure 8.14 demonstrates the Compare window of the two schema versions.

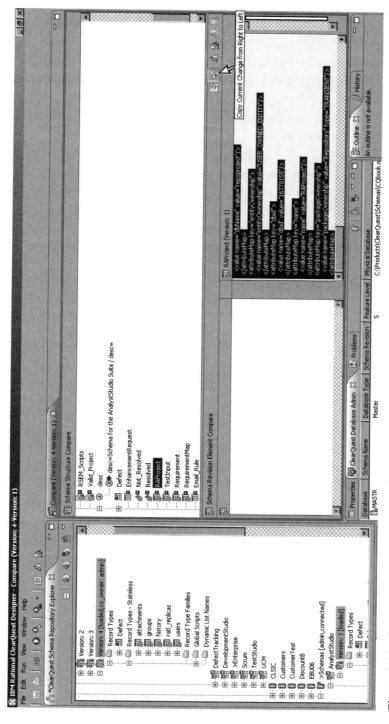

Figure 8.14 Comparing two schemas and Copy record type

5. Focus on the element that needs to be imported by double-clicking on it.

   The content is displayed in XML format in the lower section. Figure 8.14 shows the content of the selected record (RAProject) in the right lower window.

6. Click on the button Copy Current Change From Right to Left (or Left to Right depending who is copying from whom).

   This button is located on the toolbar that is below the Schema Structure Compare section. Note that the schema elements are copied to the left section, but not yet to the main schema. Other buttons in the toolbar allow you to copy all non-conflicting changes and to navigate between changes.

7. Save the schema to actually copy the elements to the main schema.

   If the imported record types have reference fields, ClearQuest will fix references and show you the fixes.

   Figure 8.15 shows the Reference Repair window, ready for the user confirmation to perform the repair. To better understand reference repair, let's look at an example. The reference to the "ratl_replicas" record type needs to be fixed because the "dbid" field values in the two schemas are not the same. ClearQuest will report an error if there is a reference to an object that does not exist in the new schema, so you should pay extra attention to elements that are referenced. For example, if you copy the EnhancementRequest record type, the RAProject record type should also be copied (or installed via a package) as it is being referenced.

8. Continue and copy other elements to the main schema.

   Before the next element can be compared, you will be asked to save the changes. Only after saving will you be able to see the changes in the Schema Explorer.

9. Perform tests against the test database, and verify that changes introduced actually work as expected.

10. Check in the new schema version.

The differences between the two schemas are displayed in the Schema Structure Compare window as seen in Figure 8.14. Elements can be highlighted, and their XML content is presented in the lower right window; the displayed elements can be copied to the other schema.

When fields with references are copied to another schema, the references are not valid (as the record "dbid" is different) and therefore need to be repaired. Figure 8.15 shows the identification of the required repairs.

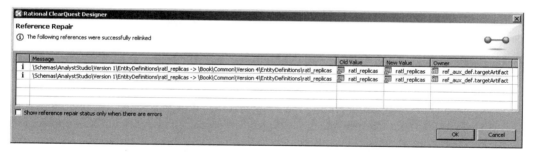

Figure 8.15 Reference Repair message after record merge

8.4 Storing Hooks Externally

The limited ability to develop in parallel and the need to check in and upgrade the production database, even for a small change, has led some organizations to develop smart techniques to store elements of the schema externally, so that changes will be possible without checking out the schema. One of the techniques is to store the code externally, that is, not in the hook itself. The hook will extract the external code, parse, validate, and execute it. The Perl hook skeleton to execute an action hook may look like this:

```
my $ActionName = $entity->GetActionName();
my $HookType = "Commit";
my $hookcode = FindCode( $ActionName, $HookType);
eval $hookcode;
```

This technique will work in Perl only because the BASIC language does not have an `eval()` equivalent. The `FindCode` function will extract the code for the relevant hook and the Perl `eval()` command will execute it. So how can we store the code externally? One way may be in a shared file repository (and possibly under version control, with ClearCase, for example), but this might be problematic in distributed environments and for ClearQuest Web users. Another way is to store the code in the ClearQuest user database, for example, in a multiline string of a stateless record type. Even with this solution we can propose several techniques:

- A record for each hook; for example, the Submit action initialization hook can be stored in one record, and the Submit action commit hook stored in another. This method is probably easier to implement because a single query can extract the required code. Also, it minimizes the chance that two schema developers will need to access and change the same hook.

- One record with all hooks stored in XML format for easy parsing.

- A combination of one record for each hook type; for example, all the action initialization hooks in one record, all action commit hooks in another; field value change hooks in one record and field choice list hooks in another, and so forth. Extracting and parsing are easier.

This method requires a special test environment. We explained in section 7.5.3, "Creating a Test Environment," of Chapter 7, "Disciplines, Part 2," how to create a test environment. When you change a hook and save it in the defined external location, it takes effect immediately. Therefore, you need to develop and/or modify the script and save it in an isolated test environment so that you can test without affecting the production environment. In most organizations where this solution is relevant, or that use an isolated development environment or an isolated test environment, this solution may be suitable.

> **Note** The technique of storing the code externally out of the ClearQuest schema was presented at the IBM Rational Software Development Conference 2006, session CCM32.

8.5 Releasing a Version to Production

The release process includes several stages. The first stage is in the development environment. Similar to the unit testing that developers perform prior to publishing their work, the ClearQuest developer performs testing and debugging on the test database. This test database does not have to be of the same type as the production database, but it has to be one that the ClearQuest designer can create and delete without the DBA's assistance.

The next step is promoting the changes to the test environment. This environment is similar or identical to the production environment. System tests should also be performed here by the stakeholders who approve the changes. The last step is the promotion to the production environment. We provide the suggested steps for the promotion that includes schema, data, and queries and reports.

8.5.1 Developer Testing

The schema developer should configure the test environment. From ClearQuest Designer select File > Test Configuration. In the wizard select the New Configuration icon (or right-click on ClearQuest and select New) and type the test configuration name. The configuration wizard has two pages. Figure 8.16 shows page one, where you define the test database or create a new one by pressing the Create a Database button.

The second page is for the definition of the client type to be executed. Click the Client Setup tab and define each of the clients you need to test. Click on the Client Type radio button and verify that the definition is correct, and modify it as required. As previously mentioned, you should test each environment that the users are using.

Figure 8.17 shows the Client Setup page, with the Web client definition.

To run the test, mark the test database and click the Run button. For subsequent test execution click on the menu button Rerun Test Work.

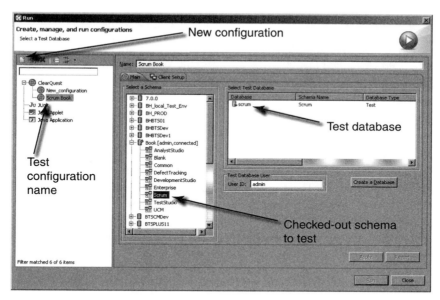

Figure 8.16 Setting the test database configuration

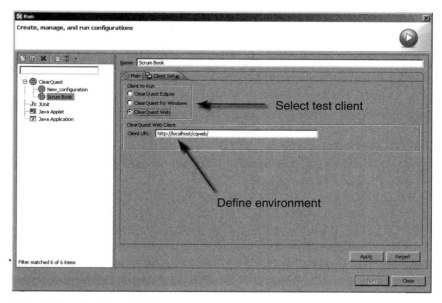

Figure 8.17 Setting the test client type

Testing with the Web Client   When you run Test Work, ClearQuest Designer performs schema validation, and if validation is successful, the test database is upgraded to the last revision. When you set up the client to ClearQuest Web, the database is *not* upgraded. So to test the Web client, first test your changes with the Windows or Eclipse client and then with the Web client.

8.5.2 System Testing

If there are several developers, each one performs similar tests on his or her environment until they all integrate their changes in one of the ways we explained in section 8.2, "Parallel Development." When all changes are merged into the main schema, we can start more general tests, similar to system integration tests. These tests will probably be performed on a test database that is similar to the production database. Intensive tests should be carried out; sometimes performance tests are required, especially if you expect an increase in the number of users, or if the schema changes include time-consuming hooks. In large deployments performance tests should be considered in each major release.

   If the stakeholders were not involved in the development process, user acceptance tests should probably be carried out.

8.5.3 Promotion to Production

We assumed that all the tests were performed in a test repository, so we should promote the release from the test environment to the production environment. First, get approval for the promotion. Second, export all the changes, including

- A new schema version
- Possibly new queries, charts, and reports that were built
- Data for dynamic lists
- Data import for new stateless record types

The process includes, but is not limited to, the following activities:

1. Prepare a checklist of all the activities that you should perform, similar to this list but including the detailed commands.
2. Export the schema version using the command `cqload exportintegration`.
3. Export dynamic lists with the command `importutil exportlist`.
4. Export new queries: from the ClearQuest client workspace select a query, Right-click, and select "export query."
5. We assume that the data for stateless record types was already imported to the test database from files, so we do not need the export again, but if this is not the case use the Eclipse client Export Tool to export the data.

Now that we have all the data exported, we can copy all the files to the shared directory, if they are not already exported to one.

To import the data to the production environment perform the following activities:

1. Get approval for the upgrade, including approval for downtime.

2. Import the schema version using the command `cqload importintegration` (or with Eclipse Designer compare and merge).

3. Inform all the users of the upgrade time, requesting that they log out. Send the message one day before the upgrade, and a reminder a few minutes before the upgrade. It is best to perform the upgrade at times when the minimum number of users is active.

4. Check in the schema and upgrade the production database.

5. Import dynamic lists with the command `importutil importlist`.

6. Import queries to the ClearQuest client workspace: right-click on the folder and select "import query."

7. Import data records to the stateless record types using the Eclipse client Import Tool.

8. Perform a sanity check to be sure nothing is missing. Perform regression tests.

9. Inform the users when the process is complete.

8.6 Globally Distributed Development (GDD) Considerations and ClearQuest MultiSite (CQMS)

Customers using ClearQuest MultiSite (CQMS) need to take into consideration the following subjects related to the development process:

- The schema upgrade process
- Mastership changes
- Testing mastership issues

8.6.1 Upgrading the Schema

The ClearQuest MultiSite automatic synchronization process does not deal with upgrading the user database. Therefore, the schema administrator must set up a manual procedure for checking in the new schema version, transporting the changes to the other sites, upgrading other sites' databases, and turning on automatic synchronization.

This procedure is described in ClearQuest Help > Administering > Administering Rational ClearQuest MultiSite > Database replicas administration > Upgrading a schema version.

8.6.2 Addressing Mastership Changes

In a multisite environment the ClearQuest record can have mastership in different sites along the record workflow. This is common when testing is performed in one site and development in another site. When assigning a new owner from another site, mastership will change. There are cases when a user in a site that currently does not have mastership needs to modify the record.

This problem can be solved in a few ways:

- Develop a command-line utility that connects to the remote site and updates the mastership. Users will have to wait for the next synchronization to be able to make the change.

- Send an e-mail to the E-mail Reader in the remote site to change the mastership. This solution is slow and less reliable because of technology.

- A user that is defined in both sites can log in with the Web client to the other site and change the mastership or even make the required modifications. This solution does not require any changes or development.

Note that to change the mastership via the GUI, the ClearQuest designer should include the field "ratl_mastership" in the form.

See also ClearQuest Help > Administering > Administering Rational ClearQuest MultiSite > Mastership management > Transferring mastership of a record, as well as the following:

> Staff, IBM Rational, "ClearQuest MultiSite Project Management and Integration Hooks," *IBM developerWorks*, www.ibm.com/developerworks/rational/library/4518.html#firstmajorhead, 2003 (accessed February 24, 2011).

8.6.3 Testing the Mastership

After you have developed the required schema changes, you should test your work. In a multisite environment the record mastership is usually changed from site to site, so testing is more complex than usual. We assume that you have set up an isolated test environment that includes repositories that are similar to the production environment.

The first step would be to upgrade all clans as discussed in section 8.6.1, "Upgrading the Schema."

The second step is to run tests in your master site. That is no different from any test case execution. When you change state and change the owner of a record, this record mastership may move to another site.

The third step is to continue the test in the new master site. Make sure that the synchronization occurred and start ClearQuest at the remote site. You can do this by Remote Desktop Connection or by using the ClearQuest Web client of the new master site.

Warning   Do not change mastership to your site just for the sake of easy testing from one site. This is not reliable enough testing for a multisite environment.

8.7 ClearQuest Script Debugging

The ClearQuest Designer IDE does not include debug options either in the Windows version or in the Eclipse version, so how can we debug our ClearQuest schema?

- You can instrument the code to output messages with variables values.
- You can use the ClearQuest diagnostics to trace the program.

To output variable values from a VB script use the `MsgBox()` calls or equivalent. `MsgBox()` interrupts the execution and requires the developer to manually hit a button in the message to continue the execution.

The other method to output the values of variables is to use the session method `OutputDebugString()`. The output is viewed with another utility such as DBWin32.exe, which we shall discuss in section 8.7.2, "Employing the `OutputDebugString()` Method."

You can also trace various types of messages with IBM Rational ClearQuest Diagnostic Output.

8.7.1 Employing the `MsgBox()` Function

The `MsgBox()` function will pop up a message window with the string that you pass as parameter. You can include additional parameters to set the button style and the titles, but for debug purpose a single string parameter is enough.

For example, we want to debug a hook that builds the record URL so that we can include it in the e-mail notifications. To verify that the script is building the URL string correctly, we can use the `MsgBox` function.

This function can be used as is in a BASIC script; the next line of code demonstrates how to display the value of the field `RecordURL`. The output is similar to the output in Figure 8.18.

```
MsgBox "RecordURL:" & GetFieldStringValue("RecordURL")
```

In Perl scripts the usage is a bit different; we have to use the Win32 library. The following Perl code is equivalent to the BASIC code:

```
use Win32;
my $url = $entity->GetFieldStringValue("RecordURL");
my $msg = "RecordURL: ";
Win32::MsgBox($msg . $url);
```

This function call creates the message shown in Figure 8.18.

Figure 8.18   Message box from Perl hook

A few notes about the usage of `MsgBox()`. This call is not practical for debugging Web client behavior as the message pops up on the Web server machine. You must remember to remove the `MsgBox` after you have finished debugging. After removing the call, you must test your application again. We have witnessed cases where programs behave differently with and without the `MsgBox` call, especially in choice list loops. So our suggestion is not to use `MsgBox()` for debugging. However, the fact that the program stops while the message window is on can be an advantage for debugging,

In organizations that do not use the Web client, the `MsgBox()` function can be used to interact with users.

8.7.2 Employing the `OutputDebugString()` Method

The `OutputDebugString()` is a session method that outputs a string to the debugger. You construct a string and pass it as parameter to the method. It is very similar to what we have shown with the `MsgBox()` function.

It is important to include a new line at the end of your string; otherwise all messages will appear on one line.

The following is an example of VB code that outputs a field value to the debugger:

```
url = GetFieldStringValue("RecordURL")
msg = "Defect_Validation >>>> RecordURL: "
session.OutputDebugString msg & url & vbcrlf
```

Here is the same example in Perl:

```
my $url = $entity->GetFieldStringValue("RecordURL");
my $msg = "Defect_Validation >>>> RecordURL: ";
$session->OutputDebugString($msg . $url . "\n");
```

We suggest constructing the message in a way that will be clear not only to you but also to others. For example, we can include in the message the hook name and field name that we preset in the message. Also include some special characters to easily differentiate your messages and system messages.

Let's look at an example. You are required to include in the e-mail notification the URL of the work item. You write a global script to construct the URL. An example of such a script is shown in Listing 8.7.

Listing 8.7 Using `OutputDebugString` in a Script

```
sub getEntityURL()
{
# Purpose: Construct the entity URL
# Input   :
```

```
# Output  : return entityURL
#            Web server name is stored in dynamic list
# Format  : http://{webserver}/cqweb/restapi/
#            {db-set}/{userdb}/RECORD/{id}
#            &format=HTML&recordType={rectype}&noframes=true

$session = $entity->GetSession();
my $list_values = $session->GetListMembers("WebServer");

my $servername = $$list_values[0];
$session->OutputDebugString("getEntityURL>> >>server= $servername
.\n");

  my $S_URL = 'http://' . $servername . '/cqweb/restapi';
  my ($dbDesc, $dbSet, $dbName, $entID);
  $dbDesc = $session->GetSessionDatabase;
  $dbSet  = $dbDesc->GetDatabaseSetName;
  $dbName = $dbDesc->GetDatabaseName;
  $entID  = $entity->GetDisplayName;

# Get the current entity name
my $entitydefobj = $session->GetEntityDef($entity->GetEntityDefName());
my $objectname = $entitydefobj->GetName();

$session->OutputDebugString("getEntityURL>> >>URL=$S_URL .\n");
my $retval = "$S_URL/$dbSet/$dbName/RECORD/" .
             "$entID?format=HTML&recordType=$objectname&noframes=true"
return ($retval);
}
```

While this script is not very complex, the URL format must be accurate and debugging can be very helpful in finding small errors. The following examples are related to this record URL.

The screen shot in Figure 8.19 shows the DBWin32 window. Note that the last line is an output from the Defect validation hook. The two lines preceding the last one are output from the global script getEntityURL() that we have provided before. Note the special comment that we have used to make it clear from which script the message is sent.

Another advantage of the OutputDebugString() is that you can leave it in the hooks, with no serious performance impact on the application.

Figure 8.19 DBWin32 debug window

Tip In the DBWin32 top menu select Edit > Clear Buffer to clear the window of previous and unnecessary messages.

8.7.3 Debugging with Tracing Information

IBM Rational ClearQuest provides a wealth of tracing information that helps in debugging the application. You can control the debug level and the output.

Controlling the trace diagnostic is done by a set of Windows registry key values.

The key is

[HKEY_CURRENT_USER\Software\Rational Software\ClearQuest\Diagnostic]

The important value names are

- **Trace:** a list of what information to collect
- **Report:** what additional information to include in the output, such as times, sequence numbers, and so forth
- **Output:** where to send the data, for example, a file path or debugger

---

Note IBM Rational ClearQuest tools read these keys only when they are started. So if you change a key value, restart your ClearQuest application.

There are almost 60 different kinds of traces that you can choose depending on the application area you need to trace. The most common are the following:

- **HOOKS:** annotates the output with which hook is firing
- **THROW:** reports exceptions thrown by the ClearQuest core

- **API:** includes all ClearQuest API calls in the trace, showing their parameters and return values

  This is probably the most used diagnostic key. You can set a higher trace level by specifying the level number, such as API = 2.

- **SQL:** shows all calls made to the database

To collect the trace output you have to specify the data in the registry value Output. If you set the value to ODS (OutputDebugString), it can be collected with a suitable monitor utility such as one of the following:

- **DBWin32:** provided with IBM Rational ClearQuest. The file is located in <InstallDir>\ Common.

- **DebugView:** a more capable free utility that can be downloaded from www.sysinternals .com/utilities/debugview.mspx. Output can be filtered and highlighted, and it is timestamped.

- **A file name:** the path to a file to collect the trace in, for example, "Output"="C:\\temp\ debug\\cqtrace.log".

Figure 8.20 is provided as a visual comparison of DebugView and DBWin32.

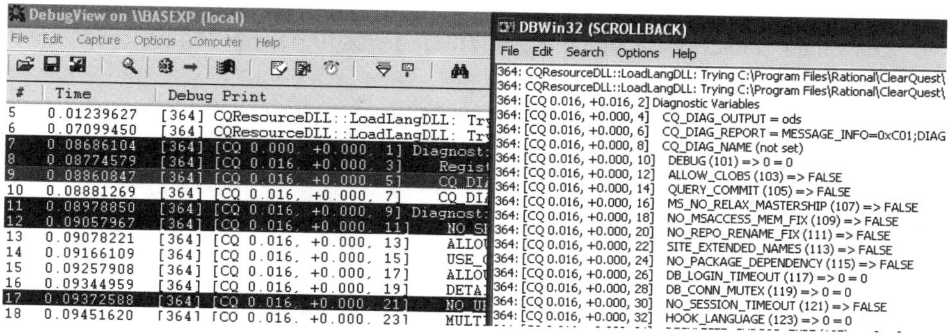

Figure 8.20 DebugView versus DBWin32
Courtesy Alan Murphy

Here is an example of the registry file that you can import with the registry editor (regedit.exe):

```
Windows Registry Editor Version 5.00
[HKEY_USERS\.DEFAULT\Software\Rational Software\ClearQuest\
Diagnostic]
"Trace"="API;CHARTS;CODEPAGE;DB_CONNECT;DBDESC;EDIT;EMAIL;HOOKS;
LICENSE;MAINS;METADATA_INIT;ODS;PACKAGES;PERL;RESULTSET;SESSION;
```

```
SYSTEM_UPGRADE;THREAD;THROW;TIMER;USER_ADMIN;VBASIC;"
"Behavior"=""
"Report"="MESSAGE_INFO=0X1309"
"Output"="ODS"
```

Debug flags can be set on either platform via environment variables. On UNIX, debug flags are set with calls like the following:

```
setenv  CQ_DIAG_TRACE   Throw;Db_Connect=2;SQL=2;API
setenv  CQ_DIAG_REPORT  MESSAGE_INFO=0x70B
setenv  CQ_DIAG_OUTPUT  trace.log
```

On Windows, debug flags are set with calls like the following:

```
set CQ_DIAG_TRACE=Throw;Db_Connect=2;SQL=2;API
set CQ_DIAG_REPORT=MESSAGE_INFO=0x70B
set CQ_DIAG_OUTPUT=c:\trace.log
```

If your scripting language is VBScript, you can use the Microsoft Script Debugger or the debugger from Visual Studio, Visual InterDev components, which will allow more advanced debugging. You will be able to set breakpoints, to stop and proceed with a single step, and even to set variables values.

To use the Microsoft Script Debugger do the following:

1. Download the Script Debugger engine from Microsoft, "Script Debugger for Windows NT 4.0 and Later," Microsoft Download Center, www.microsoft.com/downloads/en/details.aspx?FamilyID=2f465be0-94fd-4569-b3c4-dffdf19ccd99&displaylang=en, 2005 (accessed February 24, 2011).

2. Install it.

3. Enable the Debugger.

   First enable it in Internet Explorer: Tools > Internet Options > Advanced.

   Ensure that the Disable Script debugging options are unchecked.

   Enable just-in-time debugging.

4. Run Regedit.exe and edit this key:

   HKEY_CURRENT_USER\Software\Microsoft\Windows Script\Settings.

   Set JITDebug = 1.

8.8 Other Development Considerations

Other development issues to consider are listed below in no specific order. Some may be of high importance to some customers; others may be of minor importance but can make a difference in some situations.

8.8.1 Choosing a Scripting Language

As you know, the current options for scripting are Perl and BASIC. If your organization has both Windows and UNIX operating systems as practitioners' desktops, there is no option—you must select Perl as your scripting language because BASIC is not supported on Linux and UNIX. Each language provides some advantages and we cannot recommend one over the other. Some examples:

- ActiveX controls are supported only in BASIC.
- The ability to execute hooks stored externally is supported only with Perl.
- BASIC provides more advanced debugging utilities.

8.8.2 When Is a Stateless Record Type Required?

Stateless record types are good as data containers; they are meant to collect data that is logically related in a physical element. When is it recommended to create a stateless record type? If you have more than one field that is related to the same logical unit. An example is Project; if you need only the project name, use a field in the work item. If you need in addition the project manager name, the project description, and the project status (Active, Planned, Obsolete), then a stateless record type for Project is a good choice.

Read more on stateless record types in section 4.3, "Stateless Objects," in Chapter 4, "The Data."

8.8.3 Dealing with Records That Have More Than One Field as Unique Key

Unique keys allow you to select one or more fields that define the database primary key. For state-based record types the primary key is the record ID, which is unique and automatically created by the system. For stateless record types the default unique key is the field DBID, but you can change it to a more meaningful and useful field. For example, the unique key for the record type Project would be the Project Name field. A more complex example is a record type like Component. It is possible that two projects will have two different components with the same name. (For example, the component Infrastructure in the project Portal is not the same component as Infrastructure in the project SAP.) In this case we shall have to select a second field as unique key, and because the component is unique in a project, it is correct to select the Component Name as the first unique key and the Project field as the second unique key.

In some cases we even have to select three fields to define the uniqueness of the record. See Figure 4.15 in Chapter 4, "The Data," for an example of how to define three fields as a combined unique key for the record type Roles.

See section 4.4.4, "More on ClearQuest Unique Key," in Chapter 4, "The Data," for detailed information and code examples of how to construct the key, get the entity, and retrieve data from stateless records.

8.8.4 Organizing Global Scripts

The best way to organize global hooks is by subject. For each subject create a global script. In each script you can add several subroutines and functions. In this way the list of global scripts will not be very long, and it will be easier to manage and easier to find hooks during development. Do not move or change scripts that are created by packages.

Figure 8.21 is an example of a global scripts folder in the Schema Repository Explorer.

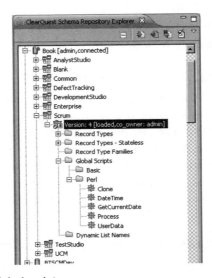

Figure 8.21   ClearQuest global scripts

In this example the script UserData contains a few subroutines to deal with user data, such as `convertLoginToFull()`, `getUserGroups()`, and similar.

8.8.5 Devising a Naming Convention

When developing the schema, you have to decide on the names of fields, actions and states, subroutines, function names, and variable names.

Decide on the naming convention to use prior to developing the schema. Publish this naming convention to all people involved in the schema development, so they will use the same naming convention. This will prevent errors, increase readability of the code, and increase productivity.

The following is not necessarily the best or our recommendation for naming conventions but is more of an example:

- **Fields:** The field name should start with a capital character. If the field contains more than one word, each word should start with a capital letter. Examples: Owner, DefectType.

- **Actions:** The same as for fields, but use active verbs. Examples: Submit, Assign.

- **States:** The same as for fields, but use passive verbs. Examples: Submitted, Assigned.
- **Functions and subroutines:** Method names should be verbs, in mixed case with the first letter lowercase and the first letter of each internal word capitalized (Java style). Examples: getParentObject, constructUniqueKey.
- **Variables in hooks:** There are several types of variables that can be used in hooks:
  - **Regular variables:** The first letter should be capitalized. Examples: ParentID, Role.
  - **Session variables:** These should start with an underscore. Examples: _ParentID, _TargetState.
  - **Object variables:** The first letter should be a lowercase *o* and the first letter of each internal word should be capitalized. Examples: oSession, oEntity.

8.8.5.1 Reserved Names

Object names cannot be the same as any reserved keywords for the database. ClearQuest interfaces will change the database column name if it is identical to a reserved word. In Figure 8.22 you can see that the field name is Date but the DB Column Name is "newfield." Although this is not an error, we do not recommend using reserved words.

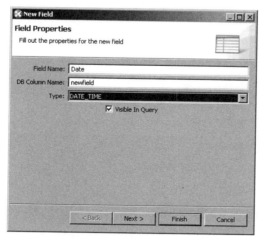

Figure 8.22 ClearQuest reserved names used in a field name

See also ClearQuest Help > Developing > Rational ClearQuest schemas > Naming restrictions.

8.8.6 Storing the old_id Field for Future Import

When you import records to ClearQuest, it is wise (even necessary) to store the old ID for reference. Old_id is very useful for validating migrations and for users moving from a legacy system into ClearQuest. If you need to import updates to existing records, you will need a field that contains a unique identifier for each record. For state-based records it is the field ID. But the ClearQuest Import Tool cannot use it and requires another field. Figure 8.23 shows this in the Import Tool settings wizard.

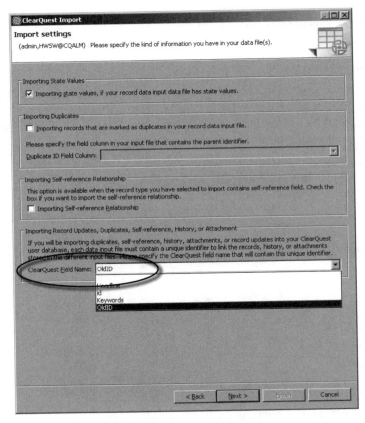

Figure 8.23 ClearQuest Field Name for importing updates

Now you can see that the old_id field pays off. We strongly recommend including this field in any state-based record type. In the Submit action validation hook, insert the record ID to the field old_id using this single line:

```
$entity->SetFieldValue ( "old_id" , $entity->GetDisplayName );
```

<hr />

Warning   Do not include this hook in the old_id field Default_Value hook or in the Submit initialization hook. Users can use the utilities Save as Default and Load Default, and this runs *after* the field default_value and action initialization hooks and will override the value set by the hook.

<hr />

8.8.7 Dealing with Long Selection Lists

In many situations the user has to select an item from a very long list. This list can be a user name from all the organization's users, or a part number from a list of thousands of parts. The user's selection operation tends to be slow and annoying. To improve the operation and the user experience you can do one of the following:

- Cache the list to speed up the operation.
- Break the list into several lists.
- Create a tree-like list.

In the following sections we discuss these options.

8.8.7.1 Recalculating and Invalidating the Choice List

When the list of one field (for example, Module) depends on the value selected in another field (for example, Product), the list must be refreshed as it is not valid at all times. One easy and somewhat inefficient method of ensuring that the choice list of a field is always valid is to select the Recalculate Choice List property for the field.

By selecting the choice list properties, you can mark the Recalculate Choice List as shown in Figure 8.24.

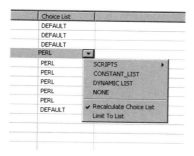

Figure 8.24   Recalculate Choice List property

Instead, you can write a field Value_Changed hook in one field that invalidates the choice list of another field.

In section 12.2, "User-Defined Fields in ClearQuest," in Chapter 12, "Sample Applications and Solutions," we give an example of user-defined fields that are dependent on the project; in this example we used the Recalculate Choice List. In Listing 8.8 we shall use the same example but with the call to `InvalidateFieldChoiceList()`. This hook shows how to write a Value_Changed hook in the field Project to invalidate the choice list of the dependent fields (`UserFieldValue_1` and `UserFieldValue_2`).

Listing 8.8   Invalidate Dependent Fields

```
Sub project_ValueChanged(fieldname)
  ' fieldname As String
  ' record type name is Defect
  ' field name is Project
  ' Start User Code

  REM Porpose: Populate the project fields names
  REM          Clear & Invalidate the dependent fields choices

  proj = GetFieldValue(fieldname).GetValue()
  If proj <> "Null" Then
    name1 = GetFieldValue("Project.FieldName_1").GetValue()
    name2 = GetFieldValue("Project.FieldName_2").GetValue()
    SetFieldValue "UserFieldName_1", name1
    SetFieldValue "UserFieldName_2", name2
  End If

  SetFieldValue "UserFieldValue_1", ""
  SetFieldValue "UserFieldValue_2", ""
  InvalidateFieldChoiceList "UserFieldValue_1"
  InvalidateFieldChoiceList "UserFieldValue_2"
  ' End User Code
End Sub
```

The code in Listing 8.9 is an example of the choice list of the field `UserFieldValue_2`. (In section 12.2, "User-Defined Fields in ClearQuest," in Chapter 12, "Sample Applications and Solutions," you will understand why we gave the field such a name.) We first check the validation status and if valid, we populate the choice list.

Listing 8.9   Checking Field Validation Status

```
Sub userfieldvalue_2_ChoiceList(fieldname, choices)
  ' fieldname As String
  ' choices As Object
  ' record type name is Defect
  ' field name is UserFieldValue_2
  ' Start User Code

  Dim oProj
  set oProj = GetFieldValue("project")
  ' Check the field status
  If oProj.GetValidationStatus() = AD_KNOWN_VALID AND _
    oProj.GetValue() <> "" then
        call Populate_list("Project.Field2_list" , choices)
    End If
' End User Code
End Sub
```

We do not recommend using the previous procedure for each and every dependent field choice list. The Recalculate Choice List property is very easy to use and does not complicate the coding. However, if you encounter some performance issues during testing, and you find the root cause to be too many choice lists recalculations, then it is definitely the recommended solution.

8.8.7.2 Caching the List

Long lists that are used often in a session are good candidates for caching; for example, the list of all subscribed users may be used in various fields such as AssignTo, RequestInfoFrom, Subscribers, and so on. To cache lists we use session variables as they are active for an entire session. The code in Listing 8.10 is an example that shows how to populate a list (myList) from a cache (the variable is _SubscribedUsers).

Listing 8.10   Caching Long Lists

```
oSession = GetSession()
If oSession.HasValue ("_SubscribedUsers") Then
        REM - cache exists: populate choice list
      myUsers = oSession.NameValue ("_SubscribedUsers")
      For Each User in myUsers
           myList.AddItem User
      Next
```

continues

Listing 8.10   Caching Long Lists (*Continued*)

```
Else
            REM - cache does NOT exist:  call creation subroutine
        CreateSubscribedUsers ()
End If
```

Additional information and examples of how to create and use the session variables are provided in section 8.1.5, "Understanding Session Variables."

8.8.7.3 Creating Several Lists

In some cases a long list can be broken down into several lists. For example, a field that contains the defect cause or reason could be a very long list. A user having to select from a long list may spend quite some time selecting the right value. Instead you can break this list into several lists by defect category, so the user will first select the category and then the cause. Although two operations are required, the total amount of time is shorter and the user experience is better. If the first field is required only to ease the selection of the second field, consider autoclearing it after the second field is saved and unchecking the Visible in Query property.

The code example in Listing 8.6 is also an example of list modules broken down by products. The implementation in ClearQuest is usually by stateless record types linked with a field of type Reference_List.

8.8.7.4 Creating a Tree-like List

Arranging and displaying the data in a tree-like manner can ease the user selection work, as navigation from an upper level to lower ones is made easy. Unfortunately, ClearQuest does not have such graphic control in the GUI palette. But with some programming we can imitate the tree structure with regular list controls such as drop-down combo boxes. An important limitation of this implementation is that the maximum number of levels in the tree must be defined in Clear-Quest Designer.

Let's consider an example. To record a defect in an SAP implementation, the component_ID should be selected. The number of components is greater than 13,000, but luckily SAP components are arranged in a tree manner, so we can provide a practical solution.

Our proposed solution is to create a stateless record type having the following fields:

- ComponentID (short string)
- ComponentDescription (short string)
- ComponentLevel (integer)

In the work item record (defect or other type) add a field for each level in the tree. The user will select the first level, and the selection will populate the values for next level. The user experience is similar to tree navigation. In Figure 8.25 you can see an example of six fields supporting a six-level data tree.

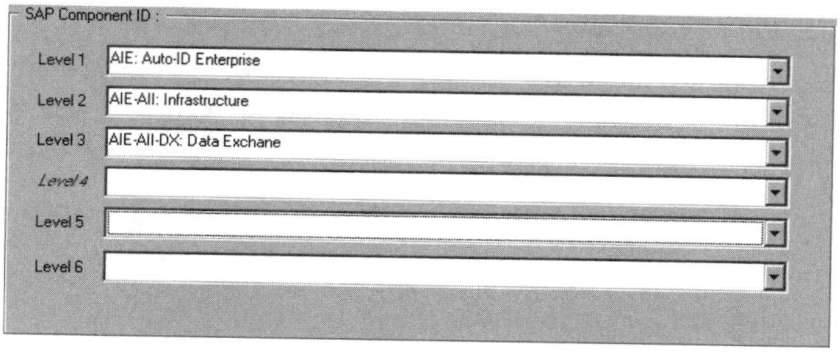

Figure 8.25 Six-level data hierarchy

As the algorithm for building the choice list for each level (except first level) is the same, it is preferable to put the code in a global hook and call it from the choice list hook. The code in Listing 8.11 is an example of the global hook.

Listing 8.11 Multilevel Choice Lists

```
sub Comp_ChoiceList {
    my($fieldname) = @_;
    my @choices;
# Purpose: build the choicelist for a tree like data structure
# Input: $fieldname as string scalar
# Output: @choices as string array
# By:   SB 25.08.09
# Comments: field name is Comp_level+numlevel
#       (ex:Comp_level1,Comp_level2 ...Comp_level9)
#             This subroutine deals with levels 2 to 9
# chop last digit from fieldname to get the current level
 my $fieldstr = substr( $fieldname, 0 , -1);
 my $numlevel = int (chop($fieldname));

 my $session = $entity->GetSession();
 my $resultvalue, $fld, $val ;
# Get the upper level ID to use in the query filter
 my $uplevelname = $ fieldstr . sprintf("%01d", $numlevel-1);
 my $uplevel = $entity->GetFieldValue($uplevelname)->GetValue();
    ($fld, $val) = split   ': ' , $uplevel ;

# Build the query:
#     select ComponentID, Description
#     from SAP_Component_ID
```

continues

Listing 8.11 Multilevel Choice Lists (*Continued*)

```
#      where Comp_Level=$numlevel AND ComponentID like 'UplevelID'
 my $queryDefObj = $session->BuildQuery("SAP_Component_ID");
 my @curid = ( $fld . "-%");
 my $filterOp = $queryDefObj->BuildFilterOperator(
$CQPerlExt::CQ_BOOL_OP_AND);
 my @mytemp = (sprintf("%01d", $numlevel));
 $filterOp->BuildFilter("Comp_Level",
$CQPerlExt::CQ_COMP_OP_EQ, \@mytemp );
 $filterOp->BuildFilter("ComponentID",
$CQPerlExt::CQ_COMP_OP_LIKE, \@curid );
 $queryDefObj->BuildField("ComponentID");
 $queryDefObj->BuildField("Description");
 my $resultSetObj = $session->BuildResultSet($queryDefObj);
 $resultSetObj->Execute();

while ($resultSetObj->MoveNext() == $CQPerlExt::CQ_SUCCESS) {
   $resultvalue = $resultSetObj->GetColumnValue(1) . ": " .
             $resultSetObj->GetColumnValue(2);
   push(@choices, $resultvalue );
 }
    return @choices;
}
```

The code in Listing 8.12 is the calling subroutine from the field `comp_level2` choice list hook. Note that the number that was chopped represents the level in the tree; also note that you can pass the field name as is and do the chopping in the global hook. Take this as an exercise. The calling hooks from other levels are the same.

Listing 8.12 Build a Choice List in Each Level

```
sub comp_level2_ChoiceList {
  my($fieldname) = @_;
  my @choices;
# $fieldname as string scalar
# @choices as string array
# record type name is RQMDefect
# field name is Comp_level2
  @choices = Comp_ChoiceList($fieldname);
  return @choices;
}
```

8.8.8 Updating a Dynamic List

Dynamic lists are lists that are linked to a field's choice list and can be updated outside the schema. If a field's choice list requires a periodic update, it is a good idea to hook it to a dynamic list so that you will not have to change the schema (as with a static choice list). Dynamic lists can be updated manually from the ClearQuest native client, by using a utility to import data to the list, or by using the API. We shall discuss each of the three update methods.

8.8.8.1 ClearQuest Client

This operation can be performed from the Windows client or the Eclipse client; each is accessed in a different way:

- Windows: Click Edit > Named Lists and select the list to edit.
- Eclipse: Click Tools >Administration > Edit Named Lists and select the list to edit.

To edit dynamic lists you need Dynamic List Administrator or Superuser privileges.

8.8.8.2 Import Utility

The command-line utility `importutil` allows importing lists to dynamic lists. The command syntax is

```
importutil importlist [ -dbset name ] login password \
  dbname listname "import_file_name"
```

The import file format is a list of members, with each member in a separate line.

8.8.8.3 Using the API

The ClearQuest API allows you to read dynamic lists and add members to the list. Listing 8.13 is an example that demonstrates how to make use of the API. If you look at the DefectTracking schema, there are two fields, Keywords and Symptoms, that are of type Multiline and connected to choice list control. This allows the user to select more than one element (multi-selection). The user can also type a value in addition to selecting a value. An organization may want to check whether the user entered a value that is not in the original list, and if so, add that value to the dynamic list. The `ValueChanged` hook in Listing 8.13 does exactly this operation.

Listing 8.13   Updating a List Dynamically

```
Sub keywords_ValueChanged(fieldname)
  ' fieldname As String
  ' record type name is Defect
  ' field name is Keywords
  ' Start User Code
```

continues

Listing 8.13   Updating a List Dynamically (*Continued*)

```
Dim session
Dim Keyvals   ' current values in the field
Dim Listmembers ' current list in the dynamic choice-list

set session = GetSession()
'Notice: Both the field and the dynamic list are called "keywords"
Listmembers = Session.GetListMembers("keywords")
av = GetFieldValue("keywords").GetValueAsList
if not IsEmpty(av) then
   Keyvals  = Split(Cstr(av(0)),vbLF)
end if

For Each keyfield in Keyvals
  isnew = 1 ' Assume it is new
  For Each keymember in Listmembers
    if (keyfield = keymember ) then
      isnew = 0 ' It is NOT new
      exit for
    end if
  Next

  if ( isnew = 1 ) then
    ' Add item to the dynamic list
   Session.AddListMember "Keywords", keyfield
  end if
 Next
 ' End User Code
End Sub
```

Note the BASIC session method that adds the member to the list:

```
session.AddListMember listName, listMember
```

8.8.9 Using Hard-Coded Data

Using hard-coded data in hooks may lead to situations where you will have to change the schema to modify the data. The code in Listing 8.14 is an example of data hard-coded in the choice list hook; the list is dependent on the target state, which is hard-coded, and the choice lists for the field Resolution are also hard-coded.

Listing 8.14   Hard-Coded Values in Hooks

```
sub resolution_ChoiceList {
    my($fieldname) = @_;
    my @choices;
    # record type name is Defect
    # field name is Resolution
    my $state = $entity->GetFieldValue("State")->GetValue();
    push(@choices, "");
    if ($state eq "Rejected") {
        push(@choices, "Cannot replicate error", "New Requirements",
            "Works as defined", "Canceled", "Test Error",
            "Out of Scope", "Deferred");
    }
    elsif ($state eq "Fixed"){
        push(@choices, "Data", "Requirements", "Code", "Configuration",
            "Build", "Documentation", "Environment", "Security",
            "Globalization");
    }
    return @choices;
}
```

In this case we can consider the choice list very much as a constant list. So if the list is unlikely to change, it is reasonable to include it in a hook. But if you anticipate that values will be added to the list, you should consider other techniques to store the data. ClearQuest offers you dynamic lists and stateless records for dynamic data.

The simplest way to use a dynamic list is to add it to the choice list in the schema and later add the values using the client. A more advanced way is to read data from the list from a hook using the method GetListMembers().

The code in Listing 8.15 is an example that enhances the ALM schema. We want to automatically assign the next role, and we need to select the primary user from multiple available roles. In the dynamic list we store the application name and the application abbreviation which is part of the role name. This allows us to identify the next role and automate the process.

Listing 8.15   Auto-Assign Next Role

```
sub GetNextRole()
{
    my( $almtype, $role ) = @_;

# Purpose: Build the the ALMRoleTypeLabel from the activity type and
#          the current role. The application and the abbreviation are
```

continues

Listing 8.15   Auto-Assign Next Role (*Continued*)

```
#          stored in a dynamic list
#          for example> WebSphere Business Modeler::WBM
# Input : $almtype- Activity type == application name
#          $role - Abbreviated role text (ex. Build Deploy Lead == BDL)
# Output: $almrole - ex. BDL-WBM

  my $list_values = $session->GetListMembers("ApplicationTypes");

# Verify if the almtype exist in the dynamic list
 foreach $Keyval (@$list_values) {
      my ($type, $abbrev)= split '::', $Keyval;
    if ($almtype eq $type) {
      $AppAbbrev = $abbrev;
        last;
    }
 }
#      Build the ALMrole name.
      my $almrole = $role . "-" . $AppAbbrev ;

      return $almrole;
}
```

Our suggestion is to store data outside the schema, even if it requires some more coding effort. Your investment will be rewarded by lower maintenance and fewer schema changes.

8.9 Web Considerations

If your users will be using the ClearQuest Web client, you should be aware of some differences in its dynamic behavior. Record scripts attached to buttons will not work if not enabled for the Web. Dependent choice lists that need to be recalculated when another field value is changed must specify for Web execution which is the dependent field.

8.9.1 Enable Button Hooks

If a pushbutton control has pre-action or post-action hooks, they must be set to "Enabled for web." This is defined in the button Properties window, under the Button Hooks tab. See Figure 8.26 for an example of hooks PreClone and PostClone that are enabled for the Web.

Other button types that have hooks associated with them must also be checked to be "Enabled for web" in the same way.

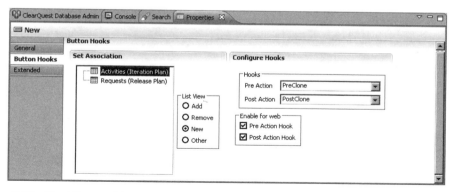

Figure 8.26 Enabling pushbuttons for the Web

8.9.2 Field Dependency

If a field has a choice list hook and the result of this hook is dependent on the value of another field, then the choice list needs to be recalculated each time the dependent field value is changed. To update the choice list associated with the dependent field, click Recalculate Choice List on the choice list of the field. The contents of the list are recalculated before the list is displayed. But this is not enough for Web clients.

To make a form with dependent fields available in Rational ClearQuest Web:

1. When adding the field to the form, use one of the following form controls for the parent field and its dependent fields: drop-down list box, combo box, drop-down combo box.

2. Open the Properties window of the parent field control (right-click the control field and click Properties). In the property sheet for the control, use the Web Dependent Fields tab to specify the fields that depend on the respective field value.

3. On the Web Dependent Fields tab, select the appropriate child fields from the Available list and click the arrow to add them to the Selected list. Only the parent field of the dependency must be Web-enabled.

Figure 8.27 shows the Properties window of the field Type; the field Owner was selected as dependent. This ensures that when the value in the field Type is changed, the choice list of the field Owner will be recalculated.

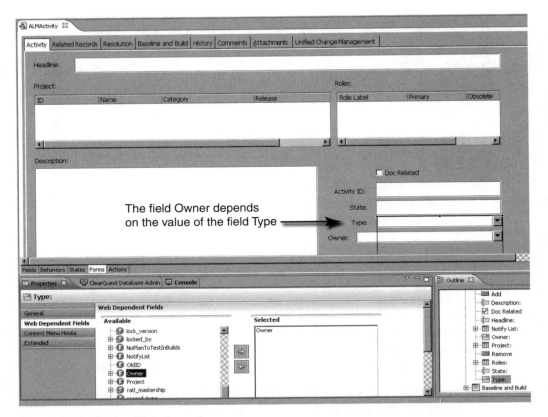

Figure 8.27   Setting Web dependency

8.9.3 Other Limitations

Another limitation of the Web client is that context menu hooks are not supported on any form control. Also, as previously discussed, message boxes (launched with MsgBox) will not be displayed on the Web client. They will be opened on the Web server. Many open messages may lead to crashing of the Web server.

For more information on the dynamic behavior of ClearQuest Web, see ClearQuest Help > Developing > Developing schemas with the ClearQuest designer > Customizing the ClearQuest Web.

Also see

> IBM Rational, "Writing ClearQuest Hooks to Run in ClearQuest Web 7.0.x," *IBM Technote*, www-01.ibm.com/support/docview.wss?uid=swg21238816, 2008 (accessed February 24, 2011).

8.10 Preparing for the Future

In many cases you get list of requirements and you develop the features based on the priorities of the requirements. When you develop one feature, bear in mind what will be required in the future. You can save yourself a lot of schema development time by considering future development. Here is an example:

You need to develop a new record type, and you have all the detailed definitions for it. You can start working according to the definitions. But if you know that in a future release your organization plans to adopt UCM and integrate to ClearCase, you may prepare your record type for that. The UCM package imposes some constraints, such as having a short field called Headline and a reference field to Users called Owner. If these fields are already in the schema, it saves you the need to create new fields in the future, as well as the significant effort of copying data from the old fields to the new ones. To continue with the same example, the UCM enforces some rules on the state machine; it is therefore best to be ready with a state machine that would be easily enabled for the UCM package.

You should also consider maintenance issues. For example, even if the use case does not require a Modify action in all states, it is advisable to add a Modify action, with Access_Control to the administrator only, to deal with maintenance issues in the future. We also suggest adding a special action that will allow the administrator to modify even fields that are in read-only mode. To do this you can implement the Superuser Modification pattern as described in section 8.1.2.7, "Superuser Modification Pattern."

Another maintenance suggestion is to create a stateless record type that will store system-wide or project-specific information. This project information will be used by the hooks you develop. Some examples for such data are maximum single attachment size, total attachment size, special notification lists, and physical name of Web server.

8.11 Resources

8.11.1 ClearQuest

King, Amber, "Extending IBM Rational ClearQuest: Dynamic Hook Code and Configurable Field Behavior," presentation CRMA41 delivered at the Rational Software Developer Conference, Orlando, FL, June 10–14, 2007.

Murphy, Alan, "Superscripts—Advanced IBM Rational ClearQuest Scripting Techniques," presentation CRMA34 delivered at the Rational Software Developer Conference, Orlando, FL, June 1–5, 2008.

8.11.2 Jazz

Patterson, Scott, "Introduction to Jazz Foundation Application SDK," https://jazz.net/wiki/bin/view/Main/AppSdkIntroduction, December 1, 2010 (accessed February 22, 2011).

The Jazz Foundation Application provides a set of libraries, samples, tools, and documentation. This reference outlines the current capabilities of the Jazz Foundation Application SDK.

Lemieux, Jean-Michel, "Integrating and Extending Rational Team Concert (the SDK)," https://jazz.net/wiki/bin/view/Main/RtcSdk20, November 19, 2010 (accessed February 22, 2011).

Welcome to the development resources for integrating and extending Team Concert. This information is intended to provide a reference to developers building integrations with Team Concert that require code or scripts to be written.

Streule, Patrick, "Resource Oriented Work Item API 2.0," https://jazz.net/wiki/bin/view/Main/ResourceOrientedWorkItemAPIv2, April 13, 2010 (accessed February 22, 2011).

In a nutshell, the API described here allows you to get, create, modify, and query work items and other resources using standard HTTP methods.

Lemieux, Jean-Michel, "Extending Rational Team Concert 2.0," presentation SDP023 delivered at the Rational Software Developer Conference, Orlando, FL, May 31–June 4, 2009, https://jazz.net/wiki/pub/Main/RtcSdk20/RSDC2009-extendingrtc.ppt (accessed February 22, 2011).

"Extending Team Concert," http://jazz.net/forums/rss.php?f=2 (accessed February 22, 2011).

8.12 Summary

In this chapter we covered advanced considerations related to the development of ClearQuest and Jazz-based applications. The chapter started with ClearQuest schema development, selecting the base schema to start, and using packages and design patterns. We provided examples of implementing several design patterns in ClearQuest and Jazz. We described how to create and reuse assets of various types such as code, forms, record types, and schema portions.

We continued with a discussion of subjects that are appealing to many large organizations, such as parallel development, storing hook code externally to improve maintainability, and creating and using the test environment to improve system quality.

We briefly discussed some development considerations for customers using ClearQuest MutiSite, such as mastership and testing.

The chapter ended with many development topics, among them creating a tree-like hierarchy, dealing with long lists, updating dynamic lists, and many more. We discussed the general development issues of naming convention, script organization, hard-coding data in hooks, and various development considerations for Web clients.

Metrics and Governance

In today's world of investments gone bad, projects being canceled because of budget constraints, and other financial hardships, one thing is more certain than ever before: if you can't measure the results of your process or investment, you have no idea what the real cost of the effort is. Many tools capture all kinds of data about many things. Many organizations focus on the usage model and workflows of their systems to improve their process governance. These are all needed, but they are not enough. A very important aspect of any system is the ability to easily get data from it on which to base business decisions. You may have the best ClearQuest schema in the world, and it may do a lot of cool stuff, but if you don't have the ability to generate key reports, you are only realizing half the value from your tool investment.

In the first part of the chapter we will explore various types of metrics that can be created with ClearQuest or with the Jazz-based system.

The second part of the chapter is about change management (CM) governance. We discuss process control, access control, user permissions, and monitoring the processes. We continue by demonstrating how you can establish various levels of CM governance with ClearQuest and with the Jazz tools.

9.1 Metrics

This section explores types of metrics, strategies organizations can adopt, and tools they can use to measure and show improvement.

Metrics are usually categorized in four levels depending on the organizational level and role that will be using the metrics. The levels are individual, team, project, and organization.

The organization should define a strategy to create reports that provide the status of each process in the software development lifecycle. A good strategy will ease the discovery of process flaws and help the organization to improve performance.

To generate these metrics you can use the reporting utilities provided with the tool and external tools that extract the data from the tool repositories. We describe the reporting tools in section 9.1.4, "Tools."

9.1.1 Types of Metrics

Organizations typically categorize their metrics in three or four levels:

- **Individual:** used to measure individual productivity and efficiency

  These metrics are typically related to counting source lines of code (SLOCs) per unit time, bugs fixed per unit time, or requirements generated per unit time. This list is not all-inclusive, but the idea is simply to examine the effectiveness of the individual or outsourced individuals. Examples of this are metrics based on headcount cost and lines of code, code complexity, and defects generated.

- **Team:** used to measure a small team's productivity and efficiency within a project

  These metrics are very similar to the individual metrics but focus on a team rather than an individual. For example, in the Agile practice, team productivity can be measured by team velocity, requirements delivered, and defects found.

- **Project:** the typical project metrics

  These include the project management metrics such as actual cost of work performed (ACWP), estimated total cost (ETC), and budgeted cost of work performed (BCWP). These also include the development metrics: requirements volatility, test coverage, requirements to test traceability, defect density, and so on. The good news is that ClearQuest can generate these easily. The bad news is that each organization is slightly different, so not every organization or project will want to see every metric. For a prescriptive set you can start with the Measured Capability Improvement Framework (MCIF) set of metrics.

- **Organization**

  These metrics are strongly tilted toward the business and project portfolio metrics and away from the development metrics. There is also a strong tilt in the development metrics toward the test and quality metrics at this level.

9.1.2 Metrics Strategy

A common strategy for metrics is to look at the software development lifecycle (SDLC) as a series of processes with work items and artifacts flowing through it. A good metrics strategy will produce a series of reports such as the following:

- A graph of work items open, resolved, and closed. The work items can be use cases, features, or requirements in the definition phase; defects or tests in the maintenance phases; or however the planning granularity is tracked. The graph shows time so that trends can be examined and decisions can be made about probable completion dates. An example is shown in Figure 9.1.

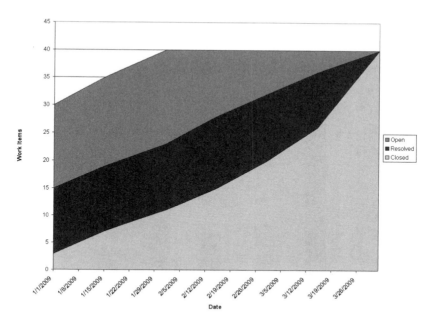

Figure 9.1   Work item status over time

- A histogram of the estimated size of the work items is also useful. This is typically done in terms of effort. An example is shown in Figure 9.2. In the chart you can see that there are about 75 work items for which the estimated work effort is less than one day, and there are 20 records for which the estimated work effort is between five and seven days, and so on.

- For Agile projects a graph of the velocity is useful for an iteration, with the velocity being defined as the number of work items done per unit time. In Agile projects the unit of time should not be greater than one to two days. An example is shown in Figure 9.3.

- A chart can also show work items in terms of planned and unplanned work. A large amount of unplanned work has a tendency to slip deadlines. Figure 9.4 shows an example.

- Reports you do for work items in general can also be done for each type of work item, such as defects. As the number of defects starts to rise during the project, they should get fixed and the open defect rate should fall as shown in Figure 9.5. Of course things are not ready to ship yet.

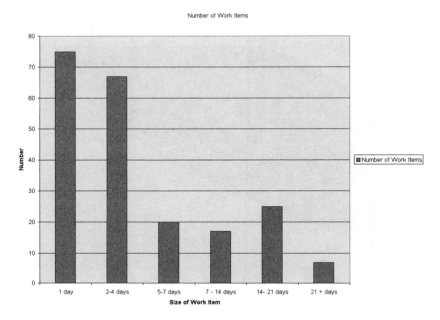

Figure 9.2   Work item size estimation

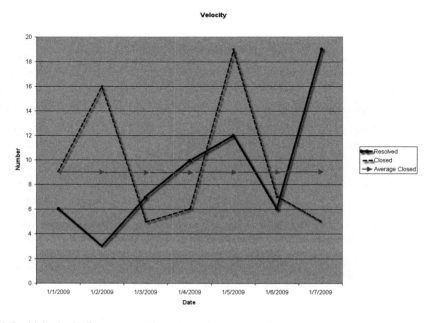

Figure 9.3   Velocity indicator: work item completion over time

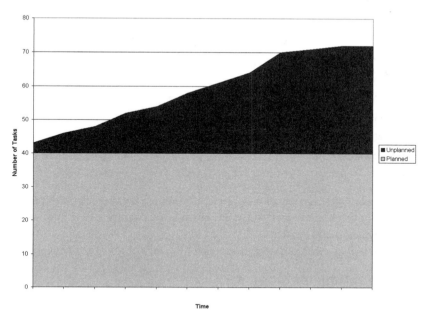

Figure 9.4   Planned versus unplanned work items

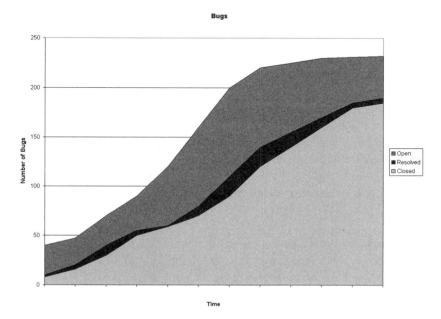

Figure 9.5   Work item resolution rate: open, resolved, and closed bugs over time

- Build reports are very important as well. Each failure should be reported on as well as the cause of each failure.

- The following quality indicators should be placed on a single report to provide overall trends to the testing teams:
    - Code churn
    - Tests passed
    - Percentage code coverage
    - Tests failed
    - Tests not completed

These are a few reports that have been used to help troubleshoot projects in the past. We could build similar sets with requirements and requirements traceability. We could also do similar things with design classes and services.

Reports such as these would be useful to each of the roles that Rational covers in the SDLC.

9.1.3 Supporting Data for Metrics

When you define your metrics strategy, you need to analyze your schema metadata to find out whether you have the supporting data to derive the metrics required. For example, if you want to derive a histogram of the estimated size of work items in a project, you need to have at least a field containing the estimated effort of each work item. This field is a default in a Jazz work item, but for ClearQuest you will have to add such a field to each work item type. If your strategy requires more precise analysis, you may need more than one field, such as estimated effort for development and estimated effort for testing and maybe more.

For ClearQuest you will have to consider the units of time measured. In a Jazz work item the user can select the units (3 d for three days, 20 h for 20 hours); with ClearQuest it is not that easy (although it is possible with scripting). We suggest defining a field of type Integer and using hours as a unit of measurement, but of course this is not the only option and for some implementations it may not be suitable.

Another example would be measuring project status; for that you would need at least fields for a due date and an actual date. Jazz work items have the due date field by default; there is no actual date field, but this information can be retrieved from the history, although not as easily as retrieving the data from a dedicated field of type Date.

9.1.4 Tools

Generating the metrics requires a tool and sometimes more than one tool. The tool is required to collect data from one or more repositories and present the results to the user in the required format. Formats can be textual reports, various types of charts, lists, and more.

To generate individual and team metrics, many of the work item management tools include internal reporting utilities. For example, ClearQuest includes the following:

- Internal query wizard and SQL query to display a matrix of field data
- Internal chart wizard to display trend charts, distribution charts, and aging charts
- Crystal Reports, integrated with ClearQuest, to generate textual and formatted reports

These tools and utilities can access a single repository and can provide metrics for individuals, teams, and some of the project-level metrics.

Another product that can generate ClearQuest reports is Rational SoDA (Software Document Automation). This product can access the repositories of several Rational tools such as RequisitePro, ClearCase, and ClearQuest and generate documents that combine data from all repositories. The disadvantages of using SoDA are the complexity of the definition of the reports and the long time it takes to generate them. The advantages are the ability to access more than one repository and the fact that it uses the popular Microsoft Word application to define the templates and generate the reports.

9.1.4.1 Crystal Reports

Crystal is a reporting tool from Business Objects (SAP) that allows you to create ClearQuest report formats. A report format is the report layout that specifies where and how to display the fields on the report form. Note that Crystal Reports Designer does not work over the Web.

To complete the report you need a query that defines which records will be retrieved from the database. Figure 9.6 demonstrates the definition of a report that includes the selection of the report format and the query.

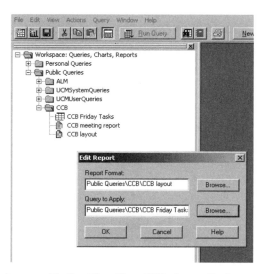

Figure 9.6　Definition of a report in the ClearQuest Windows client

> **Note** The report format in Figure 9.6 was created with Crystal Reports Designer. The query was created with the ClearQuest query wizard.

For more information on Crystal Reports visit the product Web site: "SAP Crystal Solutions—SAP Crystal Reports," www.sap.com/solutions/sap-crystal-solutions/query-reporting-analysis/sapcrystalreports/index.epx.

For detailed instructions on how to create reports and report formats, see ClearQuest Help > Managing Change and Releases > Using the Rational ClearQuest for Windows Client > Viewing query results in reports > About creating and editing report formats.

9.1.4.2 Business Intelligence and Reporting Tools (BIRT)

BIRT is an Eclipse-based open-source reporting system for Web applications. BIRT has two main components: a report designer based on Eclipse, and a runtime component that you can add to your application server. For more information on BIRT visit "Business Intelligence and Reporting Tools," www.eclipse.org/birt/phoenix/ (accessed February 24, 2011).

To learn about deployment options visit ACTUATE, "Datasheets and White Papers to Better Help You Understand BIRT-Based Products," www.birt-exchange.com/be/products/product-resources/ (accessed February 24, 2011).

9.1.4.3 Report Management with the Report Server for ClearQuest

You can use the Report Server for ClearQuest to manage and run ClearQuest reports.

ClearQuest reports can be designed with Crystal Reports or with the open-source BIRT designer included with the ClearQuest Eclipse client. The reports can then be uploaded to the Report Server for ClearQuest. The Report Server for ClearQuest provides services to manage and run ClearQuest reports.

The Report Server interaction with ClearQuest is demonstrated in Figure 9.7.

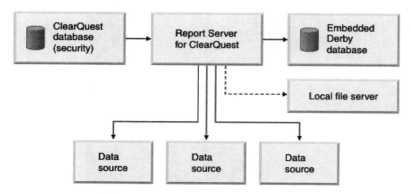

Figure 9.7   Report Server for ClearQuest

To learn more about the Report Server functionality, possible configurations, and deployment, see ClearQuest Help > Administering > Administering Rational ClearQuest Web > Planning and configuring the reporting environment > Reporting deployment configuration > About the report server for ClearQuest.

9.1.4.4 Rational Publishing Engine

Rational Publishing Engine is a solution for document generation from data held in Rational ClearQuest, Rational Quality Manager, Rational Team Concert, Rational DOORS, Rational Tau, Rational RequisitePro, Rational ClearCase, and third-party applications including any XML data source. You can run the document generation manually or in batch mode for unattended use. You can either use the predefined templates or design your own using the Document Studio application.

For more information visit the Publishing Engine Web page: IBM Rational, "Rational Publishing Engine—A Document Publishing Automation Tool," www-01.ibm.com/software/awd-tools/pubengine/ (accessed February 24, 2011).

9.1.4.5 Rational Insight

Rational Insight is not just a reporting tool; it is an ETL (extract, transform, load) engine that extracts data from various sources (such as ClearQuest and RTC repositories) and presents the required data for each role in a Web-based view. For example, Insight reports can be optimized by role; you can evaluate actual results against business or project goals and receive e-mail alerts.

Insight can be configured to support multiple projects and multiple products and will work in a geographically distributed environment. Rational Insight is coupled to Rational's Measured Capability Improvement Framework (MCIF) for best practice measurement guidance; it enables organizations to capture the right information so that they can measure and improve their software delivery processes over time.

For more information visit the following Web pages:

> IBM Rational, "Rational Insight—Real Insight. Real Results. Real Progress," www-01.ibm.com/software/rational/products/insight/index.html (accessed February 24, 2011).

> IBM Rational, "Rational Insight—Systematic and Consistent Project Performance Evaluation and Tracking," http://jazz.net/projects/rational-insight/ (accessed February 24, 2011).

9.2 Governance

Governance consists of the processes and actions that management takes to enforce the policy and rules the organization has decided upon. It involves measuring performance and taking action to reduce risks. We usually talk about business governance and IT governance, but in this book we are interested in a narrower view. In this chapter we shall focus on how work items are used in the governance of the process of change.

Work item management provides some level of governance with the capabilities incorporated into the tools:

- Process control and automation
- Permissions (access control and security)
- Monitoring

We shall first discuss each of the capabilities and later explain the usage with ClearQuest and Rational Team Concert.

9.2.1 Process Control and Automation

The ability to define a workflow that specifies the change request lifecycle enables IT to enforce a process that conforms to the organization's rules. This process can be as rigid as required, meaning that no work-arounds are possible; on the other hand the process can be more flexible when less control is required. For example, if the process requires that an SCCB must approve every major change, that rule can be enforced in the work item workflow. In addition, the process should be set up in a way that only a person having the role SCCB is allowed to perform an action (Approve, Reject, or Defer) that is a result of the SCCB decision.

Every action in the workflow can be controlled in the same way. Here are some examples: Only the role Test Manager can approve the correctness of a fix; only the role Development Lead can approve a change resolution; build should be approved by the Build Manager and Development Manager roles; closing a change request is performed by the Submitter role.

Another method of governing the process, probably the best way, is by automation—actions are performed automatically and executed by a set of rules—although this is not always possible. Here are some examples of automation:

- Change the state of a work item based on internal conditions.
- Set the due date based on the severity and the required fix effort.
- Auto-assign a user based on the work item type.
- Launch automatic testing upon a developer's Deliver action.

9.2.2 Permissions (Access Control and Security)

User permission is a broad term and is related to several levels in the change management application and to several objects in the work item.

System access is the user permission to log in to the system. This is the first security control element. The administrator can grant a user access to a repository, set the user's role, and allow the user to have access to tools and utilities. System access is related to user authentication, which can be performed at the tool level (users are defined in the tool repository) or in an external directory such as LDAP.

Access control is the user permission to perform an action on a work item, for example, permission to submit an enhancement request or permission to close a defect. Access control can be set for individuals, user groups, or roles. Using roles is probably the best way, as we discussed in Chapter 5, "Roles."

Field permission is the user permission to modify the value of a specific field in a specific state of the work item lifecycle. Field permission can be read-only, optional, or mandatory.

Record security is the permission to see the content of a specific record. ClearQuest record security completely hides the records from users who are not members of groups that have the permission to see the record. Security record permission is usually set by project or product. (This feature is not supported in the Jazz work item.)

Electronic signature is a method that requires the user to provide an electronic signature before a sensitive operation. This procedure is common in medical and financial processes. The additional signature ensures that the person performing the action is indeed the person who is logged in to the system.

9.2.3 Monitoring

Monitoring involves the capability to trace historical information or to capture current and historical project status. Examples of historical monitoring are the following:

- Who has performed a specific action?
- Who has changed the value of a field (for example, reduced the severity level) and when?
- What were the values of the record fields before and after the user's action?
- Who has authorized this work?

These are examples of project status monitoring:

- Which are the high-priority defects that are waiting to be resolved?
- Show me the list of requirements not covered by work items in the current release.
- What is the total number of lines of code developed by each team in the last iteration?
- Which are the work items that are not closed and are past their due date?

Monitoring current work status involves getting data in real time (or close to real time); here are some examples:

- Knowing what work items each team is working on
- Knowing what work item each individual is working on
- Getting a notification of when delays are detected in the project
- Being alerted to new risks that have exceeded some threshold value

Monitoring can be achieved by data pulled or pushed to the requestor. Pushed data includes e-mail notifications, RSS feeds, and dashboards. Pulled data includes execution of queries, charts, and reports that generate the required data.

9.2.4 Governance with ClearQuest

In this section we explain how to implement each of the governance elements discussed above (process control and automation, permissions, and monitoring) with ClearQuest.

9.2.4.1 Process Control and Automation with ClearQuest

Define the state transition matrix in each of the ClearQuest stateful record types to implement the organization workflow. (Workflow was discussed in detail in Chapter 3, "The Workflow.")

For each action in the workflow set the Access Control hook, either by selecting the allowed user groups or by selecting a script that will dynamically set the allowed users by their roles. Role was discussed in detail in Chapter 5, "Roles."

Process automation can be performed in ClearQuest by developing hooks with the Clear-Quest API. In section 3.4, "Dynamic Workflow," in Chapter 3, "The Workflow," we discussed this in detail.

9.2.4.2 Permissions with ClearQuest

The first permission level is system access. In the ClearQuest User Administration tool you subscribe users to databases. Users will not be able to log in to a database to which they are not subscribed. Figure 9.8 shows the User Properties window; you can see that the user is subscribed to all databases. Also, you can turn LDAP authentication on to improve the security of the system. Because ClearQuest does not enforce any rules on the user password, active directory

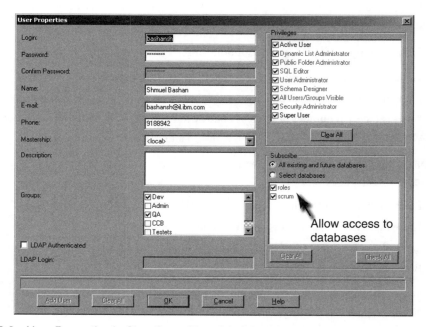

Figure 9.8   User Properties in ClearQuest User Administration

authentication will improve the security of the system. The User Properties dialog also defines the groups that a user belongs to, the privileges for various operations, and the database subscription.

Each action that a user can perform includes an Access Control hook. In Figure 9.9 you can see that Access Control to all actions is set by User Groups, but you can also set it with a BASIC or Perl script by clicking the Access Control box and selecting SCRIPTS > Add Perl Script, as shown in the figure.

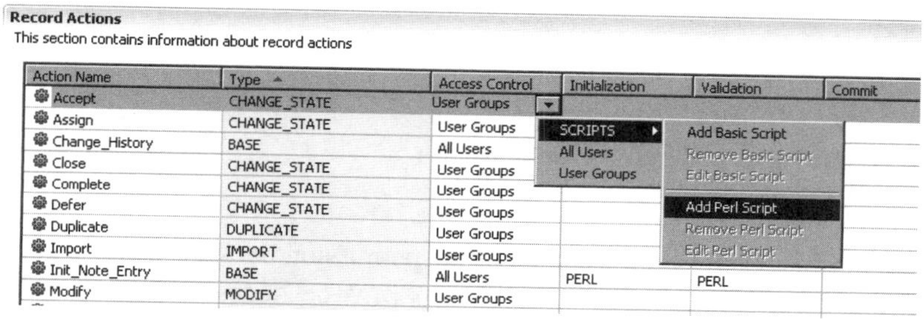

Figure 9.9   ClearQuest Access Control hooks

Field permission is the user permission to modify the value of a specific field in a specific state of the work item lifecycle. To set the field permission, modify the Field Behaviors Section of each record type. For each field select the required behavior in each state. See the field behaviors table in Figure 9.10.

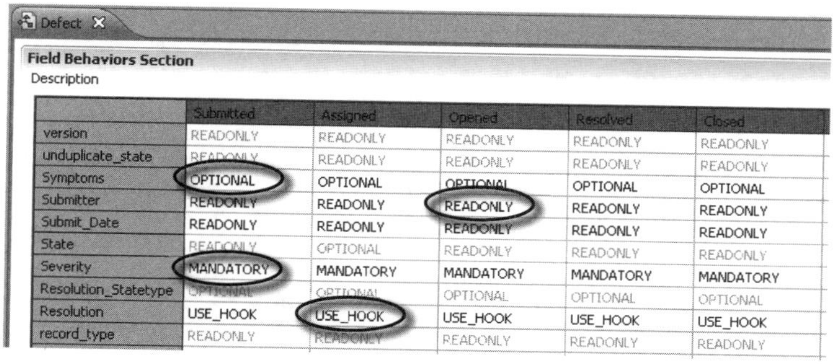

Figure 9.10   ClearQuest field behaviors in each state

The behaviors READ_ONLY, OPTIONAL, and MANDATORY are static for each state. To set a dynamic behavior you have to select the USE_HOOK value, as shown in Figure 9.10 for the field Resolution. The USE_HOOK behavior will require you to write a hook. This hook is written in the field permission area. Figure 9.11 shows the Record Fields section of the record type and the permission hook location.

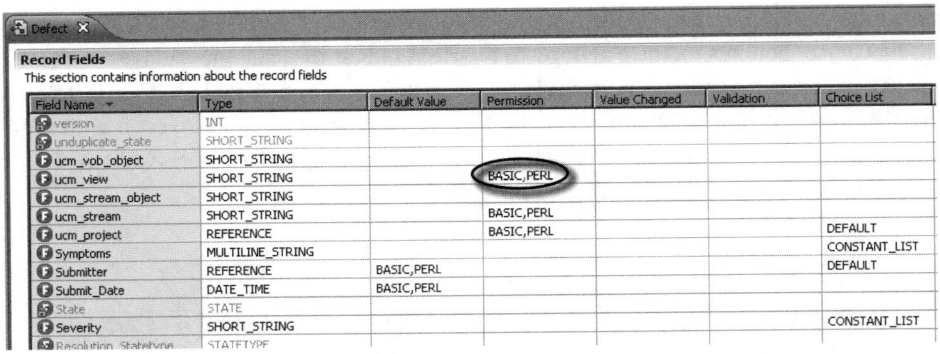

Figure 9.11   ClearQuest field permission hook

The code in Listing 9.1 is an example of the permission hook of the field `ucm_view`. The hook returns the value `$CQPerlExt::CQ_READONLY` or `$CQPerlExt::CQ_OPTIONAL` to dynamically set the field behavior to read-only or optional.

Listing 9.1   Setting Field Permission

```
sub ucm_view_Permission {
    my($fieldname, $username) = @_;
    my $result;
    # $fieldname as string scalar
    # $username as string scalar
    # $result as long scalar
    # record type name is Defect
    # field name is ucm_view
    # Start User Code

    # Set default value to return
    $result = $CQPerlExt::CQ_READONLY;

    # check if the session variable is defined
    my $variable_defined_flag = $session->HasValue("EDIT_CQACT_CTX_TYPE");

    if ( $variable_defined_flag ) {
      # defined, get the value
      my $edit_ctx_type = $session->GetNameValue("EDIT_CQACT_CTX_TYPE");
      if ( $edit_ctx_type eq "EDIT_ENTITY" ) {
            $result = $CQPerlExt::CQ_OPTIONAL;
      }
    }
```

```
    # End User Code
    return $result;
}
```

9.2.4.3 ClearQuest Security Context

Record security allows you to define which user groups can see a specific record based on a given record field value. For example, if your organization works on classified projects, you may wish to set the security record by project. In this way only the users defined as members of a classified project will be able see the records created in the project context; for other users the project and project records will be completely hidden.

This feature is very powerful if you want to open the database to external users, such as customers, vendors, and contractors. It restricts the external users' view to records that you allow. Figure 9.12 shows the relationships of the record types involved in setting ClearQuest security.

Figure 9.12 Security Context record relationships

The Security Context field is a field of type Reference that points to a stateless or state-based record type. If we follow the previous example, the field Project is the reference to the stateless record type Project. You just have to check the Security Context box in the field Properties window, as highlighted in Figure 9.13.

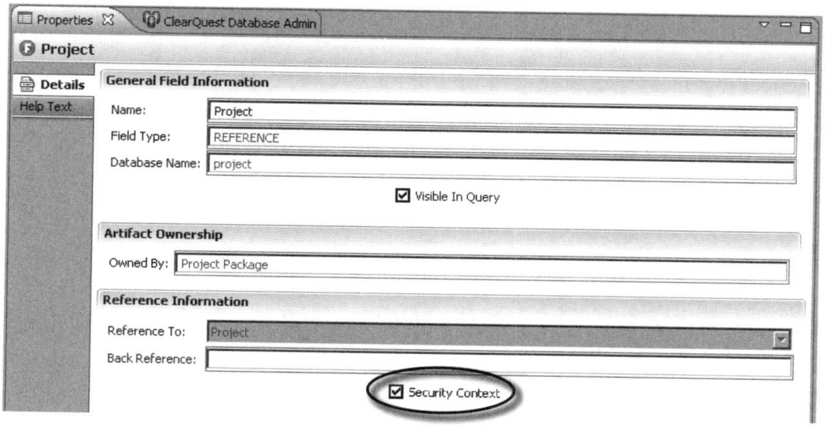

Figure 9.13   Setting a field's Security Context

After marking the Security Context, you must save and reload the schema to view the Security Context changes to the project record. A new field of type Reference_List that points to the Groups record type was created. Also a new tab, Ratl_Security, was created and the newly created field control was put on it. Figure 9.14 shows the tab, the field control, and its properties.

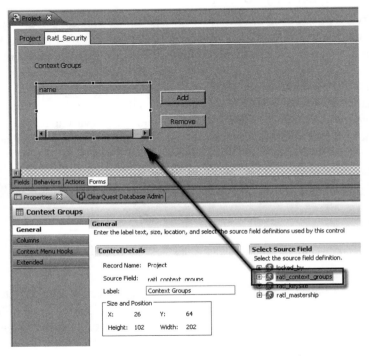

Figure 9.14   New tab and field created in the Security Context record type

After checking in the schema and upgrading the user database, you need to define the groups associated with each project. Let's look at an example. Assume an organization has three projects: Alpha, Beta, and Gamma. Alpha and Beta are classified and Gamma is not. One solution is to create a user group for each project that includes the members of each project. For the project Gamma we can use the group Everyone. Figure 9.15 shows the projects and their associated groups in the query result grid.

Everyone Group   The Everyone group includes all the subscribed users; it became available in version 7.0.1.

For more information see ClearQuest Help > Developing > Developing schemas with the Rational ClearQuest Designer > Creating Security Model.

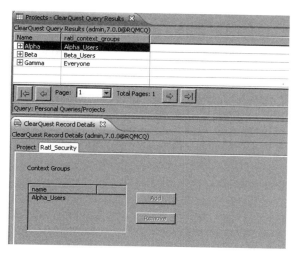

Figure 9.15 Definition of context groups in the Security Context record

9.2.4.4 Electronic Signature in ClearQuest

Electronic signature is a method that requires the user to provide a secret code, such as a password, before performing a sensitive operation. This is common in medical and financial processes. The additional signature ensures that the person performing the action is indeed the person who is logged in to the system.

The electronic signature method of security is enabled through configuring the Electronic Signature package. You can set up the signature to be requested on state change or for specific actions. Usually it is set up to fire on Postpone, Approve, or Close actions.

Figures 9.16, 9.17, and 9.18 demonstrate the usage of the electronic signature during a promotion approval in a banking application. The promotion requires one, two, or three signatures, depending on the target environment. To approve the promotion the relevant role selects the action SignApproval as seen in Figure 9.16.

Figure 9.16 Selecting an approval action that requires a signature

The record is editable and the requiredness of the fields User Name and Password is Mandatory. The logged-on user must enter name and password as shown in Figure 9.17. The User Name is checked to be equal to the current logged-on user. Also notice that the check box Application Signature is marked to identify the signature stage.

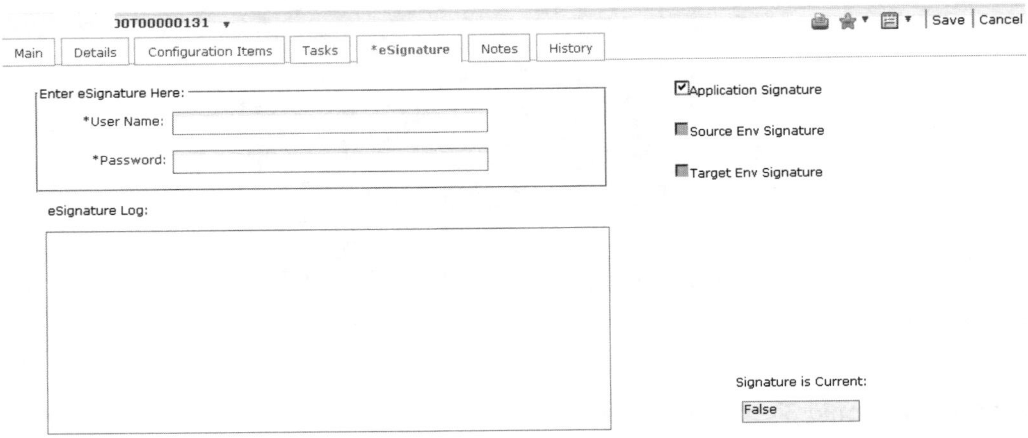

Figure 9.17   Electronic signature fields

The details of the user who signed the approval are logged in the eSignature Log field. Figure 9.18 shows the log field after two approvals.

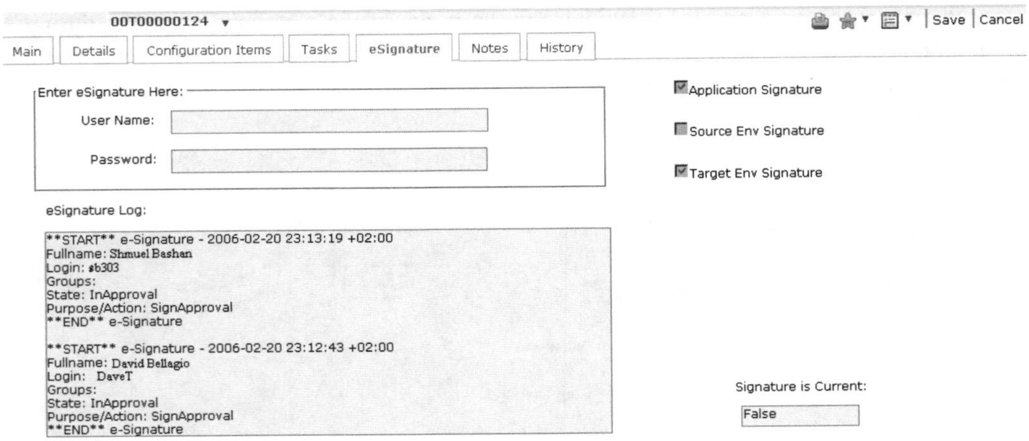

Figure 9.18   Log of signature details

9.2.4.5 Monitoring with ClearQuest

To monitor real-time activities with ClearQuest you will have to run a query periodically, such as every 15 minutes or so, to look for all modified work items since the last time you checked. From the query result set list, you may want to explore certain fields to make decisions in the short term. This can be done manually, or preferably by a script that includes alerts.

A better way to monitor a ClearQuest repository is using a tool like Rational Insight that displays dashboards to managers.

9.2.5 Governance with the ClearQuest ALM Schema

The ClearQuest ALM schema includes some built-in components that enable the organization to govern the process of change without schema changes.

9.2.5.1 ClearQuest ALM Process

The process in the ALM schema is built on three elements: the request, the task, and the activity. Each element (or record type) has a workflow, and the three workflows create the full change workflow. The ALM implementation allows each project to customize the process according to the project's needs. For example, a project can reduce the process to two elements or even one instead of three and by that shorten the change lifecycle.

9.2.5.2 ClearQuest ALM Security Context

In the example described in section 9.2.4.3, "ClearQuest Security Context," we used an existing record type (Project) as the Security Context record, and an existing field (Project) in the Defect record type as the Security Context field. Another approach is to create a dedicated Security Context record type. This approach is used in the ClearQuest ALM schema where the ALMSecurityPolicy stateless record type serves this purpose. It includes the field "name" and the field "ratl_context_groups" which is a Reference_List to the record type "groups." This method allows the definition of various security policies with a single record type. You can use the ALMSecurityPolicy to define security policy for projects, products, components, and other domains by using the Category Security Context.

Figure 9.19 demonstrates the relationship between the SecurityPolicy record type and the Project, Role, Role Label, and Group record types. The numbered items indicate the sequence of operations in creating the security policy.

Figure 9.20 shows the Security Policy field (reference to the ALMSecurityPolicy record) in the History tab of the ALMTask record.

The Security Policy field exists in the following ALM record types:

- **State-based record types:** ALMActivity, ALMTask, ALMRequest, ALMProject, and BTBuild (in BTBuild the field control is in the ALM tab and not in the History tab)

- **Stateless record types:** ALMBaseline, ALMCategory, ALMComment, ALMIteration, ALMPhase, ALMRole, and ALMWorkconfiguration

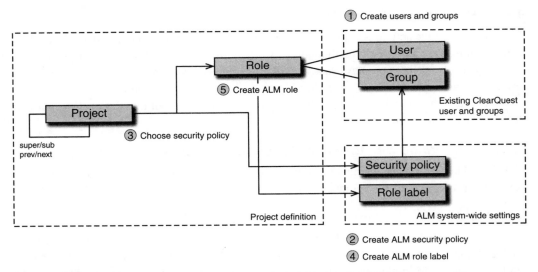

Figure 9.19 ALM Security Policy record type relationship to other record types and the record creation order in defining the ALM security

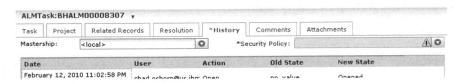

Figure 9.20 ALM Security Policy field in the History tab

9.2.5.3 ClearQuest ALM Roles

The ClearQuest ALM schema includes stateless record types:

- ALMRoleLabel, which defines the role name and what actions are allowed on each record type.

- ALMRole, which defines for each project which members have that role, who is the primary role, and the permitted actions for the project. The project's permitted actions may differ from the ALMRoleLabel permitted actions.

For more information see section 5.5, "Roles in the ClearQuest ALM Schema," in Chapter 5, "Roles."

9.2.6 Governance with Rational Team Concert

In this section we explain how to implement each of the governance elements previously discussed (process control and automation, permissions, and monitoring) with Jazz.

9.2.6.1 Process Control with Jazz

In the Jazz Process Configuration you can define a workflow that includes states, actions, and a state transition matrix. The workflow can be bound to work items to implement the organization's process. Workflow was discussed in detail in Chapter 3, "The Workflow."

9.2.6.2 Permissions with Jazz

Users should be defined as members of a project area to access the project area. With project area access control the Jazz admin can configure which users have read access to the project area (source control and work items). Each user is assigned to one or more roles. In the Jazz Process Configuration you define the permitted actions for each role. This can be done in Project Configuration or Team Configuration; click on Permissions to open the permission definition section. Figure 9.21 demonstrates permitted actions for the Test Manager role.

See section 5.6, "Roles in Jazz," in Chapter 5, "Roles," for more information on roles and permissions in Jazz.

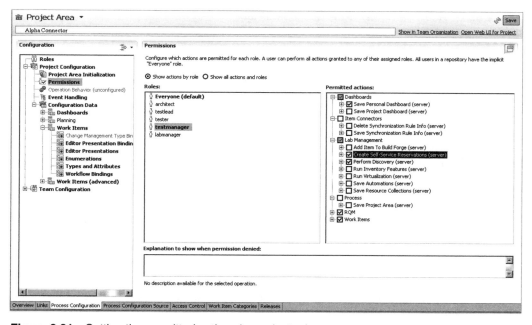

Figure 9.21   Setting the permitted actions by project role

9.2.6.3 Monitoring with Jazz

Monitoring in Jazz is performed mainly in the dashboard. For example, in Rational Quality Manager you can create dashboard viewlets to monitor subjects such as test execution status, lab resource utilization, defect submission rates, and many others. Figure 9.22 shows a viewlet to monitor Execution Status by Owner using Weight. On the left you can see the list of available viewlets to choose from.

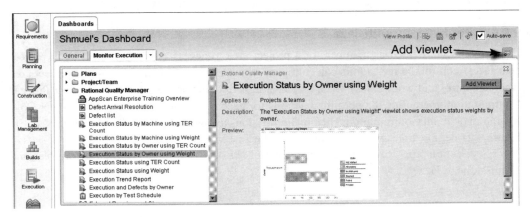

Figure 9.22   Adding a viewlet to the Dashboards tab

Rational Team Concert users can create various dashboard viewlets to monitor defect density and trends, build health, resolution latency velocity, and many more. We suggest reading "Create a Performance Measurement Dashboard" in Rational Team Concert Help > Collaborating > Collaborating using Rational Team Concert > Managing dashboards in the Web interface.

From a Jazz dashboard you can monitor other Jazz servers or other servers that were defined as friendly servers. This enables you to see in your Jazz dashboard various ClearQuest query results. For instructions on how to create a remote repository viewlet see Rational Team Concert Help > Collaborating > Collaborating using Rational Team Concert > Managing dashboards in the Web interface > Adding and organizing content on a dashboard > Working with viewlets > Adding a viewlet from a remote repository.

You can organize the viewlets in the viewlet chooser in the way your organization categorizes metrics. Open the Rational Team Concert Eclipse client, and in the Process Configuration tab select Project Configuration > Configuration Data > Dashboards > Viewlet Chooser Entries.

In this form you can create new categories and subcategories and add viewlets to each one of them. Figure 9.23 is an example of a new category, Monitoring, with subcategories for the product.

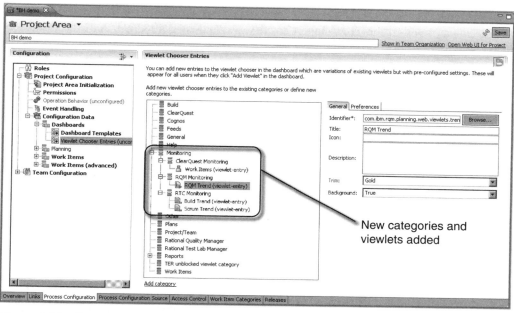

Figure 9.23 Customizing Viewlet Chooser by category in RTC

9.3 Resources

9.3.1 Metrics and Governance

Measured Capability Improvement Framework (MCIF) article and e-kit: IBM Rational, "Rational Measured Improvement Overview," www-01.ibm.com/software/rational/mcif/ (accessed February 23, 2011).

The Rational dashboard product information and whitepaper: IBM Rational, "Rational Dashboard," www-01.ibm.com/software/awdtools/dashboard/?S_CMP=swhpmid3 (accessed February 23, 2011).

The Rational Executive Dashboard demo: IBM Rational, "Rational Executive Dashboard," http://jazz.net/projects/rational-insight/executive-dashboard/ (accessed February 23, 2011).

Wikipedia, "Corporate Governance of Information Technology," http://en.wikipedia.org/wiki/IT_governance (accessed February 23, 2011).

Ishigaki, Doug, "Effective Management through Measurement," *IBM developerWorks*, www.ibm.com/developerworks/rational/library/4786.html, 2004 (accessed February 23, 2011).

IBM Rational, "Feature for ClearQuest Schema Repository Properties for Hook Level Security," *IBM Technote*, www-01.ibm.com/support/docview.wss?uid=swg21282694, 2007 (accessed February 23, 2011).

Williams, Ben, Eric Larsen, and Jon Chard, "Improve Project Success with Better Information," *IBM White Paper*, http://jazz.net/library/content/articles/insight/improve-project-success.pdf, 2009 (accessed February 23, 2011).

Hauser, John R., and Gerald M. Katz, "Metrics: You Are What You Measure!" www.mit. edu/~hauser/Papers/Hauser-Katz%20Measure%2004-98.pdf, April 1998 (accessed February 23, 2011).

9.3.2 Jazz Reports

IBM Rational, "Getting Started with Jazz Reports," http://jazz.net/library/article/35, December 4, 2007 (accessed February 23, 2011).

The Team Reports component in Jazz provides the ability to create, deploy, and generate reports. This document describes how to set up and start using reports to track the progress of your software development.

Moody, James, "Reports Central," https://jazz.net/wiki/bin/view/Main/ReportsCentral, December 13, 2010 (accessed February 23, 2011).

The Reports component provides a library of more than 50 out-of-the-box reports with Rational Team Concert 2.0. However, there are reports that we'd like to share with you that don't ship with our products.

Moody, James, "Out-of-the-Box Reports," https://jazz.net/wiki/bin/view/Main/ReportsOutOf-TheBox20, December 8, 2010 (accessed February 23, 2011).

Rational Team Concert ships with a useful library of report templates that you can use in your own development projects. While many of these templates are automatically deployed to new project areas created with the Eclipse Way and OpenUP process templates, users authoring their own process templates, or wishing to add new reports to their project areas, might want a complete list of all of the example reports.

Moody, James, "Reports Component Home," https://jazz.net/wiki/bin/view/Main/ReportsMain, December 14, 2010 (accessed February 23, 2011).

The Reports component in Rational Team Concert provides a rich library of out-of-the-box reports, a data warehouse, and integrated report viewing in both the rich client and the Web UI.

Peter, Kimberley, "Reports about the Guidelines," https://jazz.net/wiki/bin/view/Main/Reports-AboutTheGuidelines, August 2010 (accessed February 23, 2011).

In the course of creating dozens of reports containing over 75 charts during the past several releases of Jazz and RTC, we gained a lot of knowledge about the design of graphs, tables, and reports for the visual display of quantitative information. Through the application of this knowledge, trial and error, and feedback from our users, we learned more about the kinds of information that are useful to an ALM customer, and how best to present that information to communicate the important messages clearly and effectively.

Moody, James, "Creating and Deploying a New Report," https://jazz.net/wiki/bin/view/Main/ReportsCreatingANewReport20, September 1, 2009 (accessed February 23, 2011).

Jazz has many example reports that you may use to gain insight into your software development process. However, you are not limited to these reports. This article will guide you through the steps required to write your own report from scratch, using data from the data warehouse, and deploy the report to a Jazz repository.

Lavin, Matt, "License Usage Reporting," https://jazz.net/wiki/bin/view/Main/LicenseReporting, May 25, 2010 (accessed February 23, 2011).

All license usage data is collected and stored on the license server. The server that is connected to the license server does not collect data of its own. There are two ways to collect data about the license usage on a license server: historic usage snapshots and a full license usage log.

RTC 2.0 InfoCenter, IBM Rational, "Tracking Data with Reports," http://publib.boulder.ibm.com/infocenter/rtc/v2r0m0/index.jsp?topic=/com.ibm.team.reports.doc/topics/t_report_overview.html (accessed February 23, 2011).

Use reports to track progress and monitor other data for your project areas and teams. The Jazz Team Reports component provides you with the ability to create, deploy, and generate reports.

Moody, James, "Creating a Report in Rational Team Concert 2.0: Open Work Items," http://jazz.net/library/video/286, June 26, 2009 (accessed February 23, 2011).

This video is a "Hello world" introduction to creating reports in Rational Team Concert 2.0. It demonstrates how to create a report that shows the historical data of open work items.

Jaouani, Rafik, "Custom Report for Reporting across Item Links in Rational Team Concert 2.0," http://jazz.net/library/video/285, June 26, 2009 (accessed February 23, 2011).

This video is a quick tutorial on authoring a report template that reports across item links.

9.3.3 Data Warehouse

Moody, James, "Introduction to the Data Warehouse," https://jazz.net/wiki/bin/view/Main/DataWarehouseIntroduction, June 19, 2007 (accessed February 23, 2011).

The data warehouse in the Jazz repository is an extensible storage mechanism for aggregated historical data. Out of the box, the Jazz reports component collects a number of data points related to work items, builds, and source control that one may want to visualize in a report. The articles linked from this page are intended to introduce the reader to data warehouse concepts and walk through the contents of the data warehouse.

Moody, James, "Data Warehouse Concepts," https://jazz.net/wiki/bin/view/Main/DataWarehouseConcepts, June 19, 2007 (accessed February 23, 2011).

This article is intended to introduce the reader to some fundamental data warehouse concepts.

Moody, James, "Data Warehouse Snapshot Schemas," https://jazz.net/wiki/bin/view/Main/DataWarehouseSnapshotSchemas20, November 16, 2010 (accessed February 23, 2011).

Rational Team Concert 2.0 ships with several predefined snapshots that collect and store information in the data warehouse. This article describes each of these snapshots and the tables and views that they create.

9.3.4 BIRT Reports

Moody, James, "FAQ: Writing Jazz Reports with BIRT," https://jazz.net/wiki/bin/view/Main/ReportsBIRTFAQ, September 1, 2009 (accessed February 23, 2011).

This list of frequently asked questions details some tricks that we (the Reports team) have discovered while writing reports for Jazz with BIRT. Some of these FAQs are not Jazz-specific but might be useful for anyone using the BIRT Report Designer.

See also the article by James Moody, "Creating and Deploying a New Report," listed under "Jazz Reports" above.

9.3.5 C/ALM Reports

Williams, Benjamin, "Out-of-the-Box Reports," https://jazz.net/wiki/bin/view/Main/CALMReportingOOTBReports, February 17, 2011 (accessed February 23, 2011).

Each of the products making up the RTC 3.0 release provides a library of reports for the end user. These include out-of-the-box reports written in BIRT and RPE, and advanced reports written in Cognos. Some of these reports are what we call "traceability" reports, which report on artifacts from multiple domains (such as defects and test cases together in one report), and others are single-domain reports.

CLM Reporting Feature Team, IBM Rational, "CLM Reporting," https://jazz.net/wiki/bin/view/Main/CALMReporting, February 21, 2011 (accessed February 23, 2011).

The C/ALM Common Reporting feature team aims to bring cross-product reporting to the Jazz family of products. These wiki pages describe the team and our work.

Moody, James, "CALM Reporting Goals," https://jazz.net/wiki/bin/view/Main/CALMReportingGoals, May 11, 2010 (accessed February 23, 2011).

The primary goals are to create a common reporting component for use by C/ALM products, which will enable point-product reporting and cross-product reports. There are a number of incidental goals as well. This page expands on these.

C/ALM Common Reporting Team, IBM Rational, "Dashboard: Common Reporting," https://jazz.net/jazz/web/projects/Jazz%20Collaborative%20ALM#action=com.ibm.team.dashboard.viewDashboard&team=Jazz%20Collaborative%20ALM%20Development/Feature%20Teams/Common%20Reporting, 2011 (accessed February 23, 2011).

A central view of the reporting and data warehouse work for CLM 2011. Here you'll find a top-down view of the plan items and stories, as well as links to the wiki and other important documents.

9.4 Summary

This chapter is divided into two main sections that are related to each other. The first section is about metrics. We discussed the four types of metrics (individual, team, project, and organization). We explained what a good metrics strategy should be and provided several examples of required reports. We explained that the work item management tool needs to have the required data to support the strategy, as well as a reporting tool. We discussed some of the tools that can help in deriving your metrics reports.

The second section of the chapter was about governance. We explained that governance consists of the processes and actions that management takes to enforce the policies and rules the organization has decided upon. It involves measuring performance and taking action to reduce risks and improve quality.

We discussed the governance capabilities incorporated in ClearQuest and Jazz work item management in three areas: process control and automation, permissions (access control and security), and monitoring.

## CHAPTER 10

Test Management
and Work Items

This chapter was meant to be a discussion of ClearQuest Test Management (CQTM), but during the writing of the book Rational announced the end of marking of CQTM. We decided instead to focus on the new product for test management that is based on the Jazz foundation, Rational Quality Manager (RQM). This chapter is neither about test management nor about using Rational Quality Manager but rather on the work item objects of Rational Quality Manager, the methods of customizing test work items, and how work items are used in the testing lifecycle.

10.1 What Is Rational Quality Manager?

IBM Rational Quality Manager is a collaborative, Web-based tool that offers comprehensive test planning, test construction, and test asset management throughout the software development lifecycle. Rational Quality Manager is designed as a full replacement for Rational Manual Tester, Rational ClearQuest Test Manager, and Rational TestManager.

Rational Quality Manager is based on the Jazz platform and inherits many characteristics from that platform. One part of the Jazz foundation is work item management, which is the essence of this book.

The Rational Test Lab Manager (RTLM) is a product, as its name implies, aimed at managing the test lab assets, managing and executing requests for test asset provisioning and test execution. RTLM is not a stand-alone product; it is built on top of Rational Quality Manager.

The Jazz-based work items are the main collaboration tool among the team members. For more information on the Jazz platform see http://jazz.net and www.ibm.com/software/rational/jazz/.

10.2 Understanding Test Entities and Work Items

All test objects are created in a project area, which is the base repository entity; currently test elements cannot be shared between projects but can only be copied.

Many of the test artifacts are independent entities in the Quality Manager repository. You can create relationships between these artifacts, or the artifacts can remain completely independent. Usually you create test cases and add them to a test plan, but you can also work with test cases in the Quality Manager outside the context of a test plan.

Figure 10.1 shows the relationships between these test artifacts.

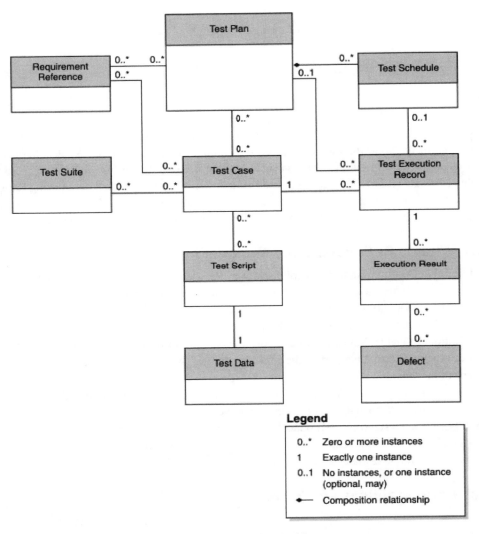

Figure 10.1   Test artifact relationships in Rational Quality Manager

Full descriptions of the test artifacts and their relationships can be found in Rational Quality Manager online-Help > Reference > General reference for Rational Quality Manager > Test artifact relationships.

As mentioned in Chapter 1, "Work Items," test objects are not always considered as work items. But some test objects have their own lifecycle, data, and user interaction forms and thus conform to our definition of a work item. Let's examine each of the elements in Figure 10.1 to determine if they conform to that definition.

The Defect and the Requirement are defined in the Jazz foundation as work items. Indeed, these are the same work items that you can find in Rational Team Concert (RTC), and we can all agree that they conform to our definition.

Let's continue to examine the other test artifacts to see if they conform to our definition of work item. A test case is created, assigned to a user by role, reviewed, implemented, and approved (for execution in a specific release) and thus has a workflow. A test plan has a similar workflow. So test plans and test cases do conform to our definition. Actually, in ClearQuest Test Management (CQTM) these objects are state-based record types just like defects and enhancement requests.

In Rational Quality Manager the test plan and test case objects also have a lifecycle, but they are of a different type from work items like defects, enhancements, and requirements. In the Jazz foundation, test plans and test cases are not considered work items and do not appear in the work item list, although they have all the elements that conform to the work item definition.

Other objects like test execution and test results do not have a workflow and cannot be considered as work items.

In the Rational Quality Manager screen shot in Figure 10.2 you can see in the left bar the Requirements icon to access the requirements work items, and the Defects icon to access the defects work items. Actually both icons will allow you to create any Jazz work item that is permitted in your system. After you have selected Create Defect and the defect form is loaded, you can change the value of the field Type to Task, Requirement, or any other available work item type, and the form will be adjusted to the newly selected type. Also note that the test plan is in state Under Review and the current selected action Approve will transition it to state Approved. The Summary section contains fields (Product, Release, and Description) that the user can select or enter values. These fields can be customized by the Rational Quality Manager administrator; we shall discuss this in section 10.4, "Customization." Also note that you can create from each test plan section an additional work item; see on the right side of the Summary section the link Work Item: Create; these additional work items are used to assign some of the test plan work to other practitioners. This is also shown in Figures 10.3 and 10.4.

There is, however, a difference in the workflow between a test case and the Jazz work item. A test case is not closed; it can be reused again and again in each product release, as long as the product needs to be tested.

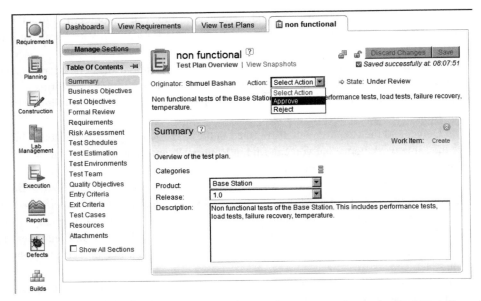

Figure 10.2   Rational Quality Manager test plan interface: user action in the Test Plan Overview
section

10.3 Work Items in the Test Process

In the previous section we identified the Rational Quality Manager entities and their relationships. Some of those entities correspond to the definition of a work item. The following procedure describes a general test process and explains how work items are used.

Note   Different organizations may adopt different processes. We deliberately ignore the
operational and logistics steps in the test process as they are not the focus of this book.

---

1. **Analyze the requirements.**

   The first stage in the test process is to analyze the requirements and to establish the test
   strategy. Requirements can be Jazz work items in Rational Quality Manager or external
   records in tools such as Rational RequisitePro or Rational Requirements Composer or
   Rational DOORS.

RequisitePro to Rational Quality Manager Integration   This integration creates links
between RequisitePro requirements and Rational Quality Manager work items of type
Requirement.

---

2. Create a test plan.

The next step is to create a test plan and in some cases more than one test plan. Each test plan will be linked to the list of requirements. The test plan goal is to ensure that the application is tested and verified to meet this list of requirements.

In Figure 10.3 you can see the Requirements section of the test plan. Note the warning in requirement ID 20; it means that the requirement was changed after it was included in the test plan. Also note the Create Work Item link; it is used to assign the completion of the Requirements section to a team member.

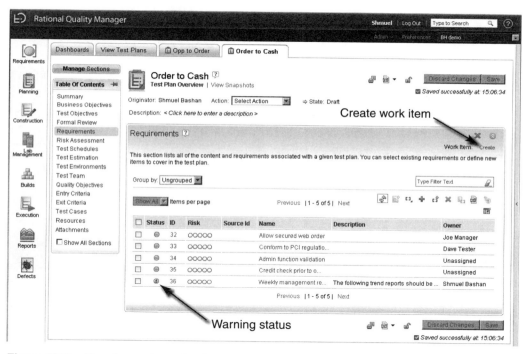

Figure 10.3   Requirements section in a test plan

3. Assign members to complete test plan tasks.

The test plan owner is responsible for filling in all the sections in the test plan. The owner can delegate some of the work by creating work items. For example, to request a team leader to fill in the Test Objectives section, the test plan owner navigates to the Test Objectives section and clicks on Work Item: Create. This will create a Jazz work item of type Task-Quality that includes the task description and a reference to the test plan. The owner will select the team leader name to complete the assignment. The same procedure can be performed on each and every section of the test plan.

Figure 10.4 shows the creation of the work item. Note that a simplified form is opened (not the full work item form) and a default summary test is included.

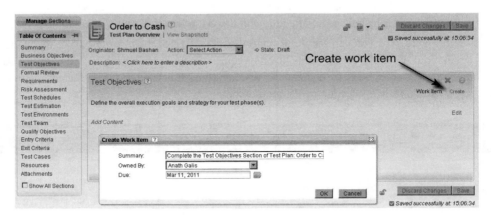

Figure 10.4   Creating a work item to assign tasks

Process Notice 1   The Jazz administrator can set rules that will prevent the test plan from transitioning to the Under Review state unless all the relevant Task-Quality work items are completed. In Figure 10.5 see the State Transition Constraints rules; the second rule is marked, meaning that all Task-Quality work items assigned to the test plan must be resolved in order to allow the transition to the next state.

Figure 10.5   Test Artifact State Transition Constraints

4. Review the test plan.

The test plan owner can set up a formal review process that is visible at all times to all members of the larger project team. The test plan includes a Formal Review section; within this section the test plan owner can select team members to review or approve the test plan or some sections of the test plan. The owner selects the type of task (Review or Approve) and the assigned user; this will create a Jazz work item of type Task-Review. Note that the work item of type Task-Review is created for both reviewing and approving the test plan. The assigned user can see the tasks in the Personal Tasks view in a dashboard. In Figure 10.6 you can see that two tasks were set, one user selected as reviewer and one as approver.

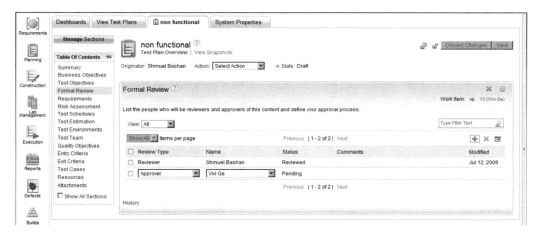

Figure 10.6 Using a work item for the review process

In the Formal Review section, it is possible to assign a person to a Quality-Task work item (by clicking on the work item link) to complete this section, that is, selecting reviewers. It is not the same as assigning a person to a Review-Task, which mean reviewing the test plan or parts of the test plan.

Process Notice 2 The Rational Quality Manager administrator can set rules that will prevent the test plan from transitioning to the Approved state unless all the relevant Task-Review work items are completed. In Figure 10.5 see the State Transition Constraints rules; the third rule is marked, meaning that all approvals in the Task-Review work items assigned to the test plan for approval must be resolved (approved) in order to allow the transition to the next state.

---

5. Create test cases and associate them with the test plan.

The test case contains the information about what needs to be tested, when, how, and by whom. There are additional fields for information such as preconditions, post-conditions, configuration, risk assessment, and possibly other customized fields. The test case is not a Jazz work item although it has similar workflow elements. As in the test plan, the test case contains sections; within each section there are fields with the test case data. The owner can assign other team members to fill in one or more sections of the test case, by creating a work item for each required section.

Process Notice 3   The test case also includes a formal review-approve process with features similar to those described for the test plan in the previous item. The administrator can set state transition constraints on test cases. In Figure 10.5 the line "Execute approved Test Cases only" is not checked, meaning that the tester can run a test case even before final approval.

Figure 10.7 shows how to create a test case from a test plan; this will associate the test case automatically with the current test plan. Selecting the + sign (next to the Create New Test Case icon) allows adding an existing test case to the test plan.

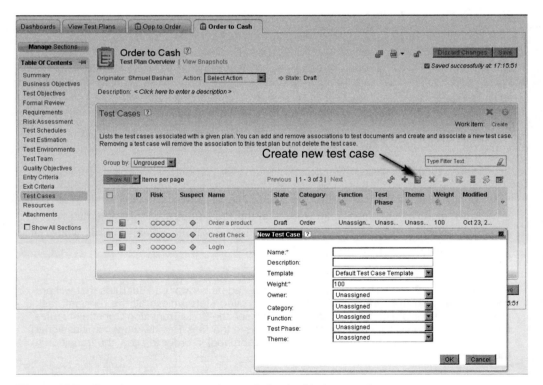

Figure 10.7   Creating a test case and associating it with the test plan

6. Associate test cases with requirements, and verify coverage.

Test cases are created so that we can test that application features correspond to the requirements definitions. To ensure that all the requirements are covered by test cases, we link each test case to one or more requirements. This allows us to easily identify uncovered requirements. We can also identify test cases that are not related to any requirement and are probably redundant. Figure 10.8 shows the Requirements section of a test case.

Figure 10.8 The Requirements section of a test case

7. Create test scripts and associate them with the test cases.

Test cases are meant to be executed. The artifact that contains the test steps that are executables is the test script. A test script can be manual as provided by Rational Quality Manager, or automatic, which will be created with a dedicated tool such as the Rational Functional Tester or other supported tools.

Tip Automatic test tools such as RFT perform the same operations that a human tester will do, while interacting with the application GUI. It will type text, press on buttons, verify return values, and do these things faster and more reliably.

In Figure 10.9 you can see the Test Scripts section in a test case. You can assign more than one script to a test case, but when executing a test case a single script has to be selected for execution.

Figure 10.9   The Test Scripts section of a test case

8. **Create a test suite.**

    The test team usually organizes the execution test cases in suites. A suite is a test artifact that contains a list of test cases in a specific order and can execute them according to the included instructions. For example, a regression test suite contains all the test cases that ran successfully in a previous release.

9. **Execute the tests.**

    Execution of a manual test requires the tester to perform the instruction on the application under test (AUT) and verify that it behaves correctly.

10. **Report defects.**

    If the testers find an error, they can report a defect immediately, while the test is still in execution, or they can report one or more defects at the end of the test from the test results log as shown in Figure 10.10. The defect is a Jazz work item, and it is linked to the test results, so that other team members working on resolving that defect will have easy access to the test result log.

    Automatic tests are usually unattended; the testers examine the results at the end of the test run. They can report a defect and relate it to an error in the test results.

10.4 Customization

There are different types of customization. The Jazz work items are customized via the Rational Team Concert Eclipse client (in RTC 3.0 also with the Web client); we discussed this subject in Chapter 3, "Workflow," and Chapter 4, "The Data." But there are the test-specific work items or artifacts—*test plan* and *test case*—for which Rational Quality Manager provides the ability to customize certain aspects. In the next sections we shall explain what can be customized in each of the test work items and how this is done.

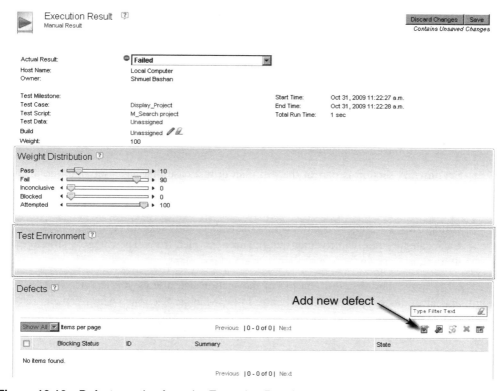

Figure 10.10 Defect creation from the Execution Results log

10.4.1 Customizing Jazz Work Items

The default Rational Quality Manager process template comes with the following Jazz-based work items:

- Defect
- Requirements
- Task
- Task-Quality
- Task-Review

Defect, Requirements, and Task type work items are well known and used in many systems. Task-Quality is a work item type used to assign some of the test plan and test case creation tasks to the relevant team members. Task-Review is a work item type used to assign the task of formal reviewing of the test plan or test case to the relevant team members.

You can open a project with the Rational Team Concert Eclipse client and use the Process Configuration to customize each work item. You can add fields, modify the workflow, organize the presentations, define roles, and set permissions. This is identical to customizing Rational Team Concert work items as described in Chapter 4, "The Data," and section 3.6, "Jazz Workflow," in Chapter 3, "Workflow."

Also refer to section 1.4.1, "Which Work Item Elements Can Be Customized?," in Chapter 1, "Work Items."

10.4.2 Testing Specific Work Items

Rational Quality Manager provides the ability to perform some customization of test plans and test cases. The customizable elements are

- **Sections:** A section is part of the test plan or test case that has a tab and one or more fields depending on the section type. A customized section has only one rich text multi-line field.

- **Categories:** A category is a collection of fields usually used to categorize the test plan. Each category has list of values that the user can pick from. The category structure and definition for test cases are similar to those of test plans.

The Manage Sections button, on top of the section list, allows you to select the sections that will appear in the test plan or the test case. In the Manage Sections wizard you can remove sections you do not need and add available sections that are not used. You can set the order of the sections. The Manage Sections screen is shown in Figure 10.11.

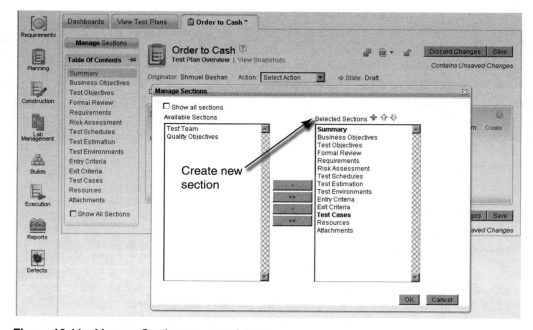

Figure 10.11   Manage Sections screen of a test case

You can also create a new section by clicking the + sign, which will open a dialog to define the new section. See Figure 10.12 for the Custom Section wizard.

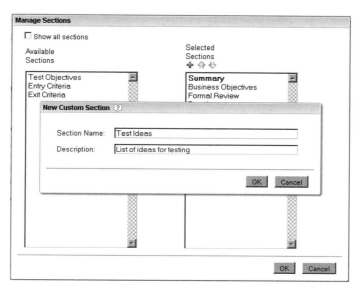

Figure 10.12   Adding a new section to a test plan

After the test plan is saved, the new section is part of the test plan. See Figure 10.13 for a sample new section, Test Ideas, and the rich text field in the section. The new section includes the Work Item: Create capability, to create a new work item (of type Task-Quality) and assign a user as the owner of this section, just like any other section.

You can create additional sections for test plans and for test cases. Also note that marking the check box Show All Sections will change the user interface and all sections will be displayed one after the other on a single page. The user will also be able to access a section by scrolling.

Figure 10.13   A new section, Test Ideas

10.4.2.2 Organizing Information with Categories

Categories are fields that help organize the information in the test plan and the test case. They allow easy viewing of the information needed. Instead of building a rigidly structured test plan hierarchy, categories allow you a more powerful way to view and find data.

The definition of the category types (fields) and the categories (values) of each type can be performed in two ways. The first way is by the administrator via

```
Admin->system properties
```

In the interface that opens, select Test Plan Configuration or Test Case Configuration to define and modify the configuration types. See the example of Test Plan Configuration in Figure 10.14.

The second way to enter the Edit Category wizard is from the Summary section of the test plan or the test case. Click on the three bars icon, as indicated in Figure 10.15, to open the category wizard. The capabilities are the same as if you entered from the admin system properties, assuming you have the permission.

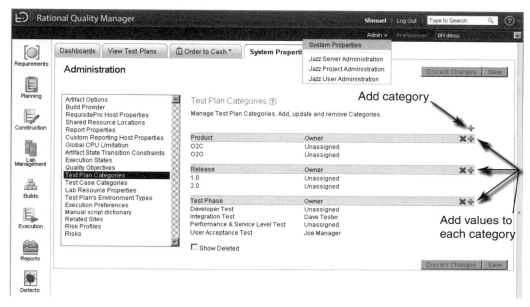

Figure 10.14 Test plan categories: administrator setting of category types and their values

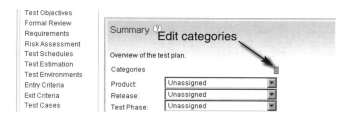

Figure 10.15 Editing categories from the test plan

10.4.2.3 Setting Permissions for Customization

Permission to customize the categories and sections is set with the Rational Team Concert Eclipse client. This is configured in the following steps:

1. Open the project area.
2. Select the Process Configuration tab.
3. Expand Project Configurations.
4. Mark the permission.
5. Select the role to allow the permission.

6. Under the Permitted actions tree mark Save Category (server) and Save Category Type (server). The administrator can set the permission of roles to create, edit, or archive category or category type.

In Figure 10.16 you can see that the role Tester has the permission to create and edit categories but does not have the permission to create and edit category types.

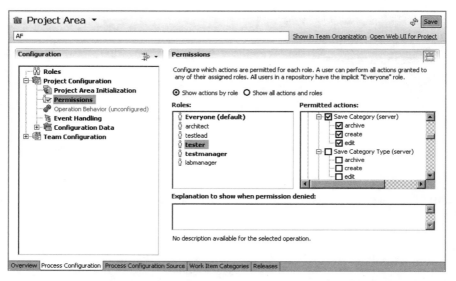

Figure 10.16   Category and category type permissions: defining the permitted actions for a role

In a similar way the permission to create and edit sections of a test plan and test case is set with Rational Team Concert Process Configuration, in the Permitted actions under the Rational Quality Manager tree: Save Test Case (server) and Save Test Plan (server). In Figure 10.17 you can see that the role Tester has the permission to create and edit test cases but does not have the permission to create or remove a section of a test case.

10.4.2.4 Testing Execution States

Test execution states are not state machine states that describe a workflow but are the statuses of the test results. As there are more than just pass/fail values for a test, the organization can define and customize the test result states to be incomplete, stopped, and so on.

To customize the execution states select

```
Admin->system properties
```

In the form that opens you can select and enable the Execution States, as well as define new states. The Manage Execution States page is shown in Figure 10.18.

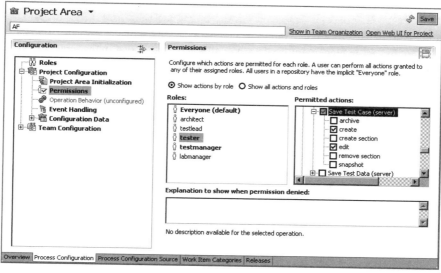

Figure 10.17   Test case permissions: defining the permitted actions for a role

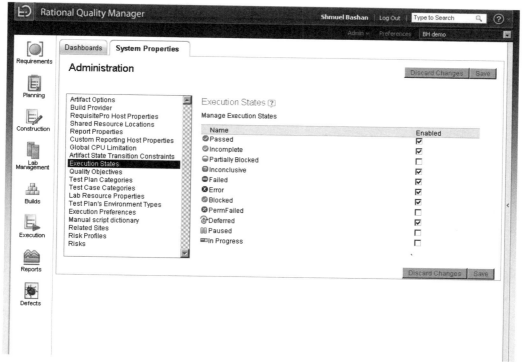

Figure 10.18   Rational Quality Manager Execution States

10.5 Summary

This chapter is somewhat different from other chapters because it discusses work items in a different context: in the test management process. We all know that defect management is an inherent process of testing because the majority of defects are created by the testing team. In this chapter we demonstrated how other types of work items are involved in the test process, work items such as requirements, tasks for review, tasks for approval, and tasks for general quality work.

We discussed the characteristics of test plans and test cases and showed that test plans and especially test cases have workflow, data, and presentations that are the elements that define other work items, and therefore we can consider test plans and test cases as work items. We explained how test cases and test plans can be customized with Rational Quality Manager by adding and modifying sections and defining category types and categories. The Jazz administrator can give permission to customize categories and sections by roles and also set some rules that control the test process, including preventing state transition if all tasks are not complete.

Managing Agile Projects

Many software projects are moving to Agile methods. This chapter is not about teaching Agile development; you can read about Agile in many articles and books. Instead, it is about realizing Agile with Rational Team Concert (RTC) and ClearQuest.

While Rational Team Concert was developed with Agile methods in mind, Rational Clear-Quest is an older product and was developed with more traditional methods in mind. Luckily ClearQuest is highly customizable, so we can develop schemas with a process that meets the modern development environment.

In this chapter we shall explain in brief the Agile method concept, just to set the right context for the rest of the chapter. The Scrum process is becoming more popular with all types of software development projects. We will use RTC's process enactment of Scrum to illustrate some of the methods within this Agile process. We shall later explain how to build a schema with Clear-Quest that will help Agile teams and stakeholders manage their projects smarter to help produce better products.

ClearQuest users using Application Lifecycle Management (ALM) will learn how to configure a project to meet the needs of Agile teams.

11.1 Defining Agile Development

There is no single definition of what Agile development is. There are some principles that many agree upon, and teams can adapt them as it suits their organization. Scott Ambler (see "Resources" at the end of this chapter) defines Agile software development as follows:

- Agile is an iterative and incremental (evolutionary) approach to software development
- which is performed in a highly collaborative manner
- by self-organizing teams
- with "just enough" ceremony

- that produces high quality software
- in a cost effective and timely manner
- which meets the changing needs of its stakeholders.

We shall later see how both Rational Team Concert and a ClearQuest schema we propose respond to this definition.

The Agile system development lifecycle is described in Figure 11.1.

11.2 Agile and Scrum in a Nutshell

Scrum is a framework for managing Agile software development projects. A Scrum project starts with a definition of the items that the system should include and address, including functionality, features, and technology. These items are often called *requests*. The list of requests is called the *product backlog* (or project backlog). The requests can be of various types: textual requirements, use cases, test cases, stories, defects, enhancement requests, and so on. The requests are likely captured in an external tool such as Rational Requirements Composer (RRC) and are referenced or linked from the change management tool.

Requests can be submitted by any team member, affected users, or stakeholders. The request content is elicited from various sources, but the requests are prioritized by the product owner only and not by the development team. The product backlog is dynamic; it changes and evolves as the project advances.

During the first phase of the project, often called *warm-up*, the requirements are analyzed by SMEs to determined feasibility, cost, effort, and risk. This phase is done with the close participation of the stakeholders. The analysis gives the stakeholders a better basis for setting their priorities.

Agile projects are divided into iterations; the iteration has a fixed duration of a few weeks, usually two to four. In Scrum the iteration is called a *sprint*.

The Scrum team's responsibility is to take the requirements from the backlog and develop a usable product or component that has real value to the project, within the sprint period. The team is cross-functional and performs all activities related to the delivery. The team as a whole is responsible for delivering the requirements.

The sprint starts with a team planning meeting. Each team takes one or more top-priority requests from the product backlog, as many as they think they can develop and deliver during the sprint. A sprint must finish with delivery of a new, executable product; thus each sprint consists of all lifecycle disciplines: design, development, testing, and so forth.

The team creates a list of activities (or tasks) from the requirement(s) they have selected. This is called the *sprint backlog*. The activities represent the way the team decides to implement the requirements. Each activity is assigned to a team member (or sometimes to team pairs).

Each Scrum team is autonomous; the team decides how to develop work products from a requirement. Teams are organized in a way that they could be autonomous, thus having expertise in various domains. The team decides which of the Agile development methods to use—XP, pair

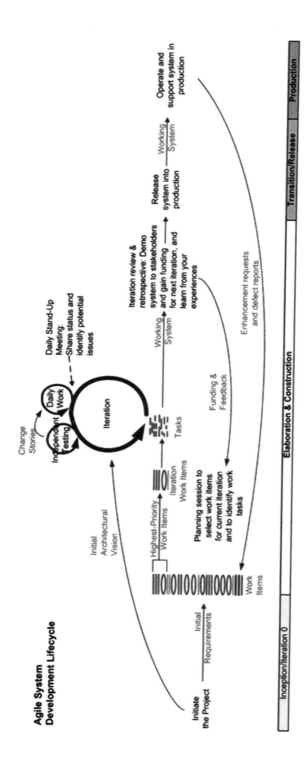

Figure 11.1   The Agile System Development Lifecycle (copyright Scott W. Ambler)

327

programming, test-driven development, or another method. They decide how much modeling to do. However, the team must adhere to regulations, standards, and rules that the organization has set.

An important role within the Scrum process is the Scrum Master. This role facilitates and guides the teams in adopting the agreed-upon practices and removes impediments. The Scrum Master is not part of the team and does not give orders to the team.

Every day the team gathers for a short (15-minute) stand-up meeting called a Daily Scrum Meeting. The purpose of the meeting is to share status and identify potential issues. During the Daily Scrum Meeting the team progress is reviewed and impediments are identified for removal by management. The Scrum Master facilitates the daily meetings, tracks progress, and works to resolve any inhibitors raised by team members.

Each Scrum member briefly reports on three items:

- What was accomplished since the previous meeting?
- What is planned to be accomplished before the next meeting?
- What prevents the member from accomplishing the activities?

The report should focus on information that helps other team members gain knowledge, learn a lesson, or contribute from their experience. Important practices in the meeting are honesty and transparency.

At the end of the sprint, the team is gathered for a Sprint Review Meeting with the stakeholders. The team reviews the work that was completed and that was not completed. The products developed are demonstrated to the stakeholders to examine their value. They will make a decision about whether to make use of the products and obtain funding for the next iteration. Additional elements of the meeting are to learn from the experience in order to make an improvement for the next iteration. Some teams conduct a different meeting for that purpose; members give their opinions on what went well and what needs improvement. This meeting is called a Sprint Retrospective.

The Sprint Review usually results in some adaptation of the product backlog. Enhancement requests are added, defects are submitted, and maybe new features are introduced. The remaining items in the sprint backlog are moved to the product backlog. The team can add an activity, for example, to learn and experiment with a new technology, or to perform more performance tests. Stakeholders and product owners may decide to change the priorities of some backlog requirements.

Now a new sprint starts again with teams selecting top-priority requests for development. The sprint cycles continue until the stakeholders think they have enough value and quality to release a product. This stage is called the Release Iteration or the End Game. During this iteration final system testing and acceptance testing are performed. Stakeholders may request some defect fixing. The team finalizes system and user documentation. Users and administrators are trained, and the system is deployed to production.

The Scrum project process is often described using the schema illustrated in Figure 11.2.

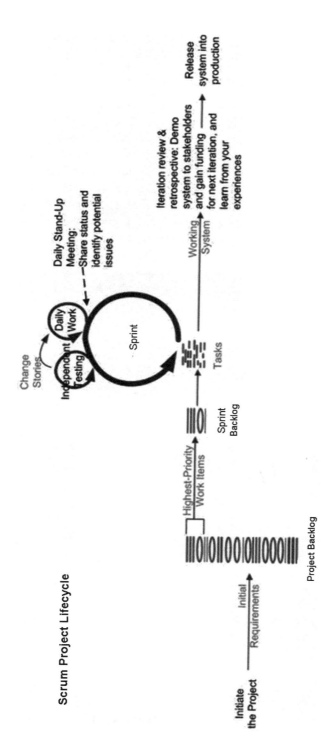

Figure 11.2   The Scrum Project Lifecycle (copyright Scott W. Ambler)

11.3 Realization with Rational Team Concert

Out of the box, Rational Team Concert has a process template that enacts the Scrum process. This chapter will discuss what Scrum is in terms of how Rational Team Concert realizes it. By using a tool's out-of-the-box process, your organization can be more Agile, as you will spend less time designing, creating, and testing a custom solution. Within Rational Team Concert, the Scrum project starts with a definition of all the items that the system should include and address, including functionality, features, and technology. These items are called *stories*. Rational Team Concert has built in an Agile planning feature through its Web interface. The lists of stories are presented in a product backlog plan. This plan interface is the main focus during the team planning meeting to decide what to work on in the first sprint. The product backlog list is shown in Figure 11.3.

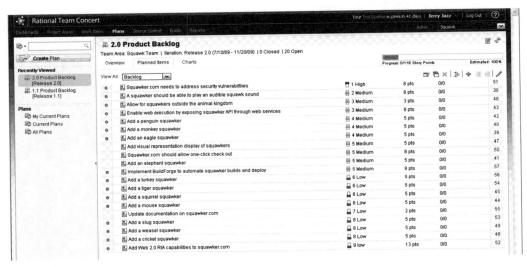

Figure 11.3   The product backlog of Release 2.0

The user stories can be submitted by any team member, affected users, or stakeholders. They are submitted against the backlog category and will show up in the product's backlog plan and are not assigned to any individual yet. The story content is elicited from various sources. A work item of type Story is shown in Figure 11.4.

The product backlog is dynamic; it changes and evolves as the project advances. Certain items may become more important than others during a sprint. Sometimes this process of prioritizing is called *ranking*. With Rational Team Concert you can easily drag stories around to rank them relative to their position in the list. You also get a visual display of unranked items. All stories should be ranked to make sure they are not missed. A product backlog ranked list is shown in Figure 11.5.

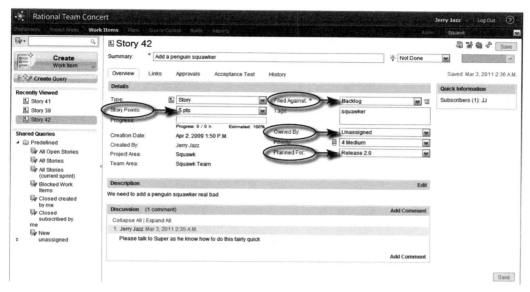

Figure 11.4 The Story work item

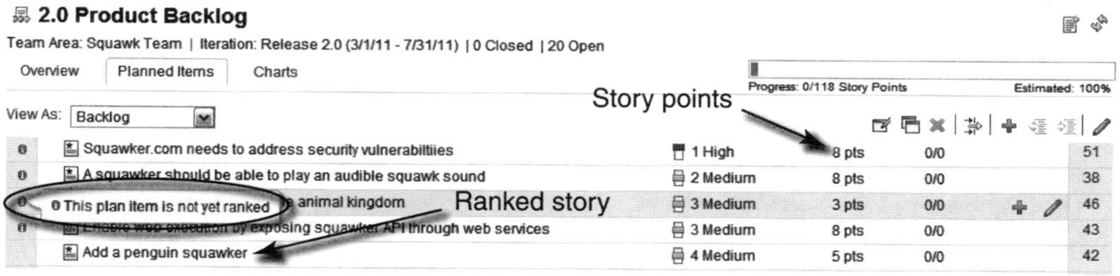

Figure 11.5 Ranking user stories

Within Rational Team Concert you have the ability to attach complexity of effort to a story. The attribute of the Story work item used to convey complexity is Story Points. The larger the Story Points, the more difficult it will be to implement the Story.

In Rational Team Concert you can set up multiple teams working on multiple releases; each release plan has its own current sprint (see Figure 11.6).

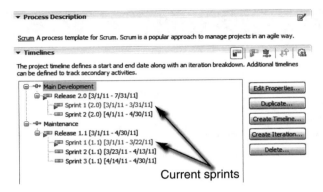

Figure 11.6   Sprints of different releases

Figure 11.7 shows the backlog and the sprints (iterations). The backlog contains a list of work items (in this figure of type Story) that should be assigned to teams in a specific sprint.

2.0 Product Backlog

Team Area: Squawk Team | Iteration: Release 2.0 (3/1/11 - 7/31/11) | 0 Closed | 20 Open

| Overview | Planned Items | Charts |

Progress: 0/118 Story Points   Estimated: 100%

View As: Iterations ◄──── View backlog with iterations

Release 2.0
Closed Items: 0 | Open Items: 20   Progress: 0/118 Story Points   Estimated: 100%

⊖	Squawker.com needs to address security vulnerabiltiies	8 pts	0/0	1 High		51
⊖	A squawker should be able to play an audible squawk sound	8 pts	0/0	2 Medium		38
⊖	Allow for squawkers outside the animal kingdom	3 pts	0/0	3 Medium		46
⊖	Enable web execution by exposing squawker API through web services	8 pts	0/0	3 Medium	+ /	43
	Add a penguin squawker	5 pts	0/0	4 Medium		42
	Add a monkey squawker	5 pts	0/0	4 Medium		40
	Add an eagle squawker	5 pts	0/0	4 Medium		39
	Add visual representation display of squawkers	5 pts	0/0	5 Medium		47
	Squawker.com should allow one-click check out	8 pts	0/0	5 Medium		50
	Add an elephant squawker	5 pts	0/0	5 Medium		41
⊖	Implement BuildForge to automate squawker builds and deploy	8 pts	0/0	5 Medium		57
	Add a turkey squawker	5 pts	0/0	6 Low		56
	Add a tiger squawker	5 pts	0/0	6 Low		54
	Add a squirrel squawker	5 pts	0/0	6 Low		45
	Add a mouse squawker	5 pts	0/0	6 Low		44
	Update documentation on squawker.com	2 pts	0/0	7 Low		55
	Add a slug squawker	5 pts	0/0	8 Low		53
	Add a weasel squawker	5 pts	0/0	8 Low		49
	Add a cricket squawker	5 pts	0/0	8 Low		48
	Add Web 2.0 RIA capabilities to squawker.com	13 pts	0/0	9 low		52

Current sprint has no work defined

Sprint 1 (2.0)   No Work
Closed Items: 0 | Open Items: 0   Progress: 0/0 Story Points   Estimated: --

Sprint 2 (2.0)   No Work
Closed Items: 0 | Open Items: 0   Progress: 0/0 Story Points   Estimated: --

Figure 11.7   Release 2.0 backlog showing iterations

In Rational Team Concert you facilitate sprint planning meetings by simply dragging and dropping a story from the product backlog to your sprint; this is shown in Figure 11.8.

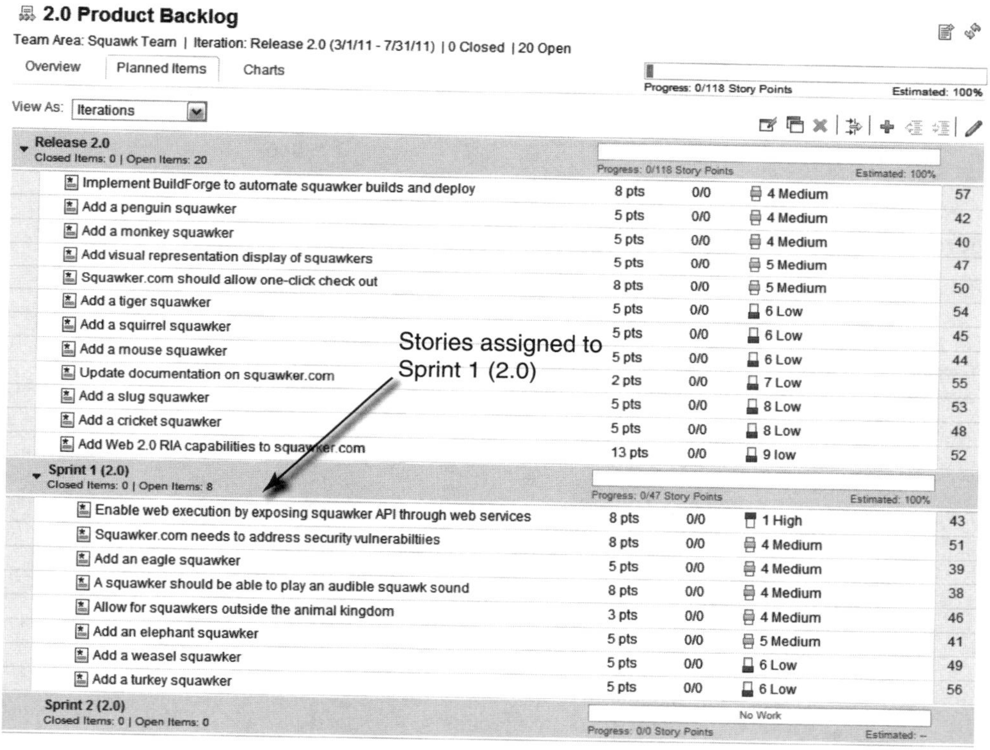

Figure 11.8 Assigning stories from the product backlog to a sprint

Rational Team Concert can easily show a plan of any iteration. Once a team creates its Sprint backlog, it can be easily communicated and worked further through the Web planning interface of Rational Team Concert. Figure 11.9 shows sprint backlog stories ordered by priority.

Through the use of Rational Team Concert's Agile planning through the Web interface, you can easily create child tasks from a story. You can drag and drop tasks to make them children of stories, and promote and demote them as needed; this is demonstrated in Figure 11.10.

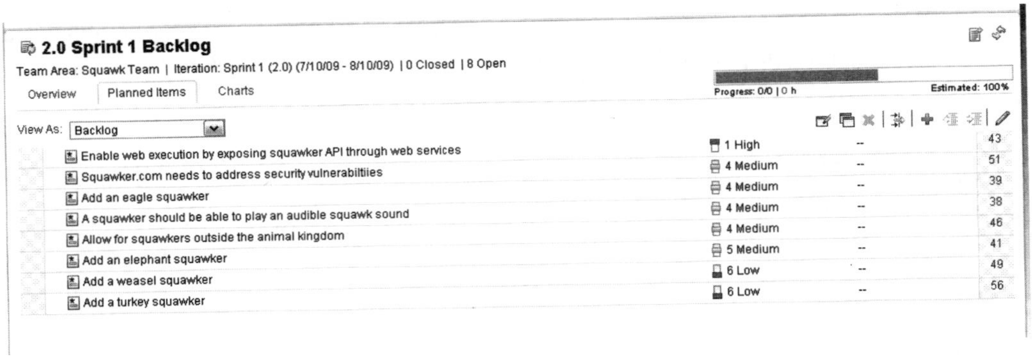

Figure 11.9   The sprint backlog

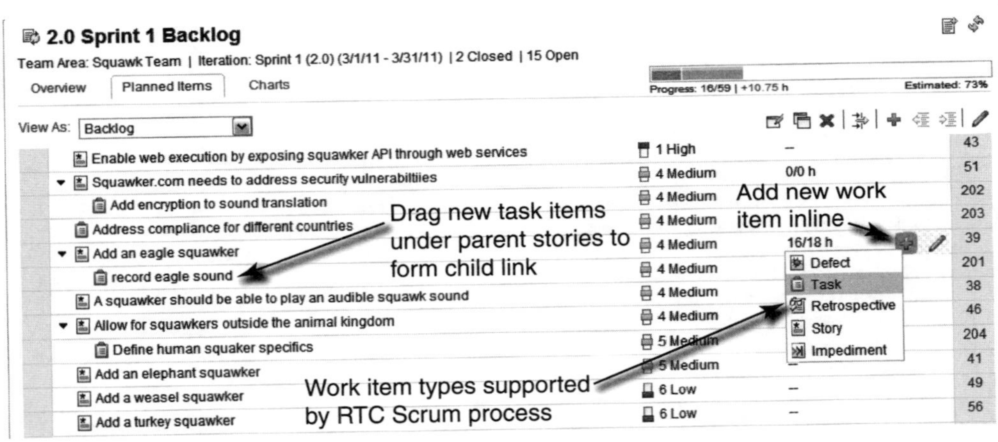

Figure 11.10   Working with the sprint backlog

In order to make sure work gets done, you want to assign tasks to individuals. Rational Team Concert supports Agile assignment of work through drag and drop, making it easier to use the tool to run a sprint planning meeting. As you are assigning work to people, you can also easily enter the amount of task time remaining. This is used to calculate the burndown metric. This work breakdown view of the backlog and the progress bar is shown in Figure 11.11.

Within Rational Team Concert, the Scrum Master role and the other Scrum roles are part of the out-of-the-box process supporting Scrum as shown in Figure 11.12. The administrator can define new roles as required.

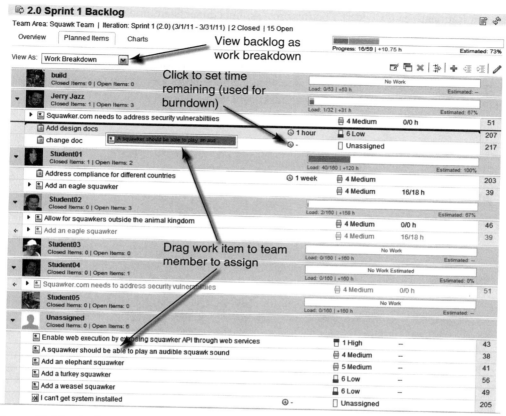

Figure 11.11   Assigning tasks to individuals

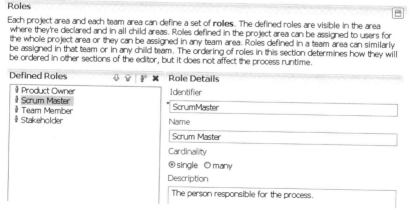

Figure 11.12   Process roles in Scrum

In Rational Team Concert's Scrum process, impediments are implemented as work items and follow a workflow of open → resolved, so they can be submitted, assigned, and managed just like any other work item. Rational Team Concert also provides another useful view for Agile planning through the Web interface called the Developer Taskboard. This view is perfect for the Daily Scrum Meeting as you can easily see what team members are working on, what they have completed, and other data. The Developer Taskboard view is shown in Figure 11.13.

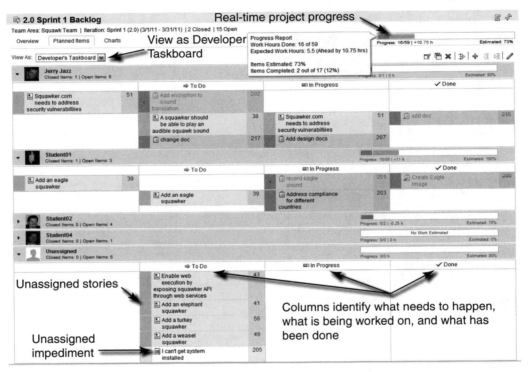

Figure 11.13   Using the Developer Taskboard in the Daily Scrum Meeting

Another Agile communication vehicle within Rational Team Concert is the dashboard. This is a way that stakeholders and executives can keep informed on the progress of any project. Much of the information contained within Rational Team Concert can be presented easily through feeds to a dashboard. Any Rational Team Concert user (assuming the user has authorization) can set up a dashboard to collect and present items of interest. A sample Rational Team Concert dashboard is shown in Figure 11.14.

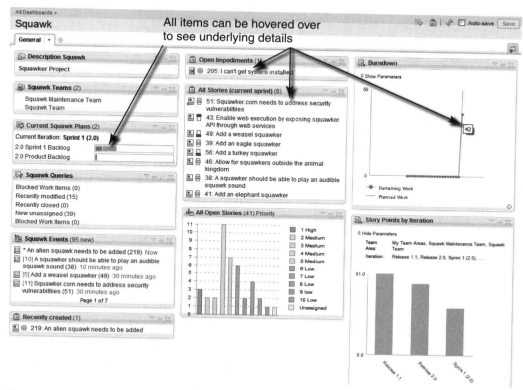

Figure 11.14   Project dashboard showing real-time status of events of interest

One of the types of work items that Rational Team Concert supplies out of the box in the Scrum process is a retrospective. You use this work item to log and track the issues that you discuss during the Sprint Retrospective.

11.4 Realization with ClearQuest

In section 11.2, "Agile and Scrum in a Nutshell," we described the Agile process and the Scrum in particular. Unlike Rational Team Concert, which has a built-in process template to support Scrum, ClearQuest does not have an Agile built-in schema. In this section we shall explain how to build a schema to support Agile projects. Reading the process description in section 11.2, we can identify data objects and workflow scenarios. Now let us take out the data objects from the description. These are

- Request
- Product backlog of requests

- Sprint
- Activity
- Sprint backlog of activities
- Team
- Iteration

Let's discuss each of these data objects a bit more.

- A request (or CR or any other name that may fit your environment) is realized by a state-based record type. We shall describe the fields of this record type in the next section, but one important field should be the RequestType. Types could be Defect, Enhancement, Feature, Story, Test Case, and so on. Another important field is Priority; the team will select Requests to implement in the iteration based mainly on priority.

- The product backlog of requests and sprint backlog of activities are lists of work items. We do not need to create a special object for these; the reason is that the logs will be realized with queries whose result set is the backlog. The project backlog is a query on the Request record type that filters all of the analyzed requests (ready to be selected for the sprint), sorted by priority. The sprint backlog is a query on the Activity record type that filters all of the opened activities (not completed) that are referenced from a specific sprint, sorted by priority.

- A sprint is realized by a state-based record type. This record type will have fields of type Reference_List to the Requests and the Activity record types, and fields of type Reference to the Team and Project record types.

- An activity (or task or work item or any other name that may fit your environment) is realized by a state-based record type. As stakeholder requests are usually high-level and nontechnical, the team will break down requests into activities. Each activity will be assigned to a team member.

- The team is realized by a stateless record type. The Team record type contains a list of team members, specific roles in the team such as Team Leader, and users having a role.

- Iteration is realized by a stateless record type. The Iteration record type contains the iteration name, the start date, and the end date.

The record types and their relationships are described in Figure 11.15.

We have realized some of the data objects with state-based record types and some with stateless record types, and we have realized the product backlog and the sprint backlog with queries.

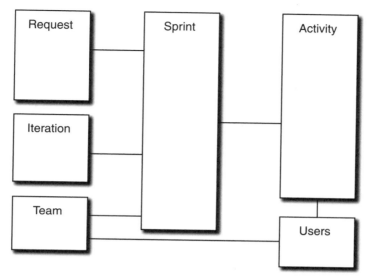

Figure 11.15 Entities relation diagram for the Scrum schema

11.4.1 Required Data

In this section we describe the fields for each record type that are essential for the solution. It is assumed that each implementation will include additional fields based on products developed, organizational culture, regulations, and other considerations.

Table 11.1 describes the suggested fields for the Request record type.

Table 11.1 Request Suggested Fields

Field Name	Field Type	Comments
Headline	Short_String	
Description	Multiline_String	
CR_Type	Short_String	Closed choice list of request types
Priority	Short_String	
Requestor	Reference	Reference to the user submitting the request
RequestForProject	Reference	Reference to the project record (optional)
Activities	Reference_List	List of the activities this request breaks down to
Iteration	Reference	Reference to the Iteration record
EstimatedEffort	Integer	Estimated effort in hours to deliver the request; mandatory in the analysis

Figure 11.16 is a screen shot of the Request record, with several of the fields listed in Table 11.1.

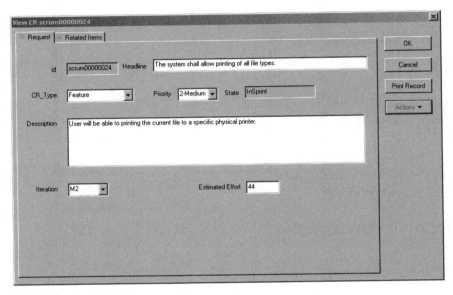

Figure 11.16   Request record: main tab

Table 11.2 describes the suggested fields of the Sprint record type.

Table 11.2   Sprint Suggested Fields

Field Name	Field Type	Comments
Headline	Short_String	
Description	Multiline_String	
Iteration	Reference	Reference to the Iteration record
StartDate		Display only, derived from Iteration.StartDate
EndDate		Display only, derived from Iteration.EndDate
Requests	Reference_List	Reference to the Request record; optionally include back reference
Activities	Reference_List	List of the activities this sprint breaks down to
Team	Reference	Reference to the Team record
Review	Multiline_String	

Note We have not included the back reference for the Requests and Activities fields. It is not required for the Scrum process as suggested in this chapter. However, it may ease the creation of several queries and reports.

Figure 11.17 displays the Sprint record main tab; it shows the sprint details, the responsible team, iteration name, end date, and other information. You can see the list of requests that will be realized by the team in this sprint, in this case one new feature to develop and one defect to fix.

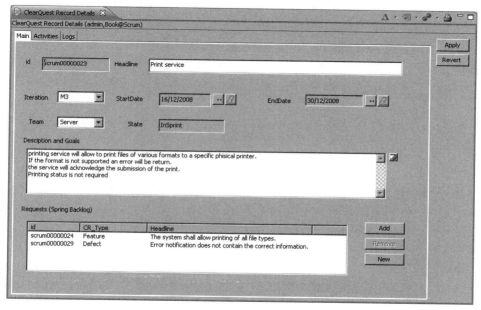

Figure 11.17 Sprint record: main tab

Table 11.3 describes the suggested fields of the Activity record type.

Table 11.3 Activity Suggested Fields

Field Name	Field Type	Comments
Headline	Short_String	
Description	Multiline_String	
ActivityType	Short_String	Closed choice list of work items/activity types

continues

Table 11.3   Activity Suggested Fields (*Continued*)

Field Name	Field Type	Comments
Priority	Short_String	
Owner	Reference	Reference to the user who is the solution provider
DueDate	Date_Time	Optional
ResolutionDescription	Multiline_String	
ActualDate	Date_Time	Optional
EstimatedEffort	Integer	Estimated effort in hours to deliver the request; mandatory in the analysis
ActualEffort	Integer	Actual effort in hours (optional)
UnitTest	Short_String	Unit test name; may be an automated script name

Figure 11.18 is a screen shot of the Activity record main tab, with several of the fields listed in Table 11.3.

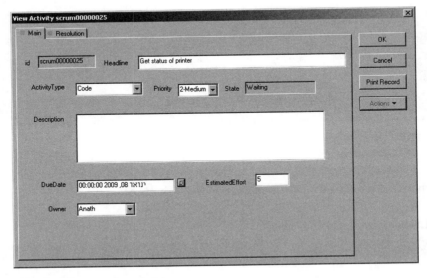

Figure 11.18   Activity record: main tab

Figure 11.19 displays the Activities tab in a Sprint record. The team has created five activities of different types, to realize the two requests that are shown in the Requests field.

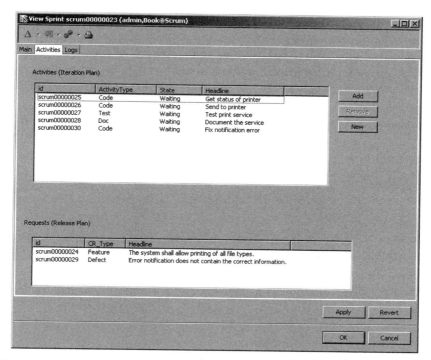

Figure 11.19   Activities and Requests related to a sprint

We have seen in this section the record types and the fields that construct the Scrum schema.

11.4.2 Understanding the Workflows of Each Record Type

After creating the three state-based records types and the fields in each one, we need to define the state machine for each record type. In the next section we describe the workflow for each record type.

11.4.2.1 Request

The workflow for the Request record type depends a lot on the organization, the stakeholders, and the regulations enforced. We propose the flow shown in Figure 11.20.

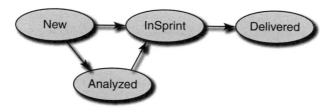

Figure 11.20   The Request record type workflow

The Request is submitted to the New state and analyzed to identify feasibility, effort, priority, possible impacts, risks, and so on. After it is analyzed and priority is given by the stakeholders, it can be picked by a team to be developed in a sprint. At the end of the sprint during the Retrospective (review meeting) the deliverables are evaluated. If the deliverables are found to meet the stakeholder request and have the desired quality, the Request can be moved to the Delivered state.

In some cases a Request can be moved from the New state directly to the InSprint state, for example, in the case of a defect or a request submitted by the team. In either case the Request must get a priority value by the stakeholder.

11.4.2.2 Activity

The workflow for the Activity record type is similar to the CMBaseActivity record type of the UCM package. We suggest that this record type be integrated with your version control system. If you are using ClearCase, add the UCM package to the schema and enable the Activity record type to the UCM package. The Request and the Sprint record types should not be UCM-enabled because artifact changes are controlled with the Activity record.

The state machine includes four consecutive states: Waiting, Ready, Active, and Complete (see Figure 11.21).

Figure 11.21   The Activity record type workflow

11.4.2.3 Sprint

The Sprint record type is used for project management as explained in the previous section. During the sprint planning meeting (or before) the record is created and its state is Submitted. When the sprint starts (the sprint iteration start date is reached), the team performs the action StartSprint which moves the record to the state InSprint. When the sprint ends (the sprint iteration end date is reached) and during the sprint Retrospective meeting the team performs the action Close, which moves the record to the state Closed. So the Sprint record type has three consecutive states: Submitted, InSprint, and Closed (see Figure 11.22).

Figure 11.22   The Sprint record type workflow

In this section we have described the suggested workflow for each of the record types that construct the Scrum schema.

11.4.3 Understanding Metrics in Agile Development

We discussed metrics in detail in Chapter 9, "Metrics and Governance"; we include here just a few words on metrics in Agile projects. Metrics measure data of direct business value to the organization. In the repetitive cycles of Agile projects, improvement can bring value, and to improve we need to measure. Working with ClearQuest, we can measure by means of charts and reports provided by the tool.

Figure 11.23 is a screen shot of the ClearQuest client displaying some typical queries and charts for Scrum projects in the workspace. The executed chart shows Planned Effort, and it displays the estimated effort of requests in each iteration.

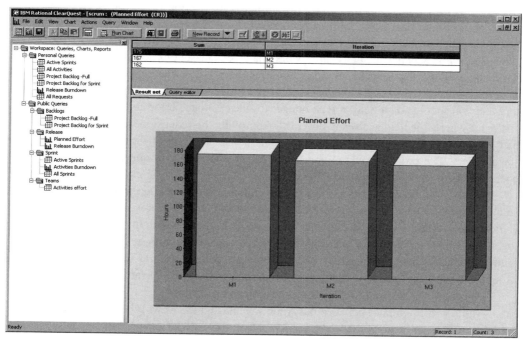

Figure 11.23   Planned Effort for Iteration chart

The "classic" release burndown charts and velocity charts cannot be created with the Clear-Quest chart wizard, but you can create reports and distribution charts that display the closed activities per iteration, or the actual/estimated effort of activities in an iteration, which will provide similar information. Also, using tools such as Rational Insight will allow you to present burndown and velocity charts.

Creating the "Total Effort per Iteration" Chart   Use the ClearQuest Windows client to create a new chart. For record type select Sprint, and for chart type select Distribution Chart. In the Vertical Axis (Y) select the field Activities.ActualEffort (this is an Integer field); in the Function select Sum. This will sum the effort of all the activities in each iteration. In the Horizontal Axis (X) select the field Iteration.Name.

11.5 Agile with the ALM Schema

Companies that have decided to adopt the CQ-ALM (ClearQuest Application Lifecycle Management) schema on an enterprise-wide basis may still need to deal with projects and teams that are using an Agile development method. Those companies may ask if they need an additional schema for these teams. Our answer is that they do not; they can use the ALM schema. We shall explain how they can configure an ALM project in an Agile way. We assume that you are familiar to some degree with the CQ-ALM and the ALM terminology. Section 12.4, "ClearCase, ClearQuest ALM, Build Forge Integrated Solution Architecture," in Chapter 12, "Sample Applications and Solutions," includes additional discussion and examples of the CQ-ALM schema.

The ALM schema includes three work management state-based record types: Request, Task, and Activity. The Request record is similar to the one described in the previous sections. A Task record is created when the request is approved for development. Priority behavior is mandatory and you should add a field of type Integer for the estimated effort unless you are using CQ-ALM 1.1 where this field is already provided. Approving the request means that it was analyzed by both the technical and the business teams, and it was prioritized by the product owner or the stakeholders. The product backlog is a list of tasks generated by a query that displays all the opened tasks of a given project sorted by priority.

The ALM schema defines project phases and iterations. Agile projects do not use phases, so the ClearQuest admin can create a single phase record and name it with a dummy name such as Iteration or Sprint. The next step is to create iteration records with the numeric values of the iteration. For example, create iteration records and label them with 1, 2, and so forth. Using numeric values is only a suggestion; you can use any method, such as week in the year. When using the system, you will have Iteration 1, Iteration 2, or Sprint 1, Sprint 2, and so forth.

Figure 11.24 shows an ALMTask record assigned to Sprint 2.

Another differentiator between our Agile schema and the ALM schema is the use of roles. Agile projects usually adopt the whole team practice; the skills of the whole team are what matters and team members' roles are less relevant. So we suggest creating a Role Label record for each team, using names like Team-A, Team-B, and so forth. In the Members tab add the team members to the Members field and the team leader to the Primary field. If relevant to your project add additional role labels such as TeamLeader or ScrumMaster (see Figure 11.25).

In the Scrum schema described in the previous sections we used a record type called Sprint. Do we need to create such a record type in the ALM schema? The answer is no.

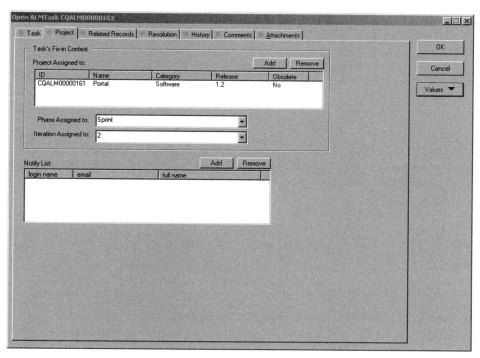

Figure 11.24   ALMTask record assigned to sprint (iteration)

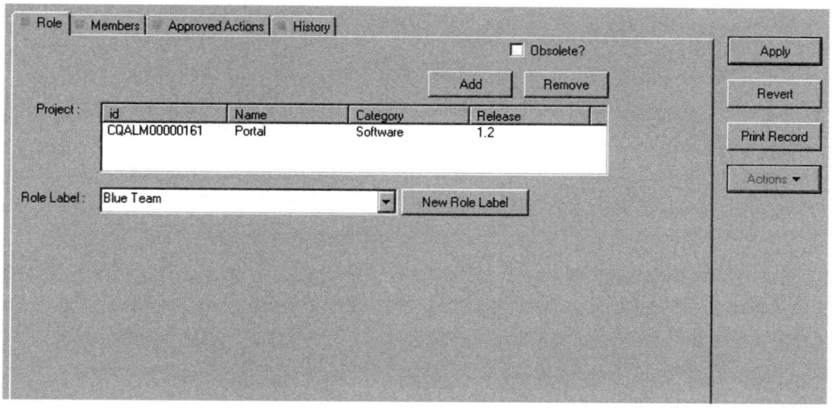

Figure 11.25   ALMRole record assigned to an Agile team

A sprint is a team effort for a given iteration. What we need to do is to link the Request, Task, and Activity to the team and the iteration (see Figure 11.26). Among the many possible solutions we shall mention three:

- Add a field called Sprint to each of the Request, Task, and Activity record types. The team will fill in a value that uniquely identifies the sprint. The field value should be automatically copied when a child record is created. Although this solution is simple, it requires a schema change.

- The second solution uses existing fields. The Task record already has the field Iteration that references the ALMiteration record that has fields such as start_date, end_date, status_label, description, and others. The Activity and the Request record types have references to Task, so for each record we can find the iteration that the record was assigned to. We also need to relate the record to the team working on it; this is done using the ALMRole record as previously explained.

- The third solution is similar to the second one. We previously explained that we gave the phase a dummy value, so instead of using a dummy value we can set the phase name to be the team name. Now we have for the iteration a meaningful value that is the team name and the iteration name. The user will see in the Iteration field Team-A 1, Team-A 2, and so on, which identify the sprint numbers for Team-A.

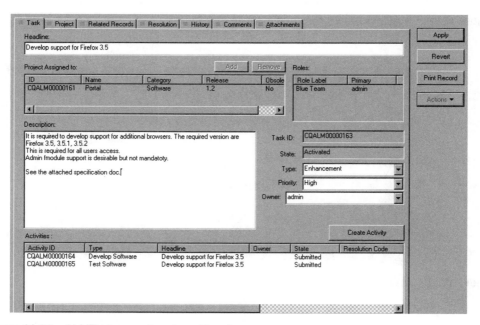

Figure 11.26   ALMTask record assigned to a team

The team (field Roles) in Figure 11.26 is automatically selected when the task type is selected. This is defined by creating an ALMWorkConfiguration record with the following fields: Project, Record Type, Type Label, Roles.

The three solutions allow you to create queries to see the sprint status, cumulative effort, status of each activity, defects reported against a specific sprint, and other sprint queries, charts, and reports as required.

During the sprint planning meeting the team creates one or more activities for each task. Each activity is assigned to a team member. The number of child activities that will be created per task and the types of those activities can be defined and set by each team in the ALMWork-Configuration record. This is a powerful and useful feature of the ALM schema.

In the Sprint Review Meeting, if the team found the tested deliverables to have the required quality, the team can Complete (an action) the Activated (a state) Tasks. Now the stakeholder can Accept (an action) the related Requests to release the deliverables and to Close the sprint (see Figure 11.27).

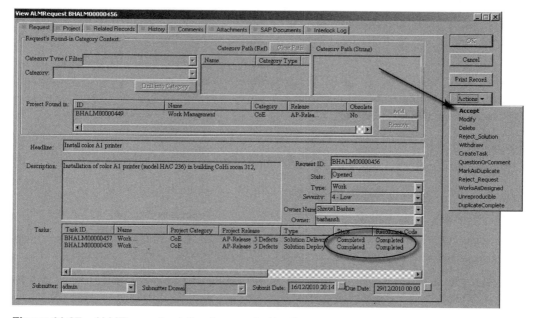

Figure 11.27   ALMRequest solution is accepted by the requestor

The ALMRequest record is accepted by the requestor (stakeholder) after the ALMTask is completed with resolution code Completed.

11.6 Resources

11.6.1 Materials by Scott Ambler

Ambler, Scott, "Agile Modeling—Effective Practices for Modeling and Documentation," www.agilemodeling.com, 2007 (accessed February 23, 2011).

Ambler, Scott, "Scott Ambler's Articles and Other Writings," www.ambysoft.com/onlineWritings.html, 1997–2011 (accessed February 23, 2011).
      This page provides links to books and Web-based writings.

Ambler, Scott, "The Agile System Development Life Cycle (SDLC)," www.ambysoft.com/essays/agileLifecycle.html, 2005–2010 (accessed February 23, 2011).

11.6.2 DeveloperWorks Articles

Pampino, Carolyn, and Robert Pierce, "Application Lifecycle Management with Rational Clear-Quest 7.1.0.0," *IBM developerWorks*, www.ibm.com/developerworks/rational/library/edge/08/mar08/pampino-pierce/, 2008 (accessed February 23, 2011).

Ellingsworth, Millard, and Thomas Starz, "Scrum Project Management with IBM Rational Team Concert Version 2," *IBM developerWorks*, www.ibm.com/developerworks/rational/library/09/scrumprojectmanagementteamconcert-1/index.html, 2009 (accessed February 23, 2011).

Lee, Kevin A., "Agile SCM and the IBM Rational Toolset," *IBM developerWorks*, www.ibm.com/developerworks/rational/library/jun06/lee/index.html?S_TACT=105AGX15&S_CMP=EDU, 2006 (accessed February 23, 2011).

11.6.3 Other Information

"Agile Alliance," www.agilealliance.org/, 2011 (accessed February 23, 2011).

"OpenUP," http://epf.eclipse.org/wikis/openup, 2011 (accessed February 23, 2011).

"Scrum Alliance," www.scrumalliance.org/, 2011 (accessed February 23, 2011).

Wells, Don, "Extreme Programming: A Gentle Introduction," www.extremeprogramming.org, 2009 (accessed February 23, 2011).

Wikipedia, "Lean Software Development," http://en.wikipedia.org/wiki/Lean_software_development, 2009 (accessed February 23, 2011).

Schwaber, Ken, and Mike Beedle, *Agile Software Development with Scrum* (Upper Saddle River, NJ: Prentice Hall, 2002).

11.7 Summary

In this chapter we started with a short explanation of Agile principles and continued with a somewhat more detailed description of the Scrum method. We later explained how Scrum is realized in Rational Team Concert using the provided Scrum process template.

We continued with an explanation of how to create a ClearQuest schema to manage Agile projects and specifically Scrum projects. It is important to mention that the proposed solution can be modified and adapted to each company or project. The same principles can be applied to extend existing schemas. Some examples of metrics derived with ClearQuest charts are explained.

The ClearQuest schema described will be available to download from the IBM developer-Works site. The schema serves as a skeleton and does not pretend to be a complete solution. Use it as a basis for your schema; add fields and hooks to create rules and to automate operations.

In the last section we explained how organizations that use the built-in CQ-ALM schema can configure an ALM project to support Agile teams. We proposed several solutions that require only minimal modifications or no modifications to the schema.

## CHAPTER 12

Sample Applications and Solutions

This chapter provides examples of applications and solutions developed using ClearQuest and Rational Team Concert. Some of the examples are not typical solutions and are not related to change management or work item management, but because the flexibility of the tools allows such freedom, users are taking advantage of developing applications with that powerful platform. Other examples include extensions to existing applications.

The solutions described are

- Collaborative Application Lifecycle Management (C/ALM) with Jazz-based tools
- User-defined fields, a ClearQuest solution that allows each project to define project-specific fields and pick lists without the need to change the schema
- Service level agreement (SLA), a ClearQuest solution to define SLA rules and techniques to notify and alert prior to contract breach
- ClearCase, ClearQuest, Build Forge Integrated Solution Architecture, a ClearQuest schema based on the Application Lifecycle Management (ALM) schema that is integrated with ClearCase and Build Forge to provide the customer with a governed development and build process
- Manage release promotion with ClearQuest

12.1 Collaborative ALM with Jazz-Based Tools

What is ALM and what is Collaborative ALM? There are several definitions of ALM; the Rational C/ALM project adopted the following from Forrester Research, Inc.:

> The coordination of development life-cycle activities including requirements, modeling, development, build and testing, through: Process Automation, Traceability and reporting across activities of all disciplines.

Forrester has defined five criteria for an ALM 2.0 solution:

- Common services available across practitioner tools
- Microprocesses and macroprocesses governed by externalized workflow
- Practitioner tools assembled out of plug-ins
- Features available across arbitrary asset repositories
- Use of open integration standards

In the next section we explain how these criteria are met in the C/ALM solution using the Jazz platform.

12.1.1 Jazz C/ALM

Looking at collaborative teams, we see people having specific roles who are collaborating via tools to deliver a desirable change to an application. The team's work is governed by a set of disciplines; they collaborate by sharing and exchanging data from one or more repositories.

In today's world many teams work in a distributed environment and use Agile development methods. This requires even more collaboration during the process of a change.

The process of changing an application involves several disciplines: requirements management, design, development, build management, test management, project management, and others. In each discipline there are workflows and activities, usually performed with dedicated tools that store data in a dedicated repository. Collaboration across the disciplines is key to transforming from silo-oriented disciplines to collaborative software development teams. The lifecycle service integration layer ensures that collaboration on the server side enables cross-discipline collaboration.

C/ALM involves several disciplines and several integrated tools. Figure 12.1 describes in a schematic way the relationships and coordination of the elements we have described.

The Jazz-based Collaborative Application Lifecycle Management (C/ALM) is a solution that is based on the following:

- **Data integration:** Artifacts are linked across tools and repositories using RESTful interfaces (OSLC).
- **Collaboration:** Practitioners can link, navigate to artifacts, chat with other team members, be notified of status, and otherwise interact.
- **Transparency:** Team members can track the status of work across the entire lifecycle, not only in their discipline.
- **Automation:** Process automation improves product quality and project performance.

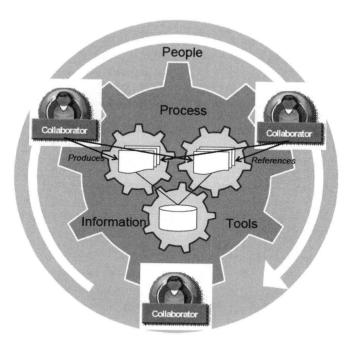

Figure 12.1 The coordination of people, process, information, and tools in ALM

The Rational Jazz Collaborative Application Lifecycle Management project incorporates four components (see Figure 12.2):

- C/ALM scenarios

  Provide real-world, role-based and task-based user experiences that explore end user goals and their needs to access data throughout the lifecycle.

- Open Services for Lifecycle Collaboration (OSLC)

  RESTful integration to unlock the information buried within development tools; open and agreed-upon interfaces are needed that allow different tools to share and exchange the data that they produce.

- Jazz Integration Architecture (JIA)

  A set of interconnected technologies and specifications consisting of reference architecture, API specifications, a set of common services, and tool building blocks.

- Jazz Foundation

  An implementation of the Jazz Foundation Services and optional toolkits to aid in the construction of Jazz applications.

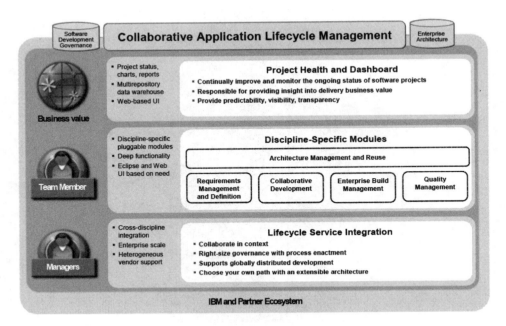

Figure 12.2 Collaborative Application Lifecycle Management blueprint

This material has been reproduced by Addison-Wesley with the permission of International Business Machines Corporation from IBM Redbooks publication SG24-7622: *Collaborative Application Lifecycle Management with IBM Rational Products* (http://www.redbooks.ibm.com/abstracts/sg247622.html?Open). COPYRIGHT © 2008 International Business Machines Corporation. ALL RIGHTS RESERVED.

So the Jazz C/ALM is not only about the Jazz tools, but about the integrations between the tools that allow synchronized activities, information sharing, asset traceability, and governed processes.

See the "Resources" section at the end of the chapter for more information on ALM and Collaborative ALM.

12.2 User-Defined Fields in ClearQuest

Here is a common enterprise scenario: You have defined a schema for the entire organization and obtained agreement from all the stakeholders. You have developed the schema and deployed it. After some time a project manager requests that you add a field that is specific to a project. Later another project manager asks for just two fields that will help in the analysis phase, and the story continues with requirements for specific projects, products, or teams. If you implement these changes, after a few years you will find yourself with a schema that has many fields that are used by just a small group of practitioners.

A recent engagement we were involved with had a similar problem. We decided to create project-specific fields to address the issue. The idea was to have some fields that have general (internal) names such as UserDefined_1, UserDefined_2, and so on. The caption for those fields is blank, but the end user sees a "caption" that is actually the value of another field. The value of that field is set by the project team and not by the schema designer.

The end user sees a form similar to the one in Figure 12.3.

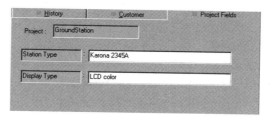

Figure 12.3   User-defined fields in a ClearQuest form

The form has five fields:

- The upper field is a text box control that displays the value of "project.name"; it is not mandatory to include this control, but advisable.

- The two fields in the left column are read-only fields that serve as the displayed names (captions or labels) of the fields in the right column.

- The two fields in the right column are the fields where the end user will put the values for his or her project.

In this example the project is Ground Station with two fields named Station Type and Display Type. Those names are project-specific. Each project manager can enter the relevant fields for his or her project.

Now let's see the internals, how this is done in ClearQuest Designer.

First we have modified the Project record type. As the fields were defined for a specific project, it make sense to put these fields in the project record, but other ideas such as a designated stateless record type will work, too.

We have added two fields of type Short_String; these fields will store the *names* (caption or label) of the project-specific fields. In the Project record type we have added a tab for these fields, and it looks like the form in Figure 12.4.

Note   Note that the fields in Figure 12.4 are defined in the Project record type.

It is clear that you can add as many fields as are required. We have found that five fields are usually enough to cover the needs of most stakeholders. You have seen the four fields that we added to the Defect record type (two fields to store the names and two to store the values).

Figure 12.4   User-defined field names in ClearQuest Designer

The names are entered with a ValueChanged hook of the field Project. Thus, when a user selects a project, a hook will copy the content of the names from the Project record.

The hook code in Listing 12.1 fills in the field names for the specific project (assuming the field Project is of type Reference and points to the Project record type).

Listing 12.1   Setting Field Names

```
proj = GetFieldValue("Project").GetValue()
If proj <> "Null" Then
 name1 = GetFieldValue("Project.FieldName_1").GetValue()
 name2 = GetFieldValue("Project.FieldName_2").GetValue()

 SetFieldValue "UserFieldName_1", name1
 SetFieldValue "UserFieldName_2", name2
End If
```

This strategy is very simple, but there is a caveat. If users want to query on project-specific fields, they will not find the same field names. To overcome this problem we suggest doing one or more of the following:

- Train the users on the solution strategy.
- Include help text with the internal field name.
- Add the internal name as a visible caption.

12.2.1 Defining Choice Lists

Now let us take one step forward. A project manager has requirements that are more complex. For example, suppose someone wants to have choice lists for the project-specific fields. We cannot use a Constant_List. We could use many Dynamic_Lists, a set of lists for each project, but that does not scale, especially if there are many projects.

One solution is to create a list for each field in the Project record type. The list can be stored in a Multiline_String, one value per line as in our example (another option is to separate the values with a special delimiter).

To achieve this we add one multiline field for each project-specific field. In the Project record it looks like the screen shot in Figure 12.5.

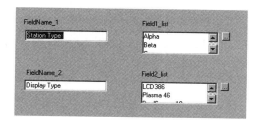

Figure 12.5 Definition of the fields in the Project record

In the Defect record type the control for the field should be a drop-down combo box. This control allows both selection and typing, to respond to the needs of all projects (a list box control allows selection but does not allow typing). The tab in the Defect form is displayed in the screen shot in Figure 12.6.

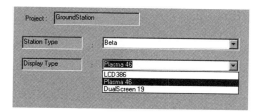

Figure 12.6 User-defined fields with a choice list: end user view of the user-defined fields in the ClearQuest client

The additional task that we have to perform is to write the hook that will populate the choice list. We suggest writing a global hook that will be called from the field choice list hook. The reason is that all the project-specific hooks will be almost identical, so by reusing code we gain simplicity and reduce maintenance costs.

The global subroutine will have two parameters as follows:

```
Populate_list(field2read, choices)
```

- The `field2read` parameter is the name of the field in the project stateless record type, which contains the list of values for the choice list.

- The `choices` parameter is a reference to the field choices object, where the values will be populated.

The next code line shows the calling hook example. Here we use the dot notation to access the field `Field2_list` in the referenced stateless record type Project:

```
call Populate_list("Project.Field2_list" , choices)
```

The BASIC code in Listing 12.2 is an example of the called global subroutine.

Listing 12.2   Populating a Choice List

```
Sub Populate_list(field2read, choices)

' Purpose: Get the list values from the project record
'                     and populate the choice list
' Input  : field2read As String
' Output: choices As Object
' Created by: SB on 20  Nov 2008
' Date modified:

REM - read values
      flist = GetFieldValue(field2read).GetValueAsList
      if not IsEmpty(flist) then
      Keyvals  = Split(Cstr(flist(0)),vbLF)
REM - populate the choice-list
            For Each keyfield in Keyvals
               choices.AddItem(keyfield)
            Next
      end if
End Sub
```

12.2.2 Defining Requiredness

Now let's take another step forward.

A more complex stakeholder requirement might be to set the project-specific field requiredness differently for each project. Look at the ClearQuest behaviors table; if we want project-level behaviors, we actually need one table per project. Instead of using a table for each project, we shall use a list of pair values for each user-defined field: State::Requiredness. To achieve this solution, we will use the same method we used for the choice list. In the Project stateless record type we create fields of type Multiline_String, one field for each user-defined field.

In the screen shot in Figure 12.7 you see for Field_1 and Field_2 three supporting fields:

- The visible name of the field (caption or label)
- The choice list values
- A list of pairs of state and field permission (similar to an entry in the behaviors table)

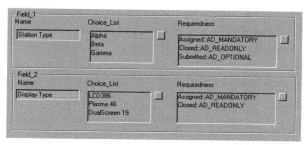

Figure 12.7   Definition of the choice list and the requiredness

---

Note   Note that the definitions in Figure 12.7 are performed at the project level.

We have modified the form of the Defect record type. When the field is mandatory, the column sign becomes red. Since there is no caption for this field on the form, this is not a very visible indication. So we have changed the caption to be "==>" which is more visible and understandable. (Actually this caption is as good as any sign you see fit.) Figure 12.8 shows the Defect record type with the two mandatory fields.

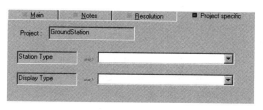

Figure 12.8   Annotation of the user-defined fields when requiredness is Mandatory

Let's review the logic behind this solution. First change the behaviors table and select the USE_HOOK permission of all states of the fields UserFieldValue_1, UserFieldValue_2 … UserFieldValue_n.

UserFieldName_1, UserFieldName_2 … UserFieldName_n should be READONLY, as these are the captions of the corresponding fields UserFieldValue_n (see the field behaviors in Figure 12.9).

UserFieldValue_1	USE_HOOK	USE_HOOK	USE_HOOK	USE_HOOK	USE_HOOK	USE_HOOK	USE_HOOK	USE_HOOK
UserFieldValue_2	USE_HOOK	USE_HOOK	USE_HOOK	USE_HOOK	USE_HOOK	USE_HOOK	USE_HOOK	USE_HOOK
UserFieldName_1	READONLY	READONLY	READONLY	READONLY	READONLY	READONLY	READONLY	READONLY
UserFieldName_2	READONLY	READONLY	READONLY	READONLY	READONLY	READONLY	READONLY	READONLY

Figure 12.9   The behaviors table definitions for the user-defined fields

To set the field permission (or requiredness) we write a global function. This function gets the name of the field in the Project record where the list of permissions for the current project is stored. The function returns to the calling hook the permission value; note that the return value is of type Long.

The calling field permission hook, for the field `userfieldvalue_2`, looks like this:

```
userfieldvalue_2_Permission =
                SetRequiredness( "Project.Field2_requiredness")
```

The BASIC code in listing 12.3 is an example of the called global subroutine.

Listing 12.3   Setting Field Requiredness

```
Function SetRequiredness( ReqFieldName )
'
' Purpose: Get the permission value from the project record
'          convert to Long and return to field_permission
' Input:   ReqFieldName As String
' Output:  requiredness As Long
' Created by: SB on 27  Nov 2008
' Date modified:

     SetRequiredness = AD_OPTIONAL
     stat = GetFieldStringValue("State")

REM - Get the list values from the project record
     flist = GetFieldValue(ReqFieldName).GetValueAsList
     if not IsEmpty(flist) then
     Keyvals  = Split(Cstr(flist(0)),vbLF)
REM - Get correct value for current state
           For Each keyfield in Keyvals
              freq = Split(keyfield, "::", 2, 1)
           If( freq(0) = stat) Then
                   ' Return value is of type Long
                      SetRequiredness = ConvertEnum( freq(1) )
                      Exit For
```

```
                    End If
          Next
      end if
End Function
```

A few comments on Listing 12.3:

- The `split()` function uses the textual delimiter `: :` and splits the `keyfield` string into two strings, `freq(0)` and `freq(1)`.
- The function `ConvertEnum()` gets the permission string value and converts it to a Long.

The credit for the idea described in this section goes to Dr. Alexander Karnovsky.

12.3 Service Level Agreements (SLAs) in ClearQuest

ClearQuest is flexible enough to allow you to build various applications such as a help desk. Some of these applications require governance and monitoring of the SLAs. In this section we shall propose a method for defining SLA rules and how to monitor and alert to approaching events. We describe how to define and build an SLA in the ClearQuest schema. The solution not only verifies that the SLA is met, but also sends notifications and alerts prior to contract breach.

12.3.1 Background

An SLA is defined as a contract or agreement between the service provider and the client or the stakeholder.

We usually talk about SLAs in the context of SOA, CRM, and ERP systems. One may ask why this is relevant to ClearQuest.

We can build a help desk system with ClearQuest (as many have done), and SLA is very relevant to such a system. In the context of other applications that can be built with ClearQuest, such as defect tracking, enhancement requests, or any other change request system, we can broaden the term SLA by including internal policies and performance measurements that deal with each type of request.

Here are some examples of SLAs:

- A service provider will initially reply to a help desk ticket within four hours for a normal ticket and two hours for an urgent ticket.
- The SCCB will reply to a high-priority enhancement request within seven days.
- A blocking defect will be assigned to a solution provider within 24 hours.

Each rule includes alert and notification options:

- Who should receive an alert
- Who should receive a notification

- How long before the due date the alert should be sent
- How long before the due date the notification should be sent

In this chapter we shall propose an SLA solution that can be added to most ClearQuest schemas.

12.3.2 The Topic

In order to be able to govern the SLA rules, we need to provide the following to the administrators and the stakeholders:

- A means of defining the SLA rules in ClearQuest and the ability to easily modify them or inactivate them
- A means of checking the ClearQuest database records against the SLA rules
- A means of notifying the solution providers when a critical time is approaching
- A means of notifying the stakeholder and/or the responsible manager when a critical time is overdue
- A means of providing governance and status reports for various roles

12.3.3 SLA Definition

An SLA consists of one or more rules. Each rule is defined in a stateless record. This stateless record type contains the fields shown in Table 12.1.

Table 12.1   Suggested Fields of the SLA Record

Field Name	Field Type	Comments
Name	String	The SLA name. Set this field to be the unique key.
RecordType	String	The entity definition of the record type in context (defect, enhancement request, ticket, etc.). The rule applies to records of that type. It is advisable to set this field as a secondary unique key.
IsActive	String	Define if the rule is active (values: Y/N).
BaseAction	String	Define the initial action from which performance/time is to be measured.
NextAction	String	Define the next action after the initial action that must be performed.
DueTime	Integer	Time (in hours) that NextAction has to be performed after the BaseAction occurred. This is also the manager alert time.

Table 12.1 Suggested Fields of the SLA Record (*Continued*)

Field Name	Field Type	Comments
NotifyTime	Integer	Time (in hours) that a notification has to be sent to the solution provider if it has not performed the NextAction.
SolutionProvider	String	The name of the field in the RecordType that contains the solution provider (example: Owner).
ServiceManager	Reference	A reference to the user who will be alerted if NextAction has not been performed within the DueTime.
Priority	String	Minimum RecordType priority to activate the rule (example: 3-High).
Severity	String	Minimum RecordType severity to activate the rule (example: 4-Showstopper).

You may add other fields to support your specific organization's needs; some examples are shown in Table 12.2.

Table 12.2 Suggested Optional Fields of the SLA Record

Field Name	Field Type	Comments
Reminder	Integer	Time (in hours) that an additional notification has to be sent to the solution provider if it has not performed the NextAction
Ignore	Long String	Pairs of FieldName::FieldValue that if one exists in the record the rule should be ignored

12.3.4 Activate the SLA Rules

To check the ClearQuest database records against the SLA rules and activate the relevant rules, we need a time-based event, which does not exist in ClearQuest.

The way to do it is by writing an external program or script, then activating that program via tools like AT scheduler in Windows or Cron in UNIX. The program will query the database and test each record against each SLA rule.

12.3.5 Notifications

If the SLA rule is found to be valid (as explained above), we need to find out whether this is an alert or a notification and send an e-mail to the relevant person. The way to send e-mail from an external script (not via ClearQuest e-mail rules) is explained in several assets published in developerWorks. See the examples in the following:

Staff, IBM Rational, "E-mail: Sample Hooks for Users of IBM Rational ClearQuest," *IBM developerWorks*, www.ibm.com/developerworks/rational/library/4513.html, 2003 (accessed February 24, 2011).

12.3.6 Providing Governance Reports

It is important to allow managers to have status reports so that they can understand the root cause of poor service and take proactive action to improve the services they provide.

Reports, charts, and queries can be easily created in ClearQuest as explained in Chapter 4, "The Data," and in Chapter 9, "Metrics and Governance."

12.3.7 The External Program

As mentioned previously, the solution requires writing an external program that checks the SLA rules, identifies the records in context, and sends notifications and alerts.

One approach for such a program can be to loop on each record in the database, and for each record to find if it responds to one of the SLA rules. Although this is relatively easy to program, it may require extensive resources for large databases and many rules. A similar approach is used in the following hook:

Staff, IBM Rational, "External VB Application to Do 'Something' with Records Not Touched in 14 Days," *IBM developerWorks*, www.ibm.com/developerworks/rational/library/3895.html, 2002 (accessed February 23, 2011).

Another approach is to write an SQL query that identifies the records that respond to the SLA rules. This query requires knowledge of SQL and may be platform-dependent.

An example of such a query is demonstrated in Listing 12.4.

Listing 12.4   Sample SQL Query

```
-- Raanon Reutlinger, IBM Toronto DB2 Labs (Israel), 2010


sla_rule_check
AS
(
  SELECT h.*, s.duetime, s.notifytime
        , LAG( action_timestamp, 1)
            OVER (PARTITION BY entity_dbid
              ORDER BY action_timestamp) prev_action_ts
      FROM  history h
      ,       sla_table s
```

```
        WHERE
            h.entitydef_name = s.recordtype
        AND   h.action_name = s.baseaction OR h.action_name = s.nextaction
)
,
sla_check
AS (
    SELECT s1.*
    ,CASE WHEN TIMESTAMPDIFF(8, CHAR( action_timestamp - prev_action_ts))
     BETWEEN notifytime AND duetime THEN 1 ELSE 0 END past_notify
    ,CASE WHEN TIMESTAMPDIFF(8, CHAR( action_timestamp - prev_action_ts))
     > duetime THEN 1 ELSE 0  END past_due
    FROM   sla_rule_check s1
)
SELECT *
FROM sla_check
WHERE past_notify = 1
   OR past_due = 1
;
```

Notes   The ClearQuest SLA record type name is `sla_table`.

In the `TIMESTAMPDIFF` the `8` in the first parameter means the hours interval.

This query was tested with IBM DB2; adjustments may be needed for other database vendors.

You can identify table columns with our field definitions.

You can create two queries, one for `past_notify` and one for `past_due`.

12.4 ClearCase, ClearQuest ALM, Build Forge Integrated Solution Architecture

This section describes a solution developed for a customer; the solution is composed of three integrated products: ClearCase to manage the software configuration control, ClearQuest to manage the change control, and Build Forge to manage the build process and automation (see Figure 12.10).

The ClearQuest ALM schema was customized to meet the required process.

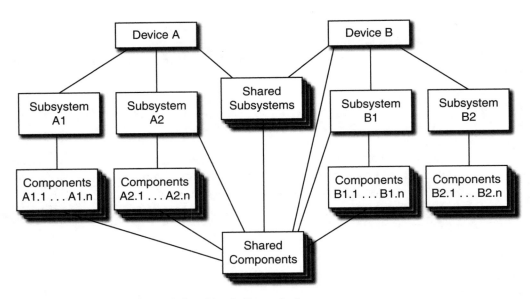

Figure 12.10   Component relationships in the project

12.4.1 Understanding the Work Projects

These types of projects are the most common projects within ClearCase UCM. These are the projects where developers perform their changes. This is the UCM project where developers check out, check in, and continuously validate changes. UCM work projects have development streams, shared streams, and other stream configurations that satisfy the working requirements of the developers using the work project.

Configuring ALM   Every ClearCase UCM work project must have a corresponding Clear-Quest ALM project. This UCM project is where work will be performed within ClearCase against development activities contained within the ClearQuest ALM project.

12.4.2 Developers Work on Activities within a Project

To work on ClearQuest ALM activities that are assigned to a developer, the developer must first "join" the UCM project. If the developer uses the normal Join Project wizard of UCM, he or she will eventually be left with a development stream on the UCM project with a view attached to it, as well as an integration view attached to the UCM project's integration stream. The developer will "set" into his or her development view and associate an ALMActivity to this view using the command

```
cleartool setact ...
```

Figure 12.11 outlines the relationship between UCM and ALM objects.

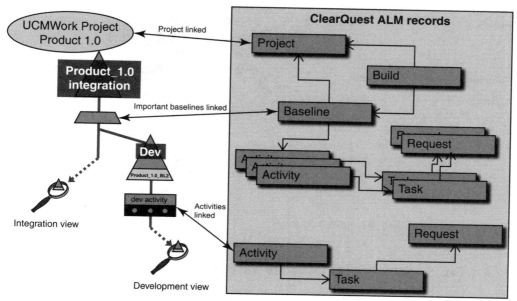

Figure 12.11   UCM objects linked to ClearQuest ALM objects

Developers work on their activity in ClearCase UCM by checking out versions of elements, making changes, validating those changes, and checking their changes back into ClearCase. Once they are done with their changes, they will use ClearCase UCM to "deliver" their changes to the integration stream. At this point their development activity in ClearQuest ALM is Complete with a resolution code. However, it has not been validated yet in the integration stream.

Configuring UCM   You can configure a UCM project to autotransition a ClearQuest activity to a Closed UCM state type upon delivery. Doing so may pop up a ClearQuest dialog box to fill in required fields, such as Resolution. This GUI pop-up may not be supported on all client interfaces, so it's best to have the developer manually complete the activity.

12.4.3 Continuously Validating through a Build and Validation Process

Once changes have been delivered to the integration stream, they are candidates for the periodic build and validation process. A scheduled Build Forge project can wake up every hour (or at some other interval) and attempt to validate the integration stream. This process can be performed after every delivery, or on a time-based schedule. This type of build also does not create any records within ClearQuest ALM. Only important baselines should be logged in ClearQuest ALM. This periodic build project performs the steps outlined in Figure 12.12.

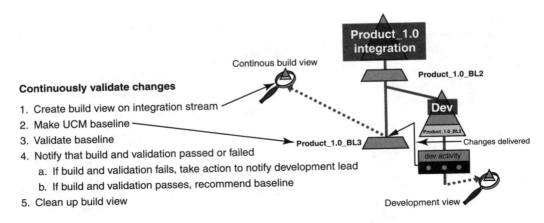

Continuously validate changes

1. Create build view on integration stream
2. Make UCM baseline
3. Validate baseline
4. Notify that build and validation passed or failed
   a. If build and validation fails, take action to notify development lead
   b. If build and validation passes, recommend baseline
5. Clean up build view

Figure 12.12   Continuous build process

12.4.4 Creating the Task to Integrate the Baseline That Includes a Defect Fix

When a request of type Defect is submitted against a project, there is normally a development task created to hold the work activities. A common extension to ALM is to create the integration task record against the projects that depend on the current project's released baseline. This allows for the consuming projects to be notified that there is a potential defect that they may be exposed to. If the consuming projects wish to wait for the fix, they can set this integration activity to the Open state and wait for the underlying integration activity to be created. If they don't care, they can simply close out the integration task with the appropriate resolution code.

Configuring CQ-ALM   A common strategy to keep track of an ALM project's consuming ALM projects is to use the ALM project's Super Project relationship to other ALM projects.

Figure 12.13 shows the integration task relationship to the initial request.

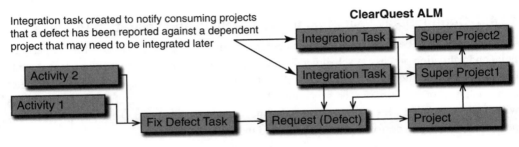

Figure 12.13   The integration task associated with the defect request

Using the strategy outlined above, you can keep abreast of defects that may affect you as a consuming project and how the development activities for this defect are progressing.

12.4.5 Releasing Periodically through Stable Composite Baselines

Periodically it is good to expose others to your changes. A scheduled Build Forge project can perform a release for your project team. This type of release will be tracked within ClearQuest ALM. It will also use a UCM project to collect the various baselines into a composite release baseline. A typical strategy within UCM is to use a Release Project that is read-only to all components. This Release Project is used to track the composite relationship of the various baselines it is consuming. Some of the baselines being consumed may also be composite baselines.

A major benefit of using ClearQuest ALM integrated with ClearCase UCM is the ability to automatically notify consuming projects that they have an integration task to be performed on this baseline. A step within the Build Forge Release Project (step 13 in Figure 12.14) fires a process that will interrogate ClearCase's knowledge of the baseline relationship of the previous project's baselines and the UCM projects that consumed them. This list will be gathered and integration ALMActivities will be created on the consuming CQ-ALM project's integration task.

To accomplish the desired functionality, the process must

1. Gather all projects that consume the last baseline in the release project

2. Look at all the activities being fixed in this baseline

3. Go up to their task level and find all integration tasks that are in the Open state

4. Make this list unique and attach the Integrate Baseline activity to each Open task of this type

    If a project is found that does not have an integration task associated with it, the integration activity needs to attach to the default integration task for the ALM project. This would indicate that ClearCase thinks the project is a valid consumer but was in the Super Project list.

5. Grab the activities being fixed in this baseline and associate them with the integration activity as related records

This process will notify the integrator that there is a new set of functionality ready to be integrated. This release build project will perform the steps outlined in Figure 12.14.

Figure 12.14 shows creating a release view for the baselining of the writable components of Product_1.0. Contained within the project are also steps that deal with the Release Project. Steps 8 and 9 specifically deal with marking the composite release that consuming projects will want to integrate. This composite baseline within ClearQuest ALM simply aggregates the various baseline records with ClearQuest. To align the activities with the correct baseline records in ClearQuest, the following ClearCase command is used:

```
cleartool diffbl
```

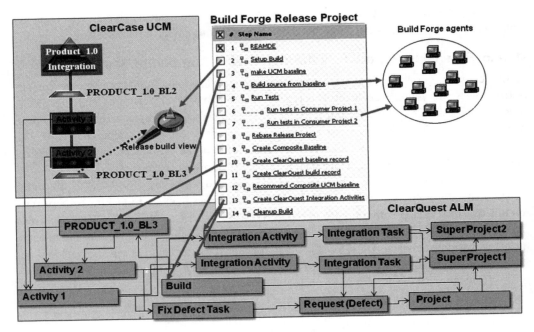

Figure 12.14   Release build process

Figure 12.15 shows the composite baseline structure within ClearQuest ALM.

12.4.6 Working on Test Artifacts

In many cases there is a time period when the source code is frozen and only critical defects are worked on. During this time frame development of test assets may continue but not source assets. With a ClearCase UCM stream strategy you can model this in UCM as a test project with writable access only to the test assets and read-only to the source. In some cases the tests and source are contained within the same components. In this case you can simply have the test development occur on its own stream which has a foundation baseline of the frozen source baseline.

You can also use ClearQuest ALM to "turn off" development activities in the work project's ALM work configuration by only creating Test Development activities in your project, and only assigning the test developers to a role that is allowed to work on artifacts during this stage. Figure 12.16 shows a UCM project in this phase and its related ClearQuest ALM records.

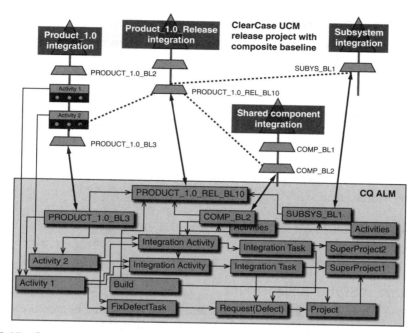

Figure 12.15 Composite baseline structure within ClearQuest ALM

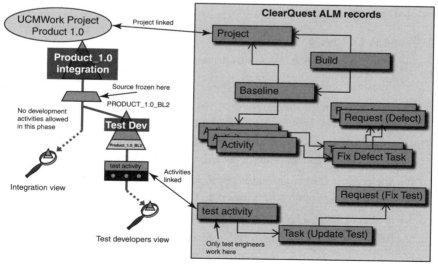

Figure 12.16 Only tests allowed to be developed

12.5 Manage Release Promotion

A financial organization used to manage its software promotion process in a manual manner with spreadsheets. Promotion is a process of movement of a software configuration item from one environment to a higher environment, according to an Information Technology division work plan, to create a new software release. The environments in this context are development, integration, preproduction (or user acceptance test), and production. The organization has several IT platforms such as IBM mainframe, UNIX-based systems, and Microsoft-Windows-based systems; each one is running many applications.

The software promotion process started with preparing a detailed request for promotion (a spreadsheet form). This request required approval, and after the approval process, the task of promotion was assigned to several support teams that would actually perform the promotion activities.

The organization realized that the existing method did not provide them with the governance and quality needed, so they decided to develop a system to manage the release promotion. We shall describe that system in the following sections.

12.5.1 Current Status Assessment

This section briefly describes the current status assessment of the promotion process. Each system edition may include several applications/projects that should be released together. Project managers are responsible for preparing request for promotion documents for the configuration items (CI) in their projects. Usually each project prepares several promotion request documents, which means that a promotion for major releases includes a huge number of promotion request documents that are managed manually.

12.5.1.1 Process Lifecycle

The following tasks are performed by the various roles in the process lifecycle:

1. The requestor prepares a request for promotion by filling in a spreadsheet form.

2. The requestor asks for the approval of the Application Manager, Source Environment Manager, and Target Environment Manager.

3. Each of the three roles—Application Manager, Source Environment Manager, and Target Environment Manager—approves or denies the request for promotion.

4. After the request for promotion is approved, the project manager assigns tasks to the relevant technical support teams for doing the technical promotion.

5. Each technical support team confirms when its own task is completed.

6. The release manager manages, follows up on the process, and closes the request.

12.5.1.2 Problems in Current Status

All the operations related to the promotion process are manual, which causes the following problems:

- There is no effective permission policy or security enforcement.
- Assignment of the request for approval or for an action is performed by sending an e-mail with the request form attached to the e-mail. There is no easy way to know if the request was received or if work is in process.
- The follow-up and auditing of the process by the release manager are performed by telephone calls.
- There is no way for a manager to get real-time project status.
- In many cases two versions of the same document circulate in the system. Some even use older versions of the request form that did not conform to the IT standards.

12.5.2 Solution

It was clear to management that they needed a tool with a central database to store all requests and to be able to query the status of specific promotions and the status of a release promotion. The IT division should be able to customize the tool metadata to support the process defined by the organization. A workflow engine is required to support the defined process. Security should be enforced to support the banking regulations.

12.5.2.1 Scope

Development of an application was required to control the promotion process from one environment to the next environment only. The process starts with a request for promotion for a certain environment and ends when all of the technical tasks related to this request for promotion are completed and the promotion request is closed.

Target environment promotion rules allow promotion from the following source to target environments:

- Development to integration
- Integration to UAT (user acceptance test)
- UAT to production

12.5.2.2 Tools

The tool that was selected to develop the promotion application was IBM Rational ClearQuest. Other tools that are in use by the organization and will be integrated with this application, in the future, are IBM Rational RequisitePro and IBM Rational ClearCase.

12.5.3 Process Components

This section provides an overview of the ClearQuest components and elements that will be used in the process.

12.5.3.1 Process Roles

The activities described in the process model are performed by employees who are working in a specific development or IT operations role. A single employee can perform many roles, but any given task is performed in the context of one role. The following process roles were defined:

- ClearQuest Admin
- Application Manager
- Project Manager (usually the promotion requestor)
- Environment Responsible
- Technical Support Team (for each CI type)
- Release Manager

Only ClearQuest administrators interact directly with the schema repository. The ClearQuest administrator must grant database access to a user before the user can operate on a promotion request record.

Figures 12.17 and 12.18 demonstrate how roles are defined in the stateless record types. For each configuration item type the responsible users are defined in the CI_Type record type.

In a similar way the approvers for each environment are defined in the Application record type as shown in Figure 12.18.

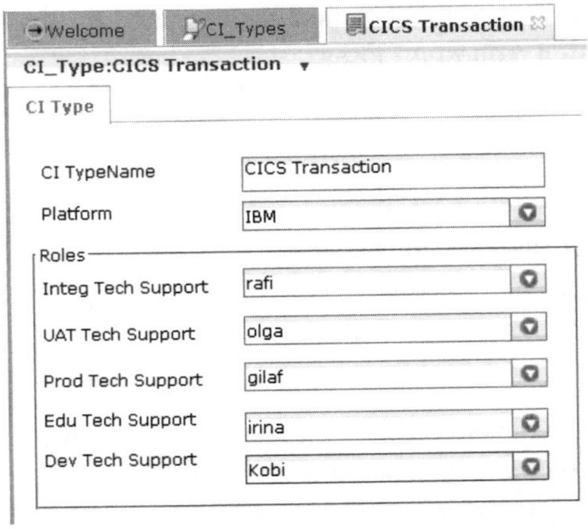

Figure 12.17   Tech support roles defined in the CI_Type record: roles definition for the CICS Transaction configuration item

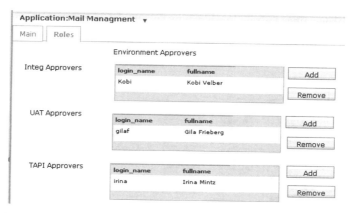

Figure 12.18   Approver roles defined in the Application record: defining the approvers of the Mail Management application for each environment

12.5.3.2 Process Entities

Each promotion request is represented as a record within the ClearQuest user database. The promotion request represents the basic unit of work that is authorized to be created, modified, or destroyed by the project. The activities of the process model are focused on manipulating individual records or reporting on the state of the records within a database.

Additional entities are needed to support the promotion request model. Table 12.3 describes the set of process entities defined in the promotion request system.

Table 12.3   Process Entities of the Promotion Request System

Entity Name	Entity Type	Description
Promotion	Stateful	Promotion request general details.
Configuration_Item_Type	Stateless	Contains all CI type details, related platform, and technical support team for each environment.
Configuration Item	Stateless	Configuration item details (name, type, etc.) for the use of technical support teams.
Project	Stateless	Project details. Project includes one or more applications.
Application	Stateless	Application details and corresponding units, roles, and project.
Task	Stateful	Promotion request tasks. One task is related to all the CIs having the same type within a promotion request.
Environment	Stateless	Contains environment details.
Component	Stateless	ClearCase component details.

Figure 12.19 describes the relationship between all the ClearQuest record types (entities) in an ERD-like schema. Note also the fields in each entity.

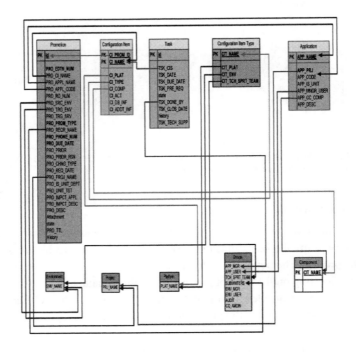

Figure 12.19   The ERD of the promotion solution

12.5.3.3 Business Rules

The operations available to the ClearQuest user are controlled by the set of policies and rules that apply in the context of the user role (see Table 12.4). Access to change state actions and modify actions is controlled at multiple levels:

- Access to the user database is controlled through database subscriptions. Only authorized users are allowed to log in and operate on the records within the database.

- Within a database, access to specific actions is controlled based on the user role that is related to group membership.

- At the lowest level, control can be implemented on an individual user basis using the login ID.

- Access can also be defined based on a custom implementation.

Table 12.4 Role-Based Access Control Actions That Are Allowed to Each Role

ClearQuest Role	Access Rights
Application Manager	New Request, Renew, Delete, Request for Approval, Request for Promotion
Environment Responsible	Approve, Deny
Auditing reports and queries	Read-only, queries and reports
ClearQuest Administrator	All activities
Technical Support Team	Confirm Promotion
Project Manager	New Request, Renew, Request for Approval, Delete
Applications-related users	Request for Approval, Request for Promotion

12.5.3.4 The Process Lifecycle

A promotion request follows a process lifecycle that is captured in the ClearQuest state transition matrix. ClearQuest automatically controls the states and actions available, as well as event notification. In the next sections we shall describe the process model of stateful record types involved in the process: the promotion and the task.

12.5.4 The Promotion Process Model

This section presents the activities and states for the Promotion Request record type. The action names are annotated above the action arrow, and the responsible role that is allowed to perform the action is annotated below the action arrow (see Figure 12.20).

12.5.4.1 Process Rules

The Promotion Approval action is allowed based on the Application Name, the Environment, and the Promotion Type. Each approval requires an electronic signature. Some applications require three signatures, and others may require only one, depending on the business rules. See Figure 12.22 for the eSignature tab of the Promotion record.

The Request Promotion action will generate a task for each CI type (all CIs of the same type will be linked to a single task). Each task (related to CI type) is assigned to a corresponding technical support team. The configuration item promotion is controlled by the Task record flow.

Figure 12.21 shows the main tab of the Promotion record. The Configuration Items tab contains a field of type Reference_List to the CI record type. The tab Tasks contains a field of type Reference_List to the Task record type.

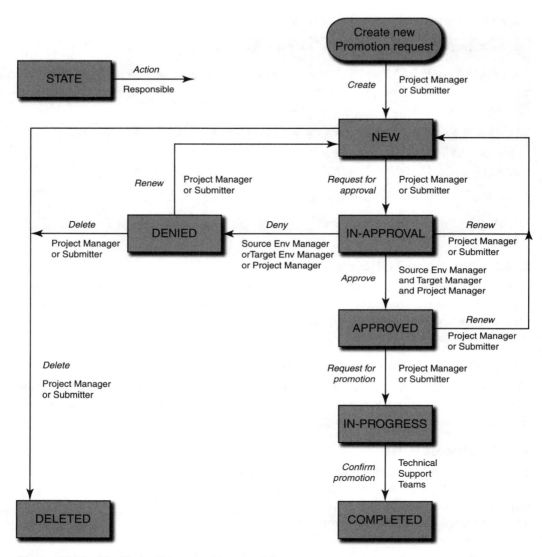

Figure 12.20   The Promotion record type workflow

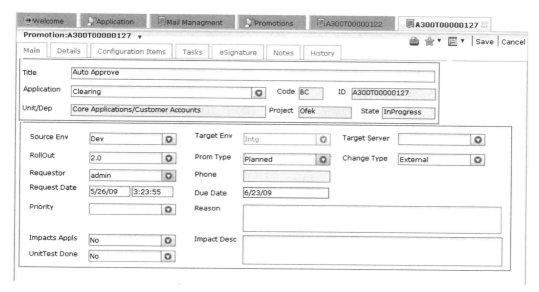

Figure 12.21   A sample Promotion record: main tab

12.5.4.2 Automation

The following automations are required in the process (see Figure 12.22). The automations are implemented by hooks.

- Tasks are created automatically by the action Request for Promotion in the Promotion record. For all the CIs of the same CI_Type *one* task is created.
- Do not allow one task to start before the other is finished.
- Notify the task owner to start task activities.
- Allow the user to set dependency based on special conditions of specific configuration items.
- Automatic dependencies are based on the CI_Type.

  For example, if the CI_Type is CICS Transaction and the transaction is a *new* transaction, then create three tasks and allow the tasks to be processed in parallel (the opposite of the rule that tasks should be processed in sequence).

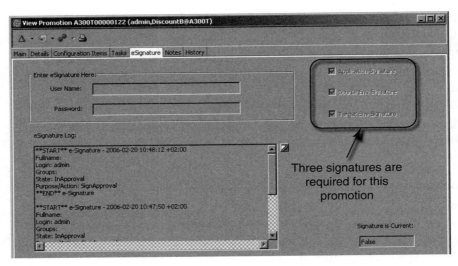

Figure 12.22   A sample Promotion record: electronic signature tab

12.6 Resources

12.6.1 Solutions Developed by Customers and Rational Staff

O'Neill, Tony W., "SOX Compliance Using IBM Rational ClearCase and ClearQuest," *IBM developerWorks*, www.ibm.com/developerworks/rational/library/05/1227_oneill/index.html, 2005 (accessed February 23, 2011).

This article explores the process of implementing IBM Rational's ClearCase and Clear-Quest tools to address Sarbanes-Oxley compliance.

Staff, IBM Rational, "Examples and Sample Schemas," *IBM developerWorks*, www.ibm.com/developerworks/rational/library/05/1227_oneill/index.html, 2003 (accessed February 23, 2011).

Dubovitskiy, Pavel, "ClearQuest Email Notification Package," http://cqadmin.org/wiki/ClearQuest_Email_Notification_Package, 2006 (accessed February 23, 2011).

This URL points to a free ClearQuest package.

This is an alternate ClearQuest Notification package. This e-mail package has several advantages over the original Rational ClearQuest Notification package: it maintains a message queue; no client setup is required; it has advanced formatting and enhanced notification conditions. It provides some SLA capabilities. The new ClearQuest EmailPlus package addresses some of the original issues as well.

12.6.2 SLA

Myerson, Judith, "Use SLAs in a Web Services Context," *IBM developerWorks*, www.ibm.com/developerworks/webservices/library/ws-sla/index.html, 2002 (accessed February 23, 2011).

Staff, IBM Rational, "External VB Application to Do 'Something' with Records Not Touched in 14 Days," *IBM developerWorks*, www.ibm.com/developerworks/rational/library/3895.html, 2002 (accessed February 23, 2011).

Greiner, Lynn, and Lauren Gibbons Paul, "SLA Definitions and Solutions," www.cio.com/article/128900/SLA_Definitions_and_Solutions, June 18, 2009 (accessed February 23, 2011).

12.6.3 ALM and C/ALM

Gothe, Mats, Carolyn Pampino, Philip Monson, Khurram Nizami, Katur Patel, Brianna M. Smith, and Nail Yuce, *Collaborative Application Lifecycle Management with IBM Rational Products, IBM Redbook* (Poughkeepsie: IBM, International Technical Support Organization, 2008), www.redbooks.ibm.com/abstracts/SG247622.html (accessed February 22, 2011).

Forziati, Rich, and Mats Gothe, "Collaborative ALM Interoperability," *IBM White Paper*, www-01.ibm.com/support/docview.wss?uid=swg27017757, 2010 (accessed February 22, 2011).

Pampino, Carolyn, Erich Gamma, and John Wiegand, "Scaling Agile with C/ALM (Collaborative Application Lifecycle Management)," www.infoq.com/articles/scaling-agile-with-calm, June 29, 2009 (accessed February 23, 2011).

Pampino, Carolyn, "Simplifying Application Lifecycle Management with IBM Rational Clear-Quest Software," IBM White Paper, ftp://ftp.software.ibm.com/common/ssi/sa/wh/n/raw14039usen/RAW14039USEN.PDF, 2008 (accessed February 23, 2011).

12.6.4 Application Lifecycle Management with Rational ClearQuest

Pampino, Carolyn, and Robert Pierce, "Application Lifecycle Management with Rational Clear-Quest 7.1.0.0: Part 1," *IBM developerWorks*, www.ibm.com/developerworks/rational/library/edge/08/mar08/pampino-pierce/index.html, 2008 (accessed February 23, 2011).

Pampino, Carolyn, and Robert Pierce, "Application Lifecycle Management with Rational Clear-Quest 7.1.0.0: Part 2," *IBM developerWorks*, www.ibm.com/developerworks/rational/library/edge/08/apr08/pampino-pierce/index.html, 2008 (accessed February 23, 2011).

Pampino, Carolyn, and Robert Pierce, "Application Lifecycle Management with Rational Clear-Quest 7.1.0.0: Part 3," *IBM developerWorks*, www.ibm.com/developerworks/rational/library/edge/08/may08/pampino-pierce/index.html, 2008 (accessed February 23, 2011).

12.7 Summary

In this chapter we provided some examples to solutions developed by customers using Clear-Quest. The solutions usually involved customization of an existing schema or developing a new schema. Some solutions were utilities developed with scripting languages or programming languages and using the ClearQuest API to access the database.

The fact that ClearQuest is highly extensible allows many customers to develop applications that are not necessarily related to change management. Some examples are a corporate help desk, activities management, promotion management, and others.

Some solutions are based on integrations of products that build a more complete solution, for example, the Collaborative Application Lifecycle Management Jazz project that is based on RRC, RTC, and RQM. In Chapter 6, "Integrations," we discussed tools integration; in section 12.1, "Collaborative ALM with Jazz-Based Tools," we looked at the integration from a broader view: the entire software development and delivery process, including information sharing, traceability, and governed processes.

Section 12.2, "User-Defined Fields in ClearQuest," presented a detailed description of a ClearQuest solution that enables project managers to define their own fields and lists without the need to modify the schema. The solution allows several projects running on the same database to see different fields and different values and behaviors.

In section 12.3, "Service Level Agreements (SLAs) in ClearQuest," we proposed a solution to govern SLAs in the following way:

- Define SLA rules using stateless records.

- Develop an external program that queries the rules and the candidate records.

- Use e-mail for notifications and alerts.

This provides both solution providers and managers with a means to control the level of service that they provide to their customers and to prevent breaching the agreement ahead of time. To complete the solution you can use ClearQuest packages that provide charts and reports on your SLA status.

In section 12.4, "ClearCase, ClearQuest ALM, Build Forge Integrated Solution Architecture," we described a solution that combines three integrated products. The ClearQuest packaged integrations were used to integrate with ClearCase and BuildForge. The ClearQuest ALM schema was customized to meet the required process; fields were added to include data from the customer-specific environment (embedded systems), and hooks were developed to respond to the rules the customer needed. The integrated solution enabled the customer to have better control of the development process, reduced the time to build the application, and reduced the total development costs.

The message is you can do many things, enhancing your solutions with products that allow customization and can be easily integrated.

Section 12.5 described a ClearQuest system to manage the promotion of a software release in a complex heterogeneous environment. The new system was implemented in a short time, teams were trained, and the system was deployed. Managers saw an immediate improvement in all parameters. The process is now governed and managers have full control; errors in the process were dramatically reduced. Delays have been reduced as people are notified about tasks, and management can view project status by simply executing a query.

Index

A

A (active) state type, UCM, 54
Access control
    compared with permissions, 3
    governance and, 288–289
    hook providing security in ClearQuest, 128
    roles in, 127, 144–145, 379
    rules governing, 11
    workflow rules, 46
Accessing records, 114–115
Action hooks, ClearQuest, compared with Jazz
    Operation Access Control. *See also* Hooks,
    Access Control
    behavior or extensions, 3
    Commit hook. *See* Hooks, Commit
    Initialization hook. *See* Hooks, Initialization
    Notification hook. *See* Hooks, Notification
    Validation hook. *See* Hooks, Validation
Actions
    comparing ClearQuest action with Jazz
        action, 2
    customizing work items, 15
    dedicated, 70–76
    in Jazz workflow, 67
    hooks. *See* Action hooks
    reassignment, 70
    roles in automation of, 127
    rules governing, 11
    workflow rules, 46
ActiveX
    applets, 12
    integration with ClearQuest and, 171–172
    supported in BASIC not Perl, 261
Activities
    describing ClearQuest data objects for Agile
        process, 338
    subclasses of, 5–6
    workflows in activity diagrams, 44
Activity record type

    in ALM schema, 346, 348
    suggested fields for, 341–343
    workflows of, 344
ACWP (actual cost of work performed), 280
Administrative activities, 5
Administrators
    dependent integration of IBM administrator
        with ClearQuest, 158
    implementing roles with ClearQuest groups,
        133
    performance benchmarking by Web
        administrators, 200
    training, 206
Agile development
    in ALM schema, 346–349
    applying Agile practices to requirements, 28
    in ClearQuest. *See* ClearQuest, Agile schema in
    defining, 325–326
    in Jazz. *See* RTC (Rational Team Concert),
        Scrum process in
    overview of, 325
    resources for, 350
    Scrum framework for, 326–329
    summary, 351
    use of graphs in metrics strategy, 281
Agreement, getting regarding requirements, 28
ALM (Application Lifecycle Management)
    schema. *See also* C/ALM (Collaborative ALM)
    Agile development in, 346–349
    common schema in development, 222
    creating task to fix defect, 370–371
    governance in, 297–298
    in integrated solution architecture, 367–373
    periodic releases in, 371–372
    process control in, 297
    resources for, 195, 383
    roles in, 140–141, 298
    security context in, 297–298
    workflows in, 65–66

ALMActivity, 5, 65, 140, 370

ALMRequest, 348–349

ALMRole

comparing Agile and ALM schema, 347

overview of, 140–141

stateless record types in ALM security, 298

ALMRoleLabel

overview of, 140

stateless record types in ALM security, 298

ALMTask, 347–348

Amount of effort. *See* Effort required

AMStateTypes, 53

Analysis

data providing information for, 81

in workflow item lifecycle, 50

Analysis & Design discipline

choosing database, 32–33

defining client types, 29–30

defining data fields, 35

defining infrastructure architecture, 30–32

defining workflow, 35

design patterns in, 36–40

designing user interface (forms), 36

overview of, 29

resources, 40

reviewing/signing off on design models, 40

schema high-level design in ClearQuest, 33–34

summary, 40–41

Applets, performing background operations, 12

Applications/solutions

ClearQuest example. *See* ClearQuest, example
solution

external impacts and, 89

installing during deployment, 202

integrated. *See* Integrated solution architecture
(ClearCase, ALM, and Build Forge)

Jazz-based C/ALM, 354–356

resources for, 382–383

summary, 384–385

Approval tracking, Jazz, 2

AppScan, integration of RQM and RTLM with,
185–187

Architecture

defining infrastructure architecture, 30–32

for integrated solution. *See* Integrated solution
architecture (ClearCase, ALM, and Build Forge)

JIA (Jazz Integration Architecture), 192–193, 355

Areas

defined, 130

role implementation and, 133–136

user roles in different areas, 131

Asset reuse, 191

Assign action, notification and, 58

Assignees, assigning solution providers, 91

Assignment

auto-assignment, 145–149, 273–274

issues/typical problems addressed by roles,
128–129

members to test tasks, 311–312

reassignment, 70

roles in, 127

Association, by field label in Eclipse Designer, 109

Attachments

data, 100–103

HasAttachment hook, 120–121

Limit Attachment size hook, 121–122

to work items, 11

Auto-assignment, of roles, 145–149, 273–274

Auto-change state, 58–59

Automation

in ClearQuest governance, 290

in governance, 288

in Jazz-based C/ALM solution, 354

roles in, 127

setting choices based on Multiple role,
146–147

setting Responsible based on role object,
147–149

setting Responsible based on Single role,
145–146

Single roles and, 130

B

Back Reference field, in object relations, 110–113

Balking pattern, 36

Baselines

fixing defects and, 370–371

periodic releases and, 371–372

BASIC

choosing scripting language and, 261

creating new ClearQuest integrations, 167–172

storing hooks externally, 249–250

use of session variables, 240

BCWP (budgeted cost of work performed), 280
Benchmarking, performance, 200
Bill of materials (BOM), in preparing for
    deployment, 201
BIRT (Business Intelligence and Reporting Tools)
    as metrics tool, 286
    resources for, 303–304
Blocking assignment, 129
BOM (bill of materials), in preparing for
    deployment, 201
Budgeted cost of work performed (BCWP), 280
Build engines, RTC integrations, 190–191
Build Forge
    continuous build and validation process,
        369–370
    dependent integration with ClearQuest,
        161–162
    in integrated solution architecture, 367–373
    RQM integrations, 187
Build reports, in metrics strategy, 284
Build work items, 6
Builds
    continuous build and validation process,
        369–370
    subflow for build approval, 76–78
Burndown charts, releases and, 345
Business Intelligence and Reporting Tools (BIRT)
    as metrics tool, 286
    resources for, 303–304
Business rules, 378–379
Buttons, enabling button hooks in Web
    development, 274–275

C

C/ALM (Collaborative ALM)
    Jazz-based, 354–356
    overview of, 353–354
    reports, 304–305
    resources for, 383
C (complete) state type, UCM, 54
Caching choice lists, 267–268
Capability Maturity Model Integration (CMMI),
    83, 103
Cardinality, roles in Jazz, 130
Categories
    customizing test work items, 318

organizing test information using, 320–321
setting permissions for test customization,
    321–322
CCRC (ClearCase Remote Client), 172
Change management
    defining change process, 207–208
    process diagram, 47–48
    roles in, 131
    RUP (Rational Unified Process) applied to,
        21–22
    system elements, 28–29
    Unified Change Management. *See* UCM
        (Unified Change Management)
Change requests
    activities for breaking down into smaller
        elements, 5
    documenting in change management database,
        28–29
    roles in, 131
    types of changes and, 4
Change_State actions, ClearQuest
    overview of, 56
    subflow for gathering more information, 69
Chart wizard, 285
Charts
    comparing ClearQuest and Jazz customization
        areas, 17
    in metrics strategy, 281
Child Control pattern
    design, 38
    implementing, 38, 229–231
Child records, creating from parent record, 123–126
Choice list, Clear Quest
    allowed actions list, 150
    caching, 267–268
    compared with Jazz Enumeration, 3
    creating multiple lists, 268
    creating tree-like lists, 268–270
    defining requiredness, 361
    hard-coded data in, 272–273
    hooks, 114, 144, 150, 236–238, 270-271
    improving performance of long lists, 265
    populating based on role objects, 147–148
    populating based on roles, 146–147
    recalculating/invalidating, 265–267
    in solution example, 358–360
    for user-defined roles, 150

Classification of work items
  activities, 5–6
  change requests, 4
  overview of, 4
  project-related work items, 6–7
  test elements, 6
ClearCase
  ActiveX controls in establishing integration
    with, 171–172
  CM API and, 172–175
  in integrated solution architecture, 367–373
  integrating with ClearQuest, 156–157
  in managing release promotion, 375
  UCM work projects and, 368–369
  working on test artifacts, 372–373
ClearCase Bridge
  ClearCase Connector compared with, 188–190
  connecting to RTC, 188
ClearCase Connector
  compared with ClearCase Bridge, 188–190
  RTC integrations, 188
ClearCase Remote Client (CCRC), 172
ClearQuest
  ALM schema. *See* ALM (Application Lifecycle
    Management) schema
  comparing ClearQuest and Jazz terminology,
    2–3
  comparing customization elements and terms
    with Jazz, 15–17
  customizing record types, 18–19
  databases supported by, 32–33
  design patterns built into, 36
  implementation tasks, 198
  implementing roles with ClearQuest groups,
    132–133
  integrations. *See* Integration, ClearQuest
  representation of data in, 117–118
  schema high-level design in, 33–34
  scripts for data representation in ClearQuest,
    120
  setting up customizations during deployment,
    203–204
  setting up environment during deployment,
    202–203
ClearQuest, Agile schema in
  metrics, 345
  overview of, 337–339

requesting required data for, 339–340
  suggested fields for Activity record type,
    341–343
  suggested fields for Sprint record type, 340–341
  workflows in, 343–345
ClearQuest Bridge, 180–183
ClearQuest Connector
  integration at data-level, 154
  Jazz integration with ClearQuest, 177–180
  RTC integrations, 188–190
ClearQuest Designer
  comparing Eclipse and Windows versions of,
    18–19
  moving user databases, 214–216
  user-defined fields in, 357–358
  viewing database properties, 213–214
  Windows version, 213
ClearQuest, example solution
  defining choice lists, 358–360
  defining requiredness, 360–363
  SLAs (Service Level Agreements) in, 363–367
  user-defined fields, 356–358
ClearQuest, governance in
  electronic signatures in, 295–296
  monitoring in, 297
  permissions in, 290–293
  process control and automation in, 290
  security context in, 294–295
ClearQuest Maintenance tool
  creating test environment with, 214
  QATest, 212
ClearQuest MultiSite (CQMS), 253–254
ClearQuest to Project Tracker integration, 158–159
ClearQuest Test Management (CQTM)
  overview of, 6
  RQM replacing, 307
  state-based record types in tests, 309
ClearQuest Tool Mentor
  creating test environment with ClearQuest
    tools, 214–216
  creating test environment with database vendor
    tools, 212–214
  importing records with references, 208–210
  importing updates, 210–211
  overview of, 208
ClearVision Subversion, ClearQuest integration
  with, 176

Clients
    CCRC (ClearCase Remote Client), 172
    defining client types, 29–30
    Eclipse. *See* Eclipse client
    interactions with resources on server, 173
    representation of data in ClearQuest and,
        117–118
    Web clients, 119, 252, 276
Cloning hook, for creating parent from child
    record, 123–126
Closing pattern
    implementing in ClearQuest, 223–224
    implementing in Jazz, 224–225
    overview of, 37
    suggested fields, 222–223
Closure stage, in workflow item lifecycle, 51
CM (Configuration Management) API, creating
    new ClearQuest integrations, 172–175
CMMI (Capability Maturity Model Integration),
    83, 103
Code generation, list of RTC integrations by
    category, 191
Code reuse, 105
Collaboration
    in Jazz-based C/ALM solution, 354
    list of RTC integrations by category, 191
Collaborative ALM. *See* C/ALM (Collaborative
    ALM)
Comma-separated value (CSV) format, importing
    and, 204
Communication diagrams, workflows in, 44
Communication Manager (CM) API, creating new
    ClearQuest integrations, 172–175
Components
    internal impacts on, 88
    in promotion process, 376–379
    relationships in integrated solution architecture,
        368
Convert Full_Name to Login_Name hook,
    122–123
Corrective actions
    assigning solution providers, 91
    data related to, 82
    documenting, 92
    prioritization of, 91
CQ-ALM schema. *See* ALM (Application
    Lifecycle Management) schema

CQ CM API JNI (Desktop) provider, 172–173
CQ CM API WAN (Network) provider, 172
CQMS (ClearQuest MultiSite), 253–254
CQTM (ClearQuest Test Management)
    overview of, 6
    RQM replacing, 307
    state-based record types in tests, 309
Crystal reports, as metrics tool, 285–286
CSV (comma-separated value) format, importing
    and, 204
Custom Section wizard, 319
Customer role, in defect and change management,
    131
Customizing test work items, in RQM
    default work items, 317–318
    execution states, 322–323
    organizing test information using categories,
        320–321
    overview of, 316–317
    setting permissions for customization, 321–322
    testing specific work items, 318–320
Customizing work items
    ClearQuest record types, 18–19
    comparing ClearQuest and Jazz customization
        elements and terms, 15–17
    elements that can be customized, 14
    Jazz work items, 17–18
    overview of, 13–14

D

Dashboards
    comparing ClearQuest and Jazz customization
        areas, 17
    creating monitoring viewlets, 300
    in RTC Scrum process, 336–337
Data
    accessing records, 114–115
    attachments, 100–103
    Back Reference field, 110–113
    Convert Full_Name to Login_Name hook,
        122–123
    corrective actions, 91–92
    creating parent from child record, 123–126
    customizing work items, 14
    defining fields, 35
    description of work items, 83–86

Data (*continued*)
    environment information, 87–88
    external impacts, 89–91
    hard-coded data in hooks, 272–274
    HasAttachment hook, 120–121
    history of work items, 96–98
    import/export, 163–164
    importing initial data during deployment,
      204–206
    integration at data-level, 154
    integration in Jazz-based C/ALM solution, 354
    internal impacts, 88–89
    Limit Attachment size hook, 121–122
    links, 115–116
    location information, 86–87
    metrics, 284
    multiple relationships, 108–109
    object relations, 106
    ownership of work items, 99
    purposes of accumulating, 81–83
    quality assurance and, 103–104
    references to unique keys and, 113
    referencing objects, 114
    replacing unique keys, 115
    representation in ClearQuest, 117–118
    representation in Jazz, 118–119
    requestor information, 98–99
    scripts for data representation, 120
    single relationships, 106–107
    state-based objects, 105
    stateless objects, 105–106
    storing in fields, 7
    summary, 126
    test artifacts in RQM, 308
    test-related, 95–96
    time-related, 92–94
Data Hierarchy pattern
    implementing, 233
    overview of, 39
Data warehouse, in Jazz repository, 303–304
Database servers, in infrastructure architecture, 30
Database vendor tools, for creating test
    environment, 212–214
Databases
    change management database, 28–29
    choosing type in Analysis & Design, 32–33
    determining number to create, 33

hook for performing lookup on external, 171
    moving, 214–216
    system test and database size, 200
    test configuration for, 251
    viewing properties of, 213–214
Dead End pattern
    design of, 39
    implementing in ClearQuest, 231
    implementing in Jazz, 232
Debugging
    BASIC utilities for, 261
    using MsgBox() function, 255–256
    using OutputDebugString() method,
      256–258
    using tracing information, 258–260
Decision stage, in workflow item lifecycle, 50–51
Dedicated actions, in subflow for gathering more
    information, 70–76
Default work items, 317–318
Defects
    change requests due to, 4
    creating task to fix, 370–371
    default work items in Jazz, 317
    key roles in defect and change management, 131
    quality assurance and, 103
    reporting, 200, 316
    test artifacts in RQM, 308–309
    tracking, 191
Defect_Validation hook, 147–149
Deferring stage, in workflow item lifecycle, 52
Deleting stage, in workflow item lifecycle, 52
Demilitarized zones (DMZs), defining
    infrastructure architecture, 30
Dependent integrations, ClearQuest, 158–162
Deployment discipline
    following up on system adoption, 207
    importing initial data, 204–206
    installation phase, 202
    overview of, 201
    preparation phase, 201
    setting up environment, 202–203
    training phase, 206
Deployment plan, 201
Description field, for work items, 84
Descriptive data, 83–86
Design. *See* Analysis & Design discipline
Design models, reviewing/signing off on, 40

Design patterns
in Analysis & Design, 36–40
implementing Child Control pattern, 229–231
implementing Closing pattern, 222–225
implementing Data Hierarchy pattern, 233
implementing Dead End pattern, 231–232
implementing Parent Control pattern, 226–229
implementing Superuser Modification pattern, 233–234
implementing Triage pattern, 224–225
Designing forms and tabs, 243–245
Developer Taskboard, in RTC Scrum process, 336
Developers
data providing historical information for, 81
defining client types, 30
testing releases, 250–252
work on activities in integrated solution, 368–369
Development
being prepared for future requirements, 277
Child Control pattern, 229–231
choosing scripting language, 261
Closing pattern, 222–225
coding hooks for parallel development, 241
with common schema (ALM), 222
comparing/merging schema versions, 245–249
CQMS (ClearQuest MultiSite) issues, 253–254
Data Hierarchy pattern, 233
Dead End pattern, 231–232
dealing with long selection lists, 265–270
debugging using MsgBox() function, 255–256
debugging using OutputDebugString() method, 256–258
debugging using tracing information, 258–260
designing forms and tabs, 243–245
developer testing, 250–252
exporting/importing schema portions, 237–238
hard-coded data and, 272–274
list of RTC integrations by category, 191
naming conventions, 262–263
organizing global scripts by subject, 262
overview of, 221
packages, 238–239
parallel development, 240–241
Parent Control pattern, 226–229
promoting release to production, 252–253
record types in parallel development, 241–243
releasing versions to production, 250
resources for, 277–278
session variables in, 239–240
storing hooks externally, 249–250
storing old_id field for future import, 264
summary, 278
Superuser Modification pattern, 233–234
system testing, 252
Triage pattern, 224–225
understanding when stateless record type is required, 261
unique keys and, 261–262
updating dynamic lists, 271–272
Web-related considerations, 274–276
writing reusable code, 234–237
Diagrams. See also Graphics
defining and documenting requirements, 25
entity relationships. See ERD (entity relationship diagram)
in high-level design, 34
process diagram in change management, 47–48
state transition, 45–46
states, 47
workflows in activity diagrams, 44
Disciplines
Analysis & Design. See Analysis & Design discipline
ClearQuest Tool Mentor and. See ClearQuest Tool Mentor
Deployment. See Deployment
Implementation, 197–199
Jazz Tool Mentor and, 217–219
Maintenance, 207–208
overview of, 197
Requirements. See Requirements discipline
resources for, 220
summary, 220
Testing, 199–200
DMZs (demilitarized zones), defining infrastructure architecture, 30
Documentation
changes affecting, 90
of corrective actions, 92
gathering initial, 23
of requirements, 25–28
DOORS, RQM integrations, 185
Duplicating stage, in workflow item lifecycle, 52–53

Dynamic change state, 60–61
Dynamic lists
    adding to choice lists, 273
    updating, 271–272
Dynamic workflow
    moving automatically between states, 57–59
    overview of, 56
    record types in, 56
    single record type having multiple state
        machines for each issue type, 59–61
    single record type having state machine for
        each issue, 61–65
    state transition and, 56–57

E

E-mail notification. *See* Notification
E-mail Reader service, example of ClearQuest
    integration, 164–167
Eclipse client
    creating process template using, 217–219
    creating project using process template,
        217–219
    customizing work items, 17
    import/export tool in, 163–164, 208
    setting permissions for test customization,
        321–322
Eclipse Designer
    association by field label, 109
    comparing/merging schema versions, 241,
        245–249
    comparing with Windows version of
        ClearQuest Designer, 18–19
    exporting forms with, 244–245
    supporting parallel development, 241
Editor presentations, Jazz, 2
Effort required
    estimating in requirements gathering, 27–28
    storing in work tasks, 93–94
Electronic signatures
    in access control and security, 289
    in ClearQuest governance, 295–296
Elements, work item
    applets, 12
    attachments, 11
    customizing work items and, 14
    data, 7
    links to other work items, 11–12
    overview of, 7
    pictures or graphics, 12
    presentation forms, 7–9
    roles, 13
    rules, 11
    workflows, 9–10
Enhancements
    change requests due to, 4
    test artifacts in RQM, 309
Entities, defining data fields, 35
Entity relationship diagram. *See* ERD (entity
    relationship diagram)
Enumeration, Jazz, 3
Environment
    creating test environment with ClearQuest
        tools, 214–216
    creating test environment with database vendor
        tools, 212–214
    data related to, 82
    fields related to system configuration, 87–88
    setting up during deployment, 202–203
ERD (entity relationship diagram)
    creating record types in ClearQuest, 198
    creating work item types in Jazz, 199
    in high-level design, 34
Errors, fixing import. *See also* Defects, 205–206
Estimation of man-hours, in requirements
    gathering, 27–28
ETL (extract, transform, load), Insight tool for, 287
Excel, importing record from, 168
Execution states, in RQM test process, 322–323
Export. *See* Import/export
External impacts
    applications and, 89
    data related to, 82
    documentation affected by changes in, 90–91
    training materials impacted by changes, 91
    users and, 89
Extract, transform, load (ETL), Insight tool for, 287

F

Features, change requests for adding, 4
Field behaviors, ClearQuest, 3
Field hooks
    choice list. *See* Hooks, choice list

default value. *See* Hooks, default value
permission. *See* Hooks, permission
value changed. *See* Hooks, value changed
validation. *See* Hooks, validation
Fields, ClearQuest
category fields for organizing information,
320–321
compared with Jazz Work item attribute, 2
customizing edit permission, 15
defining, 35
mapping record fields during import, 210
permissions, 289, 291–292
storing data in, 7
storing test data in, 95–96
time-related, 94
user-defined, 356–358
Fields, making Web forms with dependent fields,
275
Firewalls, 30–32
Forms, ClearQuest
compared with Jazz Editor presentations, 2
designing, 243–245
Presentation forms, 7–9
representation of data in ClearQuest, 117–118
user-defined fields in, 357
Forms, Jazz. *See* Editor presentations
Forms, making Web forms with dependent fields,
275
Functional requirements, listing, 27
Functional Tester. *See* RFT (Rational Functional
Tester)
Functionality packages, 238

G

GDD (Globally Distributed Development),
253–254
Glossary, in defining and documenting
requirements, 25
Governance
in ALM, 298
in ALM schema, 297
in ClearQuest, 290
electronic signatures, 295–296
monitoring and, 289
monitoring in ClearQuest, 297
monitoring in RTC, 300
overview of, 287–288
permissions and, 288–289
permissions in ClearQuest, 290–293
permissions in RTC, 299
process control and automation and, 288
process control in ALM, 297
process control in ClearQuest, 290
process control in RTC, 299
reports, 366
resources for, 301–302
roles in ALM, 298
in RTC, 298
security context in ALM, 297–298
security context in ClearQuest, 294–295
summary, 305
Graphical user interface (GUI), designing forms
and tabs and, 243–245
Graphics. *See also* Diagrams
defining and documenting requirements, 25
in metrics strategy, 280–281
presentation insertions, 12
Group box, ClearQuest, 2
Groups, ClearQuest
implementing roles with, 131–133
query listing members for access control,
144–145
GUI control, ClearQuest, 2
GUI (graphical user interface), designing forms
and tabs and, 243–245

H

Hard-coded data, 272–274
Hardware, location information for, 87
HasAttachment hook, 120–121
Headline field, in work item description, 83–84
Hide data, customizing work items, 15
Histograms, in metrics strategy, 280–281
History
data and, 83
reasons for saving history of work items, 96–98
History view, in Eclipse Designer, 245–246
Hooks
access control, 128, 144–145
Action hooks, in ClearQuest, 3
automation implemented with, 381–382
button hooks in Web development, 274–275

Hooks (*continued*)

Choice List hook, 114, 144, 150, 236–238, 270–271

cloning hook for creating parent from child record, 123–126

code reuse with, 234–237

coding hooks for parallel development, 241

Commit hook, 230

Convert Full_Name to Login_Name hook, 122–123

default value, 266

external storage in Perl not BASIC, 261

hard-coded data in, 272–274

HasAttachment hook, 120–121

initialization, 64, 70–72, 224, 235

Limit Attachment size hook, 121–122

for lookup on external database, 171

notification hook, 58, 60, 62

organizing global scripts by subject, 262

permission, 293–294, 364

storing externally, 249–250

validation, 33, 76–78, 147–149, 228

value changed, 73–75, 84, 135, 266–267

HP Mercury Test Director and Quality Center, 176

I

IBM Administrator, dependent integration with ClearQuest, 158

IBM PureCoverage, 157

IBM Purify, 157

IBM Quantify, 158

IBM Rational Build Forge. *See* Build Forge

IBM Rational ClearCase. *See* ClearCase

IBM Rational ClearQuest. *See* ClearQuest

IBM Rational DOORS, 185

IBM Rational Requirements Composer. *See* Requirements Composer

IBM RequisitePro. *See* RequisitePro

IBM RTC. *See* RTC (Rational Team Concert)

IBM TeamTest, 159

IBM Tivoli. *See* Tivoli

IBM Unified Change Management (UCM). *See* UCM (Unified Change Management)

Icons, in Jazz workflow, 68

IDEs (Integrated development environments), list of RTC integrations by category, 191

Idioms. *See* Design patterns, implementing

Implementation discipline

ClearQuest tasks, 198

Jazz tasks, 199

purpose of, 197–198

Import/export

creating new ClearQuest integrations, 163–164

fixing import errors, 205–206

importing data during deployment, 204–205

importing records with references, 208–210

importing updates, 210–211

Process Template, 217–219

schema portions, 237–238

validating imported data, 206

Import tool, ClearQuest, 205

Independent integrations, ClearQuest, 156–158

Individual level metrics, for productivity and efficiency, 280

Information gathering subflow, 69–76

Infrastructure, defining infrastructure architecture, 30–32

Initialization pattern, ClearQuest, 36

Insight tool

for metrics, 287

release burndown and velocity charts, 345

Installation phase, of deployment, 202

Integrated development environments (IDEs), list of RTC integrations by category, 191

Integrated solution architecture (ClearCase, ALM, and Build Forge)

component relationships in, 368

continuous build and validation process, 369–370

creating task to fix defect, 370–371

developer work on activities in, 368–369

overview of, 367

periodic releases, 371–372

working on test artifacts, 372–373

Integration, ClearQuest

built-in, 156

CM API and, 172–175

creating new, 162

dependent, 158–162

E-mail Reader service example, 164–167

import/export and, 163–164

independent, 156–158

OSLC REST API and, 175–176

overview of, 155–156

Perl and BASIC API and, 167–172
resources for, 195–196
summary, 196
third-party offerings, 176–177
Web services and XML and, 176
Integration, introduction to, 153–155
Integration, Jazz
build engines, 190–191
Build Forge, 187
building new integrations, 192
ClearCase Connector, 188
ClearQuest Bridge, 180–183
ClearQuest Connector, 177–180, 188–190
IBM Rational DOORS, 185
JIA (Jazz Integration Architecture), 192–193, 355
list of RTC integrations by category, 191–192
overview of, 177
Rational test automation tools, 185–187
RequisitePro to RQM, 183–185, 310
resources for, 195
REST API and, 193–195
RQM (Rational Quality Manager) and, 177
RTC (Rational Team Concert) and, 187–188
STAF (Software Testing Automation
Framework), 187
summary, 196
SVN (Subversion), 190
Integration packages, 238
Internal impacts
on components, 88
data related to, 82
on releases, 88–89
Interviews, in requirements gathering, 23–24
Issues, data in description of, 81
Iterations
in ALM schema, 346
describing ClearQuest data objects for Agile
process, 338
planned effort for, 345–346
in RTC Scrum process, 332–334

J

Java APIs, 172–175
Jazz. *See also* RTC (Rational Team Concert)
Agile, Realization in RTC, 332–339
C/ALM (Collaborative ALM) and, 354–356

comparing ClearQuest and Jazz terminology,
2–3
comparing customization elements and terms
with ClearQuest, 15–17
customizing work items, 17–18
databases supported by, 33
governance and. *See* RTC (Rational Team
Concert) governance
implementation tasks, 199
integrations. *See* Integration, Jazz
monitoring with Jazz, 302
process control with Jazz, 301
permission with Jazz, 301
report resources, 302–303
representation of data in, 118–119
roles in, 142–143
setting up customizations during deployment,
204
setting up environment during deployment,
202–203
types of links to Jazz work items, 115–116
workflow, 66–68
Jazz Foundation Services, in C/ALM solution, 355
Jazz Integration Architecture (JIA)
building new Jazz integrations, 192–193
in Jazz-based C/ALM solution, 355
Jazz Tool Mentor
creating project using process template,
217–219
overview of, 217
JIA (Jazz Integration Architecture)
building new Jazz integrations, 192–193
in Jazz-based C/ALM solution, 355

L

License servers, defining infrastructure
architecture, 30–31
Limit Attachment size hook, 121–122
Links
to attachment files (CQ), 101–102
types of (Jazz), 115–116
to work items, 11–12
List View, Back Reference field and, 110
Lists
choice lists. *See* Choice list, Clear Quest
dynamic lists. *See* Dynamic lists

Location information
    in describing physical artifacts involved in
        change, 86–87
    locating items/components that must be
        changed, 82
Login name, converting full name to, 122–123
Lookups, hook for performing lookup on external
    database, 171

M

Maintaining requirements, 28–29
Maintenance discipline
    defining change process, 207–208
    improving maintainability, 208
    ongoing support, 208
    overview of, 207
Manage Section wizard, 318
Management (decision makers)
    benefits of integration to, 154
    data providing information for managers, 81
    getting agreement regarding requirements, 28
Manual Tester, RQM replacing, 307
Mastership, in multisite environment
    addressing changes to, 253–254
    testing, 254
MCIF (Measured Capability Improvement
    Framework), 287, 301
Members, 311–312
Metrics
    BIRT (Business Intelligence and Reporting
        Tools), 286
    categorizing by levels, 280
    ClearQuest, creating Agile schema in, 345
    Crystal reports, 285–286
    data supporting, 284
    Insight tool for, 287
    overview of, 279–280
    Publishing Engine for document generation,
        287
    Report Server for managing ClearQuest
        reports, 286–287
    resources for, 301–302
    strategy for, 280–284
    summary, 305
    tools for, 284–285
    units for time-related data, 94

Microsoft Visual Source Safe, integration with
    ClearQuest, 161
Modeling. *See also* UML (Unified Modeling
    Language)
    list of RTC integrations by category, 191
    promotion process, 379–382
Monitoring
    in ClearQuest, 297
    in governance generally, 289
    in Jazz, 300
MsgBox() function, debugging with, 255–256
Multiple relationships, object relations in
    ClearQuest, 106, 108–109
Multiple roles
    implementing implicitly, 134
    overview of, 130
    setting choices based on, 146–147

N

Naming conventions, in schema development,
    262–263
New session, notification hook, 58
Notification pattern, 36
Notifications
    Assign action and, 58
    customizing work items, 16
    in debugging, 256
    roles in, 127
    rules governing, 11
    setting environment, 202
    SLAs and, 365–366
Not_Resolved state type, 54

O

Objects
    relations. *See* Relationships
    state-based, 105
    stateless, 104–106
    test artifacts, 308–309
old_id field, storing for future reference, 264
Ongoing support, in maintenance discipline, 208
Open Service for Lifecycle Collaboration.
    See OSLC (Open Service for Lifecycle
    Collaboration)
Open Unified Process (OpenUP), 45

OpenUP (Open Unified Process), 45

Operating systems (OSs), environment information and, 87–88

Operation behavior or extensions, Jazz, 3

Organization level metrics, for productivity and efficiency, 280

OSLC (Open Service for Lifecycle Collaboration)
  building new Jazz integrations, 193–195
  in Jazz-based C/ALM solution, 355
  REST API compliance with, 175–176

OSs (operating systems), environment information and, 87–88

`OutputDebugString()` method, debugging with, 256–258

Ownership
  assigning solution providers in process of taking corrective actions, 91
  data, 99
  defined, 130
  misassignment of, 128–129
  unassigned changes and, 128

P

Packages (in ClearQuest)
  creating, 239
  enabling for editing, 239
  overview of, 238–239
  types of, 238

`packageutil`, creating packages with, 239

Parallel development
  coding hooks for, 241
  designing forms and tabs, 243–245
  overview of, 240–241
  record types in, 241–243
  storing hooks externally and, 249–250

Parent/Child control, 110–112

Parent Control pattern
  design of, 38
  implementing, 226–229

Parent records, creating from child record, 123–126

Performance benchmarking, by Web administrators, 200

Performance Tester. *See* RPT (Rational Performance Tester)

Perl
  choosing scripting language and, 261

Convert Full_Name to Login_Name hook, 122–123

creating new ClearQuest integrations, 167–172

HasAttachment hook, 120–121

Limit Attachment size hook, 121–122

storing hooks externally, 249–250

use of session variables, 240

Permissions
  in ClearQuest, 290–293
  in governance, 288–289
  in Jazz, 299
  Jazz permissions compared with ClearQuest Access control, 3
  roles and, 13, 142–143
  for test customization, 321–322
  workflow rules, 46

Petri nets, modeling workflows with, 43

Pictures, as presentation insert, 12

Plans, Jazz, 2

Postponing stage, in workflow item lifecycle, 52

Preconditions, Jazz, 3

Preparation phase, of deployment, 201

Presentation
  customizing work items, 15
  Jazz Presentation compared with ClearQuest GUI control, 2
  representation of data, 118

Presentation forms, 7–9

Prioritization
  of corrective actions, 91
  in requirements gathering, 27

Process Configuration, customizing work items, 317

Process control
  in ALM schema, 297
  in ClearQuest, 290
  in governance, 288
  in Jazz, 299

Process entities, in promotion request system, 377–378

Process lifecycle
  managing release promotion and, 374–375
  promotion requests and, 379

Process Template, Jazz
  compared with ClearQuest Schema, 2
  creating new project area with imported template, 219

Process Template, Jazz (*continued*)
exporting, 217–218
generating, 217
importing, 218–219
Processes
components in promotion process, 376–379
integration at process-level, 154
representation in workflows, 45–49
rules in promotion process model, 379–381
WBM (WebSphere Business Modeler), 47–48
Product backlog
describing ClearQuest data objects for Agile
process, 338
ranking Jazz stories in, 330–331
showing Jazz iterations in, 331–332
Project level metrics, for productivity and
efficiency, 280
Project management, list of RTC integrations by
category, 192
Projects
classification of project-related work items, 6–7
work projects in ClearCase, 368–369
Promotion process
model for promotion process, 379–382
overview of, 374
process components, 376–379
solutions, 375
status assessment, 374–375
Promotion work items, 6
Publishing Engine, for document generation, 287
PureCoverage, integration with ClearQuest, 157
Purify, integration with ClearQuest, 157

Q

Quality assurance
benefits of integration to, 154
data related to, 83, 103–104
Quality indicators, in reports, 284
Quality management, list of RTC integrations by
category, 192
Quality Manager. *See* RQM (Rational Quality
Manager)
Quantify, integration with ClearQuest, 158
Queries, comparing ClearQuest and Jazz
customization areas, 17
Query wizard, 285

Questionnaires, in requirements gathering, 24–25
Quick Information section, Jazz, 2

R

R (ready) state type, UCM, 54
Ranking stories, in RTC Scrum process, 330–331
Rational AppScan, integration of RQM and RTLM
with, 185–187
Rational Build Forge. *See* Build Forge
Rational ClearCase. *See* ClearCase
Rational ClearQuest. *See* ClearQuest
Rational CM API. *See* CM (Configuration
Management) API
Rational DOORS, 185
Rational Functional Tester (RFT)
automating test scripts with, 315
integration of RQM and RTLM with, 185–187
Rational Insight tool. *See* Insight tool
Rational Performance Tester (RPT)
integration of RQM and RTLM with, 185–187
test simulation with, 200
Rational Publishing Engine, for document
generation, 287
Rational Quality Manager. *See* RQM (Rational
Quality Manager)
Rational Requirements Composer (RRC). *See*
Requirements Composer
Rational RequisitePro. *See* RequisitePro
Rational Team Concert Eclipse client. *See* Eclipse
client
Rational Team Concert (RTC). *See* RTC (Rational
Team Concert)
Rational test automation tools, 185–187
Rational Test Lab Manager. *See* RTLM (Rational
Test Lab Manager)
Rational Unified Process (RUP). *See* RUP
(Rational Unified Process)
Rational University, 206
Reassign action, 70
Recalculate Choice list property, 265–267
Record forms, representation of data in
ClearQuest, 117
Record type family, ClearQuest, 2
Record types, ClearQuest
compared with Jazz Work item type, 2
creating parent record from child record, 123–126

customizing, 18–19
in dynamic workflow, 56
in parallel development, 241–243
single record type having multiple state machines for each issue type, 59–61
single record type having state machine for each issue, 61–65
stateful, 56
stateless, 104–106
user-defined roles and, 137–138
using roles stateless record type with static roles, 136–137
Records
accessing via referencing, 114–115
importing updates to existing, 210–211
importing with references, 208–210
mapping fields during import, 210
with more than one field as unique key, 261–262
permissions for access control and security, 289
Security Context and, 293
test artifacts in RQM, 308
Reference_List
Back Reference field and, 110–113
types of object relations in ClearQuest, 106, 108–109
References
importing records with references, 208–210
to objects, 114
pointing to unique keys, 113
types of object relations in ClearQuest, 106–107
Rejecting stage, in workflow item lifecycle, 52
Relationships
accessing records, 114–115
Back Reference field in object relations, 110–113
links, 115–116
multiple, 108–109
overview of, 106
references to unique keys and, 113
referencing objects, 114
replacing unique keys, 115
single, 106–107
between test artifacts, 308–309
Release work items, 6
Releases
burndown and velocity charts, 345

developer testing, 250–252
internal impacts on, 88–89
managing promotion process, 374
model for promotion process, 379–382
overview of, 250
periodic, 371–372
process components, 376–379
promoting to production, 252–253
solutions, 375
status assessment, 374–375
system testing, 252
Reloading records, notification hook for, 58
Reopening stage, in workflow item lifecycle, 51–52
Report Server, for managing ClearQuest reports, 286–287
Reports
comparing ClearQuest and Jazz customization areas, 17
defects, 316
in metrics strategy, 281
test defects, 316
Representation of data
in ClearQuest, 117–118
in Jazz, 118–119
scripts in ClearQuest, 120
Request record type
in ALM schema, 346, 348–349
describing data objects for Agile process, 338
suggested fields for, 339–340
workflows of, 343–344
Requestor information, 98–99
Requirements Composer (RRC)
documenting requirements, 25–26
Requirements discipline
Agile practices applied to, 28
analyzing requirements in establishing test strategy, 310
default work items in Jazz, 317
defining and documenting, 25–28
gathering initial documentation, 23
getting agreement regarding, 28
interviews for gathering, 23–24
maintaining, 28–29
overview of, 23
questionnaires for gathering, 24–25
resources, 40

Requirements discipline (*continued*)
    section of test plan, 311
    summary, 40–41
    test artifacts in RQM, 308–309
    verifying test case coverage of, 315
Requirements management, list of RTC
    integrations by category, 192
RequisitePro
    analyzing requirements in establishing test
      strategy, 310
    dependent integration with ClearQuest, 159
    documenting requirements, 25
    managing release promotion and, 375
    RQM integrations, 183–185
Reserved names, in schema development, 263
Resolution pattern, 40
Resolution stage, in workflow item lifecycle, 51
Resolution states, 53–55
Resolutions
    effort required for, 93
    in Jazz workflow, 67
Resolved state type, 54
Resources
    client interactions with resources on servers,
      173
    enhancements in Jazz version 2.0, 19
Responsible
    defined, 130
    setting based on role object, 147–149
    setting based on Single role, 145
    unassigned changes and, 128
REST API
    building new Jazz integrations, 193–195
    creating new ClearQuest integrations, 175–176
Results, test artifacts in RQM, 308
Reusable assets
    code reuse, 105, 234–237
    exporting/importing schema portions, 237–238
    list of RTC integrations by category, 191
    overview of, 234
    packages, 238–239
Review, of test plan, 313
RFT (Rational Functional Tester)
    automating test scripts with, 315
    integration of RQM and RTLM with, 185–187
Risk work items, 6
Role-based access control, 379

Roles
    in access control hook, 144–145
    in ALM governance, 298
    in ALM schema, 140–141
    areas and groups and, 131
    auto-assignment of, 145–149, 273–274
    change request process and, 131
    comparing Agile and ALM schema, 346–347
    customizing work items, 16
    defined, 130
    implementing implicitly, 133–136
    implementing with groups, 132–133
    issues/typical problems addressed by, 128–129
    in Jazz, 142–143
    in Jazz governance, 299
    organizing questionnaires by, 25
    overview of, 127
    in process model, 376–377
    in Scrum process, 334–335
    security and, 139
    stateless record type and, 136–137
    summary, 151
    terminology related to and types of, 130
    user-defined, 137–139, 150
    users activities and, 13
    workflow rules, 46
RPT (Rational Performance Tester)
    integration of RQM and RTLM with, 185–187
    test simulation with, 200
RQM (Rational Quality Manager)
    Build Forge integration with, 187
    ClearQuest Bridge, 180–183
    ClearQuest Connector, 177–180
    combining with DOORs in Jazz integrations,
      185
    combining with RequisitePro in Jazz
      integrations, 183–185
    creating dashboard viewlets for monitoring,
      300
    customizing work items, 17
    databases supported by, 33
    integration at data-level, 154
    integration with ClearQuest, 163, 180–183
    integration with Rational test automation tools,
      185–187
    integration with STAF, 187
    integrations, 177

roles in, 142
setting up Jazz environment during
deployment, 203
test entities and relationships, 307–310
test plan and test case objects in, 6
testing work items. *See* Testing work items, in
RQM
what it is, 307
RTC (Rational Team Concert)
as ALM tool, 7
Build engines, 190–191
ClearCase Connector, 188
ClearQuest integration with, 188–190
customizing work items, 17
databases supported by, 33
dependent integration with ClearQuest, 163
implementing Closing pattern, 224–225
integrations, 187–188
Jazz integration with ClearQuest, 180–183
listing integrations by category, 191–192
representation of data in Jazz, 118–119
roles in, 142
setting permissions for test customization,
321–322
setting up Jazz environment during
deployment, 203
support for customization from Web clients, 119
SVN (Subversion) used for source control, 190
RTC (Rational Team Concert) governance
monitoring in, 300
overview of, 298
permissions in, 299
process control in, 299
RTC (Rational Team Concert), Scrum process in
dashboards, 336–337
Developer Taskboard, 336
iterations and sprint planning, 332–334
Scrum roles, 334–335
setting up multiple teams for multiple releases,
331–332
stories, 330–331
RTLM (Rational Test Lab Manager)
based on RQM, 307
built-in integrations, 177
integration at tools-level, 154
Rules
customizing work items, 16

governing change process, 11
workflow definition, 46
RUP (Rational Unified Process)
applying to change management, 21–22
definition of roles, 127
workflows in software development, 44–45

S

SCCB (Software Change Control Board), 131
Scenarios, in Jazz-based C/ALM solution, 355
Schedules, test artifacts in RQM, 308
Schema packages, 238
Schemas
ClearQuest schema compared with Jazz
Process Template, 2
comparing/merging schema versions, 245–249
componentizing, 241–243
exporting/importing schema portions, 237–238
high-level design in ClearQuest, 33–34
upgrading, 253
use in development, 222
Scripts
choosing scripting language, 261
cloning hook for creating parent from child
record, 123–126
Convert Full_Name to Login_Name hook,
122–123
for data representation, 120
for executing tests in RQM, 315–316
function Defect_AccessControl, 132
function Defect_Validation, 145, 147
function GetLoginfromFullName, 123
function SetRequiredness, 362
HasAttachment hook, 120–121
import script, 169–171
Limit Attachment size hook, 121–122
organizing global scripts by subject, 262
sub allowedactions_ChoiceList, 150
sub ALMActivity_Validation, 77
sub AssignApprover, 78
sub attachments_ValueChanged, 120
sub Bug_Initialization, 223
sub ChildrenStatus, 228
sub ChoiceList, 236
sub Comp_ChoiceList, 269
sub comp_level2_ChoiceList, 270

Scripts (*continued*)
  sub Defect_Commit, 229
  sub Defect_Initialization, 234
  sub Defect_Notification, 58
  sub Defect_Validation, 227
  sub EnhancementRequest_Initialization,
    71–72
  sub feature_CloneParentCR, 124
  sub getEntityURL, 256
  sub GetLoginfromFullName, 122
  sub GetNextRole, 273
  sub Issue_Initialization, 64
  sub Issue_Notification, 60, 62
  sub keywords_ValueChanged, 271
  sub Limit_Attachment, 121
  sub note_entry_ValueChanged, 75
  sub Populate_list, 360
  sub project_ValueChanged, 266
  sub resolution_ChoiceList, 273
  sub responsible_ChoiceList, 146
  sub SetLog, 73
  sub ucm_view_Permission, 292
  sub userfieldvalue_2_ChoiceList, 267
  test artifacts in RQM, 308
Scrum
  dashboards, 336–337
  Developer Taskboard, 336
  framework for Agile development, 326–329
  iterations and sprint planning, 332–334
  Realization with ClearQuest, 339–348
  roles, 334–335
  setting up multiple teams for multiple releases,
    331–332
  stories, 330–331
Section, Jazz
  compared with ClearQuest Group box, 2
  customizing test work items, 318–320
  representation of data and, 118
  setting permissions for test customization,
    321–322
Security
  Access_Control hook in ClearQuest, 128
  defining infrastructure architecture, 31
  governance and, 288–289
  roles and, 139
Security Context feature, ClearQuest
  in ALM schema, 297–298

  in ClearQuest governance, 293–295
  overview of, 139
  records and, 293
Security testing, list of RTC integrations, 192
Selection lists. *See* Choice list, Clear Quest
Sequence diagrams, workflows in, 44
Servers
  client interactions with resources on, 173
  defining client types, 30–31
  installing during deployment, 202
  for managing ClearQuest reports, 286–287
Service Level Agreements. *See* SLAs (Service
  Level Agreements)
Service Request Manager (SRM), 154, 172
Session variables, 239–240
Single relationships, types of object relations in
  ClearQuest, 106–107
Single roles
  implementing implicitly, 134
  overview of, 130
  setting Responsible based on, 145–146
SLAs (Service Level Agreements)
  activating rules, 365
  background and examples, 363–364
  defining rules, 364–365
  external program for, 366–367
  governance reports, 366
  notifications, 365–366
  overview of, 363
  resources for, 383
SME (subject matter expert), 208
Software
  internal impacts on components, 88
  location information, 87
Software Change Control Board (SCCB), 131
Software development processes
  OpenUP (Open Unified Process), 45
  RUP (Rational Unified Process), 44–45
Software Testing Automation Framework (STAF),
  187
Solution providers
  assigning in process of taking corrective
    actions, 91
  data providing information for, 81
  key roles in defect and change management,
    131
Solutions, in promotion process, 375

Sprint record type
    suggested fields for, 340–341
    workflows of, 344–345
Sprints
    in ALM schema, 348–349
    describing ClearQuest data objects for Agile
        process, 338
    in Scrum process, 332–334
SQL query
    listing group members for access control,
        144–145
    listing in SLA, 368–369
SRM (Service Request Manager), 154, 172
STAF (Software Testing Automation Framework),
    187
Stages, of workflow, 50–53
Stakeholders
    getting agreement regarding requirements, 28
    interviews for gathering requirements from,
        23–24
    key roles in defect and change management,
        131
    questionnaires for gathering requirements
        from, 24–25
State-based objects, 105
State group, Jazz, 2
State pattern, 36
State transition
    diagramming, 45–46
    in dynamic workflow, 56–57
    moving automatically between states, 57–59
    test artifact state transition constraints, 312
State transition matrix, ClearQuest
    compared with Jazz Workflow, 2
    creating, 49
    workflow design with, 9
State transition tables, 9
State type, ClearQuest
    compared with Jazz State group, 2
    workflow and, 53–56
Stateful record types
    ALM Security Context and, 297
    overview of, 56
Stateless objects, 105–106
Stateless record types
    ALM schema roles, 140

    ALM Security Context and, 297
    importing, 205
    overview of, 104–106
    understanding when they are required, 261
    user-defined roles and, 137–139
    using roles stateless record type with static
        roles, 136–137
States
    auto-change, 58–59
    comparing ClearQuest state with Jazz state, 2
    customizing test execution states, 322–323
    diagramming, 47
    dynamic change state, 60–61
    in Jazz workflow, 66–67
    workflow rules, 46
Static roles, 136
Status assessment, in promotion process, 374–375
Steps to Reproduce field, in work item description,
    85
Stories, in Scrum process, 330–331
Storyboards
    defining and documenting requirements, 26
    for functional requirements, 27
Subflows
    for build approval, 76–78
    deviation needed to gather more information,
        69–76
    overview of, 68–69
Subject matter expert (SME), 208
Submission stage, in workflow item lifecycle, 50
Submit forms, representation of data in
    ClearQuest, 117
Subversion (SVN), 190
Superuser Modification pattern
    design of, 39–40
    implementing, 233–234
Supplementary specifications, in requirements
    gathering, 27
Support, in maintenance discipline, 208
SVN (Subversion), 190
System
    access permissions in ClearQuest, 290–291
    defining scope of in requirements gathering,
        26–27
    following up on adoption, 207
    tests, 200, 252

T

Tabs
comparing ClearQuest with Jazz, 2
designing, 243–245
representation of data in Jazz, 118
Task-Quality, default work items in Jazz, 317
Task record type, in ALM schema, 346, 348
Task-Review, default work items in Jazz, 317
Tasks
activity subclasses, 5
assigning members to, 311–312
creating task to fix defect, 370–371
default work items in Jazz, 317
Team Concert. *See* RTC (Rational Team Concert)
Team level metrics, for productivity and efficiency,
280
Teams
describing ClearQuest data objects for Agile
process, 338
in Scrum process, 331–332
TeamTest, integration with ClearQuest, 159
Telelogic Harmony, 44–45
Termination dates, for actions, 92–93
Test Case field, in work item description, 85–86
Test cases
associating with requirements and verifying
coverage, 315
categories for organizing information in,
320–321
creating and associating with test plan, 314
creating scripts for executing, 315–316
creating suite of, 316
customizing test work items, 316
test artifacts in RQM, 308–309
Test elements, in work item classification, 6
Test environment
creating with ClearQuest tools, 214–216
creating with database vendor tools, 212–214
promoting release to production, 252–253
storing hooks externally, 250
Test Lab Manager. *See* RTLM (Rational Test Lab
Manager)
Test plan
assigning members to tasks, 311–312
categories for organizing information in,
320–321
creating, 311

creating test cases and associating with test
plan, 314
customizing test work items, 316
reviewing, 313
test artifacts in RQM, 308–309
Test suite
creating, 316
test artifacts in RQM, 308–309
Testers
data providing historical information for, 81
in test process, 312–318
Testing stage, in workflow item lifecycle, 51
Testing work items, in RQM
analyzing requirements and establishing test
strategy, 310
assigning members to test plan tasks, 311–312
creating scripts for executing test cases,
315–316
creating suite of test cases, 316
creating test cases and associating with test
plan, 314
creating test plan, 311
customizing test execution states, 322–323
customizing test work items, 316–317
default work items, 317–318
executing tests, 316
organizing test information using categories,
320–321
reporting defects found during testing, 316
reviewing test plan, 313
setting permissions for test customization,
321–322
summary, 324
testing specific work items, 318–320
verifying test case coverage of requirements,
315
TestManager, RQM replacing, 307
Tests/testing
data related to, 82–83
developers in, 250–252
effort required for, 93
fields for test data, 95–96
integration of RQM and RTLM with test
automation tools, 185–187
key roles in defect and change management, 131
overview of Testing discipline, 199–200
system testing, 252

working on test artifacts for integrated solution, 372–373

Third-party integrations, with ClearQuest, 176–177

Time-related data
amount of effort required, 93–94
overview of, 82
termination dates, 92–93

Tivoli
SRM (Service Request Manager), 154, 172
TPM (Tivoli Provisioning Manager), 163

Tools, for metrics
BIRT (Business Intelligence and Reporting Tools), 286
Crystal reports, 285–286
overview of, 284–285
rational Insight tool for, 287
Rational Publishing Engine for document generation, 287
Report Server for managing ClearQuest reports, 286–287

Tools, integration at tools-level, 154

TPM (Tivoli Provisioning Manager), 163

Tracing information, debugging with, 258–260

Training materials, external impacts on, 91

Training phase, in deployment discipline, 206

Transitions. *See also* State transition, 67

Transparency, in Jazz-based C/ALM solution, 354

Triage pattern
design of, 37–38
implementing in ClearQuest, 224–225
implementing in Jazz, 225

TSRM (Tivoli Service Request Manager). *See* SRM (Service Request Manager)

U

UCM (Unified Change Management)
integration with ClearQuest, 160–161
periodic releases, 371–372
state types and, 53–55
work projects in ClearCase, 368–369
working on test artifacts, 372–373

UML (Unified Modeling Language)
in high-level design, 34
modeling workflows with, 43
workflow design with, 9

workflows in, 44

Unified Process. *See* RUP (Rational Unified Process)

Unique keys
dealing with records with more than one field as unique key, 261–262
references to, 113–115
replacing, 115

Units of work
measuring time-related data, 94
time measurements, 284

Updates
dynamic lists, 271–272
importing, 210–211

User acceptance testing, in release process, 252

User-defined fields
in ClearQuest solution, 356–358
defining requiredness, 361–362

User-defined roles
ChoiceList hook for, 150
overview of, 137–139

User interface
defining, 36
designing forms and tabs, 243–245

Users
benefits of integration to, 154
business rules, 378–379
defining client types, 30
external impacts and, 89
following up on system adoption, 207
getting agreement regarding requirements, 28
ongoing support, 208
permissions for access control and security, 288–289
roles, 13
roles in different areas, 131
training, 206

User's privileges, ClearQuest, 3

V

Validation
continuous build and validation process, 369–370
hook. *See* Hoocks, validation
of imported data, 206

Velocity charts, releases and, 345

Version control, list of RTC integrations by category, 192

VersionOne, ClearQuest integration with, 177

Visual Source Safe, ClearQuest integration with, 161

Vocabulary control, glossary in defining and documenting requirements, 25

W

W (waiting) state type, UCM, 54

WBM (WebSphere Business Modeler), 47–48

Web administrators, performance benchmarking by, 200

Web clients
  limitations of, 276
  support for customization from, 119
  testing releases with, 252

Web-related development considerations
  enabling button hooks, 274–275
  limitations of Web clients, 276
  making forms with dependent fields, 275
  overview of, 274

Web servers, defining infrastructure architecture, 30

Web services, ClearQuest integration with, 176

WebSphere Business Modeler (WBM), 47–48

Windows version, of ClearQuest Designer, 18–19, 213

Work item attribute, Jazz, 2, 7

Work item type category, Jazz, 2

Work item type, Jazz, 2

Work items
  classification of. *See* Classification of work items

comparing ClearQuest and Jazz terminology, 2–3

customizing. *See* Customizing work items

defined, 1

elements. *See* Elements, work item

summary, 20

in test process. *See* Testing work items, in RQM

what's new in 2.0 work items, 19

Workflows
  in ALM schema, 65–66
  in clearQuest, creating Agile schema in, 343–345
  customizing work items, 15
  defining, 35
  dynamic. *See* Dynamic workflow
  Jazz, 66–68
  Jazz workflow compared with ClearQuest State transition matrix, 2
  overview of, 9–10, 43
  process representation, 45–49
  software development processes, 44–45
  stages in, 50–53
  state types, 53–56
  subflows. *See* Subflows
  summary, 78–79

Workspace Versioning and Configuration Management (WVCM), 172–173

WVCM (Workspace Versioning and Configuration Management), 172–173

X

XML, ClearQuest integration with, 176